Salt and Steel

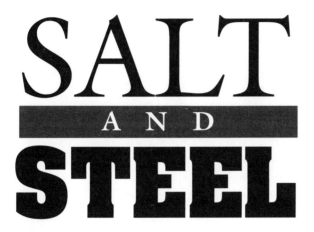

SALT AND STEEL

Reflections of a Submariner

EDWARD L. BEACH

NAVAL INSTITUTE PRESS
Annapolis, Maryland

Library of Congress Cataloging-in-Publication Data
Beach, Edward Latimer, 1918–
    Salt and steel : reflections of a submariner / Edward L. Beach.
       p.   cm.
    Includes index.
    ISBN 1-55750-054-1 (alk. paper)
    1. Beach, Edward Latimer, 1918– . 2. United States. Navy—Officers—Biography. 3. United States. Navy—Submarine forces—Biography. I. Title.
    V63.B43A3 1999
    359.9'3'092—dc21
    [b]   98-47175

Printed in the United States of America on acid-free paper ∞
06 05 04 03 02 01 00 99   9 8 7 6 5 4 3 2
First printing

There is only one person to whom this story of my life could be dedicated: the lovely eighteen-year-old girl who became my partner during a hectic period of wartime leave, and has been that ever since, through the good times and the bad, sharing everything. She has been a fantastic Navy wife, supporting me in all my Navy duties, and everything else besides. We have had four children, and she's as beautiful as ever, inside and out.

Rise from the darkness
Dive to the depths beneath
In Salt and Steel

Bonded together
Mates for eternity
In Salt and Steel

Braving the awesome sea
Peels of thunder
Over, under
Engulfed in Salt and Steel

Captain's your father
Friend and your brother sealed
In Salt and Steel

Colorless faces
Pride of the races yield
In Salt and Steel

Called to defend the free
Guard the ocean
Stop oppression
We are here
In Salt and Steel

KENNETH-MICHAEL VELTZ

Contents

Preface

The United States Navy: 200 Years, to which this book may be considered something of a companion, was written as an appreciation of our Navy. It had some of the hallmarks of a history, though as I carefully wrote in its introductory chapter, I did not try to describe every one of the naval events in our nation's few wars, nor all that went on between them. Rather, my purpose was to tell about our Navy as an organization of people with a single objective that always lies before them: the world ocean that covers three-quarters of the surface of our planet. Underlying everything, so far as the Navy is concerned, there has always been the great leveler, the sea itself. Although it is one of the most stable, predictable elements of the world structure, the sea is fluid in nature, and this is what enables it to encompass the continual changes in employment that mankind has imposed.

The half-century soon to end saw an extraordinary explosion in nuclear and electronic capability. It has brought more change to naval warfare—change to all warfare, but it may be argued that the Navy has been most affected—than the whole of past history. Partly as an outgrowth of these changes, Europe being a prime example, the nations of the world are coalescing into much bigger regions of common interests. The past half-century in fact may have eliminated future all-out war between nations, at least in the traditional historical sense. The capabilities of the weapons, and their vehicles, have become simply too much to be handled in the old way.

Aircraft, submarines, and electronics, each of which had a massive effect on how the military does its business, have been subsumed into the nuclear age. Historically speaking, this has happened in an incredibly short period of time. The new ideas, the consequent change in how we think about "sea power," have been extraordinary. "Control of the sea," that glib phrase, no longer even remotely carries the operational concepts it accumulated over the previous centuries of naval warfare.

For all of history, the sea has been a two-dimensional boundary between impenetrable environments, upon the surface of which man could freely move about, and which has been extremely useful to him. The nation with control of that boundary membrane upon which moved the commerce of the world could control that world, in effect "own" it. This England proved during centuries past, and Alfred Thayer Mahan, to his everlasting credit, articulated the lesson better than anyone else.

During the past century, however, within a single lifetime, the sea has become three-dimensional. The surface of the sea is now beyond any previous concept of ownership except in limited areas and in the most temporary sense. It is still useful, now most extraordinarily so, but these days it cannot be controlled. The most powerful navy in the world—ours—can think of controlling only small parts of the great world ocean, and these for very short periods, barely long enough for specific missions. Even that short-time control is subject always to instant intrusion and possibly catastrophic change. To whatever use of the sea we may now aspire, in the traditional sense of inexpensive transport of important cargo, in war it has become the objective of a contest that must go on continually, far above it, and far below.

It is not, however, the sea that has changed, but its uses and the way we think of it. The objective of sea warfare, and of navies, now refers not only to use of the boundary between air and water, but to use of the air and space above it, and the depths below. Man has changed, and so have his instruments. The vehicles by which he carries the tremendous power now at his command have changed beyond imagination. The sea now provides a hiding place for extraordinary weapons that can strike without warning and with fearsome accuracy, exploding out of a peaceful sea in a blink of an eye, flying faster than the speed of sound, to devastate huge areas of land thousands of miles away, and blot out everyone thereupon.

Mankind consequently now has the enormous problem not of controlling the sea but of how to control the terrible weapons he has created. It was against this backdrop of the Old Navy that I came to experience some of our Navy's crucial transitions into today's world. I was privileged to participate in some of its greatest achievements. Nevertheless, this book does not essay full coverage and proper proportions of emphasis. It flows, instead, with the contingencies of my own life in the Navy, which, in the large view, has not yet ended.

I offer here first-hand accounts, personal memories, and some reflections spun from them. While the intersection of my own life with the ongoing panorama of naval history must be limited, and of course patchy, nonetheless it spans a remarkable period: from the unrealistic years before World War II which almost cost us victory in that Armageddon of all wars, into the foundation of the electronic-nuclear era now well upon us; from the closing of the two-dimensional sea into the development of our Navy as a three-dimensional fighting force able to project our national ideals throughout the world.

The problems we face today, as the twentieth century drifts across the 2,000-year mark into the twenty-first, are different from any the United States has ever before seen, and this is as true of the U.S. Navy as anywhere else. The single constant remaining, on which we will always be able to depend, is that rapid change will henceforth be the norm, not the exception.

It has been an enormous privilege to have been in on some of the Big Bang we have recently seen in human capability. In many ways I greatly envy the young men and women today entering into naval service, because they will be the ones exercising this extraordinary new competence.

In some ways, however, I don't.

Acknowledgments

Very special thanks to Kenneth-Michael Veltz of Vienna, Virginia. Ken has written a very nice piece of music and poem, titled "Salt and Steel," that honors the Navy and our men who served in submarines. I'm proud to have been able to help him shape a couple of the lyrics. Now Ken has most graciously agreed to go along with my use of these words in the title of this book.

It happens that Peter Padfield, one of England's best writers about her navy—for that matter, about all war on the sea, or under it—used that same title for a novel. It also should be recognized. All the same, a book title cannot be copyrighted, or so I'm told. As with *Run Silent, Run Deep,* a good one will resurface from time to time.

Salt and Steel

Chapter One

The Beginning of a Naval Career

I became a part of the Navy during an era of astonishing change: the latter two-thirds of the twentieth century. It was not my original intention to write an autobiography, but as this manuscript began to take shape it took on some elements of such an effort, even though it is still my intention to concentrate on Navy development that I have observed or participated in, instead of on my personal career. Looking back, it is evident that the period it covers encompasses a most extraordinary set of changes in the Navy as a whole, of greater magnitude than those of any comparable span. A single career could not begin to cover all that has taken place during the present epoch, nor could a dozen different careers.

My idea is to describe that which I know something about, with the thought that there will be others undoubtedly doing the same, so that to the careful student of history an accurate and cohesive whole can be assembled.

In order to lay out the scope of these changes, it might be useful to begin by describing some of my early encounters with the Navy, which began as a child. My father was a naval officer, veteran already of more than 30 years of service and holding the rank of captain, when I was born. He was, quite properly, the greatest influence on that early period of my own life, and I revere his memory.

I first saw the light of day in New York City in 1918. This was a momentous event to me, but though my role was central Mother handled it alone, and I have no memory of it. My father was on the other side of the Atlantic Ocean, in command of the battleship *New York,* flagship of the Sixth Battle

Squadron of the British Grand Fleet. This American Battle Squadron, as it was also known, consisted of five of our best and biggest battleships. Upon our entry into World War I—the Great War, as it was then called—this squadron was assigned to European waters as part of the British fleet standing guard over the German High Seas Fleet.

The Grand Fleet was based in northern Scotland at Scapa Flow, a fine body of water for a wartime fleet base but with little appeal to sailors about to go out of their minds with boredom. The mission of this big fleet of capital ships, the biggest battleship fleet ever assembled up to that time, was to mount a permanent blockade against the German High Seas Fleet based at Wilhelmshaven. It lived for the day it believed must inevitably arrive: the ultimate sea battle between these two tremendous fleets. This battle would out-Trafalgar Horatio Nelson's great victory of 1805, heretofore the epitome of what an important naval battle should be. In 1918, as it had been in the past, it would be what those great ships had been built for, what their people had spent their lives training for.

It also illustrates how slow change was in the past, as compared with recent times. At Trafalgar, England's greatest naval victory, Nelson's flagship was built of wood and may have displaced about 5,000 tons fully laden. She is still preserved at Portsmouth. As a young officer, Nelson could dream of serving on board, and possibly later commanding her. He was 10 years old at her launch, and as admiral had her as his flagship. Only a century later, at Jutland, the *Iron Duke,* British Fleet flagship, built of steel, had about six times her displacement. *Iron Duke* was infinitely more powerful than *Victory,* was only about five years old at the time of her great battle, and she was put aside, antiquated, not many years later.

To go a step farther, the carriers that won World War II were, for the most part, not yet even on the drawing boards when the war began. There are hundreds of comparable examples, all stemming from the phenomenal progress in technology of the past few years.

So far as the Royal Navy of Great Britain was concerned, to have been able to say, even half a century after Trafalgar, "I was there," was to claim a special knighthood of the sea. Nothing remotely like that tremendous fight had come its way since 1805. The Royal Navy had been thirsting for more than 100 years for an equivalent reason for existence. In 1916, however, while the Battle of Jutland rivaled Horatio Nelson's greatest and final battle in terms of forces and perceived importance, it had not been a decisive victory. It was inconclusive; it could not qualify as a "new Trafalgar." For the rest of World

War I, officers of the Royal Navy felt it imperative that they redeem what they saw as their failure at Jutland with a truly great victory at sea that would merit the "Trafalgar" accolade.

The outlook of the German navy is less clear, and because of later developments its aspirations for combat lessened while those of the British navy grew. The showdown battle between the great rival fleets never took place.

From my father's unpublished autobiography, one gets the idea that he was infected with only some of the determined enthusiasm of his allied colleagues. He does mention with some pride the day the High Seas Fleet made an unexpected sortie from base and Dad's battleship led the Grand Fleet in an all-out dash to intercept. This was purely by accident of location, the allied fleet having been also at sea for maneuvers. When information of the enemy fleet movement was received, the Grand Fleet reversed course at full speed toward the reported enemy location to begin this most ultimate of sea battles. The *New York* had been in the rear of the allied formation, and now Dad's ship was in the lead. For a short time the excitement was high.

But contact was not made, and the great battle was not to be. Whether or not the Germans got wind of this effort, they did not remain at sea; instead, they returned to Wilhelmshaven, and the British fleet, disappointed, went back to "Scapa."

No one had any idea that this would be the last time at sea for that great German fleet of World War I. When next it ventured forth it would be to surrender its magnificent warships to internment in a backwater of Scapa Flow. (There, following many anxious months, they would in the end scuttle themselves to prevent England from taking actual possession of the ships.)

As Dad told the story, during the days following the surrender ceremony, some British officers visiting the *New York* had tears in their eyes as they told of their frustration at having been denied that last big sea fight. It had become an emotional need for them. For a century they had studied Trafalgar, had lived the dream of another such. The Battle of Jutland, or Skagerrak, as the Germans called it, had on the other hand been characterized by overcaution on the parts of both commanders-in-chief. The British Fleet Commander, Adm. Sir John Jellicoe, commented that he was "the only person who could lose the war in a day"—and of course made sure he did not. Reinhard Scheer, the German admiral, had a somewhat smaller fleet, but he handled it brilliantly. However, he broke off contact when the chance to disengage presented itself, and left the British fleet, as before, in command of the North Sea. Had Scheer been a little more like "Bull" Halsey of World War II, had he stayed on the scene at Jutland and attacked aggressively instead of seizing the opportunity to escape further contact, might he have proved Jellicoe right?

No one can answer that question. In terms of ships sunk and damaged, the British fleet suffered considerably more than the German. The British ships were less damage-resistant; German gunnery, thanks to better rangefinders, was more accurate; but both fleets came out of Jutland essentially intact. The endless analyses afterward have been more far-reaching than the battle.

Although Father's visitors in the *New York* knew that many of them would not have lived through the great sea fight that did not take place, their sorrow had its probable root in subconscious historical perception. They could not have stated it in words, but in their hearts they may have felt that their failure to achieve total victory in battle at sea would, in a generation or so, spell the demise of their own navy.

Father did not see it that way, or his subconscious may have differed from theirs by embracing the probable rise of his own navy as that of his guests diminished. He also predicted, in that unpublished manuscript I have so fil-ially preserved, that naval warfare would greatly change, that with "aircraft dropping bombs from overhead and submarines firing torpedoes from below, battleships in a future war would have a hard time"—a statement that few would quarrel with today.

Mother was of a French family that had been in the export-import business in Haiti since before the expulsion of France early in the previous century. Her maiden name was Fouché, her family claiming descent from Joseph Fouché, a survivor of the French Revolution. Father's first wife, Lucie Quin, had died "without issue," as the quaint language of the time described it, the year before he met Mother.

Women are now officially included in the U.S. Navy in both enlisted and officer ranks, but it is simplistic not to understand that women and families have been in and of our Navy—of all navies—since there have been sea services. I come from such a family. Mother's service, and Lucie's also, was every bit as real as Dad's, though of a very different type. I will have a little more to say about Mother later, but while on the subject of the Navy's distaff side, I am impelled to give honest tribute to Father's first wife, Lucie Quin, who died of breast cancer after 20 years of marriage. She had no children and was therefore able to "follow the fleet" to a greater extent than other young wives (this was more common among older ones with grown children). Among Dad's old papers, of course, there are pictures, but most important is a heartfelt, handwritten statement of his anguish at Lucie's death. She was a vital part of his life, helped him with his books about the Navy, sent him off in his ship, the *Washington,* bravely concealing that doctors had told her they could do nothing for her, that she had only months to live. Finally having to give up the pretense, she sent for him, so that she died in his arms only days after emergency leave brought him home to her side. Like so many women of the Navy, she gave her husband and, through him, gave the Navy and her country the best that was in her. As she lay suffering in the presence of death, she told him he should remarry, and have the children she could not give him. Though she would not have thought of a foreigner, I know she would have liked Mother very much.

Father was thus a recent widower, nearing 50 years of age, when he met Mother. The *Washington* was in Haiti "to protect American lives and property" as one of its "revolutions," the usual way of changing administrations in that country, began to turn violent. Father's orders were only to protect American citizens, but a day or two before he arrived there had been a real revolt, as differentiated from the usual staged and mostly bloodless government upheavals. There had been rioting, a great deal of indiscriminate gunfire, and the sitting president had been mobbed and murdered in the streets of the city.

A "normal" revolution had been brewing. The president, Vilbrun Guillaume Sam, had had the usual year or so to collect the national customs duties (the entire revenue of the country) and sequester the loot in a French or Swiss bank. This was the parlous state of politics in Haiti in 1915, characterized by this sort of behavior on the parts of about a dozen presidents during the same number of years. It made them millionaires. Most of them moved to France, where they had gone to school, and their country, of course, remained with neither funds nor revenue, and with nearly all its inhabitants in abject poverty.

Sam, a former convict, resolved to break this precedent of quickly succeeding presidential administrations, and when he detected the beginning of negotiations with the same mercenary "army" of Cacos he had used himself the previous year, he decided on a ruthless countermove. Based in the north of Haiti, Cacos were armed peasants who would stage an uprising for hire. To forestall the routine Caco march to the south to the capital to install a new president, Sam imprisoned all the local citizens and members of their families, especially sons nearing adulthood, whom he suspected of being in on the plot to oust him. These included a goodly number of the very small, mostly Paris-educated, Haitian intelligentsia. The trouble began with gunshots heard from the direction of the prison: the president had sent a squad of thugs to eliminate his political enemies, which they did by going from cell to cell and shooting through the bars, then rushing in with knives and bayonets.

By the time a hastily formed rescue attempt was able to stop the carnage, nearly all the prisoners had been killed, and when their mutilated bodies were found the fury of the populace of Port-au-Prince broke all bounds. The capital's chief of police, a man named Delva, himself led a crowd of enraged citizens through a backwater creek into the center of the city, thus neatly getting in the rear of the presidential forces and directly assaulting the opulent French-built presidential palace. The national army immediately fled, and President Sam ran for sanctuary through a gate in the walled palace backyard into the adjoining grounds of the French legation. The crowd of angry people, by this time grown into a bloodthirsty mob, swept into the legation grounds, surrounded the legation building, and demanded their president be surrendered to them. When the French minister, citing the right of sanctuary, refused to give up his unexpected guest, the infuriated crowd stormed inside and, following the smell of iodine he had used on a minor injury, found Sam hiding in a locked toilet on the second floor. They dragged him out, broke both of his arms when he clung to a stairway banister, then pitched him over the legation fence into the street, where the enraged people, led by parents of some of the young victims of the jail massacre, literally tore him to bits. Then they impaled parts of his body on poles and paraded the streets with the gruesome proofs of their anger.

For the next few days, mob rule was the only authority in Haiti's capital. Armed men walked the streets searching for personal enemies and occasionally shooting into the air, looting and killing when the spirit moved them. This was the situation when the USS *Washington,* one of the fastest heavy ships of our Navy, steamed at full speed into the bay of Port-au-Prince, anchored, and sent ashore a small landing force under the command of the ship's captain, my father-to-be.

The family story has, of course, details that do not pertain to the official narrative, true and important (to us) though they might be. Mother had been orphaned at an early age by yellow fever; her father came down with the dread disease, her mother cared for him until he died, then came down with the dreadful infection herself and died a few weeks after him. Mother was left with a tiny inheritance that soon disappeared at the hand of some predatory relative. At this juncture she was befriended by the Swedish Carlstroem family, carrying on an import-export business, and was living with them in their large home on a suburban hillside overlooking the capital city, Port-au-Prince, when the Sam-inspired riots broke out. Apparently some bullets actually struck the Carlstroem house, and the family, including several younger children who because of the age difference had become Mother's charges, had taken cover in the small basement under the house. After a time, the noise of the rioting seemingly having abated somewhat, Mother, being evidently a somewhat venturesome young woman, left the crowded basement to have a look. She climbed to the third floor of the house, where there was a good view in nearly all directions, and brought a pair of binoculars.

There was not much to distinguish on the land, the mob being more interested in finding enemies in the city than in the outlying suburbs, but at sea, as she described it in later years to her children, she could see a huge warship, black smoke pouring from four tall funnels and a big bow wave extending broadly on both sides as she sliced through the water, approaching the harbor at high speed, heading exactly for her. She could not distinguish the ship's colors, but it was clearly a warship, gray paint and all, and Mother needed no more. She ran down the stairs, calling out, "Don't worry! We're saved! The American Navy has come!" Salvation from mortal danger, she told us, needs to be experienced to be properly felt; but when that happens it is a feeling like no other.

She did not meet the captain of that great ship for some weeks, and could not, of course, have had any idea of the rather momentous consequences that particular instant of time would have on her personally. Father was, in fact, not yet a widower, and had no knowledge that his beloved Lucie had already received her sentence of approaching dissolution from her doctor. In fact, the worst year of Father's life was upon him, for within a year he was to lose both his wife and his wonderful ship, both wrecked by convulsions of nature against which there was no way to fight.

As already noted, Dad's only instructions, countersigned by Adm. William B. Caperton who, as "Commander Cruisers in the Caribbean," flew his flag in the *Washington,* were to see to the safety of Americans. The admiral remained aboard ship and in radio communication with the Navy Department, while Father, possessing some knowledge of French, set up headquarters ashore and reported every night to his superior when he returned aboard. Quickly, Father found the mob's anger to be directed only at their own native black oppressors, of whom there was no apparent shortage. "Whites," whatever their nationality, were in danger only from looters seeking to take advantage of the chaotic conditions. Black Americans, of whom there were a number, were in more danger than white ones, and one of Dad's first moves was to identify all local persons who should have the protection of the United States.

This, in itself, proved not to be difficult. Everyone entitled to the safety of the American flag let his or her status be well known. The difficulty came in dealing with the fearful nationals of other countries. This question, referred to Washington, brought the immediate reply: United States policy, stemming from the century-old Monroe Doctrine, opposed use of any sort of force in the Western Hemisphere by any non-American nation. In case of emergency the United States would exert its own good offices, and would alone decide how much force might be necessary to protect foreign lives and property in the event local authorities proved unable to do so.

This was the rule guiding Father, and he liked to tell the story of how the German minister once complained about his assumption of the authority to give orders forbidding anyone, including members of the German legation, from carrying weapons of any kind, as they were in the habit of doing, within the limits of the Haitian capital. Father's response, lifted verbatim from the autobiography I have kept so carefully, was that it was "the same authority the Minister acknowledged when he asked for and still retains the United States Marine Guard" that, for his and his legation's safety, had been stationed there for weeks.

It was also through this protective operation that he met my mother, for the Carlstroem family was one of those that eagerly availed itself of the U.S. Navy's protection during those difficult days. During regular inspections of the various posts he had established, Father could not help noticing the attractive young Alice Fouché, whose parents had died of yellow fever years earlier, living with relatives in one of the well-to-do outskirts of Haiti's capital city.

All this occurred in the summer of 1915. Lucie died later that year, Father obtained emergency leave to be with her, and then almost immediately was asked by Secretary of State Robert Lansing, who apparently had noted his success in handling the difficult situation in Haiti, to return to his post as soon as possible. Father, as he described it, badly needed exactly such orders and made some kind of a speed record rejoining the *Washington* in Guantanamo Bay, where Caperton had come to await him.

A few months later, early in 1916, *Washington*, scheduled for routine overhaul, was replaced by *Tennessee*, her identical sister, sent to Caribbean waters for the purpose. Father's expertise in handling the Haiti imbroglio brought quick acceptance to the proposal by the new arrival's skipper, who wanted to avoid service in the warm Caribbean, that the two skippers swap ships. The

Washington went to Norfolk for overhaul, in the process of which her name was changed to *Seattle* to free the state name for a new battleship about to be built, while Father remained in command of the just-overhauled *Tennessee,* the new Cruiser Force flagship. He grew to like his new ship as well as her predecessor, if not a little more; in his autobiography he called her the most responsive ship he had ever handled, and mentioned his annoyance when Navy bureaucracy directed her name be changed to *Memphis.*

In August of that year (1916), with orders similar to those that had started *Washington* on her way to Port-au-Prince the year before, he anchored the newly renamed *Memphis* in the harbor of Santo Domingo, capital city of the country of the same name, which occupied the eastern two-thirds of the same island, once known as Hispaniola, of which Haiti held the western third. It was a good anchorage, like the one off Port-au-Prince, exposed, however, to the south instead of to the west. On 29 August there was absolutely no hint of the disaster that would overtake the ship that afternoon.

What happened to the *Memphis* was unprecedented in history, although Santo Domingo tradition has it that three and a half centuries earlier something like it may have happened to a "pirate fleet," probably one commanded by Sir Francis Drake, and with the same result. Without warning the sea erupted to the south, huge waves swept into the harbor, and in less than an hour Dad's great ship was hard aground against a rocky cliff in 12 feet of water (her normal draft being about 29). Today I can make claim to being the most knowledgeable living expert on that disaster, having researched all available details and laid them out in *The Wreck of the Memphis,* published by design on the fiftieth anniversary of the fateful day.

Father returned to the United States, was court-martialed for having negligently hazarded his ship in the face of an approaching hurricane which he should have foreseen, found guilty of not having been able to get under way immediately when bad weather threatened. A few years later a letter from the secretary of the Navy informed him of his final exoneration when it was determined that the extraordinary sea conditions causing the disaster resulted not from a hurricane, of which there was no evidence except the size of the seas that swept into the harbor, but from what was then called a "tidal wave." It had nothing to do with tides, nor was it a single wave. The Japanese term "tsunami" is used today for this infrequent phenomenon, which results from an underwater earthquake, a seismic shift in continental plates.

The years 1915–16 were tough for Father, alleviated only by the arrival of Mother in New York City after his court-martial. In 1917 they were married, and I came along a year later. By that time, as already stated, Dad was again at sea in the battleship *New York*. In 1919, the war over, he traveled across the country by train with his 26-year-old French-speaking wife and the infant son now telling this story.

Father's previous duty, before the *New York*, had been in command of the Torpedo Station at Newport, Rhode Island, where his mother, well along in years, had joined him and his new wife. The plan had been that after Father's detachment from Newport and departure from the fine commandant's living quarters on Goat Island, Mother and her mother-in-law, for whom she could provide company and needed assistance, would find an apartment in New York City. But my grandmother died just before Father's detachment. Mother, of course needing nonetheless to leave Newport, took a smaller apartment in New York, where she was able to find the benevolent friendship of the same order of Catholic nuns who had provided her education in Haiti (her family was Hugenot and not Catholic, but there was no other educational institution).

As for Father, like so many persons from time immemorial whose lives were embraced by the sea, he did not see me until I was nearly a year old, when his salt-streaked battleship triumphantly led her four sisters of the American Battle Squadron into the Hudson River.

My earliest consciousness was of the commandant's quarters at the Navy Yard, Mare Island, in San Francisco Bay, California, where he was next assigned. It was a big white house as I recall, and the Marine orderlies, resplendent in their blue and red uniforms, who stood sentry watch in a booth at the entrance to the grounds, seemed to take particular pleasure in keeping me from running out of its fenced yard. I now suppose they must have had special instructions to prevent the commandant's small son from escaping. As I recall, the fence, being made of vertical iron bars, was no impediment to sight, and the temptation to a fully ambulatory four-year-old was no doubt irresistible. Most of the Marine sentries did their duty in a kindly way, but at least one was most authoritative in his refusal to let me pass, and for this he sticks out in my few memories of Mare Island while the others, also having kept the situation well in hand, are only dimly recalled.

Mother had no experience in the circumscribed society of our Navy in those long-ago days, could speak only minimal English, and devoted herself entirely to the little family with which she quickly presented Father. My brother John and sister Alice, who followed me only short years apart, were both born in the Mare Island commandant's house, no doubt an unusual occurrence for that great old mansion.

She taught all three of her children to speak excellent French. We always spoke French with her, and until she died all the letters we exchanged with her were in that language. She left the running of the commandant's quarters to the staff with which it came equipped, while she did her best to fit herself into an entirely new and foreign existence. With her youth and innocence, she was, of course, the object of interest from the members of the naval society, from the distaff side in particular. Possibly in envy or some twisted illogic, a few of these caused her some uncomfortable moments that I learned about later from other sources, but the only memories she imparted to me were happy ones.

Mother did, however, figure in one of the humorous stories that went around about life in the circumscribed environment of a naval station. The houses assigned to the senior officers at Mare Island, though of slightly different sizes as befitted their positions, stood in a row along the same tree-lined street a few blocks behind the industrial area. Useful to the persons involved, since they could walk to work in minutes, this also led to a certain convenience in fulfilling the social duties falling to their wives. Reciprocating the hospitality of Father's second-in-command, who lived next door, was naturally the first order of business, but in due time Mother felt she must do something to entertain a larger group. This, she found, was easy for the wife, even the foreign-born wife, of the commandant of the Navy Yard. A date was set and the menu was decided with the help of the commandant's steward, an imperturbable Filipino of many years service who was in charge of the mansion. Invitations were sent through Father's secretary who, already veteran of many years in Mare Island, kept invitations and place cards in her desk, and knew whom to invite.

It was extraordinarily simple, not much different from what Mother had already experienced from her days in the well-to-do Caribbean society from which she had come. It was even easier, since all the functionaries she needed were so familiar with the procedures customary in the Navy and honestly wanted to help the commandant's foreign-born wife who was so dependent on them. For this dinner, the first she had given of any size, everything was organized to perfection. Genteel drinks were served in the living room (national Prohibition, passed by the Eighteenth Amendment in 1919, did not go into effect until January 1920). At just the right moment the steward announced dinner was ready, and Mother fulfilled her function by suggesting in her memorized French-accented English that the guests adjourn to the dining room across the hall. This they proceeded to do, finding their seats according to the place cards around the beautifully set dinner table. The first course was served—and then disaster struck.

The steward came in grandly, bearing an imposing turkey, browned to perfection, on a silver platter—but just as he began to approach Father's place at the head of the table, his foot caught on the rug, and he stumbled. The beautifully prepared *pièce de résistance* fell to the floor and rolled several feet toward the side of the room. Everyone was aghast, none more than Mother, who knew not what unimaginable penalty would fall on the young foreign woman presuming to carry on the social duties of the wife of the commandant of the Mare Island Navy Yard.

But the steward appeared equal to the occasion. "Just a minute, Captain, I fix!" he announced, retrieving the turkey and disappearing into the kitchen. Mother's move to rush there also was intercepted by another Filipino steward, who appeared with a bottle of fine California wine, whispered, "Wait, ma'am. Will be okay!" then went to Father at the other end of the table for the protocol-dictated ritual of approving the wine. Following this, the wine steward moved around the table punctiliously filling everyone's glass. Father had served in the Philippines during the Insurrection following our war with Spain, had come to know and admire the Filipino people in their brave but hopeless fight against subordination to the United States, and had actually, quite by happenstance, become friendly with their leader, Aguinaldo.

Father had captured a party of Filipinos, one of them a young patrician-looking woman, who had strayed into forbidden territory. The rest of the group, some men and some women, were obviously in her service. Instructions were silent on what Dad should do with captured women, so he did the gallant thing. He showed them the location of the line of demarcation they had violated, bowed formally, and released them. Some time later, when he himself was captured by a party of Filipino soldiers, he discovered whom it was he had helped that day. By direct order of President Emilio Aguinaldo, Father was escorted back to the U.S. lines and released, with Aguinaldo's personal thanks for the chivalry he had shown his wife! In Mare Island many years later, unsure of what to expect, wondering what was happening in the kitchen but knowing Filipino resourcefulness, that if his steward needed help he would ask for it, Father carried on with the table discussion as though all was well. The guests at the table, wondering what the outcome of this unusual situation was going to be, perforce had to do the same.

Then the door to the kitchen pantry opened once more, and there stood Father's head steward, once again immaculately clothed. He entered the dining room only a shade more carefully than previously, the shining silver tray balanced in his hands. On it, in place of the turkey, was an imposing roast of beef, like the turkey cooked to seeming perfection, as indeed it proved to be.

The dinner proceeded from that point without further incident, and after all the guests had departed my parents found that everyone in the kitchen, with the exception of a single scullery maid still washing the final debris, had gone home, too. Despite his overall authority, Dad was totally stymied in his curiosity, and it was Mother, next day, who discovered how the contretemps had been handled; but it was not from the mansion's Filipino steward, who, otherwise intelligent and communicative, was unable to understand Mother's poor English when she tried to interrogate him on this point.

Father's executive officer, a Captain Cox, was billeted in the second-most-imposing house on Executive Row, next door to the one assigned to us, and also had a coterie of Filipino servants. Mrs. Cox had been very helpful to Mother, had become a good friend, and frequently came over for morning coffee, a custom Mother looked forward to for part of the education in Navy ways that she needed to learn. Over coffee the morning after the dinner party, the conversation naturally went to the previous night's dinner. To her friend's question of "how it all went," Mother told the story of the disaster to the turkey dinner she had planned. But she could not understand where the chief steward found the already prepared roast beef, and at such short notice, she said, at this point a trifle uncertainly because her visitor seemed about to burst with repressed amusement.

"Now I've seen and heard everything!" Mrs. Cox finally exclaimed. "We had a dinner party last night too, though not as big as yours. But I thought we had prepared a roast beef, and I had to cover up fast when the main course turned out to be a fine turkey that I'd never seen before!"

The two women agreed that the devotion to duty of the exclusively Filipino staffs they had inherited could not be denied, but in the case of a real emergency you could also count on their loyalty to each other. The previous evening had become such an emergency, and their respective stewards, who must have known each other for years, had coped with it with the *sang-froid* the women had come to expect of them. The two ladies agreed, however, that the less said publicly about this particular example of how officers' stewards in Mare Island Navy Yard worked together the better.

. . .

I was in my fifth year when Father retired from active duty in the Navy, took a position as professor of naval and military history at Stanford University, and established residence in nearby Palo Alto, California. It was in Palo Alto that I passed my childhood years. My time in the Navy began there, too, literally at my father's knee, for my earliest recollection of it is of constantly asking that poor man to describe the disaster that overtook the powerful armored cruiser *Memphis* while under his command. The "Wreck of the *Memphis*" was my favorite childhood story, in interest far exceeding, in my eyes at least, any possible competition from the standard children's texts of the day.

At some point, possibly in self-defense, Father introduced me to Edgar S. Maclay's *History of the United States Navy from 1775 to 1901* (he had only the first volume), and then in succession to James Fenimore Cooper's *History of the Navy of the United States of America* (published in 1846), and an over-size picture book full of wonderful Navy warships. All three of these I literally "read to shreds," lying on my stomach on our living-room rug. In school I learned about Dick and Jane and their dog, Spot, and a little later also about George Washington and Abraham Lincoln. But the latter two were distant figures, if more real than the paper-thin Dick and Jane. To me the world consisted of ships and the sea and people like my father, who sailed in the ships and on the waters.

This included men like Nicholas Biddle, John Paul Jones, Joshua Barney, Edward Preble, and Stephen Decatur, for the Cooper history and the first volume of Maclay were, of course, about the sailing-ship navy. Father saw to it, however, that I also learned about David Glasgow Farragut, William B. Cushing, Rafael Semmes, and Franklin Buchanan of the Civil War; William T. Sampson and George Dewey of the war with Spain; and William Sowden Sims, Theodore Roosevelt, and Alfred Thayer Mahan of the years after that. Sometime during my early boyhood period I discovered that Father, too, had written about our Navy, and on his library shelves there reposed 13 specially bound "author's copies" of his novels about our seafaring service.

It was, I suppose, understandable that in those days I had little appreciation of how to handle treasured books, but I have since wondered how my parents could have permitted the nearly wanton destruction I so carelessly visited on them. They may have been so pleased at my obvious interest in the Navy that they shut their eyes to the damage it cost his books, particularly to the beautifully bound novels telling the adventures of Robert Drake, Roger Paulding, Ralph Osborn, and Dan Quin. Maybe they were simply glad that I was reading such heavy material at so early an age. Years later I was able to purchase a complete set from a used bookstore and had them all rebound, a set for Mother and another for myself.

For some reason I never fully understood, Father had the idea that I should become a doctor—a surgeon, he said, because of my early proclivities with tools. Apparently he didn't notice that the things I made at least theoretically represented naval ships. I had made wooden models of our battleships, putting particular care on the one representing the handsome *California,* built at Mare Island and launched during his time as commandant. I built a number of cruisers and destroyers too, but no aircraft carriers, and remember well a naval battle that took place on our living-room rug. My line of battleships was advancing toward the sofa, which for lack of sufficient ship models substituted for an enemy fleet that had, defensively, put up a large smoke screen, when from behind it, tied together with string so that they followed in column (in "line ahead" was the term Father used), a squadron of destroyers suddenly appeared, fired all their torpedoes, and totally destroyed my surprised battleline. Father had given no hint of his intended employment of my destroyer models and had used his superior naval experience to outwit me! When I complained that this was not fair he hugged me and explained that surprise was an entirely legitimate naval tactic, as I had already had thoroughly explained in the books I had been reading.

One of my models, it should be mentioned, was a submarine, complete with permanently extended periscope (a small-headed finishing nail hammered into the deck). Having been carefully ballasted with lead and fitted with bow and stern planes at suitable angles, with a gentle push this little boat could make respectable dives in the bathtub, or a pond or swimming pool. I planned a propeller with a rubber-band motor to give it more verisimilitude, but must have lost sight of this part of that foreshadowing project.

To return briefly to the *California,* out of proper chronological sequence, she, like the *Victory* to the British, held always a special place in my perceptions. Father had supervised her building and launching. Mother had kept a careful scrapbook that contained many clippings about her. Once, when I was eight or nine, our Battle Fleet visited San Francisco and Dad took my brother and me on board for a visit. Like *Victory, California* was built to be a fleet flagship, and I enviously watched the admiral, a classmate and close friend of Father's, pick up my younger brother and fling him bodily on the big bed in his cabin. Johnnie roared with delight, and I remember expecting to be flung on the bed in my turn. But Adm. Henry A. Wiley evidently thought flinging one kid was enough, or maybe I was too big. I also remember a fascinating tour of the ship that he sent us on, and have unsuccessfully tried to identify the very nice ensign who performed that chore for him, complete with an obligatory stop at the ship's soda fountain.

In 1922, shortly before he retired from active duty, Dad turned the completed *California* over to the Pacific Fleet as its new flagship. So that vessel has always been a very particular ship for me. While growing up I had pictures of her all over my room. Someday I would serve aboard, I vowed, maybe even become her skipper.

My career did not lead me in that direction, and it was aboard a submarine entering Pearl Harbor after voyaging from San Francisco Bay that I received my next and most indelible impression of that magnificent battleship. She had been sunk at her berth, water up to her main deck, listing to port. When I saw her she was afloat again, with great wounds visible, her carefully ordered topsides in hopeless disarray. Photographs taken after the attack showed her three huge main battery guns in the foremost turret punched through the canvas awning that had been stretched over her forecastle. There being insufficient time to furl the awning properly, they had been elevated through it as though intending to shoot at some enemy, assuming that anyone in his right mind would have fired a 14-inch gun in the middle of Pearl Harbor. But of course, except for the buzzing bees that had inflicted the terrible hurt, and which she could not touch with those ponderous rifles, the enemy was 300 miles away and totally out of reach. It is probable, however, that under the circumstances prevailing not many Americans there on that day remained for long in their right mind.

I recall thinking, however, not only how obsolete she appeared, but how obsolete she actually was. She was launched five years after Jutland, had been built for that battle of 1916, and was outclassed by the conditions of 1941. She should never have been put into the position she was, unable to respond to an attack by agencies and weapons not even thought of when she was designed. Far worse, our naval leadership had utterly failed to comprehend the problems she faced, the quarter-century worth of changes that had doomed her. For me, *California* so humiliated represented a first-order failure of leadership; not that the admirals in charge had been caught by surprise, but that she had been so terribly exposed in the first place. The *Victory* served as a fleet flagship in the British navy for three-quarters of a century and was never put into a situation where she could be found wanting. *California*, in a fourth of the time, had regressed from fleet flagship to an impotent, if beautifully polished hulk without ability even to defend herself. She was the perfect symbol of why we nearly lost World War II in the first six months. So was the *West Virginia*, still in drydock, her port side shattered nearly beyond repair. The speed of change had overwhelmed both of these fine ships, the others too, and the worst of it was that, apparently, no one in authority could see that the fault lay in themselves.

John Blair was one of my father's closest friends from his younger days. He was a retired lawyer whom my brother, sister, and I had been taught to know as "Uncle John." Dad had thought enough of him to name my younger brother after him (I was named after Dad, pretty much the norm in those days). Many years later, as I researched the court-martial Father had to undergo following the loss of the *Memphis,* I learned that John Blair had insisted on acting as Dad's defense attorney without pay during the trial, and Father, suffering greatly from the vicissitudes of that personally disastrous year, although he must have wondered at the advisability, could not turn down this deeply friendly offer of assistance. So far as I can recall, the matter was never mentioned at home, but it has become my personal conviction that both men later felt the move had been a tactical error, that it was not wise for a civilian to participate at all in a naval court-martial. Although the court's judge advocate (the prosecuting attorney) made no reference to this disregard of unwritten protocol, my own review of the record years later left me with the impression that while the court allowed John Blair, as defense counsel, to make a lengthy, emotional, final statement (to which it paid no attention), it did this perhaps partly out of personal sympathy for Father, and at least partly, if not probably, to avoid imputation of not having given the accused every possible opportunity for defense. If anything, John Blair's efforts, well meant though they were, could only have been counterproductive.

A Navy lawyer, member of the Judge Advocate Corps, would have known how better to present the absence of hurricane winds and thus refute the hurricane theory the court had uncritically accepted because there was no other known cause of the huge waves that had done the terrible damage. In a Navy trial, all lawyers on both sides should be members of the Navy Judge Advocate Corps.

Today, as an afterthought, I wonder whether Blair, an accomplished advocate as a civilian lawyer, may not have had a hand in the secretary of the Navy's later reversal of the court-martial verdict. Something, or someone, must have convincingly brought the unfairness of this bit of finished business to his attention. As a child I knew only that when John Blair retired from the business world he moved to California and set up his home in Palo Alto, where we also lived, possibly having heard of the salubrious climate and other pleasant things from Father.

Despite any possible shadow about the *Memphis,* the two families always remained close, and one day when I was 13 years old, Uncle John asked me to come to see him. Wondering what was behind this unusual request I came to his house at the appointed time and was ushered into his library, which looked to me something like what I imagined a lawyer's office should be, complete with a big bookcase full of impressive law books. A pair of soft leather chairs stood in front of a big desk behind which Uncle John sat, much as though I might have been a client.

"You've done well in high school, where I understand you're already a sophomore. Have you thought much about what you want to do in life, Ned?" There had probably been some preliminary conversation, but as soon as he said these words I realized this must have been why he wanted to see me. It didn't occur to me that while at my then-attained age of 13 it was perhaps time to begin to think about career plans, it was hardly necessary yet to become dogmatically firm about them. I was, however, fairly big for my age (having attained my full height) and, perhaps partly because of my somewhat precocious reading, had skipped some of the lower grades, so that I was already well along in high school and on the scholastic honor roll. It was also true that the entrance ages for the U.S. Naval Academy at Annapolis were a minimum of 16 to a maximum of 20 as of the first of April.

I answered that Father and I had several times discussed the subject, and that he wanted me to study medicine and become a surgeon, arguing that the manual dexterity I had shown in sawing wood to make model battleships would serve me well in that part of the medical profession.

"Do you want to be a doctor? Have you thought about the Navy? What do you think about going to the Naval Academy?"

John Blair must have been a good lawyer. He certainly was wasting no time, getting directly to the heart of the issue. For my part, I have never forgotten the interview, for it turned out to be crucially formative for me. In less than three years I myself would be 16, and eligible for appointment to the Naval Academy. Maybe it was indeed time I made up my mind.

I told him that I had often thought about Annapolis, but Father seemed to believe that the time away from home was a serious detriment. There were many lonely hours at sea, he used to say, sometimes long periods totally without communication, and there was frequent danger, including the ever-present one of falling overboard while performing some duty. In case of war, or the far more frequent international problems involving what might be called "minor wars" (he used to say he had been in five minor wars and two major wars, and that the minor ones had been more dangerous to him than those declared by Congress), the life of a Navy man was almost automatically on the line. It could not be called a normal life by any stretch, any more than a swaying, wracking hull in a seaway could be compared to a solidly built house with a nice yard around it.

I admitted to Uncle John, however, that the excitement and adventure of the Navy appealed to me, and that in spite of all Father had said I still wanted most to go the Naval Academy and lead a naval career, as he had.

Uncle John gravely considered what I had said. "Have you talked to your father about this?" he asked. Yes, I said, and he always argued against the Navy. "I mean," said Uncle John, "have you told him what you've just told me?"

I had to admit that I had not, at least, not quite in those terms. "Why don't you do it, then?" he said. "I think you'll find him receptive to what you have to say, if you do."

I did as John Blair suggested, and to this day remember how surprised I was at the ease with which I won my father over to my point of view. It has since been my thought that he might have been leaning over backward to be sure that I was not simply carrying on the childish infatuation he had observed. Mother, too, no doubt wanted me to be certain of what I wanted to do, and from time to time I have since wondered whether there might have been collusion between my parents and my Uncle John. If so, I can feel nothing but gratitude. It might have come out this way anyhow, but for me the way ahead was clear, with no future problems except to win one of the appointments.

Father set himself to preparing me for the competitive and entrance examinations to Annapolis. Having served a tour there as instructor, as well as having written about the Naval Academy in his novels, he was well qualified to guide my studies in this direction. As son of a naval officer, I was eligible to take a nationwide competitive examination, administered by the Civil Service, for one of 25 appointments to the Academy made annually by the president. I was also eligible for appointment by both California senators and the representative from our congressional district. One of our two senators and our district congressman announced they would give their appointments to the Naval Academy through similar Civil Service exams. In total, I had three vacancies to compete for.

My special studies began that summer, under Dad's careful guidance. He sent to the Navy Department for all extant past entrance exams, the same ones used by the several Naval Academy Preparatory schools and available to everyone on request. I had to work out the answers according to the regular (and rigid) examination time schedule for each, after which he marked my papers rigorously, and then had me correct my errors within a time-scale he devised to duplicate actual examination conditions. In some cases he made me take the exam over again.

After three years of this regime, working all summer, during weekends, full-time every day except Sunday for nearly a year after high school graduation, he deemed me ready. A week before the scheduled exams, he made me stop. Summarily, all studies ceased. Full and complete rest became his requirement. For a week I had to go to bed early, sleep late, and not look at another book. At this stage this was not difficult.

Then came the competitive and entrance exams for all three appointments, and I found myself more ready, better prepared, than for anything in my life ever before. The exams were easy. I finished them with the certain knowledge that I had done well. They were in six different subjects, and when the results were announced I had perfect grades in three of them, and wound up with my choice as to whether I would enter the academy as appointee of senator, congressman, or the president.

After serious thought, and consultation with Father and Uncle John Blair, I chose the senatorial appointment and set off for the U.S. Naval Academy in June of 1935, not quite two months after my seventeenth birthday.

Annapolis was a long three-day train ride away from California, and it was the first time I had gone anywhere alone, except for short trips of the excursion type. Father, Mother, Brother, and Sister all came, of course, to see me off, for it was a momentous occasion far superior, in my estimate at least, to the one described earlier in this chapter when I entered the world. Mother, alone, seemed to be less than enthusiastic. There were tears in her eyes when she kissed me goodbye, but I knew that all women were sentimental, and must confess I didn't think much about what this first permanent break in her family might mean to her.

Chapter Two

Early Years

Dad's fictional Robert Drake, "Stone" Stonewell, and Ralph Osborn had all gone to the Naval Academy at Annapolis around the turn of the century, roughly 35 years before my entry into that institution. In the early 1900s, Father himself was a "discipline officer" (part of the military "executive" department as differentiated from the academic department) and he used his spare time, with Lucie's help, to write about them. In spite of 35 years of time difference, and their status as only fictional characters, Osborn and Drake and their friends represented the Navy to me, and I privately felt their kinship. This was not the sort of thing one would talk much about with one's fellows, but on occasion, during my entire time at the Academy, I would imagine the advice they might give me, or their reaction to a situation I might find myself in. Somehow still much older than I—they were 17- to 19-year-old midshipmen in Dad's books, but by the time I had attained that advanced age they sounded more like old-time commanders—they were good guides in things relating to naval mores and spirit.

Soon after reporting to Bancroft Hall, the huge midshipman dormitory, I found myself a member of the United States Naval Institute, with a subscription to its magazine, the *Proceedings*. Father had ordered this for me as an indoctrination gift. I have maintained it ever since, and 13 years ago received my 50-year certificate. Early on I found out that he had once been its secretary treasurer, then its senior officer. Once again, Father's example colored my life, for, with a much wider audience than he had, the Institute has fought to maintain the standards as to traditional systems and procedures, as well as to thoughtful consideration of new ideas. Always it has held that new and sometimes unusual ideas and views should be heard, and it has often gone out of its way to carry forward consideration of them. It is not a stranger to controversy, always seeks both sides to professional arguments, and will give them both space in its pages and editorial assistance for presentation.

It well merits its international reputation as the best, most professional, most thoroughly nonpartisan organization of this nature in the world. Foreign navies put as much store by it as ours does, keeping in mind, always, its never questioned loyalty to the interests of the United States.

As a brand-new midshipman, I well remember the first thing we had to do at Bancroft Hall: indelibly and very neatly mark with name and laundry number each item of the tremendous pile of clothing thrown at us. We not only learned how to use a stencil and the right ink, but also that these marks were expected to last at least four years and that one's name was intended to be visible all the time. Second was the traditional plebe haircut, for which we had to stand in line much longer than the job itself took: less than a minute; the haircut submerged personality, made us all look more alike, more "Navy" (there was no question of this, even though, after that first painful cut, we were allowed to grow our hair back to a more normal—but nonetheless still short—length). Third was my introduction to infantry drill, rowing a cutter, tying knots, signaling by semaphore and Morse code—and more infantry drill.

We all questioned use of infantry drill by an outfit dedicated to service on water. My arrival at Annapolis was at the start of what was called "Plebe Summer," a thoroughly planned period of time, and it was carefully explained that the ability to march in unison would help us to think in unison, which was necessary for the Navy to function with its parts in unison, that the superiority of many minds aimed in the same direction, working the same way, doing the same thing together simultaneously as an organization, was the military attribute we needed most to learn. How to lead, or manage, would come later. First it was necessary to learn how to obey by rote, exactly as trained. "Nothing gets this across better than infantry drill," we were told time after time, and surprisingly, there was truth to the adage, not that any of us recognized it then.

Every minute of every day was taken up with drills or exercises. Only at night, when taps were sounded on a bugle, could we rest, and even that was by command. Lights out by 10:00; no talking, no moving around. Sleep was ordered; and sleep we did, for the routine was intentionally exhausting. Reveille was at 6:00, the day's first inspection in ranks at 6:30, then breakfast with plenty of good food, followed by half an hour to make up our rooms and clean them for inspection. Someone, in writing the regulations, had had an early idea about smoking: none was allowed before breakfast, just the period when a hungry budding addict would want to light up. Violation of this edict could easily be detected by smell and would automatically result in a week's incarceration in "the ship," the Spanish-American War relic *Reina Mercedes,* permanently moored at *Santee* Wharf on the Academy waterfront.

The *Reina* had been captured from the Spanish navy at the Battle of Santiago de Cuba in 1898. Already obsolescent, she had been maintained as a trophy, replacing the aged wooden pre–Civil War frigate *Santee* that had served in this place when Dad was a midshipman, and, having been there so long, had bequeathed her own name to the wharf (the only thing of distinction *Santee* did during her entire lengthy career). Being sent "to the ship" was, by intention, no fun, for it did not entail absence from any of the Academy routine. It resulted in longer walks to drill, or class, and deprivation of the haven represented by one's regular room in Bancroft Hall. On board the *Reina* one slept in a hammock, which had to be triced up and stowed every morning, had a tiny locker for stowage of books and essentials, was required to observe regular study hours, carry on all the regular activities. It was not a prison, but neither was it a vacation.

For severe offenses such as "Frenching out" (no one knew the derivation of this term, but it signified unauthorized absence from the Academy grounds, often involved illicit drinks at a local pub, and was considered a "class A" violation), the penalty time "on the ship" could be much longer than a week. In our circumscribed midshipman society, a month's sojourn entitled one theoretically to a "black N," comparable to a blue-and-gold block "N" awarded for athletic excellence. The "black N" was, however, not worn on sweaters or bathrobe, as were the athletic awards. Bravado though it may have been, the only place I have ever seen it flaunted was the occasional entry in the *Lucky Bag,* the annually published compendium of photographs and biographies of the graduating class. Graduation and being commissioned as an officer in the Navy or Marine Corps wiped out past history, as did survival of Plebe Summer four years previously. One began one's adult career with a clean slate.

I myself did not smoke, but soon discovered the hold the habit had on my classmates. The disproportionate punishment was just one of the risks. Since nearly all the upper classmen and officers in charge of us themselves smoked, detection was not a sure thing. More than one superior may have intentionally not noticed the odor of cigarette smoke, but to be seen too near a lighted cigarette before breakfast meant "the ship" for sure.

My arrival at Annapolis was in June of 1935. Graduation of the senior-class midshipmen had taken place a few days before. No evidence of their four years' presence was detectable that I could see. The new seniors, first classmen in midshipman lingo, and the newly promoted third classmen (sophomores) were away in a couple of old battleships on the annual midshipmen's cruise. Second classmen were spending a relaxing summer at the Academy, where the new fourth class, ourselves, known as plebes, were among their responsibilities. Above them were officer members of the executive department, the old "discipline" department of Dad's time, and we plebes were the sole objects of the attention of everyone then present at the Academy. So, at least, did our superiors impress on us at all opportunities. It was also made sure we knew that we were the lowest thing in the Navy, fit only for ridicule and discipline. There was only the barest hope that somehow we might learn a useful thing or two and, though not likely, actually amount to something.

Discipline was, of course, one of our bugaboos. The Naval Academy Regulations filled a thick volume, loose-leaf for the frequent and easy addition of more regulations. My first infraction of these came for being out of uniform. I had forgotten to put on my neckerchief. For this dereliction, I stood out conspicuously in our noon meal formation and was duly put on report. Next day I found my name on a list designated to appear at "mast." This is still the Navy term for arraignment of offenders, derived from the old days when they were brought to the quarterdeck, paraded before the ship's mizzen mast (the one farthest aft), and their crimes recited to the captain for his judgment of the punishment to be awarded.

This day in Bancroft Hall our midshipman "mast" was held in a basement hallway. Other miscreants stood in line with me, most accused of smoking before breakfast. Commander Walter Delaney, the august executive officer of Bancroft Hall, baronial in his white uniform, stood forbiddingly behind a lectern. When my turn came I shambled miserably into focus in front of it, togged out in my best summer "white works" uniform, neckerchief in its proper and this-time-not-forgotten place. Impeccably correct, I stiffly saluted the commander. Punctiliously, he returned my salute, looked me straight in the eye. The look on his face told me it was early in my career to have disregarded naval regulations.

"You're on report for being out of uniform at formation," he said severely, consulting a paper in front of him. "What have you to say for yourself?"

I had been briefed on how to handle myself. Despite his total lack of sympathy for me in my predicament, my second-class midshipman advisor had done this much for me. "Nothing, sir," I muttered, subconsciously hoping my interrogator would not hear me. "I just forgot it."

Everyone in the Navy has his day in court, even those at our low level. Commander Delaney's piercing eyes bored into me as he pondered a suitable punishment. I knew my naval career had not yet been ruined, not totally at any rate. But a couple of days on "bread and water" in the brig were a possibility. My friends caught smoking before breakfast, something nearly everyone did, not a crime at all, faced a week on the *Reina Mercedes*. I trembled internally. What would the commander see as the condign penalty in my case? Time passed leadenly as Delaney debated my fate.

Finally he seemed to have made up his mind. Eyes snapping, he delivered judgment: "One demerit!" he said. "Maybe that will help you remember!"

Again I saluted. "Thank you, sir!" (This was the correct response, even if I had been sentenced to life imprisonment or to being boiled in oil.) I stepped backward, relieved at the light punishment but thinking, all the same, that I would carry this black mark the rest of my time in the Navy. It was not till a day or so later that I read in the rules that "plebe summer demerits are wiped off the books at the beginning of the academic year."

(Years later I sat next to Vice Admiral Delaney at lunch somewhere, and took pleasure in reminding him of this little incident. I had never forgotten his admonition, I told him. His memory of the business was understandably not as good as mine, but for me it has always been a treasured recollection of my early days in the naval service.)

So far as I can recall, this was my only time afoul of the "regs" without due premeditation. I once "Frenched," but this was in the middle of the day for a necessary errand for the boat I was helping to rehabilitate, and was quickly accomplished. Having done the deed in broad daylight, not the usually chosen time for "Frenching" (at night after taps), I went completely undetected. There were a few other similar emergencies that necessitated going a little out of line, but in the main I was a pretty "regulation" midshipman. Once I capsized an Academy sailboat during a Sunday afternoon sail with two classmates and three pretty girls (they were prettier yet when soaking wet). This cost me my sailing qualification, for although the accident was not my fault I had signed for the boat and was therefore in charge of it. Another Navy lesson learned.

The Naval Academy was touchy about certain things. At meals, held in the cavernous, uninviting midshipman mess hall, since renovated and semantically upgraded to "wardroom," all four classes sat together at one of the mess tables assigned to their midshipman company, with the first class (the senior class of midshipmen) in charge. Table manners were in the purview of the first class, and they enforced them. *Reef Points*, an unofficial "how to" book issued to all of us, had a chapter on etiquette, with such important directions as how to tip a soup plate to scoop up the last drops, which knife and fork to use and which hands to hold them in, how to butter a piece of bread, and so on. Mundane items all of these, but not all midshipmen came from the same background. Criticism of our table manners was forthright, instantaneous, and often brutal. Compliance with *Reef Points* was mandatory. This was not hazing, but it is safe to say, in this department, at least, that we were totally and thoroughly indoctrinated.

In another area, the Academy authorities evidently felt it might not be equally useful to leave ballroom dancing to the uncertain conduit of upper class instruction. Plebes were mustered as in their regular formations, marched off to a large room, there required to practice the basic waltz and foxtrot steps. There was no effort to show anything fancier. Success came from going through the requisite steps in formal "platoon front," that is, as many as 20 plebes in line abreast in a "front rank," with a "rear rank" just behind, solemnly marching through the dance steps in cadence, or to a phonograph record if they were lucky. In contrast to the Navy's achievement with table manners, this program, a holdover from ancient days, was finally dropped, many years later than it should have been.

Midshipmen were not allowed to have autos in my day, nor even to ride in them within the city limits of Annapolis, the exception being when on authorized leave of absence or, for the new (soon-to-be) graduates, the "June Week" of festivities just prior to graduation. Having had my own car in high school, however, this was a rule I could not but circumvent, all the while staying on the right side of the "regs." There could be no regulation against ownership, only against riding in a car in the Academy grounds or in Annapolis, if not on authorized leave. As a midshipman I owned two different automobiles at different times, stored them quietly in a garage in town, broke none of the rules concerning them. I was admittedly ahead of my time, and the situation is very different now. Upper class midshipmen are today permitted to drive their own cars and even store them in designated spots on the Academy grounds, which are, in consequence, cluttered with them.

Not only through Stonewell, Drake, and Osborn, but also as a parental duty, Father had done a very special thing for me. Hazing, defined as unwarranted and unauthorized assumption of authority by an upper classman over a plebe, had been a scandal for years and was punishable by summary dismissal. Dad's fictional characters had all experienced this. In his novels some had received severe punishment, sometimes unfair, though all came out all right in the end. One of them, having hazed a plebe by requiring him to stand on his head, was dismissed and later, it having been shown that the plebe he had ordered to perform this feat had not yet been sworn into the naval service, reinstated on this small technicality.

A far-fetched story? Maybe, but true all the same. The admiral in command of the U.S. Fleet, who picked up my brother in his sumptuous quarters in the battleship *California* and pitched him joyously on his big admiral's bunk, could tell it better. Some 40 years earlier, it was he whose career had been saved in this way.

Things came out less favorably, despite his famous name and antecedents, for Stephen Decatur III. He had hazed someone, nothing could save him from dismissal, and Dad made sure I knew it. Partly because of this, and perhaps partly because I felt the injustice of the custom, I resolved never to haze, and never did—except once, when it was richly deserved. A plebe, having been "put under the table" (a common punishment for not knowing the menu, for example), had taken some butter with him and put it, very quietly, on the shoes of all the upper class he could identify from below. Although I had had nothing to do with putting him under the table, among the shoes receiving this treatment were mine. Butter on inspection shoes absolutely ruins the polish; I ordered him to "sit on the little green bench" (eat from a sitting position without a chair under him) until I could get the polish back, which took a few days despite diligent effort on my part. During the process, obviously an uncomfortable one for him, he visited me in my room to ask to be allowed to repolish my shoes for me—but this was a menial service and against my scruples. Never would I allow this, I told him, but I would work on them myself every spare moment, and did so. With this he had to be content. My point, which today I have some difficulty in articulating, was that he had caused me much extra work, and special risk as well, but even so I was not going to compromise my stand against hazing any further than I had already done.

The whole situation was nothing but a boyish prank enlarged by law into far more importance than it warranted, for if I had been found out my punishment might have been dismissal from the Academy and the naval service. Partly because of this imbalance between offense and penalty, the unofficial "system" almost always protected the hazer instead of the hazee. There is a world of difference between the hi-jinks of which I was guilty and "black" hazing (to coin a term). There is something intrinsically cowardly about hazing, even though often done in fun, even with good spirit all around, by superiors unaware of the background of their assumed authority. Invariably, however, someone oversteps the bounds of propriety, sadistically enjoys inflicting pain on his official inferiors. This is the root of official disapproval of the custom, which on no account should support cruelty of any sort, even ostensibly well intentioned.

Hazing harks back to medieval servitude; behavior of this nature is somewhere ingrained in the psyche. Rooting it out is mandatory, if one only thinks back to what it stands for.

Recent studies of Nazi abuses have shown that nominally "decent people" sometimes went out of their way to hurt minorities. Our own inequities relating to skin color show that we, too, thinking of ourselves as the greatest of democratic societies, can and do harbor obscene prejudices. Whether for a life of forced serfdom, or only a year of it, inhumanity to fellow man, intolerable though it may be, is evidently ingrained in the human psyche. Rationalize it though we may, and as we do, hazing has only bad features, no good ones.

Whatever "good" it may claim to do can be proved false, an excuse for dehumanizing violation, or exploitation. The target of the abuse, whatever he may be, fraternity initiate, plebe, or unwanted minority, cannot fight back. It is purely subjective rationalization to argue that enduring indignities proves one's eligibility for acceptance and his right, in his own turn, later to inflict the same abuse on others subordinate to him.

So, too, is the notion that the risk the hazer himself (now also "herself") takes, of a heavy penalty if discovered, gives him some sort of right. Under this construction the penalty of dismissal, enacted years ago at the behest of a Congress outraged by some stupidly brutal example of hazing, is self-defeating, for it engages the protective instincts of the hazer's friends, and of the "system" itself.

An opposite example, however, occurred during my plebe year when a member of the class just above ours, no doubt not fully thinking out what he was doing, lashed a classmate of mine with a section of wire cable. My friend was hospitalized with severe injury, but refused to report who had hurt him. He was praised for this, but as a result, to everyone's indignation, the malefactor was officially unknown. The story did not end there, however, for the midshipmen knew what had happened even if the authorities did not, and members of the first class let it be known that they did not approve. "Drake" and "Stonewell" had spoken. Unofficial disgrace descended, the cable-wielder was shunned, failed in his studies, and that was the end of him.

Thoughtful comment against the disgraceful custom, or some comparable manifestation of it, is found in surprising places. In 1812, one Samuel Leech served in HMS *Macedonian* during her battle with USS *United States,* and later wrote an account of the action that received wide coverage, the most recent publication being in *Every Man Will Do His Duty: An Anthology of Firsthand Accounts from the Age of Nelson,* edited by Dean King and John B. Hattendorf. Writing of the treatment of the ordinary sailor by the officers over him, Leech has this to say:

> [Officers] know what is fitting between each other as officers; but they treat their crews on another principle; they are apt to think of them as pieces of living mechanism, born to serve, to obey their orders, and administer to their wishes without complaint. This is alike a bad morality and a bad philosophy. Until every feeling of human nature is conceded . . . in naval discipline . . . perfect, rational subordination will never be attained. . . . It is this very system of discipline, this treating them as automatons, which keeps them degraded.

Leech was an American seaman, impressed into the British navy, forced to fight against his own country. His account of the famous battle was moving because of its clear and honest depiction of the grim details of combat at sea, but this particular passage almost accidentally touches on the fundamental base from which hazing, a relic of slavery, or serfdom—a crude manifestation of power—arises. More than a century old, these words should be read by everyone seeking to justify an immoral custom that is long past any excuse for continued existence.

It was clear that the Naval Academy was not for everyone. The name of the person escapes me, but one of the young men entering with my class found after only a few days that he was one of those it was not made for. He simply disappeared, and the story bandied about among us was that he had just packed up and gone home. He may have recognized (somewhat late in the game) that he was unable to face a heavily regulated military life. He might have had something disqualifying in his record that came to light at this late moment. Perhaps he had a bad, even a perverse experience at the hands of one of the officers, or one of the second class placed over him. Of none of this have I any knowledge. He might even have been a "shill," for example a reporter, put in the Academy to write an article about it for a newspaper or magazine. Whatever the circumstances, he left us after only a single day's visibility, and his name appears to have been expunged from our rolls as though it had never been there.

I had two roommates while at Annapolis. Toward the end of my sophomore or "youngster" year, as we called it, the first became a casualty in that while a member of the Academy rifle team, an outfit that had garnered many prizes in competition, he tried to survive a shooting slump in his daily practice by reporting higher scores than he had actually shot. It happened to all team members that their scores were sometimes below their best. Shooting slumps were normal, to be expected, were corrected by continual practice. Team members selected to shoot in competition were picked not only from practice scores but also on where they stood on their personal cycles at the target range. This was, of course, one of the functions of the team captain and coach, who naturally picked midshipmen at the peak of their shooting abilities to represent the Academy.

My roommate's mistake was in not realizing the cyclical nature of everyone's practice performance. When his practice scores were uniformly good from day to day, he brought suspicion on himself, was quietly investigated by the team captain, and summarily fired off the squad. This was not all, however, for a few days later he found himself on "Class A" report for falsehood. This was an unforgivable offense. Despite high grades and high potential, he had made "false official statements." Practice or not, the scores were official reports in that they bore on the selection of competitive team members. He defended himself as well as he could, possibly unwisely in some detail (he had neither counsel nor good advice), and was then accused of specious argument and prevarication in general.

It was pitiable. As his roommate and at this stage his only friend, I tried to rouse backing for him, wrote a statement of support, got a number of friends to agree it represented their views—and was called in by our company officer to be told quietly that even this small effort might be viewed as an infraction of discipline, and that I had better stop it. My roommate's distressed parents visited to plead his case, were courteously received by both the commandant and superintendent, but got nowhere. A Class A offender, the poor fellow was confined to our room except for classes and meals, and after a week of this torture his name was read out at noon formation as having "resigned for the good of the Service," and he was gone.

It was tragic for a young man of his promise. I saw him again, shortly after my own graduation, and then years later after he had entered the Coast Guard as an enlisted man for war service. He won promotion on merit during World War II and rose to the rank of captain. He died of a heart attack while skipper of one of the Coast Guard's finest cutters, only a few days before I was to see him again, and I was glad to be able to remember him at the height of a fine career in that service.

My second roommate was Emmett Bonner, whose own roommate had failed academically after two years. Almost immediately we found ourselves extremely sympatico, gradually became the very best of friends. He had an infectious humor that never ended. Both of us became volunteer crew members of a strange "inland scow" sailboat, very flat of deck and underwater hull, belonging to a fellow midshipman (this was the boat I "Frenched" for a few times). The Academy pattern shop had been set up for the purpose of making wooden patterns for casting metal machine parts for the several mechanisms midshipmen studied, and it was receptive to special requests from midshipmen desiring to do a little carpentry work. During our relatively leisurely Second Class Summer (during moments when not engaged in straightening out the new good-for-nothing plebes), five of us worked on the boat, building a tall, carefully trussed, mast for it. In October the mast was done, letting us happily take her out for a trial sail. In a blowing breeze, we tore around the Severn River inlet with delighted abandon. The boat listed far over, her windward "lee-board" high in the air, and she tore through the water with a tremendously satisfying dash.

Our delighted sailing fun did not last long, however, for in the process of enjoying our first really good sailing day, in a fine wind, our insufficiently supported mast, strongly braced but structurally weak, gave out. It was dramatic indeed to see our big stick break into three pieces, high above us, and fall on deck and in the water, shattered beyond repair as though by an enemy broadside. It was truly a catastrophe. From a steeply listing sailer, flying under a beautifully billowing sail, we were without warning converted into a flat, logy, board in the water. The scow had no height of hull, only of her mast and its big mainsail, and we members of her crew, no longer admirals of the ocean sea, found ourselves, without warning, converted into shipwrecked castaways on a bobbing raft.

We did not, however, have too long to contemplate our predicament, for almost immediately we found another benefit of being in the Navy. The station ship *Reina Mercedes,* in addition to being a prison ship for before-breakfast smokers and other midshipmen who had run afoul of the rules, also kept a lookout on sailing boats in the Severn River. It could not have been longer than about 10 minutes before a motor launch arrived from the *Reina* to tow our dismasted boat back to its moorings.

Construction of a new mast began immediately, during the two hours or so of free time in the afternoons of the Academy academic year. We also found it necessary to awaken before reveille in order to run out to the boat's moorings and pump her out. She leaked badly, had to be pumped out in the evening, too, and it was due to this that she failed to bear out her initial promise. Annual leave came (for all mids except plebes), and the month-long lack of care finished her off.

Emmett and I survived the summer and our work on the boat, despite its vicissitudes, in good order. An indication of our effect on each other came after annual leave between our second-class and first-class years. We had lived together as roommates only a single year, but my friends in Palo Alto immediately noticed that I had developed what they called a "Southern accent," and demanded to know what had happened. They hadn't noticed such a change in me before, they said, commenting that Maryland, of which Annapolis was the capital city, could hardly be considered as being in the Deep South.

"True enough," I responded, "but I have a new roommate, and Bonner's from Athens, Georgia." The story, after our return from leave, got a delighted laugh from him.

"Funny you should say that," he said. "My folks down in Athens say I talk like a damn Yankee!"

As midshipman, I attained high class rank academically and in "aptitude for the service," both legacies of the training and background Father had given me. I graduated second in the Class of 1939 (we were all ranked academically, and that was where our names thereafter stood on the Navy list). Senior year I was named regimental commander, and had the great honor of leading the Regiment of Midshipmen on the field at Philadelphia for the traditional Army-Navy football game. Sadly, we lost.

It was while I was regimental commander that the Martians "landed," with the help of Orson Welles, and I attained my highest fame in that office. By request once described in the pages of the Naval Institute *Proceedings*, the story bears repetition. A radio was permitted both first and second classmen, but members of only the first class were considered mature enough to use it discreetly during study hours. Normally, "Foxy" Bonner and I used our study hours for necessary study and did not have our radio on. On this evening, in October of 1938, a member of the second class, name long forgotten, had come in on some errand, and while he was there our neighbor in the next room (Murray Frazee, later holder of a brilliant war record in our submarine service) burst in to tell us of the breathtaking news coming in on the radio. We turned it on, heard the excited announcer telling of huge six-legged machines striding the streets dealing out death and destruction all about them. It was unbelievable! We stared at each other, not knowing what to make of it.

As we heard that the attack was taking place in New Jersey, not many miles north of our location in Annapolis, the second classman spoke up. "My class ought to have permission to hear this, too!" he said.

This was at least a concrete proposal that I could do something about. Like practically all midshipmen during evening study hour, I had already shifted to pajamas and slippers. I flung arms into a bathrobe and took off for the Main Office, three floors below and in the adjoining building, where there was a duty officer who could give the necessary permission. My bathrobe must have been sailing behind me in perfect Superman style as I pelted into the Main Office, disregarding the surprised people there, and dashed into the adjoining private domain of the day's duty officer.

Lt. (jg) Charlie Kirkpatrick, later an outstanding submarine skipper during the war, and still later an esteemed superintendent of the Naval Academy, looked sharply at me. His radio was silent, as mine had been. "What's up, Beach?" he asked.

I told him, ending with the request for the second class. Without answering directly, Kirkpatrick reached for the table behind his desk, flipped on a small desk-set radio. The strident account of interplanetary disaster in New Jersey filled the room, as it had mine, only moments before. Kirkpatrick hardly moved, but for a second, on his angularly expressive face, an extraordinary look took over. He turned positively green in color, and his mouth worked in a strange way. A novelist might say he actually seemed to gobble, as a turkey might, but only for a few seconds. With a decisive movement, he began twirling the tuning dial. Other programs filled the air, but no mention of the Martians.

Back to the original station, the situation was getting rapidly worse. Then came the welcome news that our air station at Langley Field was sending planes to New Jersey to investigate, some of them with active bomb loads for emergency use if needed. The airfield action was flashed to our station, and for a moment we could hear the engines of the planes taking off.

Then our station shifted back to New Jersey, where real destruction was now beginning to take place. Suddenly the air was filled with the noise of our aircraft buzzing the interlopers, and now the unmistakable chatter of airplane machine guns could be heard. They sounded very much like World War I airplane guns I had heard in movies, interrupted stutter and all, and suddenly Kirkpatrick began figuring with a pencil on a sheet of paper. "They can't do that!" I heard him say. "It's too far, and the guns aren't right!" He began tuning in other stations again. As before, everything was calm and normal there. He turned the dial back to the original station, and then to the others, all around the dial. Nothing. The New Jersey radio station was the only one we could pick up that was carrying this extraordinary news. By this time, Kirkpatrick's face was entirely back to its usual sarcastic look, normal color and all. He turned directly to me.

"We've been had, Beach!" he said. "Go back to your room!" He had said, "we," not "you," something for which I'll ever be grateful.

My remaining recollection of this incident is divided into three parts. The first occurred on my departure from the Main Office complex. My classmate Jack Munson had the duty as midshipman officer in charge, with his desk in the outer office which I had passed in my entering hurry, and could not have avoided being aware of my colloquy with Kirkpatrick. As I left the latter, Jack's telephone rang. "Hello," I heard him say. "*Washington Post?*—yes, this is the midshipman main office. No, we've not heard about anything like that. Right now it's study hour down here, and midshipmen aren't allowed to have their radios on. No, I'm on duty here, and I'm not allowed one either. What did you say happened?"

This was all I heard of Jack's conversation, but it was enough. "Bless you, Jack!" I thought as I passed through the door and, more slowly this time, walked back to my fourth-floor room. The second portion of my memories is not quite so happy. Numerous midshipmen had been standing in their doorways, radios blaring, cheering me on during my run to the Main Office. Now there were even more of them, but they were laughing. On my own floor, however (the third memory), in the vicinity of my room the opposite reaction had taken hold. All the doors were shut, including that to my own room. Even Murray Frazee, my next-door neighbor and very good friend who had started the whole thing, was avoiding me. Only "Foxy" Bonner held out a little comfort. "Too bad you didn't wait just a little longer," he said.

I can't say I could blame anyone, the circumstances being as they were. A few days later it fell to me to address a scheduled meeting of the Midshipman

YMCA, composed mostly of plebes required to attend. Speaking to them was not usually difficult, but it was this time. Whatever inhibitions they might have had about being disrespectful of their seniors, these had seemingly gone by the board. My appearance was greeted with jeers and laughter. Had I been more adept at comedy I might have handled the situation better, for it took several minutes before I was able to get into my prepared remarks.

In retrospect I could feel good, and not ridiculous, about one thing. Not many years later when the subject came up in wardroom conversation, one of my wartime skippers commented, "Too bad you couldn't have traded places with the young guy at Pearl Harbor who didn't report the Japanese planes his crew spotted on their new radar."

Another of my Naval Academy episodes I've never been able fully to understand. During my first-class year there came suddenly a knock on the door, and there stood a captain whom I had never seen before. He was in full service uniform, and announced that he intended to give me a surprise inspection in my room. While Emmett and I stood at attention, he asked me which side of the room was mine, and proceeded to go over my side alone with the proverbial fine-toothed comb. He had me open the safe Emmett and I shared as members of the senior class, then had me open my strongbox (the first time anyone had ever required this, inspection or no), asked which of the laundry bags in the closet was mine, went through it, finally stood up, indicating he wanted to question me. What he said was astonishing.

"Where's the whiskey?"

"What?"

"Where's your booze, Beach?"

"I don't have any, sir!" I had indeed heard him right. But it didn't make sense. There was a long pause. We stood, looking at each other, then the captain smiled.

"I guess you've got it well hidden, and you're a better man than I was. When I was a midshipman your father caught me with a bottle of whiskey, and I thought I'd repay the compliment." He turned and went out the door.

Emmett and I stared at each other. "What was that all about?" said Emmett. I didn't have any idea. Neither of us ever saw the man again, and the only viable theory we could come up with was that, if Father many years ago had indeed caught the captain with whiskey in his room, which would have merited dismissal then, as in our time, he might have been merciful. Our inspector had obviously not been forced out of the Navy. Dad might have found a less painful way to handle the situation, an idea I found not hard to believe. In that event, the captain might just have been playing a game with me, with possibly no intent actually to put me on report—his neglect even to look at any part of my roommate's gear indicated he was not making a regular room inspection. In that case, I must have been a disappointment.

When I asked Father about this incident, he, like the admired Vice Admiral Delaney in a somewhat similar situation, could not recall it. It happened not long before graduation, and probably I should have pressed him harder while I still had the chance, for I had already noticed, from his letters, that his mind was beginning to fail him (he died four years later). Whatever the reason, my mind is a blank on anything further on this subject.

Our Class of 1939 was the largest, up to that time, to be admitted to the Academy. This was partly because of a series of smaller-than-average classes as the economic depression of the early thirties forced budgetary cutbacks that resulted in fewer vacancies. In 1935, however, when '39 entered, the vacancies that had been blocked were restored. More were available for '39 than ever before. Perhaps some extrasensory perception was operating, though no one could know the depths of what Hitler had in mind. We were, however, with the accumulated vacancies of prior years, the biggest class to enter up to that time. The Class of 1939 had the largest number of graduates for several more years, and the compilation of war casualties, in the world war that began three and a half months after our graduation, gave us both the greatest total number and the highest percentage.

My time as a midshipman was not all pleasure, of course, but in retrospect it has coalesced into a warm memory. I had no difficulty with classes. Father's strenuous training preparing me for the entrance exams had a long-term effect. I wrote to him often, and it soon became apparent, to some extent at least, that he was reliving his own midshipman days through me. Advice and counsel were prevalent, but so was interest in my drills, classmates, classes—all my activities. Never far from our lengthy exchanges was the fact that his class, in 1888, had graduated only 35 "passed midshipmen," as they were called in those days, having lost more than 50 during the four-year curriculum, while, 51 years after his, mine had entered 10 times as big. In due course we graduated 576 strong, having lost, principally through academic failure, about a third of our number. In 1888, his class had lost three-fifths of theirs. There was no war in the offing, but comparably a far higher percentage of his class achieved flag rank than of mine.

The Naval Academy was founded in 1845, and 43 years later Dad was graduate number 1,935. My graduating number, 51 years after that, was 13,221. Reference to the current registry of graduates in 1998 (59 more years) gives the "anchor man" number 65,257. (The "anchor man" is the graduate standing last in academic ranking and therefore bottom man in the class, considered a position of honor since he or she had barely avoided "bilging.") The numbers show how the Navy has expanded virtually exponentially since it was founded, primarily because of the great increase in aviators. Recent classes have graduated more than 1,000 from some 1,500 entering, although these numbers are now becoming less. Even these figures do not show the whole picture for the Navy, however, since they refer only to the Academy. They do not include the many thousands of officers recruited from the enlisted ranks, or the ones from the many NROTC units augmenting the Navy during World War II and afterward.

There was one piece of unfinished business at the Naval Academy that I had to leave behind. It amounted to research into what looked like a good idea, but there was not the capability. In our navigation studies it had seemed to me that calculation of a ship's position by sighting stars through a sextant might be unnecessarily difficult and time-consuming. Modern electronic equipment (in 1938), combined with gyrocompass capabilities, could conceivably do it easier and better. In a couple of months I had become obsessed with an idea for accomplishing this, and proceeded to try to build a model. This was a mistake, for I had no idea of the complexities of such a project, even the relatively simple one of building a gyroscope.

What I needed, in brief, was a gyro with three degrees of total freedom, so that it could be depended on to maintain a set axis of rotation regardless of the motion of the earth, or of the ship or aircraft holding it as it moves on the surface. I made a number of calculations to illustrate how my contraption would work, and received encouragement from one of my navigation instructors who agreed that the idea seemed to have some merit. Father, too, thought I might have come upon something useful. I actually cast some parts with which to make a set of gymbals (the pattern shop again), but there was no way to finish them, no available sets of the necessary ball bearings. I was far out of my depth, as is now evident. Recently I came upon the old casts I had made and wondered at the simplicity of my mind at that time.

Yet the idea had the germination of what has since come to pass. The missiles that today fly to remote targets with pinpoint accuracy are guided by such devices. Three degrees of freedom are no longer impossible with magnetically supported air- or electric-driven gyroscopes turning at impossibly high speeds. Picking off the extraordinarily minute changes in configuration resulting from change in location is, with modern electronic equipment, not so difficult either. It was an impossibility for me as a midshipman, but I can be proud that the basic rudiments of the idea nevertheless came my way, too.

I called my unbuilt device a "Gyro-Navigator," wrote a letter to the Navy Department describing the idea, and received back a complimentary letter from someone who ended it with "Keep up the good work." Sometimes I wish I had been able to do this, but from 1939 through 1941 there were too many competing interests in Europe and the Far East.

Graduation came on 1 June 1939, and with it my orders to report to the new and beautiful cruiser *Chester,* based at Long Beach, California, but then completing a short repair period at Bremerton, Washington. The ship got under way for an Alaskan cruise within days, returned to Long Beach in September, and was anchored there when war broke out in Europe. A few days later, one of the radical changes Hitler was making throughout the world resulted in my sudden transfer to a destroyer in San Diego being brought back to service from laid-up status. We happened to be passing that port when the dispatch transferring me was received. I was given half an hour to gather my few possessions, got into a ship's boat with my trunk and a small suitcase, and from a dock watched my old home, where I'd been expecting to serve for three years or so instead of the three months I had actually been aboard, disappear over the horizon. My orders were to report to the *Lea,* destroyer number 118, at the time still out of commission in the reserve fleet.

Chapter Three

Two Prewar Years in the Atlantic

Over the years since World War I, "the Great War" as it had then been called, many old destroyers, the familiar slim greyhounds with four prominent stacks, had been put into mothballs in San Diego. The destroyer base where they were located was in effect a small navy yard on the outskirts of town with a few buildings housing workshops, and an ancient marine railway barely big enough to haul a World War I destroyer out of the water. The biggest ship present, the most prominent feature of the base, was the old destroyer tender *Rigel,* a repair ship permanently moored to the concrete sea wall there. She had been there so long the Navy had built living quarters—a house on top of and blended in with her capacious stern—for her skipper, in charge also of the base, and his family. The machine shops and other repair facilities had gradually extended themselves on shore, taking up quarters in whatever old buildings were available, or building new "temporary" ones in empty spaces. Most of our navy yards had begun life in just this way.

Each of several wooden piers extending from the sea wall provided moorings for up to 16 old "four-pipers," as they were affectionately called, securely attached to the pier bollards with heavy wire in groups of four to a "nest." These old destroyers, or "tincans," the *Lea* being one, had evidence of fairly recent use: they still wore peeling coats of gray paint. It was scraped and chipped from years of inactivity, rubbing against a pier piling or the old wicker fenders placed between them and an adjacent destroyer, or had larger areas of last-minute damage, but the group as a whole looked viable, if somewhat careworn. These ships, we understood, were supposed to be capable of activation within a month.

Perhaps 50 additional tincans, far more decrepit-looking, were chained in a second group to both sides of a long row of wooden pilings that had been driven into the bay bottom some distance from the active piers.

These latter ships, dull red in color, showed little or no evidence of ever having worn standard Navy gray. In general they were alive with rust, and they were missing significant items of equipage such as a gun here or there, or (more likely) an anchor removed to replace one lost by an active fleet destroyer. A few planks haphazardly spanned the distances between pilings to permit precarious passage from one rusting relic to another, but to get to the mooring at all, a boat was required. There was no direct connection to the destroyer base, or to the shore in any way. Almost certainly no one, except possibly bureaucrats who had never seen them, had ever expected members of this last sorry bunch to go to sea. Derisively called "Red Lead Row," some had been put there at the end of the Great War, right out of the building yards. Many were brand-new, had never seen deep water, and, as the World War I naval building spurt died out, construction of a number of them had not even been completed. For years they had been a source of "midnight requisitions" by active destroyers in quick need of parts.

With the outbreak of fighting in Europe, the U.S. Navy Department implemented plans to activate all these old relics of a past war, beginning with the ones most recently out of service, and issued dispatch orders to man them. I happened to have a name high in the alphabet, and that was evidently the criterion for assignment to this duty. I was not at all alone in this experience, and I remember contemplating the lengthy chain of events, beginning in Europe, 6,000 miles away, that had made such a sudden and significant change in my personal circumstances and those of all the other ensigns (likewise high in the alphabet) reporting suddenly and unexpectedly for new duties. I also noticed the tarnished brass plate on *Lea*'s mast that gave the date she had been launched: by coincidence it was the same year and month I, too, had slid down the ways.

There was not, however, much time for philosophizing. Work did more than beckon; it surrounded us, and the memory that stays most strongly with me today is of the smell. To protect their machinery, these old ships had been swathed in some sort of black fuel-oil derivative that we called "comsomol" (no doubt a form of Cosmoline, which may even be the correct word) that pervaded everything. Removing the comsomol, an inspired mixture of old crankcase oil and soft tar, was the first stage of the procedure required to restore the ships to operating condition. It had to be boiled off the engines, boilers, torpedo tubes, and guns, in some cases dissolved with spirits. Finally it was wiped off with rags (in very short supply; to us a bale of rags was like gold, and many were the stratagems devised to augment our dwindling supply when the man in charge of doling out the few available bales was not looking).

The laborious cleaning procedure put much comsomol into the atmosphere, and incidentally got much of it on the people doing the work. All the destroyers were going through the same evolutions, in various stages, and to me the destroyer base at San Diego will forever recall the redolent smell of dissolved or simply scraped-off comsomol, dumped into spaces between buildings, stuffed into empty oil drums, loaded into filthy trucks for transportation to some other unfortunate location, or just burning in a vacant place.

It was a heady time for all that. Our ship had been designated for conversion to a squadron flagship, and this involved provision of berthing and work space for a squadron commander and a staff of two lieutenants, plus a Filipino steward. More work was therefore done on *Lea* than on the other destroyers, quite a bit of actual construction work, but the smell of comsomol was the same for all.

The *Lea* was among those unrealistically designated "30 days to readiness," but it took considerably longer before we were able to get her to sea, and to Mare Island Navy Yard for final checkup. There we discovered that somehow she had lost a reel of movies during her previous commission. As the junior officer aboard, I was automatically the "movie officer," and learned that issue of any movies whatever to *Lea* was proscribed until we came up with the one lost during her previous commission, about three years before. One would have thought it an international incident. No one listened to my expostulations that recommissioning an old ship was the same as commissioning a new one, that *Lea* had begun a new life and should not be tarred with any problems existing earlier, that no one now aboard could possibly bear responsibility, or even know about, mistakes that might have been made in a previous life. I, merely an ensign, might have been talking to a deity living on the moon.

Fortunately, we were a designated squadron flagship; I was astonished to see (and hear) our squadron commander in action. He evidently liked his movies, and he drew a lot of weight in the Navy. I doubt that Mare Island has been the same since this fracas. We got our movies, the squadron commander was happy, someone was probably made to understand the error of his ways, and we headed for the Panama Canal. Our destination was Key West, Florida, our newly activated base. We were to be part of the Neutrality Patrol proclaimed by President Franklin Roosevelt.

Initiation into patrol doings was not long in coming. I was communications officer (among myriad other things), and we had barely arrived at Key West when I decoded a message directing our squadron to intercept and escort the German cruise liner *Columbus* in her attempt to return to Germany from Vera Cruz, Mexico, where the war had caught her. Her passengers had long been returned to their own countries via neutral transport, but the ship and at least some crew had been interned in Vera Cruz for months. Other Neutrality Patrol destroyers based in Galveston, watching over her attempt to break out from the harbor of Vera Cruz, had picked her up as she got under way, escorted her across the Gulf of Mexico, and turned her over to us as she approached the Straits of Florida.

A large, handsome ship she was, superstructure extending nearly the entire length of her hull, two broad business-like stacks, an oceanliner in all respects. We soon remarked, however, that not once during her entire period in our company, as we escorted her through the Straits of Florida and north toward Charleston, did we see anyone topside. She might have been an empty ship with not a soul aboard, except that she was steaming at a steady 20 knots, navigating to remain in the middle of the straits, and informing us of her intended changes of course by flaghoists in international code. We thoroughly looked her over whenever we were close enough for binocular inspection, and we watched carefully whenever she hoisted or lowered one of her flaghoists, purely out of curiosity to see whether she actually had some crew members. But never an individual did we see.

Her flag bags must have been inside the enclosed bridge; the flags simply appeared through a bridge window from which a halyard led to an overhead block, or pulley, hanging from a wire between her masts. Obviously there was someone inside pulling on the return portion of the halyard—we could readily see the flags jerk as he did so—and of course there was someone steering. There must have been someone in charge on her bridge, and an engineroom watch below as well; but despite balmy weather that brought many of our own crew on deck to enjoy it, not one person did we ever see aboard the *Columbus*. Her crew must have had orders to remain out of sight, and I remember thinking this was perhaps telling us something. To us in the *Lea*, the entire affair was something of a lark—funny business, not for real. To the *Columbus*, it was serious indeed.

We also noticed that she ran well. I do not recall ever seeing even a wisp of smoke from her stacks. The gases issuing from her broad stacks were clean, invisible over the horizon. As the days of our association ran on, we began to admire this merchant skipper. In naval terms, he ran a "taut ship." He would have been an asset to any navy, ours included.

As communications officer, it was my job to encode our squadron position report every four hours for transmission to Atlantic Fleet headquarters in Norfolk, and with some dismay I noted the simplicity of our code: after a day or so I knew some of it by heart (another reason why we seemed only to be playing games). Anyone could break this code with minimal effort. To use that particular one were the orders, however, and I dutifully followed them, wondering all the while if anyone other than someone in Norfolk might also be decoding our messages.

About the third night my question was answered. A dark shadow appeared over the horizon to starboard, overtook our little convoy, suddenly altered course to pass quietly between us and our charge, and as quietly disappeared astern. Those who got a good look at the interloper swore that she was a British cruiser, probably of the *Southampton* class. A message reporting the incident was handed to me to encode—in that same insecure code—and so far as I knew that was the only action taken. Full details must have been immediately reported to the German skipper. He would have taken a good look at the British ship himself, and with little doubt his radio room had been intercepting our messages and decoding them as easily as the British must have been. The significance of the British cruiser's appearance must have been clear, and if the German captain had not done so previously, he surely then began to prepare for what he intended to do.

Our escort services terminated as we approached Charleston, S.C. When we turned the admirable German oceanliner over to the destroyer squadron based in that harbor, our squadron commander directed the international flaghoist signal be made: "Best wishes for a safe journey." The *Columbus* instantly hoisted her own signal: "Thank you for kind services goodbye and good luck." Then she headed north in the gathering dusk, and the fate that awaited her.

She had only a few days more to live. Under escort of our Charleston-based friends, she continued north in the Gulf Stream until she reached the latitude of Norfolk. There she turned due east, and shortly thereafter, as she reached the line on the chart marking the then-claimed limits of U.S. territorial interest, there was another exchange of signals with seaman-to-seaman expressions of good will. Then the American destroyers reversed course and headed west, and as they did so, dead ahead of the German liner, the tops of a British destroyer hove into view. Tactfully, the British tincan did not ever get within sight of the Americans, nor did the bigger cruiser that had been shadowing us for a week, but at one point both Americans and British must have simultaneously been in sight from the big German liner.

The *Columbus* was too far gone to save, sinking with all hatches and portholes open, her vestigial crew, hitherto unseen, waiting quietly in lifeboats, when HMS *Hyperion* arrived close alongside.

Predictably, demands on the Neutrality Patrol progressively became more strenuous. There was a period, to the resentment of her squadron mates, when the *Lea,* being squadron flagship, spent far more time alongside her pier in Key West than they. This changed in time, however, and our whole squadron headed for the Virgin Islands for a great deal of target practice. I was now gunnery officer as well as communications officer, torpedo officer, first lieutenant, and ship's service officer. There were only four officers aboard, not counting the squadron commander, and I was the most junior, therefore holding the unofficial title of "George," as in "have George do it."

The world condition was worsening, but my own little world was of consuming interest and activity. I was busy from reveille to midnight, stood a watch in three (four hours on, eight off) under way, and day's duty every other day in port. Half the crew worked directly for me; practically all of the ship that you could see (not engines and boilers) "belonged" to me. It was up to me (and my sailors) to keep all of it neatly painted, correctly serviced, properly running. In many ways this was the most active and wonderful period of my life. I would not trade the memories of that tiny ship for anything.

One of them might be worth repeating. One of my sailors, an excellent man who really knew how to handle the ship's guns, had earned a promotion. When the advancement came through he sought me out and offered me a big green cigar, which I accepted although I did not smoke, thinking to pass it on later to our exec, who occasionally indulged in one. But I had reckoned without my man. "Aren't you going to smoke it, Mr. Beach?" he said, holding up a small device made for cutting the tip. His other hand held a lighter, "Here, sir, let me help!" I was standing on *Lea*'s midships deckhouse, in plain view of half a dozen of our crew. Feeling I couldn't help myself, I let him cut off the tip and apply flame to the other end. It was a beautiful day; the *Lea* was steaming through a calm sea, but slowly the horizon started to heave, and very quickly she began to roll heavily. I barely made it to the lifelines, pitched the cigar overboard, retched violently—and turned, with great beads of sweat on my face, to find 50 grinning sailors enjoying my discomfiture.

On a more serious note, as communications officer I soon decoded a message giving provisional instructions for a possible attack on Vichy French units holed up at Martinique. As gunnery officer I then went on to prepare our ship's attack plan (others would work out details of the ship and squadron movements). It was enough for me that as squadron flagship the *Lea* would lead the column of destroyers into the harbor of Fort-de-France in full darkness, before dawn. We had just overhauled the entire gunnery system and aligned our ancient Vickers "step by step" gun director with it. At a recent target practice every shot had hit the target, and in salvo fire the spread between shots had been phenomenally small. The atmosphere was exhilarating. My gunners were well trained and enthusiastic, and so was I.

I remember writing to someone, about this time, that the ship also had a captain, an executive officer, and an engineer, but that I had no idea of what any of them did. This was not quite true, of course, but my duties took all my time, thought, and energies. Likewise, I recall not thinking at all about the probable consequences of our surprise attack on the French ships, the death and destruction that would be dealt by our guns, the possibility the French might retaliate in kind. That was not my concern anyway. My job was to make sure our guns worked to the best of their capability.

Our targets were two: the small old aircraft carrier *Béarn* and the training cruiser *Jeanne d'Arc*, both caught on our side of the Atlantic when war began, as the *Columbus* had been, and generally in a state of low morale, presumably unalert, with portions of their crews ashore. We, on the other hand, were at the top of our training, and certainly we were alert! Well do I remember the thrill at the thought that we might be going into action. Despite her age and years of prior service, it would be the *Lea*'s first combat experience. No one aboard our ship, nor any ship in our squadron, had ever seen a shot fired in anger.

After all the preparations, however, the order to go and do it never arrived. Diplomatic solution prevailed, the French ships did not go over to the Axis, and I have since felt that most likely there never was any real intention to resort to arms. A fallback plan is, however, always a necessity, and that's what we were, if worst came to worst. Whether President Roosevelt truly contemplated using arms against Vichy at this low point in the history of France can probably never be conclusively proved, but we, at least, were ready. On the personal level it was a letdown, but all things considered it was just as well.

Things continued to change rapidly. Our squadron was shifted from Key West to Norfolk, then to Newport, and finally to Casco Bay in Maine. Somewhere along the way our squadron commander was detached, and we learned that our entire squadron, except for our own ship, had been given to the British, who were in desperate need of antisubmarine escorts. It was said that the reason for the special retention of our ship was not our new squadron commander's quarters and office setup, built only a year previously in San Diego, but the fact that I was currently dating the daughter of the officer in charge of selecting the ships to go—but there was no substantiation for this rumor, and I never believed it.

We did have use, once, for the relatively palatial squadron commander's quarters. One of our sailors, a popular character who had been sent to us as a "cook striker" (in training for the rating of ship's cook) showed symptoms of appendicitis. We were at sea, our pharmacist's mate diagnosed the problem, but, though qualified for "independent duty," he carefully explained that he was not allowed to perform the indicated operation. So we sent a message to base and put our man, stomach packed with ice, in the squadron commander's empty cabin with constant attention. For the next several days, our low-ranking sailor had a private bathroom and three meals a day brought to him by his crewmates.

He had been well liked because of his willingness to jump into any seamanlike chore that might be going on, such as splicing rope, which he loved to do. He was young, enthusiastic, and big, obviously designed to be a boatswain's mate or signalman, despite his unlikely designation in the cooking line. At his stage in the Navy, that meant mainly peeling potatoes. Clearly, he was better at splicing rope than he would ever be at peeling spuds.

En route to Norfolk he had constant ministration by worried shipmates, and on arrival our ship was met by a naval ambulance and its crew, who transferred him directly to the naval hospital in the base. Two hours later, he came walking back down the dock to rejoin us. There was nothing wrong with his appendix, and he had suffered no ill effects from enforced idleness and the icepacks! Needless to recount, after this he had a lot of rope to splice, and many friends to placate for his "vacation" at their expense on board ship. Secretly, however, we were all pleased at the outcome, and no one accused him of faking his supposed illness.

Of greater concern to me, and real regret, was that the four-inch guns and fire-control director we had so successfully used in target practice only a couple of months earlier, and which I had spent so much time and effort readying for our aborted attack on the Vichy French ships, were removed during a two-week period at the navy yard in Charleston, S.C. Three-inch antiaircraft guns without any central control at all were put in their place, and we were converted from a pretty good little (old) destroyer to a gunboat (a fast one, true), armed with nothing but ancient pop-guns. At a single stroke, uncoordinated with any of the realities of the ship herself, we lost our well-honed main battery. At the same time two of our four sets of triple torpedo tubes were removed, and our bridge, previously open at the back, was entirely enclosed.

Obviously we were being converted for antiaircraft duties and fitted out for much heavier weather than the ship had originally been built for, but there was no word as to whether the Navy Department knew what it was doing to the individual ships. One would have thought some attention might be paid to the Navy's investment in our old set of guns and the nifty, if old, gunfire director system that, with considerable Navy money for new wiring, we had been able to get working so well. Evidently no one felt it useful to inform the ships concerned that everything we had been working on for the past year was worthless.

Neutrality Patrol was boring duty. We took our turn "on station," cruising aimlessly at slow speed in a designated sector off our Atlantic coast. All ships seen were contacted by signal searchlight, their name and destination demanded for our log, and after suitable pleasantries by flashing light or sometimes via flaghoist in international code, they were permitted to go on their way. I have no idea what we'd have done had one of them announced he was a German. We had no instructions (our skipper, Lt. Cdr. Clarence Broussard, may have had some in his secret Operations Order). It was clear, in any case, that the purpose of the patrol was to establish a presence in the event of later need.

What that need might be was soon somewhat predictable in view of the war in Europe and England's dire straits. Even from our circumscribed view, at sea most of the time but able to receive commercial radio broadcasts if not too far offshore, the steady deterioration in England's position was apparent. Her navy, about the size of ours, was spread unbelievably thin, except that her big battle fleet was kept mostly together against the possibility of a great sea battle like the fabled Jutland of 1916. This was an eventuality we found hard to envision, but we soon thought of a more fundamental reason; the battleships in which England had invested so much of her naval resources could not be spread thin. The individual units were big and full of people, but they were also extremely valuable and relatively few in number.

Argue it as you might, England's maritime resources could not come close to covering the whole world. Because of aircraft and submarines, the superb battle fleet England had maintained through so much history could no longer do its job. Admiral Mahan, though he might have been shocked at the realization, would have been forced to admit it.

The *Bismarck* episode made this thoroughly clear, though the subliminal message, at least in my mind, was different from simple rationalization about the role of the battleship. To the Germans, the *Bismarck* had some of the virtues of a submarine: once free in the world ocean, she could strike anywhere she might wish. A virtually invulnerable warship, possessed of very high speed, not only could she strike by surprise, she could in addition do something no submarine could. Her shield being not the invisible ocean depths but her visible and tremendous power, there would always be a wide circle of terror around her. Thus, in terms of scaring ocean transportation off the sea, she might be more effective than any submarine, or a group of them. Could she get loose in the world ocean, she might so blockade England from a distance that the entire concept of sea warfare might be changed, the downside of Mahan's ideas demonstrated: most especially for an island nation, in war *failure* to control the sea can be disastrous.

This view must have occurred to Prime Minister Winston Churchill and other top British war leaders, but the German battleship's foray to sea was seen by most as simply a direct challenge to Britain's navy. To British naval officers, smarting since the Battle of Jutland over their inability to do the Nelsonian thing by obliterating the enemy's sea power in a single grand battle, she represented not only a challenge, the greatest target in a generation, but an opportunity to satisfy their yearnings for justification of their very existence.

Thus, whereas Germany saw *Bismarck* in the practical sense as a warlike instrument of great potential, the British navy saw her emotionally, as well, as the enemy ship, of all ships, that must be destroyed. In this respect, *Bismarck* represented far more than a single enemy battleship loose on the high seas. Her destruction was mandatory to England's self-image, as, indeed, it would be to the view other nations would thereafter hold of England. Perhaps there were some in Germany who held the same idea, and they might have supported her unique intrusion into the North Atlantic on this account. If so, they should have planned the expedition better, given her far more backing and command assistance.

It is even conceivable that *Bismarck* could somehow have brought the war to an end by destroying England's ability for further resistance to the German onslaught, but if this was their "high strategy," Hitler's admirals failed terribly in its implementation. Sending this great battleship, of all ships, to sea in the cavalier manner they did was a tremendous mistake, for the potential damage to Germany from her loss probably outweighed any possible advantage that might have accrued from even the most successful cruise. Unless, hardly truly to be expected, she had been able to hold the entire British Fleet at bay and destroy it unit by unit. This, at that particular instant in naval time, she might have been able to do had there been no aircraft to take part in the campaign against her or if she could have been adequately supported by German aircraft. There is little doubt that, for a fleeting time, carriers not yet having come into their own, she was the most powerful and effective warship in the world.

Small wonder that Churchill, who understood such matters viscerally even better than intellectually, issued the classic order, "Sink the *Bismarck!*" Her destruction, or surrender (which, after the *Graf Spee,* no one expected), would be not only an example to the world but, most important, an example to England herself. It may not be too much to suggest that had the speedy German battleship been able to escape the dragnet thrown out for her and carry on her projected cruise, the effect on England might have been disastrous. British inability to cope with her might even have brought England's resistance to an end. Would Roosevelt's ability to support Churchill have survived a defeat such as this?

The stakes attending *Bismarck*'s disastrous cruise were thus high indeed. No one can conclusively predict what might have been the result of her not having lost fuel through chance injury by one of the *Prince of Wales*'s shells, or conversely, continuing her cruise instead of heading back to port.

Well did I remember seeing HMS *Hood,* resplendent alongside her pier in Portsmouth, England. It was on a midshipman practice cruise in 1936, and I recall thinking of her as the handsomest warship I had ever seen. A young officer who took an informal group of us on a tour infected us all with his enthusiasm for his ship. Now, only a few years later, that grand ship had been instantaneously sunk by a single salvo, probably a single shell hit, fired by an even more powerful and even handsomer warship. And it fell to me, as *Lea*'s communications officer on Neutrality Patrol well into the Atlantic, to decode the message addressed to all U.S. Navy ships in the area: if we encountered *Bismarck* we were to shadow her and send hourly reports (using, this time, a more secure code than the one prescribed for the *Columbus*).

Doubtless, Churchill and FDR had conversed by telephone on the subject, and doubtless our president was fully aware of all the possible ramifications to the *Bismarck* situation. Our enmity to everything Hitler stood for was clear, as was Hitler's for us. I took the message to Broussard, whom I had come more and more to admire, not only as a ship handler but also as a compassionate human being who understood and responded to the needs of his crew. After he had read it, I told him that just before bringing the message I had looked up the known statistics of the German battlewagon. From what I had been able to discover, she was not only a million times more powerful than we, but also several knots faster. Little "shadowing" could we do in *this* circumstance. He grunted in reply. There was a small tight smile on his face, and I felt embarrassed for having assumed he might not already have done the same research. "We'll have to do our best, whatever happens," he said.

The fact is that *Bismarck* never approached our position, and at that very moment was being sunk by the greatest concentration of force ever placed against a single target. She had been disabled by a chance aircraft torpedo hit in a rudder. At one point, two British battleships, one the powerful old post–World War I *Rodney* and the other the brand-new *King George V*, approached to point-blank range with their 16- and 14-inch guns and fired without restraint at the by-then helpless and no longer able to resist German ship. No ship in history ever took as much punishment as *Bismarck* before she finally went down, and to this day her few survivors claim she scuttled herself, committed suicide, instead of *being* sunk by her enemies. Of course, this detail mattered little, except to the naval pride of her builders and small surviving crew.

And then we found ourselves among a group of destroyers, some much bigger and newer than our lurching, dancing, four-piper, escorting a convoy of transports to Iceland. Our station was in the "outer screen," nearly 10 miles ahead of the main body of transports, and it is true that we hardly ever saw them until we all arrived at the harbor designated for our use, Hvalfjordur, a spacious fjord not far from Iceland's capital city of Reykjavik. There the transports passed between us as we spread out to screen their entry, to the disgust of many a destroyer sailor who, though not seasick (perish the unworthy thought!), found it hard to await entry into calm water and a surcease from 30-degree rolls to either side.

The Atlantic, even without winter's bad weather, is always rough, and physically exhausting to the crews of destroyers. It is, in short, hell to small ships.

In the *Lea* we actually experienced 45-degree rolls, through a total arc of 90 degrees. At times, our inclinometer read an improbable 60 degrees. At such extreme angles, the edges of our decks were entering the water, our "righting force" had reached its maximum and could no longer increase. The principle under which this functioned, discovered by David Watson Taylor of our Navy and thoroughly explained at Annapolis, showed why ships of low freeboard were in greater danger of capsizing than those with higher sides. The danger point was when a ship rolled so far, for whatever reason, that the edge of her main deck was in the water. Further roll from there could not increase "righting moment," the force returning the ship to an upright position. A few more degrees would probably have rolled us completely over!

Surcease came at last, and we dropped the hook in an excellent anchorage lined with high mountains on either side, but totally lacking anything resembling trees or habitations. There appeared to be an improvised dock on one side, however, and it was there our Marines went ashore. Here, soon, there blossomed a settlement of unusual half-cylinder-shaped buildings of corrugated iron that we learned to call "Quonset huts" after Quonset, Rhode Island, where they were reputedly designed.

The brown hillsides, entirely bare of green growth, gave us no invitation for hiking or even simple rambles ashore. I seized one opportunity to visit the capital city of Reykjavik and found it to be like Hvalfjordur: cool, almost no foliage to be seen, the streets sparsely populated. The few Icelandic people I encountered, all of them in stores or restaurants, seemed cool, too.

Someone had told me that the Icelandic women were all beautiful, that everyone went swimming in the nude, and that if the place could be found it would be a wonderful sight, especially for a young American sailor just in from a lengthy stint at sea. Wandering around in Reykjavik, it occurred to me to try to find out if this rumor could be true. The pool where this delightful disportation reportedly took place was supposedly in a gymnasium of some sort in the middle of town, and sure enough, I found such a place!

One had to pay admission and rent a pair of swimming trunks to use the pool, I learned from someone who spoke English (many Icelanders spoke it quite passably), and, quite truly, the rules did not require the trunks to be kept on. For convenience there were separate changing rooms for men and women, but the pool was communal. I could hardly believe I had found the right place so easily, and distinctly remember some hesitation at going in. I had not, after all, ever indulged in nude bathing, except at a YMCA gym, where it was *de rigueur*. However, being a courageous young fellow, I screwed up my nerve, paid the fee, went into the changing room, and emerged, wearing my rented trunks, into a large, warm, well-filled, and well-lighted swimming pool. There were men and women in it, too, some as naked as the proverbial jaybird. The buzz of conversation hit me before I could adjust my eyes to the light.

About half the men were nude, and perhaps half the women as well—but there was a large canvas screen dividing the capacious pool into two parts, extending well above everyone's head, and also down into the water to its bottom. You could hear the voices of women in conversation on the other side of the screen, but the canvas was of heavy sailcloth, impervious to sight and everything else. I'd been on swimming and water polo teams at Annapolis, and greatly enjoyed the refreshing swim I got that afternoon in Iceland, but there was no visual stimulation.

The adventure provided me with one extra benefit, all the same. When I returned aboard the *Lea,* practically everyone asked if it were really true about the nude bathing, and had I seen any. "Yes, it was true," I said, and modestly admitted to having been there. I told most of the details truthfully, too, but as has been said, sometimes it's best to know what to leave out. I hope my friends won't hold my failure to mention the canvas screen against me.

Officially, Iceland had asked us for protection from possible aggression by Germany, but as I quickly discovered, considerable pressure had been exerted to bring about the formal request. Icelanders took a dim view of our "occupation" of their island. To them we represented a war that was none of their affair, that had come to them only because of their once isolated, but now unappreciated (by them) strategic location between Newfoundland and Europe.

It was not a military "occupation" by any stretch. But we did need a mid-Atlantic airfield to provide antisubmarine coverage by land-based air of the approaches to England. At this time, July 1941, less than two years after the outbreak of World War II, England was the only country in Western Europe still in defiance of Hitler.

The *Lea* carried barely enough fuel to span the distance from Boston to Iceland. Before being able to begin a return trip we had to refuel, which we did alongside the huge former commercial tanker *Salamonie,* recently taken over from Standard Oil and sent to Iceland to form part of the "fleet support train," as we'd been taught to call such tremendous ships. The *Lea* was about the size of a rowboat alongside her huge bulk, and I took the opportunity to wander about *Salamonie*'s decks to acquaint myself with what such a big ship looked like. I made a particular point to pass by the captain's quarters and note how big they were in comparison to the tiny spaces we, even our skipper, had in the *Lea*. I also noticed that there was practically no crew aboard, at least none that I could see. Perhaps they were all ashore looking for the nude swimming pool!

We were barely able to pack enough fuel aboard our little ship to make it back to Boston in one long jump, in company with a small freighter we were nominally convoying. On arrival, we sensed excitement in the air. We were required to refuel at once, again to capacity (when fully fueled *Lea* had a noticeable list to port, so fueling to capacity had an uncomfortable effect on our daily lives). At the same time, trucks came, loaded with mail sacks. Our forward fireroom was soon jammed with mail (the sacks were, at least, loaded mostly to starboard, thus somewhat lessening our port list), and we got under way the next day, quietly, alone, well before dawn. Another of my many jobs, my getting underway station was on the forecastle in charge of the anchor equipment and to see our two anchors secured for sea as we headed out of Boston's commodious harbor.

Thus it was that I exchanged personal signals with an attractive couple, a tall young man of about my age in a tuxedo, and a lovely blonde woman, also tall, in a long green dress, standing on the sea wall as we passed. They could not know where we were bound as I waved to them from the lean forecastle of my handsome little ship, nor could I have any idea about them, except that he had his arm around her waist, waved back with the other (she waved with the opposite arm). They seemed reluctant for day to break and their long and happy evening to come to a close. The scene has come back to me often. No one could know what the immediate future had in store for any of us. No doubt they were bemused at the sight of the lone destroyer on its way to sea, and for my part I have always wished them long happy lives and many handsome children—and wondered what the war that was soon to begin did to their romance.

Argentia, Newfoundland, was our objective, and we were directed to make our best speed with only half our boilers on the line, the two in the after fireroom. We charged along at a very respectable 26 knots nonetheless, using oil from portside fuel tanks and thus "burning off" our remaining port list, throwing clouds of glittering spray from our plunging bows, rolling heavily in the usual Atlantic chop. Most of us had long gotten over seasickness. Only a few poor souls had the congenital defect of not being able to adjust to the constant motion, and our attitude toward them gradually changed from superior contempt to compassion for their misery. To most of us, glorying in our strength and ability, it was exhilarating to drive our ship through the elements and vanquish them.

Why we had to be in such a hurry to get under way for Argentia, and why we nonetheless had to give up half of our steam-making potential to make room for the mail, was not explained, but we found out when we entered the harbor. Arrayed before us was the flower of the free world navies. There was a huge battleship flying British colors, not far from the spot assigned for our anchorage. There was also a handsome cruiser, nearly a twin of my old *Chester* but different, I instantly saw, because her forecastle was longer, to accommodate more staff officers, her amidships well-deck correspondingly shorter. This could only be *Augusta,* identical sister of *Houston* and *Chicago* (both of which were in the Pacific Fleet) and little more than a year later the only survivor of those three beautiful flagships.

Many other vessels were present, most of them modern U.S. destroyers, but a number showing British-looking build. As we approached I was able to recognize the British and Canadian ensigns and confirm my initial guesses as to their nationality. The battlewagon could only be one of the British *King George V* class, notable because of the four huge guns in each of her two lower turrets, one forward on the forecastle and the other overlooking the main deck aft, while the single super-firing turret, emplaced above and immediately aft of number one turret, had only two such guns.

We were not long in finding out what was going on. We had hardly dropped our "hook" when large boats came alongside demanding immediate delivery of our cargo of mail sacks. An important conference was going on between Roosevelt and Churchill, here in the foggy harbor of Argentia. The battleship, the *Prince of Wales,* the same one that had fought the *Bismarck* and hit her twice in the fuel tanks forward, therefore leading directly to her demise, had brought the British prime minister and his staff. Roosevelt, with his people, had arrived in the *Augusta.* The other ships were the various escorts for both principal parties—and, because of the contents of our forward fire-room, for a giddy few minutes we were the most important ship present.

As is now known, the conference produced some significant pronouncements, among them Roosevelt's declaration of the Four Freedoms and the Concordance of the Atlantic Charter, as it was called. More significant than these public statements were the private agreements, unannounced but clear to all, even to an ensign up to his ears in duties associated with his own little destroyer. We were definitely about to get in the shooting war. The only question remaining was when.

The day after her epochal arrival at Argentia with the mail, the once most important ship in the harbor was told off to escort another small convoy to Iceland. When we arrived, two things happened that foretold my personal future.

First, we saw two rather large submarines anchored there. From my recreational reading in *Jane's Fighting Ships,* the renowned photographic compendium of the world's warships, I recognized them as of our next-to-biggest class, either the V-1, V-2, or V-3, or, as renamed, the *Bass, Barracuda,* or *Bonita.* As communications officer, presumably to receive messages important to our ship, I was surprised at not having gotten word of their presence, so as to be able to inform Captain Broussard, and was a bit more surprised when he told me to use a signal searchlight to invite members of both crews on board our ship for the movies we regularly showed when in port.

Iceland in August still had long daylight hours. We had been in the habit of partially unrigging an awning to enclose the deck space where movies were shown, thereby making it dark enough for tolerable pictures. Destroyers were small ships, the *Lea* a very small one, smaller than either of the submarines we sent the invitation to. When movies were shown, our deck space was so cramped that half our crew habitually sat behind the screen instead of in front of it, since the picture was almost as clear on the back of the screen as on the front. This was no problem at all, if one could accommodate to 100 percent reverse English, driving on the left with steering wheel on the right, doing everything left-handed, such as saluting with the left hand instead of the right, and so on. Even with the consequent extra space, however, cramming two big submarine crews in with ours under our broken-down amidships deck awning gave me pause, for I knew it would be my job to figure out how to do it.

But I need not have worried. Back came a blinking light from one of the submarines: "Many thanks, but your hot decks burn our fanny!" Broussard laughed when he heard it, and I wondered if the subs could show movies down below somewhere.

During this period submarines had center stage in Hvalfjordur, for it was during this same sojourn that the captured German U-boat *U-570* was brought in. We were not allowed to go on board; curiosity would have to be satisfied with binoculars, but I remember remarking how small the sub was and wondering why she had such a heavy port list, far worse than ours when full of fuel. She had surrendered to a patrol aircraft, a fact also hard to take aboard. Later, we learned that this submarine had been appropriated into the Royal Navy as a prize of war, an idea that gave us quite a bit of pause inasmuch as submarines encountered at sea were always presumed to be enemy, whether or not seen, but even when fully visible this particular sub would always look like a German sub. We need not have worried, for the British were as cognizant of that concern as anyone. The U-boat was used as a test vehicle under the name HMS *Graph,* was invariably heavily escorted, and served the Allies well in evaluating techniques and capabilities.

The second pregnant thing, for me, was a dispatch directing that I take a physical examination to determine if I qualified for submarine duty. "Does this mean they're thinking of sending me off to submarine school?" I asked the captain.

"I wouldn't be surprised," he answered.

"I'd rather not go," I told him.

"Why not? Don't you think you'll like submarine duty? You're not against it, or afraid of it, are you?"

"Not at all," I told him, "but I like it here. Do I really have to take this physical exam? If I don't take it they won't send me, will they?" Somewhere in this conversation I threw in a couple of "sirs" just to prove that I still remembered my naval manners. Broussard by this time had become something of a father figure to me, for he obviously had the welfare of everyone on board, mine among them, very much in his mind.

"No, if you don't take the exam they won't send you," he said slowly, "but you've got your orders, so you have to do it."

The battleship *New Mexico* happened to be in the harbor, and of course had on board a full battleship medical department, so to her the *Lea*'s motor launch took me, preceded by an official request for the exam. Of it I remember only one thing, other than that it posed no special problems. At its end, the doctor, a medical corps commander, had me remove my shoes and socks. He sat opposite me in his swivel chair as I did so, leaned over to give my feet a fast look, then said, in a contemptuous way, "Humph! Plow boy's feet in dancing master shoes!"

I had no idea where that announcement came from, but was able to hold my tongue. He was, after all, a commander.

Back aboard the *Lea* with physical qualification for submarines in hand and a message I had composed declining the same, I again sought my skipper. I handed him the message, which said, "Ensign Beach qualified physically but does not desire submarine duty."

"They won't send me if you send this message, will they?" I said.

"No, they probably won't. But do you really want me to send it? Maybe they'll misunderstand. You wouldn't want them to think you're afraid or something, would you? Why don't you want to go?"

It was the second time he had said this, or something like it. Father had told me, "Stay in the big ships, that's where the real navy is," but through no will of mine I had been sent to a small one and had found it very much to my liking. Now, again contrary to my own ideas, the Navy wanted me to change the orientation of my career. But I didn't really know what to tell Broussard.

"It's not that I'm afraid of subs," I said. "That doesn't bother me. It's that I like it here. I know my job, I like everybody on board, and I feel good about it. Isn't submarine duty supposed to be voluntary?"

"Well, it is, but you can't send this. They'll probably misunderstand. I'll make up the right sort of message to send."

"Thanks a lot, Captain," I said. Only the captain of a ship can direct a message be sent, but I knew he would do as I asked, would also do a much better job of composing just the right message, to which he evidently attached some importance. There was a kind of a bemused look about him, however. An undercurrent of some kind was running. The look on his broad and honest face, which I had come to believe I could read fairly well, was totally beyond me.

As communications officer I was in charge of the radio room and normally saw all the messages sent before they went out, and those received before anyone else in the ship. Not this time. The message Broussard sent, possibly intentionally before I could see it, said, "Ensign Beach physically qualified. Commanding officer would like to keep him on board."

"Captain," I said as soon as I saw it in my radio-room files, "Do you think this will do any good?"

"I'm sure it will," he answered, still with that strange expression. "Now they know I'd like to keep you."

"But it doesn't say I don't volunteer," I said desperately.

"They didn't ask for volunteers, Ned. Maybe they'll not order you, but if they do, you'll like it."

With this I had to be satisfied. I hated the idea of leaving the leaning, leaking, lopsided *Lea*, for after two years in her exclusive and demanding service I had grown to love that old four-piper, and felt it very likely—as turned out to be the case—that I would never see her again. I still harbored my secret plan for overbalancing her port list by surreptitiously loading big rocks in her firerooms, even more secretly thought that in a few more years the Navy might let me be her skipper. Already I knew more about her then just about anyone aboard, except a few of the chief petty officers—but all this was only a pipe dream. It was not to be. On our way back to Boston, dispatch orders arrived directing me to report to the submarine school at Groton, Connecticut.

I left the *Lea* with a big lump in my throat. The crew assembled informally on deck to see me off, and to my astonishment gave me a lovely gold watch with "Remember the LEA" engraved on the back. I have it still, heavily worn but intact. My bags were packed and I was in civilian clothes with 10 days leave authorized and a train ticket to Palo Alto in my pocket. As I walked to the gangway, Captain Broussard came on deck in full white uniform that he had put on for me. On his left breast, gleaming in the morning sun, appeared something I had never seen before. He had put on a golden submarine pin, signifying his own submarine service!

I made it a point to follow the *Lea*'s adventures whenever possible, once saw a picture of her in a recognition manual (I would have recognized her anywhere, despite her hundreds of nearly identical sisters), and gloried in the account I read of her encounter with a German U-boat. Apparently she and a couple of other old tincans ganged up on one they had flushed, finished her off, but had to split the credit. By this time I was well immersed in our own submarine service, and found much to read between the lines. The German had gotten himself caught rather unprofessionally, I thought, but on the other hand the three tincans had behaved most circumspectly also. Absent from my evaluation, I soon understood, was the consistently unpleasant Atlantic Ocean. It was a three-cornered war out there, and the sea was always a big player. I had been in it myself and should have remembered. Compared to them, we in the Pacific had it rather easy most of the time, at least insofar as fighting the sea was concerned.

The course at submarine school had been cut from six months to three by the time I arrived there, and was pretty intense. There were only three things that I clearly remember about it, other than the demanding schedule. First was a demonstration of the new top-secret influence exploder for torpedo warheads. On the table in our laboratory were the mechanics of an exploder, removed from a torpedo warhead and of course minus the detonating charge, and as we students watched with rapt attention (sometimes this was hard to simulate, but not this time), a slightly magnetized steel rod, representing the hull of a ship, was passed over it. The device on the table gave a satisfying "click," and we were told that if it had been for real the firing pin would have detonated 800 pounds of torpex just under the target ship and destroyed it. A few of us were allowed to pass the rod over the exploder, and it clicked every time.

"See," we were told. "Top secret. Can't miss! The rod represents the hull of a ship; in reality the torpedo is going a lot faster than the ship and passes under it, instead of like this demonstration, but this exploder will make your job easy. You set your fish to pass under the target, and it blows the bottom right out of her! All you have to do is aim it right, and it will do the rest. This exploder may win the war for us!"

I recall being greatly impressed, and then thought of a question: "What's to prevent the exploder from going off too soon, if it's a big ship with a big magnetic field?" I asked.

"That's one of the first things the designers thought of," was the answer. "The exploder actually doesn't go off until the ship's induced magnetic field has risen to its highest value, which happens just as the torpedo passes under the keel. The exploder follows the field as it increases, and just as soon as it detects the slightest falling off in value, up she goes!"

I was impressed even more, and nobody had any further questions. Would that that glib response had been true! It was, instead, only a facile answer to a question that just happened to hit exactly on one of the primary, and scandalous, problems the Mark 6 torpedo exploder was to give our submarine force for half the war!

My second memory is exactly where I was sitting, and whom I was with, when I heard of the attack on Pearl Harbor. It was around 2:15 that Sunday afternoon. We were soon to graduate, and there had been a dance on the base the night before. I had invited my cousin Gertrude from New York City, a very attractive young woman who happened to share my birthday. In a few hours she was due to get on the train to return to New York, and that morning I had picked her up at her hotel and brought her back to the submarine base officers' club for lunch. We had just finished and were sitting in the lounge, when I sensed something special was happening at the bar. It was perhaps 50 feet away. When I got there it was crowded three deep with people listening intently to a radio that had suddenly appeared from under the counter.

One battleship had been sunk, we heard, but our fleet was not seriously damaged and even at that very moment was making a sortie to seek out and destroy the enemy fleet. The battleship destroyed was an old one, the *Arizona*, but the fleet as a whole was still effective and would make Japan pay dearly.

I have no recollection of any of the rest of that day, how I got Gertrude to the train, nor what time. I had already received my next assignment, to the submarine *Trigger*, then still under construction at Mare Island, California, and I knew I would soon be at war myself.

The third memory came two weeks later, as I sat in the submarine school auditorium. Our graduation ceremony was not long. The principal address was given by our commanding officer at the school, and I remember his words. "Some of you, before this war is over, will be in command of your own submarines!" I didn't believe him, but as it turned out he was right. One of my classmates, however, got the symbolic other end of the stick, not mentioned at this happy occasion; the older submarine to which he had been ordered was sunk only a few weeks later, by collision while on maneuvers off Panama, and he was not among the lucky few who survived.

Chapter Four

Wake Island and Our Asiatic Fleet

President Roosevelt, on the advice of Secretary of the Navy Frank Knox, removed Adm. Husband E. Kimmel from the Pacific Fleet command on 17 December and designated Chester W. Nimitz as his successor. The dispatch containing this unwelcome order, not unexpected in view of the Pearl Harbor calamity, turned out also to be the direct cause of another calamity because of the hiatus it left in the Pacific command at one of its most critical moments.

The situation in the Pacific was well known, in Washington command circles, to be an absolute emergency. Yet the decisionmakers there behaved as though the political decision was the only thing that mattered, regardless of how many lives it cost.

As part of the operation involving the attack on Pearl Harbor, the Japanese had mounted an extensive campaign against Dutch and English establishments in the Far East (Vichy France did not resist Japanese demands). Japan also attacked other American bases in the Pacific: Guam, the Philippines, and Wake Island. Guam, in the Marianas chain and much closer to Japan than Wake, was in no condition to defend itself and was at once overwhelmed. Wake, however, nearer to Hawaii than to Japan, was different.

A previously uninhabited coral atoll in the middle of the Pacific Ocean, where the U.S. Navy and Pan American Airways were in the process of installing a combined naval air station and stopover point for trans-Pacific flying boats, Wake was attacked only an hour and a half after Pearl Harbor. Our small force there put up a spirited defense. The first attack, quickly seen as the prelude to an invasion, was beaten off after three days of fighting. Heavy losses were inflicted on Japanese forces. Kimmel's war plans, plus his own hard-held outlook, the outcome of much staff consideration during the 10 months since he had taken over from his predecessor, Adm. J. O. Richardson, had always envisioned the necessity of defending the outpost on Wake Island should it, as expected, be attacked.

Except for the Hawaiian Islands chain with Midway at its western terminus, only half as far from Pearl, Wake was one of the few truly defendable positions in Kimmel's charge. Like previous Pacific Fleet commanders, he foresaw a major fleet action when an aggressive Imperial Japanese Navy reached for Wake. This was where he intended to have the U.S. Pacific Fleet stand in its way. In the best of all scenarios, the war's outcome might be decided right then and there. It would, in any event, be a crucially important battle.

Contrary to conventional thinking, there may be something to be gained by imagining the course of the next few weeks had Kimmel been allowed to remain in place a short time longer, between Pearl Harbor and the arrival of Chester Nimitz two weeks later. A more thoroughly fortunate choice than Nimitz could not be imagined, as his conduct of the war amply proved; but it must also be noted that in Washington apparently no thought was given to what the Pacific Fleet, or the Japanese Fleet for that matter, might be doing during those two weeks when our Pacific Fleet had no commander worth the name.

Whatever the arguments, a more uninspired temporary replacement for the sacked original fleet commander than the next senior in the chain of command, the Battle Force commander, Vice Adm. William S. Pye, could probably not have been found. Pye, nearing statutory retirement on account of age, was serving his final tour on active duty. He had been highly regarded in the peacetime navy, but as commander of combat forces he proved to be an indecisive misfit.

In justice to Pye, however, it needs to be noted that the sudden discharge of Kimmel from his duties as commander of the Pacific Fleet did amount to cashiering, an instantaneous removal from his post. Automatically this eliminated the standard relief-of-command procedure, in which the individual relieved, while still holding authority, formally briefs his designated successor on plans and operations currently in progress, and the reasoning behind them. Pye was as surprised as Kimmel when he found himself catapulted into the top Pacific command. He had no opportunity to study his new job and was deprived of a normal turnover from the man he replaced.

He had not had even the normal consultations one might have expected between senior officers because his battleships, which by definition *were* the

Battle Force, were all damaged, some quite severely. There was no way the Battle Force could participate in any Pacific Fleet function, and since Pye was not part of Kimmel's staff he was not involved in planning immediate post-attack operations. He had enough to do with his destroyed Battle Force.

Contrary to the information given out to the country, the Pacific Fleet was in great emergency. Of this there was quickly no question anywhere, regardless of how much of the official pap anyone believed. But summarily removing its commander from the middle of what retaliatory action he might be planning, without even inquiry as to what that action might be, showed that Washington was thinking entirely of its own political problems, not of the war it had brought about.

Although the U.S. battleline had been destroyed and the great naval battle between battleships thereby precluded, the rest of the Pacific Fleet, most particularly its aircraft carriers, was intact. Absent from Pearl on 7 December, these vitally important ships were unscathed. Kimmel, probably sooner than most senior nonaviators, certainly with far greater personal impact, knew from the instant of the first Japanese bomb on his battle fleet that from then on war at sea was going to be very different from what generations of naval officers had uncritically expected. Pearl Harbor crowned the carrier as the new Queen of Battles, and the Pacific Fleet still possessed its own carriers in full authorized strength, albeit many fewer in number than Japan's. Even so, Kimmel's carrier forces were at a low ebb, reduced by the absence of *Yorktown* and *Wasp,* both temporarily in the Atlantic, and the *Saratoga,* in California working up after overhaul. He had, in fact, only two effective carriers: *Lexington* and *Enterprise,* whereas the Japanese fleet at that time had ten.

A fleet engagement of battleships replaying the 1916 Battle of Jutland, as so fondly visualized by the senior officers who had devoted their careers to slow, heavily armored ships with huge guns, was out of the question, and a good thing, too. It was clear that carriers would always be superior to battleships, except in the hardly likely case that a carrier without covering aircraft might stumble under a battlewagon's big guns. This had happened once, to a British carrier in 1940 in the North Sea, but never would again. The naval aviators had been right all along; dive bombers were far more accurate than big guns, and they had many times the effective range. This was true even with aircraft-launched torpedoes, although U.S. naval torpedoes, whether built for aircraft, surface ships, or submarines, were disgracefully ineffective (which we had not yet discovered). Most of our bombs were however of good quality, being less complicated than the torpedoes, and not built at the New-port Torpedo Station.

This obvious analysis did not change the strategy. Though the Pacific Fleet had suffered a grievous blow, it had lost only an outmoded combat branch. There had been serious damage to morale, but this was because of the loss of life, because we had been caught by surprise and, most important, because our pride had been badly hurt. Among its other consequences, Pearl Harbor amounted to radical overthrow of the religion naval high priests had been preaching since the beginning of time.

One would have to search long and hard to find a more devastating rever-sal of a lifetime of accepted belief, but to men able to put the damage in per-spective, loss of battleships was not important. Loss of aircraft carriers would have been. (Some detractors of Washington policy have actually claimed the aircraft carriers were by Machiavellian design sent away from Pearl Harbor on 7 December.) There has never been any proof of this idea, but if not so, it was extreme good fortune.

Parenthetically, the Japanese high command read the signs more accurately than ours did. It was greatly disappointed our carriers were not in Pearl Harbor. Could they have been caught in port, like the battleships, they would have been unable to defend themselves (their planes could not have taken off from their immobile decks). The Japanese attackers were instructed to con-centrate on them first, to the near exclusion of all else. This would put the U.S. Navy out of action, the Japanese high command believed. Adm. Isoroku Yamamoto took his failure to damage the U.S. carriers as most unlucky for Japan, as it proved to be. One of the impelling reasons for his later attack on Midway was the intent to force our Pacific Fleet carriers into battle, where he hoped his more experienced and better trained fliers would succeed in eliminating them.

Strategists have pointed out that loss of the fuel tanks in the hills behind Pearl Harbor, or loss of the submarine base, would have been a worse setback than loss of the battleships. During the next four years those fuel tanks were to power the fleet irresistibly across the Pacific Ocean to the very shores of Japan, and once their torpedoes were fixed (this, however, took nearly two years), submarines based on that submarine base, or its subsidiaries, were to sink more than half of all the ships, naval or merchant, that Japan was able to get to sea.

To the aggressively inclined Admiral Kimmel, it was now his turn. He would not be able to fight with battleships, but under the circumstances perhaps this was just as well. It was far better to have them sunk in the shallow water of Pearl Harbor than in the deep sea, as clearly would have happened if the Japanese carriers had caught them out of port. Now he would use his carriers to implement the strategy he and his predecessors had honed so carefully. Pearl Harbor notwithstanding, the attack on Wake had come exactly as predicted by his war planners. With enemy forces stretched thin all the way from the Dutch East Indies, the agreed-on strategy called for immediate reaction. A successful outcome to this initial battle, so felt the Fleet Commander and his operational subordinates, would greatly strengthen U.S. control of its side of the Pacific, and might well shorten the war.

Furthermore, there was a loyal American force greatly at risk on Wake Island, which it was his duty to support. Fully understanding the urgency faced by the tiny garrison of U.S. Marines at Wake Island (plus about triple their number of civilian workers and a few supervisory naval personnel), and also fully realizing his own responsibility for all of them, Kimmel immediately implemented the plan for an expedition to the relief of Wake. This had the highest priority he could give it.

No less a student than historian Samuel Eliot Morison suggests, however, that he might have done better in selecting the expedition's commander. "Circumstances dictated that *Saratoga* be the one carrier of the expedition, and Rear Admiral Aubrey Fitch, one of the navy's most experienced aviator admirals, was in her. The only heavy cruisers available to accompany her were three [units] of Cruiser Division Six, commanded by Rear Admiral Frank Jack Fletcher, a naval academy classmate of Fitch, but senior in rank." Seniority put Fletcher in command, despite the greater experience in aviation of his more junior classmate, but Fitch went along because his flagship was the principal unit of the force. Although it is known that he disapproved of many of Fletcher's decisions, he apparently had no impact on any of them.

Probably Kimmel would also have been well advised, as events turned out, to have kept President Roosevelt fully informed about his plans for the relief of Wake. This perhaps could have been done through transoceanic cable and land wire, or by sending a special emissary, but in any case his need for support at this crucial juncture was more pressing than the requirements of wartime secrecy—not for self-serving reasons, but for success in the important mission on which he had set forth. Roosevelt's well-developed sense of how the public perceived things would have supported the expedition, would have kept Pye in line (for Pye would have had to inform FDR before aborting it), and might even have induced the president to leave Kimmel in command a while longer. All this is 100 percent hindsight. One could additionally suggest that a successful relief of Wake might have benefited Kimmel personally in the ordeal he was about to undergo.

Built around the handsome old *Saratoga* that had hurriedly arrived from the West Coast on 15 December, augmented with three powerful cruisers and all the destroyers that could be rounded up, the emergency task force departed as soon as the big carrier could be refueled.

The plan was for the *Lexington, Saratoga*'s identical twin, to create a diversion to the south, and the relatively new *Enterprise* to stand guard against a repeat attack on Pearl. In the meantime, *"Sara"* and her powerful task force would either engage Japanese units attacking Wake or evacuate the island should defense be impracticable.

If it had been carried out as planned, the expedition would unquestionably have succeeded. Most likely Wake would not have been captured at all. At worst, if evacuation had been decided upon, its personnel would have been spared the loss of life and the years of brutal captivity, in a number of documented cases outright murder by sadistic guards, that they were forced to endure. In the event, however, the officer who had planned and set the relief expedition in motion, Kimmel, was suddenly gone, eliminated from the scene. Pye, in effect coming from nowhere, suddenly was in overall command from his uneasy and known-to-be-temporary office in Pearl Harbor.

Fletcher, at sea in command of the relief expedition, was as indecisive as Pye. His failure to give maximum effort to the rescue of a heroic garrison was matched by his concentration on unimportant details. Keeping his destroyers fueled to a high percentage of capacity weighed higher in his mind than the desperate plight of the men on Wake. In short, Admirals Pye and Fletcher were peacetime officers weak in professional concern for the demands of war. The result was disastrous.

Fletcher moved glacially on his emergency mission across the ocean, and when nearly within striking distance stopped for two days in bad weather to refuel. Had he driven aggressively for Wake as his staff officers begged him to, he would have arrived at the most propitious possible time. The record shows that all the aviators aboard the *Saratoga*, Fletcher's own staff officers, including his chief of staff, and even Fitch, second in command of the task group, protested, some very strongly. At the last, some even urged the Horatio Nelson touch: disobedience of Pye's order to retreat. But the debacle in the high command from which he took his orders, the craven council of caution from on high, and his own fears of the unknown were too much for Fletcher: he took the easy route. The relief task force, far superior to anything the enemy had to counter it, had we but known (or had we had the intelligence later available), could have rescued everyone at Wake with ease. In all probability it would not have needed to, would instead have reinforced the fighting Marines on Wake, given a drubbing to the inferior Japanese force attacking the island, boosted our national morale immeasurably at one of the lowest points in its history, possibly even enabled us to keep Wake as an outpost during the entire war. This at least, or some version thereof, was what Kimmel hoped to accomplish.

Halsey, in Fletcher's place, or commanding from Pearl as was Pye, would have dashed forward eagerly. He would not have thrown caution to the winds, but neither would he have been mired in indecision. He would have caught the Japanese at a low point of their campaign against the tiny island, the inspired defenders flush with confidence. Not one of them doubted that their country and their navy would come to their rescue. It would have been a clear-cut victory for our forces when it was very badly needed. Sadly, nothing anything like this happened. When Fletcher resumed his dilatory advance the Japanese had already landed on Wake—and that same day Admiral Pye concluded the exchange of a series of confusing and contradictory messages by ordering him to reverse course.

The commander at Wake was sent a short message to the effect that there were to be no U.S. naval forces in his vicinity, but he was given no further instructions, not even an order to surrender to save lives. Wake was abandoned, its defenders pusillanimously forsaken (nevertheless expected to fight to the end), and the U.S. high command had not the courage to accept the responsibility.

The most powerful U.S. task force of the time, some 10,000 Navy men and Marines, far superior to the Japanese forces attacking Wake, turned away and left the island's defenders to their fate. True to their own code, the garrison, nearly all U.S. Marines, fought the useless battle until resistance was hopeless. The cost was 121 killed, including some 70 civilians, plus an unknown number of wounded, out of a total U.S. contingent, most of them civilian workers, of about 1,600. Of the prisoners, a high percentage was doomed to die in captivity. A number of the civilians were murdered in cold blood by the sadistic Japanese commander of the captured island.

The outcome of the Wake debacle is well known to America. The 449 Marines on Wake, commanded by Maj. James Devereau, did not send a message saying, "Send us more Japs," as public relations–inspired legend had it—but short on histrionics though they may have been, the defense they put up, entirely on their own, was a noble one. It was also to no purpose, because they had been given up by their country.

Nonetheless, abandoned as they were, they fought on for 16 more days. The small, unarmed naval detachment setting up the air station, 68 men and officers, fought alongside the Marines (their commander, Winfield Cunningham by name, was in fact the senior officer present and thus in direct charge of the defense). So did the five U.S. Army personnel and some (not all) of the 1,200 civilian contract workers and Pan American employees on the atoll.

Totally on their own, with no help from anyone, none at all from their own country, the Wake Island garrison wrote a heroic chapter in the history of the U.S. Navy and Marine Corps. In contrast, the conduct of the temporary U.S. Pacific Fleet Commander, and of the task force his predecessor had sent that was now under his overall command, then in perfect position to effect relief, was a cowardly, unmitigated, disgrace.

When he learned of the outcome of the Wake expedition, Roosevelt was reportedly indignant, observing that for "his navy" this was "worse than Pearl Harbor." The nation, its armed forces, and the public at large, have no right to ignore this. We did better later, but in December of 1941 our fighting forces were even more cowardly than Japan and Yamamoto expected.

So ended the first few weeks of World War II in the Pacific, a first-class debacle, its tragic details essentially unknown to the public at large. Morison, in his monumental operational history of the naval war, stated his opinion that if Admiral Kimmel had been permitted to remain in command a few days longer Wake might have been relieved and "there would certainly have been a battle" in which our forces would probably have been victorious, inasmuch as the main strength of the Japanese fleet had already been sent to the south and west.

Compounding the tragic details, not until after the war was it discovered that some of the civilian workers had been kept on Wake to operate their heavy equipment under Japanese control. After working these men for nearly two years in barbaric conditions, the Japanese Wake Island commander, Sakaibara by name, had them herded into the water and hacked to death (by some accounts they were shot in the back) on the pretext that they were not members of a recognized military force, therefore had no rights of any kind, and furthermore had assembled a clandestine radio. They therefore merited summary execution in whatever manner might be convenient for him. After the war Sakaibara was put on trial for this atrocity and hanged, but this does not come close to evening the account. Lately, Japan has apologized for some of her wartime injustices. She should do so again, to the survivors of Wake's victims. As for Sakaibara, his name will never be forgotten by the U.S. Marine Corps.

We did one thing right, however. The dilemma of civilian workers was solved by creation of U.S. Construction Battalions, nicknamed "SeaBees," so that workers setting up bases in a war zone would have all the rights of soldiers. That put a stop to arguments like Sakaibara's. A second result was that for the SeaBees a bulldozer was much like an armored tank, and knowing how the Japanese treated prisoners, they used it like one whenever they found the opportunity.

I graduated from submarine school in mid-December of 1941 and reported to the new submarine *Trigger*, then still under construction at Mare Island Navy Yard, California. What we junior officers knew about the actual damage at Pearl Harbor was gleaned more from chance contacts with Navy families evacuated from Hawaii in its aftermath, and damaged ships that came in for repair, than from any official information. No doubt more senior officers than I were more fully informed, but we juniors, and the enlisted sailors, were told nothing. Nonetheless, little by little, we found out what had actually happened. The new cruiser *Helena*, which had taken a torpedo in one of her enginerooms at Pearl Harbor and came to Mare Island for repairs, particularly impressed me. Never had I seen such a shambles as that devastated machinery space. A dozen or so men had been killed there, I was informed, but my guide, an ensign like myself, was sure there were no bodies still buried in the reeking, oil-soaked debris. Looking at the mess, realizing that a well-ordered, highly technical place, a cruiser engineroom, had been converted into this chaotic tangle in a second or so, it was difficult to believe that anyone had escaped, but this, too, I was assured, was true.

Shortly before the *Trigger* left the yard, the destroyer *Shaw*, with a ridiculously cut-off temporary bow in place of her regular one, blown to bits in one of the spectacular explosions at Pearl Harbor, steamed in under her own power to have a new bow, already partly built, welded on. By this time I had become a little more sophisticated, perhaps overly so. Seeing the miracles the shipyard workers could perform, I half expected the new bow to be installed without putting the ship into drydock.

.   .   .

One of the more real concerns we had at this time was our Asiatic Fleet. In the prewar Navy, tours in the Asiatic Fleet had always been glamorous duty, individuals rotating back full of exotic stories and eagerly volunteering for repeat tours. It was also known for being "non-reg" (nonregulation). Most of the *U.S. Naval Regulations* seemed to have been left somewhere east of the date line.

To senior officers dating from before Admiral Dewey, an Asiatic Fleet post amounted to a quasi-diplomatic job, one where it was clearly as important to represent our flag and our national interests, in concert with the all-too-few diplomatic and consular officers our State Department could maintain in the area, as to be able to defeat an enemy at sea. To the junior officers and enlisted men of the Asiatic Fleet, unconcerned with matters of state or higher strategy, duty in that section of the world, so different from our own, presented many opportunities for "the good life," whatever one might individually consider that to be.

The situation even entered into our naval vernacular: to be "Asiatic" meant to behave somewhat unusually, to follow one's own ideas and inclinations, to have greater than ordinary fondness for wine, women, and song, and somewhat less respect for the law (foreign or U.S.). A few families, mostly those of high-ranking officers, seldom with young children, set up temporary homes in apartments or hotels in Manila, Hong Kong, or Shanghai, depending on ship locations. Often they moved around, "following the ship," which was possible in those days when security was of less concern. Concubinage was not unknown if discreetly done, and the rules were even more lax for the sailors and younger officers, who were expected to sow wild oats. So long as one was on board ship when expected and able to do his duty, few questions were apt to be asked.

Now that real war had arrived, so had "pay day" for the Asiatic Fleet, and there was little dependable information to be had about it back in the States. What we did get was contradictory, hard to swallow. What we heard by unofficial word of mouth was more believable, because it was more logical, than what we heard from official reports or the newspapers. At Mare Island, this was how I learned the truth about Pearl Harbor. At first I refused to believe it. Five battleships sunk? No way! The *Oklahoma* had capsized, but was not badly damaged and would be righted and refurbished. Only the *Arizona* had been totally destroyed. This was the official line, the official announcement, but it seemed a bit illogical that a capsized battleship could be "only a little damaged," and slowly the true knowledge seeped in through the cracks. So was it with the ordeal of the ships and crews of our tiny Far East contingent.

Surabaya, unknown before the war, became a name to conjure with, a city that had a fatal disease and yet one where that Asiatic Fleet, chased out of Manila, Shanghai, and Hong Kong, had to be based. Lying upon the Dutch populace was an aura of doom, the bravura of those who saw an end coming, about which they could do nothing. Live life to the fullest, some of them must have thought, for there could be nothing but bad times ahead.

The Dutch colonials, many of them second- and third-generation inhabitants of what they liked to call "their country," with affiliation to Holland comparable to Canada's for England, particularly felt that way, but so did some of the Indonesians themselves, especially those whose connection with the Dutch could not be concealed or papered over. Many Dutch who could leave, or send their families away, did so; but some stubborn descendants of the original colonists refused to abandon the East Indies. They argued that the East Indies was a legitimate heritage of centuries of Dutch history. They had found it in a state of savagery and had made it into a viable nation with an excellent economy. Their cause was just (and blind), their determination just as strong and just as blind. They would not give up the land they had taken many years ago from a native population unable to resist their European arms. Now their armed forces, their efficient but totally outclassed navy in particular, vowed to fight to the death for "their country," and death was to be its fate.

To Americans, less emotionally attached to the area, there was no other possible outcome of this outlook, given the already observed rapacity of the Japanese and their ruthless and superbly effective armed forces.

Japan's aims, a "Greater East Asia Co-Prosperity Sphere," and its methods of creating the same, were by this time well known. The Dutch East Indies, with much wealth and produce, most especially oil that Japan greatly needed, was a natural target. In no way could determination, leadership, fairness, patriotism, strength of character, loyalty to principle, or any other of the admirable traits the Dutch possessed in abundance, make any difference in the outcome. They were stubborn in outlook, and they were doomed. In their rational moments they knew it. All the same, they clung to their ideals and vowed to fight to the end, for it was the only thing they could do. Flight, escape for their ships and crews, was disgraceful, traitorous. They would go down with their country, for to their mind the Dutch East Indies *was* their country, even though they, or their ancestors, had come from Western Europe.

The native Indonesian population had a different outlook. Some of them, employees of Dutch industry or, worse, of the Netherlands East Indies armed forces, faced as disastrous a future as did the Dutch themselves. But, by far, most Indonesians hoped to distance themselves from their colonial masters. The coming of the Japanese would have to be borne, even cooperated with, in the hope of survival. They had been under an uncompromising Dutch rule for generations; the Japanese might be equally hard with them, but workers would be needed, too.

The United States was in a dilemma. In spite of our ideals of democracy and self-determination, we were allied with the old Dutch East Indies, as were England and Australia. Although we saw nothing to be gained by the sacrifice, we had to help them fight to preserve their Indonesian nation. They were our allies and friends. We had profited from our business dealings with them, especially in oil. We could not abandon them in their hour of critical need.

The units of the Asiatic Fleet had been often in Australia (in fact, the last known photograph of the cruiser *Houston,* with the destroyer *Pillsbury* alongside, both soon to be sunk, was taken in Port Darwin only a few days before the final battle). Back they went into the Java Sea, on the far side of the nearly impenetrable barrier of the long, narrow, curved islands of Java and Sumatra. So, too, went the British *Exeter,* refurbished after her battle with the German *Graf Spee,* also the Australian cruiser *Perth,* and numerous destroyers of all three nations. Operational control was turned over to the Dutch, thus ensuring destruction of all of them in the oncoming, inevitable debacle. They fought bravely, heroically, but there could be only one outcome. Except for four old U.S. destroyers that seized a fleeting chance, after it was all over, to escape into the Indian Ocean through the shallow Bali Strait (it was not deep enough for anything bigger), and the cruisers *Boise* and *Marblehead,* victims of early damage and sent away for repair, all the ships in that gallant fleet were sacrificed for spurious national pride.

The story of their last moments is poignant. Of the fleet commanders caught in command of sea forces at the outset of the war, only Adm. Thomas C. Hart, commanding the Asiatic Fleet, survived with his reputation relatively intact. His dispositions had been well made, and he suffered no serious losses except the submarine *Sealion,* halfway through a navy yard overhaul in Cavite. The U.S. high command, however, had decided that Hart, having been receiving MAGIC (decrypted Japanese diplomatic messages), could not be exposed to possible torture or drugs. Accordingly, he was directed to turn over his fleet to operate under the Dutch East Indies command and return home.

Through a feeling of responsibility to his tiny fleet, Hart delayed doing this as long as possible, finally turned over what was left of his command in mid-February of 1942, two months after the war had begun, and only days before Japanese forces overran Java. Just prior to giving up command, Hart had determined that the *Marblehead* was too badly damaged for further effective action, but after consultation with Capt. Albert Rooks of the *Houston* decided that important ship could still function, even though one of her three main battery turrets (number three, on the main deck aft of her superstructure) was out of commission with a heavy bomb hit. Similar fateful decisions were made for the British and Australian units still in the area.

It was a sentence of death. Military men, even if they happen to hold the option of saving themselves, cannot do so if in the process they must abandon their country or their troops. Admirals Conrad Helfrich and Karel Doorman had both vowed to defend the Dutch East Indies to the end, and felt obligated to do so (although, in the end, Helfrich got away); but one can imagine the feelings of the U.S. and British decisionmakers as they added Americans, British, and Australians to the impending sacrifice.

Perhaps—probably—they did not identify with individuals. It was a policy matter; the Dutch East Indies were our allies, we had no other choice. The skippers of the ships involved, on the other hand, most particularly Captains Rooks of the *Houston*, Hector Waller of HMAS *Perth*, and Oliver Gordon of HMS *Exeter*, perceived exactly what was being demanded of them. As events turned out, Gordon survived the ensuing series of battles and the POW years, but all of that once happy-go-lucky Asiatic contingent—except for a single Australian cruiser (HMAS *Hobart*, sister to the *Perth*) and four ancient British destroyers, sent to Ceylon at the last possible moment—all the cruisers and all except the four old U.S. destroyers already mentioned are to this day somewhere submerged in the Java Sea. Both Rooks and Waller perished with their ships, and not until some time after the end of the war was it possible to piece together their final gallant moments.

The entire effort in defense of the Dutch East Indies was marked by confusion. Since nearly all in the afloat forces lost their lives, little can be done to reconstruct conditions, but it seems clear that in sum it was a fiasco of missed communications. Staff failure to provide means of effective exchange of orders and information between ships of different nations was one of the fundamental causes, although in retrospect there was no chance of a truly successful defense. There never was any cohesive organized employment made of this tiny scratch fleet of American, British, Dutch, and Australian ships coalesced under the ABDA (American, British, Dutch, and Australian) banner. Its diverse units had never operated together, nor was there ever set up any more than the most rudimentary communications protocol.

Dutch Admiral Doorman's plans were not clear to his allies either, nor are they yet to historians. Incredibly, communications even between Doorman and his superior, Helfrich, were poor; one cannot avoid the impression that Helfrich treated the campaign with some psychological disbelief, as though it were not actually happening, or were only an exercise. Such dispatches as have been found show that Doorman, reporting his fleet under constant surveillance by Japanese "snooper" planes, asked for air cover, but this was denied because of the need to maintain air superiority over the area where the enemy was expected to land after disposing of him! He made a couple of excursions (keeping his crews all night at action stations), found nothing, returned to Surabaya late on 26 February to refuel. There he was greeted in the harbor channel, even before entering port, with a peremptory message to reverse course and attack a greatly superior invasion force nearing Java farther to the east. "Pursue attack until you have demolished enemy force," said one message from Helfrich. It might as well have said, "Give your lives uselessly for the honor of the Dutch East Indies."

The dilemma of Helfrich and Doorman is understandable if one manages to place oneself entirely in their shoes. A naval or military force may not abandon its own country, must fight as long as its own people need protection. But saving itself to fight another day, this time with a chance of success, is usually a better way to serve it. It needs, however, to be noted that applying this adage to the country from which the military force came is different from applying it to an economically enslaved region. The best that can be said is that both admirals probably appreciated, so far as the Dutch East Indies was concerned, that there never would be another day. As Carthage may have sensed during the Third Punic War, this was the end of the line forever.

The parallel with Carthage is not entirely apt. In the Dutch East Indies, the Dutch masters of their colonial Far Eastern empire could not, except perhaps on a very personal level, seek salvation in escape. For the Dutch navy in Java, as a matter of honor, defeat could never be admitted in advance.

Samurai-like, the Dutch fought their fleet to the bitter end, but this was not long in coming. Doorman, at sea in his flagship the *De Ruyter,* would have to go all the way; Helfrich, sending impotent orders from his Supreme Allied Headquarters in cool and comfortable Bandung, kept, however, a means of personal escape at hand.

The Battle of the Java Sea took place on 27 February 1942, much of it at night and into the morning hours of 28 February, and has been described as "one of the most fouled-up battles ever fought." Receiving the fatal "attack at all costs" message as he neared Surabaya, and reversing course as directed, Doorman had no time to make plans, no time for anything except to turn his weary ships and crews around and steam toward his destiny at the bottom of the sea. He hoisted the signal, "Follow me," and in *De Ruyter* headed for the supposed position of the oncoming Japanese invasion force.

As it turned out, he found it: the covering warships, that is, but it would be more accurate to say the enemy found him. The Allied force had no air cover, its many requests having been denied, and high-flying Japanese snooper planes were seen early on. All hands knew what this portended. Reconstruction of the battle is nearly impossible, however, even after postwar inspection of surviving Japanese records. Apparently the enemy force consisted of four cruisers, two heavy and two light, all fresh and undamaged, plus two or more divisions of high-quality destroyers; the Allies had two damaged heavies and three light cruisers, and slightly fewer older and smaller destroyers.

Numerically, the forces were about evenly matched, but only in numbers. The Allied ships were much older and, except for the *Houston,* considerably smaller. In contrast to the Japanese, their crews were already exhausted, their ammunition criminally undependable. This was particularly true about the torpedoes. Even if they had functioned perfectly all the time, torpedoes carried by the Allied destroyers would have been a poor challenge to Japan's 24-inch "Long Lance" torpedoes. The Long Lance had approximately four times the range, half again more speed, and warheads three times more powerful than ours. In addition, Japanese torpedoes were nearly 100 percent dependable. That is, they had been so thoroughly tested at every stage of manufacture and simulated war exercise that they had phenomenal accuracy, and their warheads worked every time they hit the target. The Japanese carried Long Lance torpedoes in both destroyers and cruisers which could be fired at extreme ranges, whereas our smaller twenty-one-inch "fish" had to be brought to much shorter ranges before they could be effective—and even then, our vaunted new Mark 14 and 23 models for our submarines and the Mark 15 destroyer version, performed properly only 10 percent of the time. Earlier torpedoes, the Mark 10 used by earlier submarines for example, though of even shorter range, had had years of exercise testing before the war. They ran at slower speed than the 14s, but their record was one of reasonable, if not excellent, results. For some reason our Bureau of Ordnance assumed the higher-speed 14s, 15s, and 23s, despite numerous design changes, would start in dependability where the earlier Mark 10s left off, an unprofessional assumption that was grossly in error.

The most significant inequality between the opposing fleets, however, was that the Japanese had air reconnaissance while the Allies did not, although as the records show, this could have been provided. What earthly benefit the Dutch East Indies Command expected to achieve by keeping their aircraft away from the fleet that was the only possible impediment to a Japanese landing has never been explained. Perhaps they could not have prevented the disaster that ensued, but they would at least have given Doorman a far better fighting chance than fate had in store for him.

A speculative reason for failure must be that utter demoralization of the shore-based headquarters had set in. Nothing could stop the onward march of fate; most of the lower-level personnel, nearly all of them native-born Indonesians, were desperately trying to protect their own skins. Many, doubtless, had little reason in any case for loyalty to their rather imperious Dutch masters. The whole situation in the Dutch East Indies had best be viewed with understanding compassion. They were doomed, no matter what they did. The only hope for survival was to be as inconspicuous as possible, particularly for those in any way connected with the Indonesian military.

This may have had a bearing on the illogical refusal of air support, which, it may be noted, was equally ill-used when the Japanese landing actually took place only a few days later. It was also unquestionably a factor in the refusal by Dutch authorities to provide urgently needed fuel when, the day following the disastrous Battle of the Java Sea, the *Houston* and *Perth* stopped in Tanjung Priok, serving Batavia (now Djakarta, the capital of Indonesia), to ask for it.

The Battle of the Java Sea began in the late afternoon of 27 February. Doorman was looking for the transports bringing troops for the anticipated landing on the island of Java, upon which he might have been able to inflict severe damage, had he have found them before engaging their escort squadron. He might even have thwarted the invasion, though not for long. What he got instead was the covering force protecting the transports, vectored into contact by its snooper planes. The combat began with an exchange of eight-inch gunfire at long range, with the first advantage apparently going to the Allies. Japanese information is scarce, however, and the fragmentary Allied records are more notable for optimism than conclusiveness.

This duel continued for only a short time when HMS *Exeter* received a severely damaging eight-inch hit that cut her speed in half and effectively put her out of the fight. As the damaged cruiser slowed and turned out of line, the lack of effective communications threw everything into confusion. Doorman's only signal had been "Follow me," the *Exeter* was next astern of the Dutch flagship, and the British cruiser's distressed turn caused all the ships astern of her to follow, thinking the maneuver had been ordered by Doorman in *De Ruyter*. Disorder ensued in the Allied formation, and the disciplined Japanese, obeying doctrine, took advantage of it by firing a large number of well-aimed Long Lance torpedoes at the confusedly maneuvering Dutch fleet.

Dutch and English destroyers were obviously in the wrong place at the wrong time, for three of them were destroyed by these torpedoes (although some authorities, unable to believe Japan could have built such extraordinary torpedoes, at the time held that the losses must have been caused by mines, even while unable to suggest how the enemy might have planted them there). When the cruisers were able to regroup, with the *Exeter* detached and heading slowly for Surabaya, their escorts had been reduced by half. Doorman held on for the invasion transports, still unsure where they might be, and the Japanese covering force again interposed. As darkness fell, both forces became cautious, the action sporadic. Japanese aircraft surveillance continued. It appears that the Japanese admiral maintained situation control throughout the entire engagement, attacking when he wished to and holding off whenever he desired. He picked off the remaining Allied destroyers one after another, except for the four timeworn U.S. "four-pipers" that fired their useless torpedoes and then, short of fuel, headed for Surabaya at full speed. Finally the Allied forces consisted only of four cruisers: two small Dutch ones, the fairly new *De Ruyter* and the older *Java*, the big American *Houston*, and the smaller Australian *Perth*. Vice Adm. Takeo Takagi, the Japanese commander, was playing with Doorman as a capricious cat might with a mouse it intended ultimately to devour.

Around midnight the Japanese closed to eight-inch gun range, fired a few excellent salvos, and at the same time fired all the Long Lance torpedoes their cruisers could bring to bear. Many of the torpedoes fired during daylight had missed all targets, but this time, in the dark of the night, both Dutch cruisers, *De Ruyter* and *Java*, were hit and suddenly burst into searing flame. Doorman had only one thing left he could do, and to his enduring credit he did it: he sent a message to the two remaining cruisers in his force, *Houston* and *Perth*, directing them to proceed through Sunda Strait into the Indian

Ocean and safety. He specifically ordered them not to stand by trying to save survivors of the sinking Dutch ships. Then he died a sailor's death as his flagship went down.

Friendly historians, sympathetic to the Dutch admiral's hopeless fight against impossible odds, would say that he had done all it was possible to do with the ships he had and the odds he faced. More dispassionate history should, on the other hand, record that he had died well, but operationally had been pretty much of a failure. His planning was uninspired, his efforts against the well-organized and well-led enemy makeshift instead of thoughtful. His true mission, of which he may in fact have had an inkling—there is no doubt Helfrich thought this way even though personally avoiding sacrificing himself— was to create a tradition for the re-establishment of the Dutch East Indies after the war.

Only his self-sacrifice, and that of his crews, did he accomplish. In the more recondite effort to lay groundwork for postwar restoration of the Netherlands East Indies, Helfrich and Doorman failed totally. None of the Dutch could understand that the way of life they had established on the Indonesian island of Java was a colonial anachronism they had literally followed to its bitter end. Japan, of course, would not have understood this point either, for her sole purpose was simply to replace the Dutch as exploiters of the area's riches. The ultimate result of the convulsion and all its horrors was the establishment, after much trouble of its own and untold sacrifice of life, of the new and completely independent nation of Indonesia.

Set free to save themselves, *Perth* and *Houston* had only 24 hours to live. The two ships went first to the port of Tanjung Priok in search of greatly needed fuel, having had no time to refuel at Surabaya. They arrived at noon on 28 February, with the *Perth* especially short of fuel. They reported Doorman's demise, with his fleet, by telephone to Supreme Allied Headquarters in Bandung, in the cooler hill country about 100 miles away. Admiral Helfrich, still speaking of fighting to the death with all his forces, American, English, and Australian though some of them might be, was not receptive to the suggestion that the battle-damaged American and Australian ships head for Australia and much needed repair. He ordered them to proceed through Sunda Strait to Tjilatjap (now Cilacap), on the south coast of Java, where he said he planned to reassemble the forces he had remaining.

Unknown to all, one day earlier he had countermanded his orders for *Hobart* and her companions to proceed to Tjilatjap by the same route, and directed instead that they go on to Ceylon, where he planned to go himself, and where they were for the time safe. He may have intended the same for the two newcomers the day afterward, but there is no confirmation of this.

So far as fuel was concerned, to the amazement of the two beleaguered skippers, although oil storage in the hills was full to overflowing Dutch authorities refused to release any. Part of the excuse was that their workers, in terror of the Japanese, had disappeared, but this had been true for some days everywhere in Java, and the sailors of the ships had become adept at manhandling the fueling gear themselves. All that was needed was permission and some vouchers (even these would shortly become valueless), but realism was already a casualty. Officials that were still functioning clung tenaciously, for reassurance, to their old bureaucratic procedures. After much extremely valuable time had been spent in argument, only 300 tons of fuel were finally authorized, and for the *Perth* alone. The two ships departed in the early evening, intending to hug the coast and round the western tip of Java into Sunda Strait, between Java and Sumatra and only a few miles away, and then head south into the Indian Ocean.

There is a lot more to that story, however. It redounds greatly to the credit of Captains Rooks and Waller, and to the discredit of the Dutch authorities whom it proves to have been duplicitous in the extreme. One must make allowances, by all means, for the state of mind of the Dutch civilians and their native employees, and be sympathetic to their effort to distance themselves from Japan's enemies, now that they were about to be engulfed. Nevertheless, what was actually impelling them, it is now clear, was the classic refusal of persons, themselves trapped, to assist in the escape of others—in this case some 1,700 American and Australian sailormen—who suddenly appeared to have the means to do so. This was particularly reprehensible on the part of the senior Dutch authorities. Their own pending fate, for which individually they may have been blameless, the result of generations of exploitation of an emerging people by their European conquerors, can never excuse the conditions found by the two Allied cruiser commanders.

Japan's reputation for atrocities had well preceded her, and the resulting aura of fear pervaded everything. The principal emotion evident to the two Allied skippers in Batavia and Tanjung Priok was resentment, combined with terror of what the future was sure to bring. One of the reasons why little has been said or written about this is that, by and large, it is understood and forgiven, best expressed by forgetting about it. One has only to look at what befell the inhabitants of Java during the next four years to realize it is the least we can do.

All the same, it was true. It is totally possible that *Houston* and *Perth* might have escaped after all, three-quarters of their crews not have died, had they been given the information that was apparently available in the Dutch capital, whether or not they were provided the fuel that was also their right.

However, it must also be said that no one not actually there could today have any idea how desperate things were in Java. The enemy was within hours of landing. Fall of the Dutch government was imminent. On arrival on 28 February, the two captains found conditions utterly frenzied. There was no possibility of defense. The senior officers and politicians were casting about desperately for means of escape. Admiral Helfrich, chief of the Dutch East Indian navy, was holding one transport aircraft for himself and his staff and, indeed, they departed the next day. Rooks and Waller found themselves pariahs, or nearly so, when they appealed to the Dutch bureaucracy for fuel.

They had been informed that Sunda Strait was open, the nearest Japanese forces many miles away. To the contrary, it is now known that Supreme Allied Headquarters had already received information of a large invasion force only a few miles north of the strait, bent on making a landing on the northwestern tip of Java that very night. One cannot be certain whether Admiral Helfrich had himself been so informed, although he should have been. In any case the information, whatever the reason, was not passed on to the American and Australian skippers. Compounding the difficulties, the Dutch harbor pilot who had brought the two cruisers through the minefields into the harbor did not show up at the time appointed, and they finally departed on their own without a pilot, an additional hour late after all the previous delay, forced to trust unfamiliar charts they could only hope had been marked correctly. One might think the pilot should have been happy at the opportunity to escape on board one of the Allied cruisers. Maybe he had family members in Tanjung Priok, or other obligations he could not dodge. Or, he might have had information about the location of Japanese ships that he felt would make this an unlucky voyage.

It is hard, from present hindsight, to reconcile all these unhappy circumstances with the easy explanation that things in Java were fervid, morale at its lowest. All this was true, but there is also a thing in human nature that wants company in a disaster. There must have been jealousy over the possibility that these two big foreign cruisers might escape the oncoming disaster. One way to give expression to this is to wash one's hands of the whole thing, give no more assistance than required. Another is to fail to pass along important information. A third is quietly to give the superior information to one's own side, or kin. Given the demoralized situation then existing, it is probable that all three of these occurred. It is certainly true that Captains Rooks and Waller received very little help of any kind in Tanjung Priok that day, and that this was the principal reason why they were unable to extract their ships and crews from the death trap the Dutch East Indies had become.

A fourth speculation requires active disloyalty, direct malevolence, and can be attributable only to persons hostile to the regime, or possibly to a Japanese agent, not an unheard-of idea: someone may have passed information of the ships' prospective movements to the enemy. The Japanese destroyer *Fubuki,* almost as though she had special information about the approach of the two Allied ships, was patrolling along the line of their planned advance, and did in fact detect them as they approached Sunda Strait.

It further appears that the Dutch East Indies destroyer *Evertsen,* then in Tanjung Priok, had been directed to clear the harbor in company with *Perth* and *Houston* and accompany them as they ran toward the Indian Ocean. U.S. Adm. William Glassford, speaking by telephone from Supreme Allied Headquarters at Bandung, informed Captain Rooks to this effect. But when Rooks and Waller tried to confer with *Evertsen*'s skipper, they found him evasive, first denying that he had received any orders at all, and then claiming that ongoing repairs would keep him in harbor a little longer. The Allied skippers disgustedly left him with instructions to follow as soon as he was able.

Yet the *Evertsen* did in fact get under way within the hour. The suspicion that she might have withheld vital information from Rooks and Waller is a deduction based upon her actions. When she left port she made no attempt to overtake the doomed Allied cruisers, made a wide circle to the north and west, and apparently had the incredible good luck to see no enemy ships of any kind until she had passed entirely through Sunda Strait and was in the Indian Ocean. How her skipper, without special knowledge, could have known where to steer to avoid the enemy is hard to fathom. All that is known for sure is that he claimed he went well offshore, around everything, and did not even hear gunfire.

But then the *Evertsen*'s good fortune deserted her, for two unlooked-for Japanese destroyers, not privy to the shenanigans that might have been going on, or possibly specially sent to do the job, caught her in the Indian Ocean and drove her ashore in sinking condition with many casualties. But for this, *Evertsen* would have got away clean. One consequently wonders if her skipper possessed special information that he kept to himself, and if so where he could have got it. In any case, he was in the end also double-crossed.

Houston and *Perth*, steaming westward close to shore through the moon-lit night of 28 February, were discovered and shadowed by the Japanese destroyer *Fubuki*, patrolling well to the east of the Japanese heavy cruisers *Mogami* and *Mikuma*. Allied lookouts, essentially sleepless for days, exhausted by days of combat, did not see the enemy destroyer at first. Shortly after *Fubuki* was spotted, however, *Houston* detected great numbers of transport ships, the largest Japanese landing yet attempted, approaching the Javanese shore at Banten Bay, barely around the corner from Sunda Strait. The invasion force, of which Admiral Helfrich's staff had been informed during the afternoon of 28 February, had reached the tip of Java, was beginning an unopposed landing. It was in fact the force Doorman had been seeking, that 24 hours ago had cost him his little fleet and his own life. Ironically, the two remaining Allied cruisers had run right into it.

It was probably with some fatalistic feeling that Captains Waller and Rooks turned their ships into what they could not but have realized would be their last battle. Whatever they may have thought about the prospects of the cause for which they had been fighting these three months, they had found the enemy for whom they had been searching, and were at the same time trapped themselves inside the Malay Barrier. Both determined to give as good an account of themselves and their ships as they could, and carry the fight to the enemy all the way. After a salvo at the *Fubuki,* which retaliated with a torpedo salvo that missed and began signaling for assistance, the two cruisers headed for the transports. The ensuing melee was reminiscent of the Battle of the Java Sea only two days previous, except that this time there was no confusion on our side. Everything Rooks and Waller saw was enemy.

Walter G. Winslow, now a Captain, USN (Ret.), was a junior grade lieutenant assigned to the *Houston*'s scout plane aviation unit, and it is to him and his book, *The Ghost That Died at Sunda Strait* (Naval Institute Press, 1984) that I am indebted for the account quoted below. The book is intended as a heartfelt memorial to a great ship and crew, and it succeeds incomparably. Winslow, assigned to an aircraft that had become unusable, as a result had no regular battle station. He worked as a volunteer wherever help was needed and kept a diary, part sent home while there was still the opportunity, and part surreptitiously chronicled during his three and a half years of captivity. For him it was a long labor of love for an indomitable captain, a great ship, and a valorous crew. Real feeling for the extraordinary circumstance comes through with every word. Regarding the ship's last moments, he writes:

> Lining the western shores of Banten Bay and along the coast of Java near Sunda Strait were 56 transports, a large seaplane carrier, and a seaplane tender. Close by were the light cruisers *Sendai, Natori,* and *Yura,* with 23 destroyers and several torpedo boats. Not far away was a covering force consisting of the aircraft carrier *Ryujo,* four heavy cruisers, including the *Mogami* and *Mikuma,* and supporting destroyers. The *Houston* and *Perth* were trapped.
>
> [We made] radical and violent maneuvers to evade torpedoes launched by destroyers from every conceivable direction. . . . The constant blinding flashes of gunfire made it difficult, and at times impossible, to keep track of the *Perth.* At about ten minutes past midnight, however, she was observed dead in the water and sinking. . . . From that moment, every ship in the area was an enemy.
>
> . . . Destroyers raced in close to illuminate the *Houston* with powerful searchlights so their cruisers' big guns could find the range. The *Houston's* crew battled back. No sooner were the lights snapped on than our guns blasted them out. One destroyer . . . was torn apart by a main battery salvo, and instantly disappeared. Another, (taken under fire) by the port side 5-inch guns, had its bridge shot away. Several times confused destroyer crews mistakenly illuminated their own transports close to the beach, and the *Houston's* gunners quickly pumped shells into them. At one point in the melee enemy vessels were shooting at each other.
>
> For almost 60 minutes the *Houston* received not a single hit of consequence. A salvo of heavy shells even passed completely through the wardroom, from starboard to port, without exploding.

And so on. The *Houston* was the magnet to which all attention was attracted. Her good fortune could not last, and finally a salvo of heavy eight-inch hit her in the after engineroom, killing all hands including her chief engineer, and cutting her speed by a third. Her maneuverability reduced, she was hit on both sides by torpedoes, and after this it was but a matter of time. A hit on number two turret put it out of action, the ensuing fire necessitated flooding the forward magazines, and *Houston's* main battery was no longer functional. Motor torpedo boats, seeing their chance, dashed in to close range and fired more torpedoes (according to Winslow at least two were sunk by *Houston*'s five-inch antiaircraft battery's remaining guns, all she had left). But more torpedoes struck the dying ship, and she lost power and began to settle.

Winslow was on the bridge with Captain Rooks as he gave his last order, "Abandon ship!" He shook hands with the captain and then, not wishing to wait to go down the crowded ladder from the signal bridge, climbed instead over the rail and dropped the few feet to the deck below. As he did so a shell hit on the bridge just above him, and "from the sound, I knew it had taken a dreadful toll."

It was this hit that killed *Houston*'s heroic skipper. An account by Ens. Charles D. Smith, reproduced by Winslow, describes the scene: he and another ensign, employed in assisting the abandonment, for real this time instead of merely for drill, came upon the unconscious figure of Captain Rooks on the deck below the bridge. He was covered with blood, and the two young men realized he was about to die. They injected him with morphine from a first aid pack and covered him gently with a blanket.

As Smith describes it, after helping a couple of other wounded men he went back to where he had left Rooks, and to his astonishment found someone sitting cross-legged on deck with the captain's body cradled in his arms. It was his Chinese steward, a plump, jolly fellow known by the nickname of "Buddha" or "Buda." Rocking back and forth he paid no attention to Smith's urging that he should leave the ship, instead repeated over and over again, in soft, crooning, sorrow, "Captain die. *Houston* die. Buda die too." It is an affecting tale, giving some indication of the regard in which Rooks was held by his crew. The steward, Ah Fong by name, was never seen again and is listed as having gone down with the ship.

Although *Houston*'s guns were now silent and she was at a complete stop, listing badly to starboard, the enemy continued to pound her in the frenzy of victory. Several torpedoes slammed into her while in this condition, with her crew members struggling to come up from below through the wreckage and go overboard while there was yet time to clear the sinking ship. Winslow, now in the water, turned to see the last sight of his ship. It was an emotional moment:

The sinking *Houston* listed further and further to starboard until her yardarms barely dipped into the sea. Even so, the enemy was not yet finished with her. A torpedo . . . exploded amidships on her port side . . . [and]

the *Houston* rolled wearily back on an even keel. With decks awash, the proud ship steadied, once more upright. A sudden breeze fluttered the Stars and Stripes, still firmly two-blocked on her mainmast, and waved them in one last defiant gesture. Then, with a tired shudder, . . . our magnificent USS *Houston* vanished beneath the sea.

In his history of the war, Samuel Eliot Morison quotes notes made at the final conference at the Supreme Allied Headquarters in Bandung between British, American, and Dutch naval commanders on the morning of 1 March 1942. There were some direct statements regarding the futility of further American, British, and Australian support of the doomed cause of the Dutch East Indies, and Helfrich continued to reiterate his determination to fight to the death. The upshot of the meeting was dissolution of the so-called ABDA Command, when the British and American admirals demanded that their respective ships be released from the obviously hopeless fight. Units of the Allied combined fleet were thereupon ordered by their respective national commanders to proceed immediately to Australia. Dutch forces were to continue as before.

There were, however, no ships left. Illustrative of the strange never-never land of the Allied commanders, these decisions, like nearly all they had made previously, were already overtaken by events. *Houston* and *Perth* were on the bottom near Sunda Strait, their survivors fighting for their lives against the sea and the jungle, and (in some cases) against murderous Japanese soldiers. Japan's claim that prisoners of war were being humanely treated was, with a few notable exceptions, false and intendedly so. Of *Houston*'s 1,000-man crew, over 600 survived the sinking, but only 284 were found alive at the end of the war. Of the *Perth*'s nearly 700, only 218 came back.

One big ship remained, the *Exeter*. With half her engine power remaining, she successfully reached Surabaya after the Battle of the Java Sea, made what repairs were possible, took on what fuel could be had, and departed the evening of 28 February. She too had been directed to exit the Malay Barrier via Sunda Strait, but one wonders at the rationale behind these orders. Sunda Strait was far to the west and slightly to the north. Lombok Strait was many miles closer, just on the other side of the fabled island of Bali. In case of the *Houston* and *Perth*, sent by Doorman's last message to Tanjung Priok, passing from behind the Malay Barrier via Sunda Strait, not far from their location near the west end of Java, was geographically the obvious way out, and would have been the fastest except for the presence of the Japanese fleet. For ships in Surabaya, at the other end of Java, the opposite was true. The Strait of Bali, between Bali and Java, was immediately to hand for any ships of shallow draft; this was the route chosen by the four old American destroyers that departed Surabaya about the same time. Bali Strait was too shallow for the big English cruiser, but she could easily have gone around the small island of Bali and into deep and wide Lombok Strait. Had this been the route selected, *Exeter* and the two destroyers with her would have been clear of the barrier by daybreak and well into the Indian Ocean.

Perhaps some vestige of Helfrich's intent to concentrate his remaining ships at Tjilatjap, about midway on the south coast of Java, was responsible. Whatever the reason, the orders were fatally wrong, for they caused the three desperate ships to steam *toward* an overwhelmingly superior enemy force instead of in the opposite direction, through Lombok. The *Exeter* and her pitifully inadequate escorts were found about noon on 1 March in the northern part of the Java Sea, farther than ever from either Sunda or Lombok Strait, and sunk out of hand.

The Supreme Allied Commanders' conference in Bandung that same morning might as well not have taken place, for all the ships with which they were concerned had already been sunk or, meaning *Exeter* and her escorts, were about to be. Following the conference, Helfrich suggested the British and American admirals arrange for their own departures from the soon-to-be-captured island. He himself, having lost the entire fleet entrusted to him without any return of value to either his or the Allied war effort, embarked in the plane that had been kept at the ready for him and flew to Ceylon. He had accomplished nothing except to sacrifice the lives of nearly all the men entrusted to his command.

Chapter Five

To War in the Pacific

Trigger (SS-237) was as different from *Lea* as two ships could possibly be from each other. The submarine was brand-new, technologically the very latest thing in warships, while the poor old *Lea,* superficially of nearly the same size though of smaller displacement, was old, obsolete, and very tired. *Trigger* was crammed full of equipment, to such an extent that despite a crew only half as big, one could hardly move around without bumping into someone. Aboard the *Lea* I had thought us fairly well cramped in that little hull built so closely around her two heavy turbines and four big boilers, but I'd not yet learned the meaning of the word. And still, in *Trigger,* with approximately a quarter of the space to myself I'd had in the *Lea,* soon I found myself quite at ease.

Submariners are always asked about claustrophobia: "How can you exist in such a small enclosed space? I'd go stark raving mad," people invariably say. The answer is simple. Submarine sailors don't want "a view." They don't want to see through glass windows around them. They feel much safer inside thick, strong, steel. Besides, you don't only see the stuff of the mere ship around you. In the Navy, your mind is far away, on your job, on the condition of whatever it is you're responsible for; you feel that your hands are not attached on the ends of your arms, but out at the limits of consciousness, the perimeter of your vision, through the periscope maybe, or the throttles of a big diesel engine, reaching for the controls of your destiny.

When I reported to Mare Island, on New Year's Day 1942, the *Trigger* had already been launched and was being fitted out as rapidly as the Navy yard workers could do the job. They were already at war. By March, we had *Trigger* under way. In April we were at San Diego for initial training, and in

May she passed under the Golden Gate Bridge on a westerly course from which she was destined to return only one time. I was not on watch as we entered Pearl Harbor but found occasion to be topside, as did everyone in our crew who was free of duty. All of us were overwhelmed at the desolation everywhere, the tremendous damage Japan had dealt us in only a few minutes.

The wrecked battleships were still at their berths alongside Ford Island, except for the *West Virginia*, recently raised off the muddy harbor bottom and put into drydock. The fleet flagship *California* was once again afloat; a series of mud-and-oil waterline marks on her once-immaculate side attested to how far she had sunk, and the successive stages at getting her once again near her normal waterline. The *Oklahoma*, in which I had once made a midshipman cruise, now aptly described somewhere as resembling a stranded whale, lay belly-up, her mud- and rust-colored bottom bleached by the Hawaiian sun, her turrets nowhere to be seen, plainly buried deep into the mud beneath her hull. Her great tripod masts had evidently already been cut up and removed so as not to block harbor passage in the channel where her rolling hull had broken them off against the bottom of the bay. Structures had been built on the whale's belly, and here and there some relatively square uncovered holes could be seen.

I remembered tales of men having been trapped inside; some had been rescued, but some could not be reached. There were stories of air whistling out when a hole was cut, so that before it could be enlarged sufficiently for someone to pass through it everyone on the other side had been drowned. Perhaps this was why those strange box-like things had been built: to contain the air pressure while the hole was cut. I thought I could identify metal straps intended to hold some of them down. No doubt there had been problems keeping them properly caulked, and of course there would have had to be airtight double doors, so that one of them could always be kept closed.

We passed *Oklahoma* fairly close aboard, and everyone on our decks had a good look at her. Some of us had read somewhere that the plan was to right her and restore her to service, and I remember wondering how that could be. From my cruise in her I recalled well how big and how complicated she was, and could not visualize restoring all that complexity.

Farther away, a gigantic tripod tower leaned toward us, a pile of wreckage at its base. The *Arizona*, of course. Her entire bow blown up by explosion of her forward magazines, she had sunk on an even keel, but the damage to her forward parts had extended all the distance to her foremast and caused the drunken angle at which we saw it.

The overall impression, however, the thing that affected me most, was not the wrecked ships, dramatic though these were, but the stench. Like San Diego, but different, it too was a smell I shall never forget. Composed principally of fuel oil, it was much more prevalent than the comsomol I remembered from putting the *Lea* back in service. Even now, five months after the attack, the waters of the bay were still oily, now with a mixture of filthy mud added. Everywhere that water could reach, there was a coating of black fuel oil. It covered the shoreline of the harbor, was deposited thickly on rocks, pilings, and the occasional buoy, was choking the spaces beneath the piers. So far as anyone could discern, no attempt had yet been made at cleanup, except possibly at some official landing places.

All available boats had, of course, been pressed into service during the emergency, and they too had immediately become filthy with black oil. Still evident in many of the visible work boats, this must have added its own share of distress to their crews, who were accustomed to keeping their boats in a pristine condition. There were still great streaks of oil floating around, most of them now congealed into long strips of tar-like "gunk," ultimately to be washed up on some rock or other part of the harbor shore where they would solidify even more. Sometimes strips of cold tar that had once (somehow) been fuel oil could be picked up by hand (neither recommended nor often done), but mostly they ultimately became part of the smelly, despoiled landscape. Hundreds of thousands of barrels of "Navy Standard Fuel Oil" had been released into the harbor when the bottoms of the battleships that had held it were blown open. Once the smell had also included the unmistakable stench of traumatic death, the putrefying bodies of American sailors, but by the time I got there this was no longer discernible.

That was my impression and my memory as *Trigger* quietly nosed her way through the still-disordered debris of Pearl Harbor to her berth at the submarine base. That was the aspect of the harbor that hit me strongest; but this material memory was instantly overwhelmed by an even more indelible one, not involved in the material condition but in the mind of man. More properly, it was in the mind of everyone present at that once-lovely, violated place. I have never felt before, nor have I felt since, such a concentrated, blazing intent. If one did not believe in extrasensory perception before this moment, one would have had to believe it then. No words were spoken, no indication so far as I can recall was given of it in any way, but I knew almost immediately—and I knew that everyone else knew, too—that something

big was about to take place. The greatest battle of the war was in the immediate offing!

Incidental happenings bolstered the overall impression of pressure. We
were to be given none of the regular pre-patrol training. Our orders were to
fuel, provision to capacity, check our torpedoes and other needs, and get
under way. As communications officer I had to get new "pubs" (confiden-
tial publications), and was in the process of a hurried trip to the classified publication office in the Pearl Harbor Navy Yard, across a small branch of the
Pearl Harbor bay from the submarine base, when in the distance I saw a large
ship, an aircraft carrier, coming down the entrance channel and into the harbor. I knew very little about Navy yard protocol or procedures (and at this
stage cared less) but I remember nevertheless being surprised to find the
main drydock of the yard already open to receive her, and even more surprised when tugs that were waiting along the way went directly alongside
the arriving ship and eased her into the open drydock.

Normally, ships would come into harbor, have some sort of arrival conference, and, if needed, drydocking would be scheduled for sometime during
their stay. Not this time. This carrier, which I guessed must be the *Yorktown*,
went into the dock without even slowing down, figuratively at least. It was
of a piece with our own orders to get going right away, part of our urgency. A
crowd of workmen boarded floating stages the moment the ship was in the
dock, and another crowd was waiting to go aboard the moment gangways or
brows were placed for them. They were hard at work on her bottom, making
repairs from both sides as it became exposed, even as the water was still being
pumped out of the drydock.

The ship, from her appearance, had to be one of our best carriers and,
although curious, I was too busy checking out *Trigger*'s new pubs to have
more than a cursory look as I hurried on about the business that had brought
me there. All the same, the impression stayed that the entire procedure was
out of the ordinary, suffused with haste and something else, which later I
decided must have been aggressive determination. The entire experience was
mental, but it was a strong one; my ESP certainty that something big was
about to happen could not have been more compellingly confirmed.

The atmosphere of tension, of subconscious realization that the stakes
were very high, has never since been so vivid. Without real understanding, I
knew that it emanated from the Pacific Fleet Headquarters and that Admiral
Nimitz, our Big Boss, must be at the center of it.

. . .

The story of the Battle of Midway is well known. Less well known is the part the *Trigger* played in the battle, far from distinguished except in a negative sense.

It was the night of 3 June 1942. We were patrolling our sector on the surface some 20 miles east of Midway, when, at about 0330, according to Lt. (jg) Steve Mann, whom I came to relieve at the prescribed time (0345) as officer of the deck (OOD), the stars began to move strangely above him, the heavens changed in ways they never had before, everything became disoriented. Shouting down the hatch, he discovered that the captain had come into the conning tower and, without notifying anyone, had ordered the helm put over and the course changed. Then he went below again, without any further word. Steve was incensed and upset; but since it was the captain who had taken this liberty, there was nothing he could do except pass on to me what he did know, and promise to tell me what was going on as soon as he found out.

Navy doctrine prescribes that, in emergency, either the captain or the navigator (but only these two) may arbitrarily take maneuvering control of the ship, "the conn," at any time. In the interest of saving what might be extremely valuable time, not even the minimum of protocol or procedure is prescribed. The captain or navigator, merely by giving a direct order to the helm or engines, automatically supersedes all other authority in managing movement of the ship. The regular OOD, and all others on watch, continue to be responsible for normal routine, but the OOD's authority to handle the ship's maneuvers has been supplanted. It remains so until the captain (or the navigator) returns it to him.

Inasmuch as their responsibility for safe handling of the ship is never ending, this is prescribed in *Naval Regulations* as well as in the "standing orders" of all ships. The captain or navigator may, of course, take over the conn any time either feels the need. If no emergency exists, however, normal procedure is to say formally, as in relieving the watch, "I have the conn," or "I relieve you of the conn." In any case, whoever has or takes the conn, even the captain, must keep it until he has been formally relieved, for by definition only one officer can "drive" or "conn" the ship. This was what had angered Steve, for suddenly, without any warning, the *Trigger* was no longer going in the direction he had been instructed he should be directing her. For a short time no one, in fact, was driving at all until, learning the captain had made the change and then disappeared, Steve reasserted his duties and responsibilities as OOD. Technically speaking, he need not have. The captain, having given a direct order to the helm, took the conn back below with him to his bunk, or wherever he went. But the ship was under way, and Steve was too good an officer to stand on ceremony.

Shortly after I had pronounced the formal words, "I relieve you sir!"— even though Steve had not been able to tell me what direction I, as his relief, was supposed to "drive"—Steve sent word from the wardroom that we had received orders to close Midway to a distance of two miles in anticipation of a Japanese landing effort at dawn.

Trigger bored on toward Midway at full speed. Having no knowledge of the navigational situation, or what the captain's intentions were, I was much concerned and kept a vigilant watch, particularly ahead, where I presumed Midway must be. At no time during this period did our skipper come on the bridge, nor into the conning tower immediately below. I thought he must be doing some important work over charts in the wardroom, and when I sent down word that I was beginning to see things in the distance ahead I was startled to discover no one knew where he was. My staring eyes, fully accommodated to the darkness (I discovered later that I had been blessed with excellent night vision), had begun to make out some sort of low-lying disturbance on the horizon. I called this down to the captain, thinking he must be in the control room. Learning he had possibly gone forward to his stateroom, I asked for the navigator to be called. Penrod Schneider, executive officer and navigator, came on the bridge, admitted he did not know what was going on, had not been briefed, and was not night-adapted. Recognizing my concern, he went below to check the charts, promising to give me more information as soon as he could.

We drove on relentlessly at 18 knots, and I became aware of something glittering on the horizon. Perhaps it was my imagination; perhaps it was ships—if so, no doubt Japanese; but my strongest impression was as though lights were reflecting from the windows of small buildings upon a distant shoreline. I reported this to Schneider in the conning tower.

Shortly thereafter, the captain came on the bridge, and, after a long look through his binoculars, went below, once again without saying a word. I made several reports that I could see land and distant buildings several miles ahead. Finally, from the conning tower I was told to desist, that there should be no land in sight, that I must be "seeing things." It was understandable that we should all be pretty tense, with a Japanese landing attempt expected within hours. Finally, however, with the sight of tumultuous white water just ahead I shouted down to the conning tower that, if it was not land, I was looking at the wakes of several big ships that had just crossed our bow. Our rudimentary radar gave no indication of anything, but at this moment our quartermaster of the watch, an experienced sailor who had heard everything and was diligently searching ahead, as on the bridge we all were, shouted out in a voice full of fright, "Breakers! Breakers ahead!"

And suddenly it was all very obvious. There were great black rocks dead ahead, waves splashing violently upon them! The captain and navigator dashed up on the bridge beside me. "All back full!" roared the captain. I heard the click of the engine-order telegraphs and could sense the propellers stopping and taking a bite in the reverse direction.

"Sound the collision alarm!" our captain shouted; I heard all the ship's alarms sound, without pause, one after the other. The effect was as if they had all sounded at once: collision alarm, general alarm, and a single blast on the diving alarm. (We discovered later that the chief of the watch in the control room, startled, had rung all the alarms in sight.)

Disaster was on us. The rocks were huge, and so were the waves splashing over them. No one thought to order the rudder hard over, which might have helped the situation. Maybe I might have done it, but by giving direct orders the skipper had again taken over the conn. Nothing was done with the rudder. More important, however, when the diving alarm sounded, the electricians took the main engines off the line, shifted to battery propulsion and, following the boat's standard orders for diving, reversed the direction of the propellers a second time, putting them to "ahead full." As the result, never even slowing our headlong pace, in accordance with dive procedures we continued to drive ahead full speed on the batteries.

The diving signal is always two blasts on a special "diving alarm," in the early days actually a raucous Klaxon horn. In the *Trigger* the horn was simulated through the general announcing system, saving several seconds getting the horn motor up to speed. The first blast called for opening the forward group of main vents—hydraulically operated at the tops of our main ballast tanks—to initiate a quick dive; the second blast, normally sounded immediately as the second blast of a two-blast signal, called for opening the after group. Since the diving alarm had given one blast, only the forward vents were opened; we were immediately lower in the water, and possibly this may have made the difference in our ability to get off the reef later on. But this is speculation. It is possible no vents were opened at all. We were in utter confusion in the ship control stations, and no one knows what was done.

Helpless, having totally lost control, we on the bridge saw our boat drive full speed onto the rocks. We struck with a horrendous clang. I was looking dead ahead, right over the bow, and saw it rise irresistibly out of the water, reaching heavenward in a desperate, agonized leap. I actually thought that, somewhere behind me, we must have broken in half. I saw our bow slammed sideways to starboard, and then several more diminishing bumps as we slid forward. Finally, and very quickly, all forward motion stopped. The ship lay half out of the water at an improbable angle. That we were seriously damaged we had no doubt. Our stern was partially submerged, our bow jutted out over gray sand and big coral rocks. We had driven our ship aground at full power, and *Trigger* was stuck fair.

We had been informed the Japs were due to try to land on Midway that very morning. There was nothing we could do to help ourselves, let alone fight them. If their aircraft, or their battleships in for shore bombardment, which operation orders had mentioned as a possibility, were to see us helpless on the reef, that would be the end of us.

However, *Trigger* had not broken in half, as I had first thought. Internally there was indescribable confusion, but our super-strong submarine hull had received no damage that we could detect. Our engines were not injured, all systems functioned normally. Our stern was still in deep water; we restarted the engines and backed with full power, but finally gave up. There was no budging from our impaled position on the rocks.

A signal searchlight was brought up, and in the growing dawn we could see, now clearly outlined in the morning twilight on the far side of the Midway lagoon, exactly the buildings and shoreline I had been describing before we struck. Whatever it was that had glittered faintly now glittered strongly; and finally the insistent blinking of our signal light evoked a response. To our message that we were aground came the answer, "Are you inside the reef?" This hadn't even occurred to us, but a later look at the chart showed it was not a foolish question.

Midway is a typical coral island built upon a submerged outcropping of the ocean bottom, possibly even an extinct volcano. In common with most coral atolls, the small amount of usable land was concentrated on one side of a much larger ring of partly submerged reefs. In the case of Midway, this usable land mass was in two islets, named Eastern and Sand Islands, close to each other on the southern rim of a big but shallow lagoon, the border of which consisted of an almost circular rim of large rocks and coral growth. We had struck on the north rim of the lagoon, several miles from the buildings I had seen, which were on the opposite side. More than one sailing ship, driven by a storm in the days of ocean-going sail, has been known to strike such a reef

and carry clear across it, rip her bottom out in the process, and come to rest inside the lagoon, essentially demolished but possibly with her upper works still intact, there to remain until time and weather bring about the inevitable disintegration. The German sailing raider *Seeadler,* skippered by the famous Count Felix von Luckner, came to grief in World War I in just this fashion.

"Outside the reef!" we said. "Send tug!" We hoped for a regular Navy tug, a big seagoing ship with powerful engines. Instead, a tiny tug appeared, so small it resembled a toy. In the meantime, mindful of the Japanese attack expected at dawn, we had manned our antiaircraft battery: two .30-caliber machine guns on the bridge, and our three-inch antiaircraft type gun on the main deck. If Japanese planes appeared, we would at least shoot back, although, looking at our tiny armament, it was evident these guns were only symbolic.

The tug tossed us a heaving line, put a hawser on our stern, and began to pull. The water boiled up behind her in a very respectable effort for so small a vessel. We backed emergency at the same time with all the power our engines could give us. Nothing happened, and then the hawser broke. At this point, I felt sure our brand-new *Trigger* was doomed to spend the rest of her days on the reef; but maybe the tug had done some good, maybe a small tide had raised the water level a little, perhaps we had indeed increased our draft forward just before striking. Before the tug came we had blown our ballast tanks absolutely dry, pumped overboard much of our fuel, and all our extra water. We were preparing to jettison torpedoes through our bow tubes when someone noticed our ship had unaccountably come alive. There was definite motion as she lay among the rocks. "She's moving!" he shouted.

All hands not otherwise engaged were ordered on deck to sally ship, cause her to roll by running from one side to the other. I stood on the after part of the bridge and tried to coordinate the crew's movements with hand motions. They ran back and forth across with a will, but there seemed to be no corresponding movement of the ship, and just as I was giving up that effort as a bad job, again I heard the cry, "She's moving!" and to our delight, with her engines under maximum load, clouds of black smoke pouring out of her four main engine exhaust ports and her two auxiliaries too, our good ship slid backward off the rocks and into deep water!

It was a time for cheering, despite apprehensive glances at the sky where Japanese aircraft still might suddenly appear. Having gotten rid of everything disposable with the exception of torpedoes, we were far out of diving trim. There was no way our boat could submerge until we reballasted (got water back into our trimming tanks to equal the weight we had pumped or blown out), and this was not a rapid process. We therefore cruised about aimlessly on the surface, our pitiful antiaircraft battery manned and ready, the ship so high out of the water that her forward torpedo tubes were exposed. Below decks everyone was frantically checking everything we could think of checking in case of some unnoticed damage—who knew what air or hydraulic line might have ruptured under the sudden stress of colliding with Midway's coral sea wall—when suddenly two other U.S. submarines surfaced nearby.

We had all been ordered to close Midway to a distance of two miles, each submarine in its own pie-shaped sector. The boats to either side of us, we later discovered, seeing us on the surface thought we might know something they didn't know, or were more daring than they, so they surfaced also. The three submarines maneuvered about aimlessly in their sectors, warily watching for the enemy—none came—listened intently for news or instructions on our radios—nothing here either—and somewhere during this period *Trigger* finally got enough water in her tanks to compensate for what we had discharged in lightening her. Without any fanfare, we submerged. Once at periscope depth, we raised the periscope to check on our friends, but they were nowhere to be seen. They had concluded that indeed we knew something they didn't, and when we dived they did, too.

We remained on patrol a few days, stopped briefly at Midway, where those of us able to get ashore had a quick look at some of the damage wrought by the Japanese attackers, and then we went on our way back to Pearl Harbor for drydocking and repairs.

Looking over the damage on the island, consisting of a couple of hangars destroyed and some burned-out aircraft, I could hardly visualize that this represented most of the visible cost of a great victory at sea. It was dramatic, but the damage encompassed only a small area, and was not at all impressive in terms of what had been at stake. The battle had taken place hundreds of miles away; and none of the warships that fought and destroyed each other, except for a few submarines, ever saw even one of the other side. It was to this that we undoubtedly owed our lives, for had any Japanese aircraft appeared in force over Midway while we were on the reef, or afterward before we were able to dive, we would have been a most inviting target, and they could not have resisted making an all-out attack on us.

Once we were in Pearl Harbor, two things were on our minds. First was the extent of the damage underwater, and second was the extent to which some of us on board (myself included because I had been OOD) might be subject to court-martial or other unpleasant consequence. Running a ship aground is never a good idea. However, if one were to select the best time for having such misfortune, none more propitious could have been picked than in the midst of a glorious naval victory. When our skipper reported to headquarters to take his medicine and find out his fate, he was greeted with the jovial instruction to forget it. "We just won the Battle of Midway! Haven't you heard?"

Damage to *Trigger*'s underbody was nevertheless more severe than expected, and it showed how hard we had hit the reef. Also it showed that a submarine was the only type of ship that could have remained effective after receiving such a blow. Our pressure hull was made of high-tensile steel five-eighths of an inch thick, reinforced with heavy frames. We had been informally told it was designed to take twice the pressure of submergence to maximum allowed depth, "test depth" in submarine lingo.

We had struck the rocks with the underside of our bow, the toughest part of our submarine's tremendously strong pressure hull, designed to withstand maximum possible sea pressure. The point of contact was the ship's forwardmost "main ballast tank," blown dry when the boat was surfaced, flooded when she dived. Special emergency safety measures involving functioning at great depths had been built into this important tank. The Midway coral had torn a great hole in its heavy steel plates and ruined our fathometer, but we had received no other discernible damage, especially—our principal concern—to the vulnerable torpedo tubes just above number one main ballast. If anything, the big hole Midway punched in the tank had shortened our diving time, since, once the vent valve above was opened, water could flood it more quickly than before.

Repairs to *Trigger*'s bottom took about a week. I was amazed at the speed and flair with which the welders and shipfitters in the drydock waved an enormous piece of curved steel plate, suspended on wire cables from a huge crane, down to the drydock floor near her bow, deposited it gently, and then maneuvered it with other simple but heavy tools into exactly the place they wanted it. Within a week we were back at the submarine base, preparing this time for the training we should have had before being sent to Midway.

We had been issued a code for use during training, which, as I was communications officer, became mine to administer on board the *Trigger*, and I well remember visiting the new submarine *Grunion* (SS-216) when she arrived at Pearl Harbor shortly before our departure on patrol. Willie Kornahrens, her communications officer, was a classmate and close friend at the

Naval Academy who had once borrowed my full-dress trousers for a dress parade from which I, being on the day's watch squad, was exempt. Now Kornahrens puzzled over this new but simple code. From my position of experience with how Pearl Harbor did its business, I was able to explain it. Several other officers gathered around us in the wardroom, and I remember particularly how being the "resident expert" gave my then low spirits a lift. Because of what came after, I still remember the moment, and the feeling.

In due course, we departed Pearl Harbor for *Trigger*'s first official patrol (the Battle of Midway had taken about two weeks all together and another week of repair, but we were glad enough to forget about that). Attu in the Aleutian archipelago, the farthest island of any size in the chain, had been occupied by the Japanese at the same time as they had attacked Midway. It was believed to be the least important in Japanese eyes, and since *Trigger* had lost her fathometer at Midway she was given Attu as her patrol area. It is possible also that because of our grounding the submarine force commander in the Aleutian area considered us one of his less-effective submarines and assigned us accordingly.

Our time there was dreary and stultifying, enlivened only by an occasional sighting of ships that we seemed never able to approach close enough to attack. We spent all day submerged, well offshore, with nothing in sight but the distant outline of Attu. At night we moved still farther offshore and surfaced for our nightly battery charge. The skipper wanted two officers on watch on the bridge whenever we were surfaced, and with only six officers aboard, this forced the four of us who stood watch as OOD into a watch-on, watch-off status, two hours at a time. We did our duty loyally, but our alertness was hardly of the best. I recall wondering, with our continuous lack of sleep, how we would manage a true emergency. Fortunately, there was none. As a submarine patrol area the way we patrolled it, well offshore, Attu was dead indeed.

We had been off Attu for a week or so when the submarine *Growler*, commanded by the former Lieutenant (jg) Kirkpatrick (he of the Main Office duty four years before, when the Martians "landed" in New Jersey), reported expenditure of all torpedoes, and several ships sunk. *Growler* had been assigned to Kiska, an Aleutian island larger than Attu and more active, being the principal Japanese base during their Aleutian campaign. She was ordered off station, and we were shifted there to take her place. Here the monotony of being constantly dog-tired, nothing to do, and a humid, cold, almost constantly foggy atmosphere was relieved one day when two Japanese destroyers, proceeding at slow speed in column, went across our bow. This was *Trigger*'s first actual sighting of enemy warships. My station was on the plot in the conning tower, and I remember the demeanor of our skipper as he looked through the periscope almost continuously, dipping it frequently, tracing the path of the destroyers as they passed.

Had we increased speed only slightly, we would have been in a perfect firing position. In any case, without maneuvering, we could have fired at long range, about 4,000 yards. But nothing happened. We were not detected, we did not expose ourselves, we did not attack. In fact, we did nothing at all. My faith in my commanding officer took a nose dive, and the memory of his performance at Midway assumed greater proportions.

Among my communications officer duties was that of encoding and transmitting messages we originated and, of course, decoding those addressed to us. In my spare moments, I also decoded other messages out of curiosity, and thus I learned of the disastrous Battle of Savo Island on 9 August 1942, in which the U.S. cruisers *Astoria, Quincy,* and *Vincennes,* and the Australian *Canberra,* were caught by surprise and sunk, while USS *Chicago* (which I had seen launched at Mare Island when I was a young boy), a handsome sister of the admirable, mourned *Houston,* was badly damaged. How could such a disaster have befallen our forces, I wondered. It had been an evil day and night for them. They had been caught at night with their crews exhausted after days of high-tension alertness. When the enemy showed up they were in Condition Two (a small standdown from Condition One, or Battle Stations). The attack had come so fast they were simply not able to cope with the enormity of their danger, and were already sinking as they closed up their battle stations. An immediate and personal comparison with our own situation, also exhausted by the effort to maintain constant alertness, led me to the conclusion that in their place we'd have fared little better. The British navy claimed, so the story went, that if it ever came to another war with the United States they would keep all their ships safely in port until we had worn ourselves out, then sally forth to easy pickings.

The Battle of Savo Island was one of the proofs of this. There must be a better way, I thought, and the record of the war shows that we found one. One of the most significant changes we made in crew-handling, once the more senior officers understood that permanent battle stations was not a supportable condition, was to give formal status to crew rest. Several submarines, to my personal awareness, simply went off the line for 24 hours or so, reported the fact, and were praised by their superiors. The same procedure, more complicated because surface ships almost always operated in groups, known as "task forces," was put in place in the surface navy.

We were only a few days off Kiska when orders were received directing that the *Grunion,* which had been sent to Attu in our place upon her recent arrival in the Aleutians, was to exchange areas with us. We were to return to Attu, the reason given being that there would be more need for a fathometer-effective boat in the more-active Kiska vicinity. Also, I thought, our Dutch Harbor–based commander might have less confidence in us than in the equally untried *Grunion.*

As we were proceeding on the surface from Kiska to Attu, a submarine was sighted some distance away on the opposite course. We dived instantly and through the periscope determined the other submarine must have dived also. It might have been the *Grunion,* I thought, but I will never know.

A few days later I decoded a message from *Grunion,* stating that she had attacked a destroyer off Kiska Harbor and had been depth-charged. We had yet to hear a single depth charge, except in training. I was envious of Willie Kornahrens for having so quickly surpassed me in the experience level, and imagined him sitting in his own radio room, supervising transmission of the very message I was hearing.

Customarily, when the sender finished transmitting, he would wait with his transmitter at the ready while the receiving station checked the message over. If necessary to clear something up, the receiver would send a "procedure signal," a few letters of the alphabet, asking for all or part of a transmission to be repeated. This the original sender does immediately. When satisfied, the receiving operator sends the letter "R"—dot, dash, dot—with a special sort of emphasis that is clearly above and beyond mere electronic beeping. All hands know and understand this. The originator of the message, when he hears the "R" that informs him it has been receipted for, gives his key a quick tap, a click, unofficially informing the other operator that he is satisfied also, and is turning off his transmitter. We were not "on the line" with the *Grunion* and could not therefore participate in the dialogue with the Dutch Harbor operator, but we could listen; so I participated in a vicarious way.

From the time the patrol started, I had been spending many of my off-watch hours (when not sleeping) listening to the radio traffic in our radio room, which was of course in my bailiwick, as it had been in the *Lea.* I had learned Morse code at the Naval Academy and was fairly good at it, though nowhere near good enough to receive messages the way our professionals took them, on a typewriter. But reading over their shoulders and hearing the dots and dashes at the same time, I did find that I could recognize the timbre of the code, "read" some of the Morse code letters as they came in, and on a rudimentary basis analyze what we were hearing. I was thus in our radio room when, once again, a nearby transmitting station began to tune up. Someone nearby was about to send a message. I made a quick motion to Ben Baxley, our leading radioman, then on watch. He was as curious as I was, and as usual, glad to be told to break a few rules.

Quickly rolling a sheet of paper on top of the official log sheet in his typewriter, Baxley copied the message verbatim, procedure signals prior to transmission, shore station answer, and all. He and I both heard the loud, nearby signal, its measured cadence, the way the sender moved methodically through the sequence of five-lettered gibberish that constituted a coded message. It must be the *Grunion*, I thought. It was a U.S. code, all right, and it came in as though the sender were right alongside. Everything was distinct. I could recognize the format, and so far as I could tell it was the same operator we had heard before. Then, as Ben and I listened, we knew that something had gone wrong. The letters became hurried, their measured sequence less sure. At the end there seemed almost a desperate urgency, and then the other station, by this time no doubt *Grunion*, fell silent.

The shore station, Radio Dutch Harbor, vainly requested a repeat of the last few groups of the message. *Grunion* did not respond, never acknowledged the radio procedure signals from Radio Dutch Harbor, which that operator sent repeatedly. There was a special, studied deliberation in the Dutch Harbor keying that Baxley and I recognized immediately for what it could only be: that operator's own, personal, almost spoken plea for some sign of life. He knew what he was hearing, just as we did in the *Trigger*. Little by little, Dutch Harbor formed its Morse code letters more exactly, more precisely. They began to come a little slower, keyed in a perfect, copperplate hand, as the saying went. He wanted badly to be able to give the "received" signal, wanted more than that to hear the tiny click from the *Grunion*'s radioman.

Nothing. *Grunion* never retransmitted her last confused groups of coded characters, never received the "R" our system required her to get. Grabbing the paper from Baxley's typewriter, I headed for our coding machine with a sense of foreboding. Willie, I was morally certain, had been in his radio room as I had been in mine, and we two friends had in a sense been in direct communication with each other. I decoded the message, and it was indeed from the *Grunion*. She reported an attack on two destroyers. One she thought she had possibly damaged, but she had been slightly damaged herself, and was heading out of the area to let things cool off a bit. And then the message, which until then had decoded perfectly, became garbled. It seemed to make reference to "another attack" but that is something else no one will ever know for sure.

I could well visualize the final moments. In the overhead of the radio room was a tiny hatch, big enough only for a pair of hands, leading to the "radio antenna trunk." While on the surface, connections to the sub's antennae for both transmitter and receivers were made via this trunk, which was nothing more than a rugged piece of pipe with insulated leads to the boat's external antennae built inside it. Even though the "topside" parts of the antenna trunk could not be opened to the sea, early designers felt it might be a possible source of weakness against depth charges, therefore provided a means of isolating it. When the submarine was on the surface the hatch was open, with wires leading through it. On diving, the radioman on watch would leap up, jerk down the overhead connections, and slam shut the little hatch. The antenna trunk itself was watertight, so there was little real danger if he failed to get it shut before the boat went under. But someone had considered the needed opening in our pressure hull a weak spot, and had put a hatch there to be closed on diving. The diving procedure we always meticulously followed involved jerking down the radio antennae leads, slamming shut the tiny hatch, and dogging it down firmly.

The *Grunion* radioman had been transmitting routinely, no doubt guessing the message had to do with the recent fight with the two destroyers. He was nearing the end when suddenly the diving alarm sounded, then the general alarm, followed no doubt by orders to rig for depth charges. In furious haste, for he had only seconds left, he banged out the last few groups of coded text while the submarine was diving. Water may or may not have reached his antenna by the time he was through. He had no time to correct or check anything, reached up, yanked down his antenna connection, and slammed shut the little hatch. Then he disappeared forever into the bottom of the waters around Kiska, along with my friend Willie, who, unless he was on watch, was probably at that very moment sitting also in his radio room as this last desperate message went out. No one will ever know just how it happened, but I've always felt that I was a witness when he died.

With my bride, Ingrid, on our wedding day, about 30 hours before the landing on the coast of Normandy. *Author's collection*

This ship, first named *Tennessee* (CA-9), played a central role in my life. As a child I made Father many times repeat the details of her destruction in a tsunami. We flew her ensign over the *Triton* (SS[R]N-586) on return from our submerged circumnavigation of the world in 1960, and *The Wreck of the Memphis* was, by design, published on 29 August 1966, exactly 50 years after it happened. *U.S. Navy*

Another special ship in my life, the USS *California* (BB-44). As Commandant of Mare Island Navy Yard, my father supervised her construction and launch, and I dreamed of someday even being her skipper. *U.S. Navy*

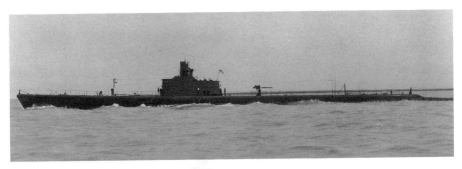

The USS *Trigger* (SS-237), fresh from the builder's yard at Mare Island. *U.S. Navy*

One of *Trigger's* "plankowners," I am the lieutenant (junior grade) closest to the camera in her commissioning ceremony. My first wartime duty was in this ship. *U.S. Navy*

The USS *Lea* (DD-118) is pictured here entering Havana harbor in 1940. She was a "four-piper" destroyer, launched on the day I was born, that I grew to love and left only reluctantly for the submarine service. *Author's collection*

A postwar photograph of the USS *Piper* (SS-409), which I skippered at the end of the war. We penetrated the Tsushima mine barrier, and were on patrol in the Sea of Japan when the ceasefire message came. She was my first command and my version of how the war ended was that the Japanese heard the *Piper* was coming and gave up in despair. *U.S. Navy*

My duty as President Eisenhower's naval aide—in this photograph functioning at a ceremony in Washington, D.C.—was one of the most exciting and rewarding of my career. *National Park Service*

Mrs. Eisenhower exuded more confidence than I when she christened the USS *Nautilus* (SSN-571). She did her duty to perfection, in part because of her practice beforehand in Washington. The strain on my face is real—our plans went awry when *Nautilus,* from having apparently stuck on the ways, began moving lickety-split and Mrs. Ike almost missed. Hopkins, cause of the problem, flinches from the spray of champagne while Janice Wilkinson, wife of the skipper, is also looking a little strained. *National Archives*

Following my White House duty, I commanded the USS *Salamonie* (AO-26), a fleet oiler not highly regarded by her crew or the rest of the fleet. Oilers are the workhorses of the replenishment force, and are most often run right into the ground. With a little luck and a lot of hard work, "Old Sal" began her climb back to being the tight ship she should always have been. *U.S. Navy*

USS *Triton* arriving in New London from her submerged circumnavigation. The flag of the *Memphis* is flying from a special fitting made for our periscope as my own personal tribute to my dad, who never lost his love for our Navy. *Bob Gomel* / Life *magazine* © *Time Inc.*

In the White House, after the ceremony honoring the USS *Triton* (SS[R]N-586) and her crew for their historic submerged circumnavigation of the world, I quietly informed Adm. Hyman G. Rickover of a reactor problem we had experienced during the voyage. Of the many men I have served with in the Navy, Rickover was the most fascinating—and at times exasperating—I ever encountered. *Hank Walker*/Life *magazine© Time Inc.*

The USS *Amberjack* (SS-522) became known as "*Anglejack*" because we pioneered the use of steep angles for changing depth. She is shown giving a demonstration in 1949 for the *National Geographic* (the picture was published in the magazine in January 1950). Jumping out of the water has no known military value, but it dramatically demonstrates the high-speed submarine's capability. *J. Baylor Roberts/*National Geographic *Image Collection*

Chapter Six

Chester Nimitz's Finest Hour

No student of World War II can fail to recognize that in appointing one Chester Nimitz to command the Pacific Fleet in place of the scapegoated Husband Kimmel, the administration in Washington did the smartest thing— with a single exception—that it could have done toward winning the war in that ocean. It would have done even better had it allowed Kimmel to stay in command until the arrival of Nimitz as his designated relief. Creating an interim of two weeks under the deplorable Pye cost us Wake Island when it could have been saved, along with the lives of most of those lost in its defense after it had been given up, but a more inspired choice than Nimitz to put things back in order could not have been found.

Typical about Nimitz was his innate modesty, his sure feel for the right and proper way to accomplish what needed to be done. In Pearl Harbor, still reeling from the Japanese attack and its aftermath, first the sacking of Kimmel and then the abandonment of Wake Island, this was not the time to stage a typical change of command ceremony. Yet it was necessary to have it happen, and have it be clear and plain. To Nimitz, an old submariner, the solution was simple. A submarine deck was not a big platform, but it could hold all those necessary. His own history as a submarine officer made it the more appropriate, and so on 31 December 1941 on the deck of USS *Grayling* (SS-208), temporarily the Pacific Fleet flagship, he simply read his orders assigning him the command, said, "I relieve you sir!" to Admiral Pye, and that was that. The circumstances were not for the usual speeches or a celebratory social affair. The occasion was strictly business, just what the situation called for.

Things seemed desperate in Australia in 1942, far more desperate than in the United States. At Pearl Harbor we had experienced the shock of our national life, but we had no thought of losing this war. Despite Admiral Yamamoto's purported boast (a misrepresentation of that brilliant man's actual words) about dictating peace on the steps of the White House, there was no immediate threat to the territorial integrity of our country. The exact opposite was true in Australia. The people there lived with the knowledge that a Japanese invasion could happen at any time.

The flower of Australia's military strength, army, navy, marines and air, excellent fighting men every one, had mostly been deployed to the sands of North Africa, where England still faced Nazi Germany's best general, Erwin Rommel. At the same time, the U.S. Asiatic Fleet, already suffering major losses, and our Pacific Fleet, with most of its vaunted battleline in the oily mud of Pearl Harbor, were seeing a major percentage of their expected support and reinforcements sent to England, in accordance with agreed Roosevelt-Churchill policy. The danger to the Free World from Hitler was deemed greater than that from Japan, and at the beginning, at least, it merited the greater effort. We cannot disagree with this evaluation today, but half a century ago our two fleets in the Pacific Ocean found this hard to accept.

It was scant comfort to the Australians, too, who viewed with the greatest of concern the speed and ease with which Japan moved into Southeast Asia. It now appears that even Japan was surprised at the absence of effective opposition, how quickly her conquests had fallen to her. Illustrative of this, without warning the Navy or even his own forces, General MacArthur declared Manila an open city on Christmas Day, 1941. Overnight, this decision required wholesale evacuation, destruction, or abandonment of all bases and supply deposits in the area, so that Japanese forces could occupy them without resistance. It was, in fact, almost similar to the debacle at Wake, where our Navy, Marines, and civilian workers were abandoned without warning or opportunity to save themselves. At Manila, there was 24 hours warning, time for the Navy to save its personnel and ships but not their vital equipment and supplies. Nor was there enough time for the army troops on Bataan, theoretically an area they could defend successfully, to move what they needed for survival to a place of safety.

Great was Admiral Hart's indignation at being summarily forced to destroy a number of valuable installations and supply dumps he might otherwise have been able to salvage. The Japanese, however, moved more slowly than MacArthur expected; they did not occupy Manila until 2 January, three weeks after the surprise attack on Pearl Harbor. Hart could have saved much more than he was allowed to, in particular the extremely valuable stock of submarine and destroyer torpedoes stored in the navy yard at Cavite. Not through bombing and fire on the day the war began, as given out at the time, but through simple abandonment by the unexpected "open city" order, this loss was felt by the Pacific fighting forces, especially those in Australia, for more than a year. (There was a fire at Cavite all right, but it was set by American forces at the MacArthur deadline, after they had removed everything they could, more than a week before any Japanese forces showed up.)

Port Darwin, Australia's principal northern harbor, was heavily bombed and put out of action in February. By the end of that month Japanese forces had landed on the northwestern tip of Java and were marching down both coasts without resistance, and the remnants of the combined American, British, Dutch, and Australian naval force, including Hart's handsome flagship, the cruiser *Houston*—all that was left of the U.S. Asiatic Fleet—had been wiped out. Two weeks more, and Java, the principal island of Dutch Indonesia, was totally occupied. Irresistible Japanese forces were only a few hundred miles northwest of Australia's north coast and going strong.

Japan's thrust into Burma simultaneously threatened India. Early in 1942, the same carrier task force that had hit Pearl Harbor severely battered British forces on Ceylon, in the Bay of Bengal, and elsewhere in the Indian Ocean. Outnumbered British naval and air forces withdrew to more secure bases west and south of the Indian peninsula. Australia could expect no help from them. To the east, America seemed hardly in condition to help anyone after Pearl Harbor. In short, Japan could go where it wished, do what it wanted, conquer what it coveted. This was, of course, just what Yamamoto had planned.

The easiest, shortest, most logical move by Japan was due south, and this seemed to be what its high command had in mind. Early in March, Japanese forces landed on the northeastern shore of the New Guinea "tail" (the reference being to New Guinea's shape, like that of a huge bird facing west, its tail drooping southeastward over the Coral Sea). Port Moresby, with a fine harbor on the southwestern side of the tail, directly across from Australia's Cape York, was their obvious objective. Immediately upon landing they started crunching overland toward it. Their air forces had already severely bombed the town and would continue to do so. Only the difficult mountain ridge along the tail's centerline obstructed approach from the land side, but this was not impossible for a determined army. Or the port could be attacked by sea, by an arm of Japan's everywhere-victorious navy. In April 1942 it seemed inescapable to Australians that Port Moresby would soon become the staging base for an invasion of the northern tip of their undefended, sparsely inhabited continent a few miles to the south. It made eminent sense to military analysts, and under the circumstances would undoubtedly have succeeded—although speculation does not extend to how long Japan could have maintained the distant and restive suzerainty that might have resulted. Heavy loss of civilian life, however, and extreme discomfort in a land heretofore acquainted only with peaceful development, was inevitable.

Today it does not appear the Japanese originally intended to invade Australia, but in early 1942, with the extraordinary momentum they had built up, they did not fail to appreciate the opportunity represented by the harbor at Port Moresby on the southern coast of New Guinea. Once that was in Japanese hands, the obvious threat to Australia, whether or not Japan chose to exploit it, would have a massive effect on Allied strategy.

The initial reaction of the U.S. Pacific forces was to attempt to divert Japan's attention back to the Central Pacific by hit-and-run raids on Japanese-occupied islands, but these seemed to have little effect on her strategy. Japan's high command pretty much ignored the raids and continued to build up Rabaul-based forces in preparation for sending them around the New Guinea tail to take Port Moresby from the sea. Then came a master stroke: the Doolittle raid on Tokyo, ordered from the White House by the president himself. The Joint Chiefs of Staff had opposed the raid as too risky for the little gain it offered—essentially morale and propaganda—but Col. Jimmy Doolittle, one of the foremost fliers of the time, was able to convince a still higher audience.

Franklin Roosevelt, of course, realized that Doolittle's bombing planes could do no important damage to Japan, but it can be believed he expected them to increase Japan's attention to the Central Pacific area. No one guessed it would speed up the timetable for the South Pacific as well, or that Japan's retaliation for the Doolittle insult would be to set in motion its most ambitious Central Pacific project of the entire war.

Admiral Yamamoto had long been urging a big movement directly eastward: occupation of Midway and the nearest Aleutian Islands. This would, he estimated, draw the U.S. Fleet into the all-out sea battle contemplated in War Plan Orange—which, contrary to the U.S. Naval War College solution, Japan expected to win. In retrospect, Yamamoto by this time, early in 1942, probably wished he had not been so successful with the battleships at Pearl Harbor, since no aircraft carriers had been caught there. He now saw that decisive elimination of U.S. naval air power would come far closer to his basic objective, destruction of American morale, than sinking outmoded battleships, which, his timing having backfired, only served to enrage us.

Yamamoto's personal thinking may already have begun to entertain nagging doubt, but he was an excellent gambler, not known for giving up easily. Doolittle's exploit was beneficial to his strategic planning, because it brought an immediate go-ahead for his Midway operation. This would, he believed, bring our carriers into action and thus give him the opportunity to destroy them, as he had wanted to do at Pearl Harbor.

Some sort of foray into the Central Pacific, in much less force than Japan in fact sent against Midway, had been expected by our side and was in fact desired, so as to relieve some of the pressure on Australia. What our leaders did not foresee was the tremendous force that would be aimed at Midway at the same time that Japan also greatly accelerated her plans in another direction, toward Port Moresby.

Yamamoto was a brilliant, daring adversary. Consolidation of gains is important in war, especially when enemy intentions are not clear, and going in two directions at the same time for this purpose was not unusual, for he gloried in the complicated orchestration necessary. To Japan's high command, taking the southern coast of New Guinea and poising its forces opposite Australia gave it freedom to aim later military moves west, south, or east, whatever might seem most called for. At the same time, as he convinced her leaders, it was not at all out of the question to make an extraordinary simultaneous cross-Pacific effort in order to consolidate the results of Pearl Harbor.

Had Yamamoto been able to succeed in both campaigns, he might conceivably have won the war for Japan right then, and gone down in history as the greatest admiral who ever lived. Japan's warriors, instead of being 10 feet tall, would have been reaching into human stratosphere. While the Doolittle raid did give the United States the shot in the arm our leaders wanted, it also proved to be somewhat counterproductive in that it increased the danger to Australia and confirmed plans for attacking Midway in greater strength and sooner than originally scheduled. No one on our side anticipated this development.

In April 1942, Admiral Nimitz, commander-in-chief of the U.S. Pacific Fleet (CINCPAC), had one important advantage: intelligence that was far superior to anything available to Admiral Yamamoto. It was also far superior to anything Admiral Kimmel ever received. Nimitz, in another of his brilliant opening moves, kept all of Kimmel's staff organization intact, now working for him loyally and with admiration, and now also fully aware of where they had failed their previous superior. Admiral Kimmel's Pacific Fleet intelligence officer, Cdr. Edwin T. Layton, now on Nimitz's staff, happened to be a close friend of Cdr. Joseph J. Rochefort, his fellow intelligencer, who occupied a basement office in the Pearl Harbor Navy Yard and was expert at analyzing radio intercepts for hints of enemy intentions.

Both commanders had personally agonized over why and how they had been unable to keep Kimmel better informed. Rochefort also happened to be the Navy's best hand at the actual decipherment of enemy messages, a talent that had sometimes excited Layton's envy when they were students together in Japan.

Rochefort had a good grasp of the Japanese language and seemed to possess nearly extrasensory comprehension of what the enemy was transmitting in its radio dispatches. He had, in short, a natural bent for Japanese codebreaking. His chain of command, however, was direct to the Office of Naval Intelligence in Washington, D.C., on which Admiral Nimitz (like Kimmel before him) was required to rely for official estimates of enemy intentions and forces. Whether Rochefort possessed information in early December that he subsequently wished he had been able to give Kimmel directly must forever remain conjecture. What is known for sure is that his talents were looked at jealously in Washington, so that he was carefully circumscribed as to whom he reported. Rochefort and Layton were appalled at the breakdown of the system so far as keeping Kimmel accurately informed was concerned.

Nimitz was well aware of the intelligence deficiencies that had contributed to the Japanese success at Pearl Harbor. Very soon after arriving there he issued a verbal order, never written but fully understood by Layton, who transmitted it, and Rochefort, who received it:

> Wherever else you send any intelligence information, if it concerns me in any way, if there is anything—*anything*—affecting the Pacific Fleet or the ocean areas under my command, I, too, must be instantly informed. *You may not keep anything from me that bears on the Fleet for which I am responsible, no matter what your instructions!*

This was only logical, and it is extraordinary today that bureaucratic battles over turf, not the national needs in war (or at any other time), were ever permitted to interfere with this so simple and so elementary a proviso. It was also exactly what the two commanders wanted to hear, and it is possible, though speculative, that Rochefort himself suggested it. In any case, thereafter Nimitz, unlike Kimmel, received raw intelligence pertaining to his job as it came off the line, hand-given to his own intelligence officer by the man who just happened to be the best of that special kind the Navy had.

Late in March Nimitz began to receive Rochefort's estimates that something was afoot regarding not only Midway but also Port Moresby and the Coral Sea. Within days after the Tokyo raid, Layton informed him of Rochefort's conclusion that the Port Moresby attack had been thereby pushed up in time instead of delayed.

The U.S. Pacific Fleet commander's great disadvantage lay in forces available. He had only four operational aircraft carriers, two in the South Pacific under Adm. Frank Jack Fletcher (still in command despite his fiasco at Wake Island), and two based at Pearl Harbor under Adm. William F. Halsey. Yamamoto had a total of ten, and he had the interior lines of communication. Though Nimitz had carefully pointed this out in March, when the Doolittle raid was directed, he could not refuse the orders of the commander-in-chief even though the operation took Halsey's whole force. The threat to Port Moresby began to become worrisomely evident, however, even as Doolittle and his planes were being embarked on board the *Hornet* at Alameda Naval Air Station, California.

(I was by then a lieutenant, junior grade, still in Mare Island readying the *Trigger* for sea. Someone—who it was I cannot recall except that he showed a proclivity for talking when he should be listening—whispered to me that something big was in the wind because of the unusually large bomber-type aircraft the *Hornet* was taking aboard. He predicted they were going to "go off and hit Japan somewhere!" I replied that whatever was going on ought not to be talked about because if his guess was right it was undoubtedly very much of a super secret. At the same time I privately felt that the security people at Alameda weren't doing much of a job, and well remember my delight when I read about the raid in the newspapers. I even felt a tiny thrill of participation at my own small personal contribution.)

With Port Moresby and Australia already on his worry list, backed up by growing awareness of the Central Pacific threat to Midway, Nimitz was at least figuratively gnawing his fingernails while the *Hornet* and *Enterprise* raced across the Pacific to the launching point. Had he been able to guess the effect the raid would have on the Japanese timetable for New Guinea, his anxiety would probably have been beyond containing. But when the latest bulletin arrived from Rochefort, advancing as well the date for the Midway attack, the near-supernatural calm with which he went about dealing with the situation was the clearest possible evidence of the depth of his concern.

The bare sequence of events illuminates the point: The Tokyo raid took place on 18 April. A week and a half later, the Japanese invasion force departed Rabaul for Port Moresby. The four-day Battle of the Coral Sea took place during the first week of May, and the Battle of Midway took place three weeks after Coral Sea was over. During the month and a half between Tokyo and Midway, our four big aircraft carriers steamed at top speed four times across the Pacific: west, then east, then south, and finally (the three survivors) north—in all, a distance equal to halfway around the world. They fought two big battles with enormous consequences, plus raiding the Japanese capital and fighting numerous skirmishes. Two of them were sunk. In the process they made history for all time, but it was a very near thing indeed.

A waterborne invasion of Port Moresby constituted an emergency that had to be defeated if at all possible. And yet, with hints of a coming attack on Midway becoming ever stronger, what might be the cost of diverting even a small portion of our strength to the south? Naval doctrine since before Horatio Nelson, and later emphasized by our own Alfred Thayer Mahan, always extolled the principle of the concentration of force. History had long proved it the only way to achieve victory at sea. This long-tested principle could be disregarded only at national and historical, not to mention personal, peril. To all of us looking back with the hindsight of half a century, whatever else might be said about Admiral Nimitz's stewardship of his trust, the way he handled the double whammy he faced at this moment must always rank as one of his finest hours.

Many have tried to visualize the dilemma in Nimitz's headquarters—in his mind—five decades ago. What to do? What more *could* he do? He radioed Admiral Fletcher, commanding the *Lexington* and *Yorktown* in the South Pacific, to be ready for action in the Coral Sea by 1 May, and he ordered Halsey to return to Pearl Harbor at full speed with the *Hornet* and *Enterprise* as soon as the Doolittle fliers were off (they were to land in China). When Halsey's two big carriers arrived, they were greeted with the news that the promised short R&R period would have to be postponed once again; after minimum turnaround time they set off, again at full speed, to join Fletcher in the South Pacific, a fifth of the earth's circumference away.

Despite all the effort, Halsey was too late. On 4 May he was still far from the battle zone when news arrived at Pearl Harbor that *Lexington* and *York-town* were in action. Anxiety mounted in Nimitz's headquarters, and not only because of this battle far to the south. Important as was the relief of Australia, Rochefort was becoming daily more insistent that the big effort for which the Pacific Fleet had to be prepared was going to be an all-out attack on Midway. Japan had the naval strength to invade both Port Moresby and Midway simultaneously; each of the two forces required could, with ease, be made superior to everything the Allies could scrape together at any single place. At the same time it was ominously more and more evident that Yamamoto's attack on Midway island was to be by far the bigger operation, and it was to take place very soon. The four U.S. carriers could not be allowed to stay one moment too long in the South Pacific, 4,000 nautical miles from where the main action was to take place—and yet the danger to Australia had not lessened a single iota.

For four days the Pacific Fleet Operations Staff slept on cots near the plotting room, measuring distance against time and the predictions of the Intelligence arm. Nimitz slept in his own office not far away. The sparse messages from Admiral Fletcher were avidly awaited, dissected to the last syllable, pondered over for hours. But Fletcher was not much of a communicator; his messages suffered also from atmospheric interference. Most of them told little, except that battle had been joined. Halsey, driving southwestward at maximum speed and in absolute radio silence, was not yet close enough to help. After four worried days, on 8 May came the wonderful news that the light carrier *Shoho*, 12,000 tons, part of the Port Moresby invasion force, had been sunk, and the Japanese landing force, bereft of its air support, had turned back.

About this time another Japanese task force arrived on the Coral Sea scene, down from the Japanese bastion at Truk, with two carriers far more powerful than the little *Shoho*. These two ships, *Shokaku* and *Zuikaku*, exchanged blows with the *Lexington* and *Yorktown*, and soon came the distressing news that our *Lexington*, three times bigger than the *Shoho*, had been badly damaged and had had to be scuttled, and that *Yorktown*, while still afloat with engines functioning, had suffered seriously.

So ended the Battle of the Coral Sea, the world's first fight between aircraft carriers. It was also the first naval engagement in which the opposing ships never saw each other (the aviators, in their fighting planes, did, of course). The result was a victory for Japan in that the United States suffered a considerably greater loss, but from the Australians' point of view the greatest invasion threat yet from Japan had been defeated. A feeling of euphoria ensued; they had not been abandoned and, more to the point, it was now evident they would not be. The cost was regrettable, but America had made its commitment clear.

With Halsey's undamaged carriers virtually in range, their presence apparently undetected, Nimitz was strongly tempted to leave him there another day in hopes of inflicting more damage on the two big Truk-based carriers, at least to even out the exchange a bit more equally. Both had suffered in the Coral Sea battle; very probably Halsey might have been successful, perhaps with little damage to his own force.

It was fortunate that Nimitz decided against this idea, tempting though it must have been; the *Shokaku* and *Zuikaku* had already started back to Truk, with moderate material damage to the first carrier and heavy casualties among the airmen of the second. The invasion of Port Moresby had been blocked, the threat to Australia at least temporarily lifted. The United States needed badly to make the most of what time and forces it had left, for it had lost one carrier, and essentially a half of another, from the paltry four-carrier force that had begun the campaign. Its Pacific Fleet would need everything it could muster very soon. And Layton and Rochefort, with Midway very much on their minds, were climbing the walls.

Yorktown was only half a ship, a crucial loss, restorable in part if she could somehow be made fit for service. There was no time for any of the fine points, even for the growing controversy over our tactics at the Coral Sea. Get the ship ready; check that her engines were working as they should be; get the flight deck repaired; patch the holes in her bottom; replace damaged aircraft and injured fliers. There was only one thing to do: get ready for another battle in the mid-Pacific against as many as 10 aircraft carriers. Halsey was directed to return immediately at best speed, but first—and this was a stroke of genius—to get within search-plane radius of the Japanese base at Tulagi, a few hundred miles northeast of the scene of the Coral Sea battle, and allow himself to be spotted. This was not hard to do, for he was practically there already.

As expected, Yamamoto heard immediately of the presence of *Enterprise* and *Hornet* in the South Pacific; knowing *Lexington* had been sunk and *Yorktown* severely damaged, the Combined Fleet commander would figure (Nimitz calculated) the two ships had been sent to replace them. Thus the Americans could manage to have at most one carrier, the damaged *Saratoga* (she had been hit by one of Japan's big 24-inch "Long Lance" torpedoes), to oppose Yamamoto's Midway adventure, about which, he believed, Nimitz as yet knew nothing. Perhaps this might reduce the force Yamamoto thought he required and thus reduce the odds faced by the Americans.

But *Saratoga* was nowhere near repaired. Halsey's two carriers pushed their engines beyond limits as they raced back to Pearl. *Yorktown*, too, returned as fast as she was able, and went directly into drydock. Repairs, it was reported, would take three months; Nimitz himself went down into the drydock to look her over and, his blue eyes blazing, directed the damage be patched and the ship returned to the firing line in three days!

By this time Rochefort had informed him that the Japanese attack on Midway would come on the third of June and that a scouting line of submarines, ordered to report all movements of U.S. Fleet units, would be in place on the first. Getting the *Enterprise* and *Hornet* beyond the enemy submarine scouting line was easy; they made it with a day or so to spare. The damaged *Yorktown* was much more of a nip-and-tuck proposition, but luck was with the Americans, combined with Rochefort's inspired intelligence; she, too, got to sea and beyond the scouting line, barely in time.

There was more good fortune. *Shokaku* and *Zuikaku*, moderately damaged and depleted in air crews at the Coral Sea, were scratched from the Midway operation (another piece of important information provided by the codebreakers). The presence of these two additional first-line carriers at Midway might have given Yamamoto the extra strength the event proved he needed. Halsey's venture into Tulagi's search radius had paid off a thousand times.

At the Battle of Midway the Japanese lost four carriers, a heavy cruiser, 322 aircraft, and perhaps as many as 2,500 officers and men. The story has been told often, and it is not my purpose to tell it here again. Rather, I aim to point out some of the dilemmas besetting Admiral Nimitz; that among the rewards it gave us was discovery of another top-class fighting admiral, Raymond A. Spruance; and to extol the inspired performance of Cdr. Joe Rochefort, who supplied Nimitz over a continuous period with the critically important information that made our victory possible against the terrible odds our forces faced.

Nimitz certainly deserved all the honors he received, but the admiral in tactical command during the critical moment at Midway was Spruance. When Halsey brought his two carriers back to Pearl Harbor, after the apparently fruitless high-speed round trip to Tulagi, he came down with a painful attack of the shingles. Although himself confined to the hospital, he convinced Nimitz that Spruance should take over in his place. This put Spruance, with two undamaged carriers, subordinate to Fletcher, who had only the quickly repaired *Yorktown,* but when that ship received additional and fatal damage near the beginning of the battle, Fletcher realized he could not command from a ship that was *hors de combat* and gave over to Spruance. It fell thus to Spruance to make the crucial decisions when to attack (he selected exactly the right time) and when to run away from Yamamoto's surface forces, who were hoping for a night action that might catch our carriers unable to fly (Japan naval aviators had trained in night flying; ours as yet had not). After some initial criticism, all students of Midway have concluded that this was precisely the right thing for Spruance to have done.

As the sea war in the Pacific developed, Nimitz realized the intellectual Spruance was his ace in the hole, and that for a counterpart to the belligerent Halsey he could not ask for a better. Ultimately, operational assignments were split between Halsey, Commander, Third Fleet, and Spruance, commanding the Fifth Fleet. The ships were the same, shifting task force designations as necessary. Only the fleet commanders and their supporting staffs were different. The two commanders, lately associated in a senior-subordinate relationship, were the best of friends although temperamental opposites, and the resulting arrangements worked ideally. Halsey, the bluff, hearty, Japanese-hater, dubbed "Bull" Halsey by the press, was complemented by the studious, methodical Spruance, who received no sobriquet; Nimitz had found the two fighting commanders he needed.

Another result of Midway, which fair-minded naval officers now deeply regret, was the niggardly treatment of Rochefort, not only during the war (in spite of Nimitz's strenuous efforts) but also afterward. He, too, made a monumental contribution to the victory at Midway. It is true he disobeyed the intelligence bureaucracy by giving Nimitz raw data, but he did so by the specific order of the Commander-in-Chief, U.S. Fleet, who was in command of the entire Central Pacific. In so doing, Capt. Joe Rochefort (the Navy finally elevated him to that rank, but it should have done much better for him) made possible one of the greatest naval victories in the history of man at sea.

Because Rochefort was right, the intelligence bureaucracy in Washington wrong, it denied him recognition for his huge contribution to the extraordinary victory at Midway. Even the posthumous award of a Distinguished Service Medal, many years later, was muted. It is only our Navy's number three medal in order of precedence, and, citing some negotiations with Japan that were theoretically important (in fact, they weren't), it was bestowed with minimal public notice, although it was done by President Reagan in the Rose

Garden of the White House. Those invited to attend were strictly limited: Rochefort's son and daughter, and a single "joint representative" of the press. Only a small handful of additional witnesses was invited to be present. (I was later privately informed that the critical text of the citation was taken from my book, *The United States Navy: 200 Years,* published in 1986. Admiral Crowe, then chairman of the Joint Chiefs of Staff, later phoned me at home to say that had he known this he would have seen to it that I, too, was present.)

The mimeographed press release about the award contained only the most routine information about Rochefort, nothing that explained why, at this very late date, any acknowledgment had seemed necessary at all. Although technically he did not risk life, he risked—and lost—his entire naval career. The proper award for him is still the Congressional Medal of Honor; and if, as the award system now stands, the requirement of risk of life itself cannot be side-stepped, then Congress should create a new and special category of its highest award to cover what he did for us.

If the Rose Garden ceremony was intended to be a public apology for the neglect Rochefort experienced all his life after Midway, extending to seeing lesser subordinates rewarded in greater measure than he for work in which he had actually led the way, it was a poor effort for which the nation ought to be embarrassed. One of the principles of restitution is that it must be wholehearted. It should be as public as the damage it is intended to counteract, and preferably more so. If the apology is posthumous, as it was for Joseph Rochefort, public action is even more important.

This man, who more than any other gave Admiral Nimitz the keys to victory in the most critically significant battle of modern times, was most shamefully treated then, and shamefully treated even after his death.

Midway has been compared with Jutland, the largest naval battle of World War I, decisive only in that Germany's High Seas Fleet never again challenged that of Britain. Since 1916, when it took place, Jutland has been studied and restudied by historians and scholars. Their general conclusion has been that Britain's numerical superiority, on the order of eight to five, provided the margin over a more effective but numerically smaller German fleet. At Midway— a far more significant battle—the winning side was inferior by odds of three or even four to one.

At Jutland the fighting was of the old school; two columns of huge steel fortresses, ponderously trying to swing into parallel lines so that their guns could blast each other. Midway, 26 years after Jutland, was different because of naval aviation. Here, only three weeks after the very first carrier battle in world history, the same unprecedented forces changed permanently the course of the greatest sea war ever fought. Yet the real differences between Jutland and Midway were only three: aircraft extended the main battery range from twenties of miles to hundreds of miles, while greatly increasing accuracy as well; timely intelligence was intelligently applied; and the battle-line, as we knew it then, did not exist. More properly, the anachronistic battle-line (that seldom fought as theoretically intended) was replaced by a new type of task force that had an entirely different concept of how to fight at sea, and did so many times during our 44 months in World War II.

The Battle of Midway was the only time this little-distinguished island achieved national importance. Although it was indeed the objective, and the name "Midway" by which the battle is known is entirely appropriate, nearly all the fighting took place far away, almost in mid-ocean.

During the remainder of the war it was used for a submarine halfway-point between patrols, and heartily disliked because, as a location for crew relaxation, it was by no means the equal of Honolulu. I visited it many times between 1941 and 1945, and returned in 1990 to find the atoll even less interesting than it had been during the war. Not a vestige of the installations of the war years remains. The submarine base paraphernalia has vanished or is overgrown; the piers and repair shops have disappeared. The aircraft hangars damaged during the battle cannot be found, although the inclined ramps for hauling waterborne seaplanes up into them still remain, at least in part. The airfield that saw our slow-flying, land-based patrol planes off for their long daily searches, and from which Marine fighter planes staged desperate sorties against the Japanese fleet, has been rebuilt into a fine modern landing strip, but planes use it only once a week. Only the original inhabitants of Midway Island are still there in force—the "gooney birds" (the Laysan Albatross). They have not changed a bit. At sea or in the air they are fantastically graceful; on land they and their numerous chicks are undisturbed by man and ridiculously humorous to observe.

After Midway, the general feeling of jubilation hid the reality that there still remained a very serious threat to Australia. Japanese troops were on the northeastern slope of New Guinea's tail, still hacking their way across the mountainous spine. Nimitz and the Joint Chiefs of Staff, reviewing the same sets of facts and obligations, came up nearly simultaneously with the identical answer. We did not have sufficient carrier strength to repeat the Coral Sea business even once more. Japan, on the other hand, would use a much stronger force next time. For the protection of Australia, it was necessary that an island base, an unsinkable carrier, be created to counter the buildup of Rabaul's magnificent harbor. Such a base was essential to enable Allied air forces to focus continual air attack on any Japanese thrust across New Guinea, and to provide our forces with secure supplies of the prodigious amounts of everything they would need for the foreseeable months and years.

The Santa Cruz Islands, not far from Guadalcanal, were selected for the new base, and the initial landing was set for 1 August—when suddenly came a patrol plane report that Japan was building an airstrip on Guadalcanal, only half the distance of the Santa Cruz Islands from Port Moresby! Despite two recent defeats at sea Japan had obviously not given up the idea of coming in on that strategically valuable harbor's seaward flanks. Guadalcanal was ideal for this, better than the Santa Cruz Islands because it was bigger, as well as closer to the military objective. An airfield there would double or triple the threat to the Australian mainland. Our decision was obvious and instant: Instead of going into the Santa Cruz Islands and permitting the enemy to establish a base *between* us and Australia, we would take over the nascent Japanese air base on Guadalcanal and make that into our staging base. Sixteen thousand Marines were told to forget Santa Cruz and start thinking about Guadalcanal. They barely had time to digest the fact that they had a new target.

On 7 August 1942, almost exactly two months after Midway, an armada of transports escorted by cruisers and destroyers brought our Marines to Guadalcanal Island under the air cover provided by three aircraft carriers (again, all there were available). The enemy was caught by surprise. Resistance was ineffective, and the airstrip Japan was building was quickly taken. Troops were still being off-loaded against only token enemy resistance when the same Admiral Fletcher who abandoned Wake Island, and later lost *Lexington* at the Coral Sea, showed he still had his penchant for keeping his fuel tanks full to the disadvantage of other objectives. In a highly questionable move, the day after the initial landing on Guadalcanal, with the Japanese reaction still uncertain, he took his carrier task force out of the area of combat for a refueling rendezvous.

This left the Marines, their transports, and the escorting ships without air cover. Shortly after midnight on the morning of 9 August, unspotted by anyone, not reported by search planes (an Australian book recently published by the U.S. Naval Institute Press, *Disaster in the Pacific: New Light on the Battle of Savo Island*, by Denis and Peggy Warner, states that such a report was made but was mishandled at the receiving end), a fleet of seven Japanese cruisers entered what became known from that day as Iron Bottom Sound, between Guadalcanal and tiny Savo Island just to the north. Five Allied cruisers (an Australian and four American) attempting to keep on the alert day and night while guarding the landing area were caught flat-footed. The actual fighting lasted only a few minutes; three U.S. ships and the Australian cruiser were sunk, and the fourth American cruiser, minus her bow, was put out of commission for months.

Only one thing lessened the disaster, and that was the Japanese admiral's decision, made because he could not conceive that there were no U.S. carriers in the vicinity, not to proceed into the landing area. This was, in fact, what he had been sent for, and had he carried out his orders we would have suffered the greatest debacle of all time. The undefended transports were at his complete mercy. Having, largely by unexpected good fortune, achieved a brilliant naval victory over a force only marginally inferior to his, he permitted his delight at this success to blind him to the fact that his mission had not yet been accomplished. In his defense is the fact that one lucky shell fired by USS *Quincy* hit his flagship, the *Chokai*, in the master chart room, killing some 34 men and temporarily ruining his picture of the action. But this is a lame excuse. When Yamamoto learned all the details, he was furious. As it was, more than 1,000 American and Australian sailors lost their lives at Savo: an expensive lesson, but it was not nearly as costly a lesson as it would have been had Adm. Gunichi Mikawa gone on as planned.

The Guadalcanal campaign began with an easy victory by an overwhelmingly superior landing force of U.S. Marines. The airfield was captured almost immediately and very quickly put in operation by our side with the name of Henderson Field, in honor of a Marine major who had been lost while commanding fighter planes at Midway. The Japanese had not yet been able to make it operational, although they would have within days. This is an indication of how close the issue actually was, for we could probably not have landed in the face of air opposition. Japan quickly understood the stakes and increased her forces on the island. We also increased our forces, because it was instantly clear that possession of that airfield was crucial to the war in that part of the world. Before the fighting ended, 50,000 Japanese troops and more than 60,000 U.S. Army and Marine Corps troops were in action there: the fighting became probably the bloodiest and the most prolonged of the entire war.

If Midway was the turning point of the Japanese advance, Guadalcanal was the beginning of the rollback. With Guadalcanal under enemy control, the Coral Sea would have become a Japanese lake. No U.S. task force would have been able to enter it. In our hands, the airfield would make it impossible for any Japanese forces to round the tail of the New Guinea bird to threaten Australia. If Port Moresby were then to be captured, it would have to be by an extraordinarily difficult over-the-mountain expedition in which the defense would have all the advantage, beginning with air cover from Henderson Field. Both sides realized fully that the battle for Guadalcanal was a battle for the future of Australia.

American casualties were high on Guadalcanal, not all from enemy action, for the hot and humid climate was something to which our men had difficulty adjusting. In spite of a massive inoculation campaign, there were many new and exotic illnesses easily caught. It was estimated that a full quarter of our men at some point suffered either from injuries received in action or illness of some kind. The Japanese had it far worse: three-quarters of their personnel who came ashore on Guadalcanal lost their lives there. At the very end (February 1943), when Japan finally began to evacuate its personnel in admission of defeat, there were only some 13,000 men desperately waiting to be picked up by destroyers sent to the northern tip of the island.

All this happened during the first 14 months of the war, most of it during the first year. U.S. forces had seesawed along exterior lines, running a route from Tokyo to the Coral Sea to Midway and back to Guadalcanal. Nimitz had been forced to scatter his fleet and run his ships all over the ocean, planning desperately how to meet all the problems at once and still be in the right place at the right time, with enough force to win when he had to. During the entire period, Japan held the interior lines and superior forces and therefore had an undisputed advantage.

Nimitz and his staff were playing against enormous odds, taking extraordinary chances. But he was doing it carefully, with full calculation of every angle of every situation, and he had the inestimable help of ULTRA, which by the end of this period was providing the capability of discerning enemy intentions so clearly and precisely that it seemed more miraculous than merely ultrasecret.

. . .

Throughout his conduct of the war, Admiral Nimitz made plain his deep affection for the sailors and officers who manned the ships of his fleet. Some two years after Guadalcanal there came a matter of great concern to the entire Pacific Fleet. Japanese propaganda broadcasts, which everyone monitored whenever possible, had begun to claim heavy losses inflicted upon us: "Dedicated Japanese aviators yesterday sank one aircraft carrier, two cruisers, and twelve smaller ships of destroyer size." "On Thursday, two carriers were heavily damaged, one new battleship sunk, three cruisers sunk or damaged, and hundreds of U.S. aviators shot down." And so on.

It was worrisome. We knew the reports must be exaggerated. The Japanese proclivity for making claims far beyond reality had to be working overtime with the bad war news they must be receiving at this stage, and we knew that propaganda was a weapon they used with little true skill. So no one placed much credence in these repeated claims of outstanding success. But, on the other hand, something must have happened. There must have been some battle of great significance that perhaps we had lost or in which maybe had suffered heavy casualties, because otherwise we would have heard of it. There would not have been any reason to conceal a victory.

Surely the Japs had exaggerated our losses, but maybe there had been some; one or two important ships might have been sunk or severely damaged. I remember how my anxiety rose. I had many friends and classmates in the various ships of our Pacific Fleet. Could some of them have been hurt, or maybe killed, in some battle I had somehow not yet heard about? For days, nothing was said by Nimitz or anyone else, and then finally everything came together. A message was broadcast to the entire fleet that said, "Contrary to Japanese propaganda claims, and to any other report you may have heard from any source, there have been no ships sunk and no major units damaged. All Japanese claims of victory or damage to our units are false. CINCPAC sends."

This was all we needed. This magically cleared the air. Admiral Nimitz had put himself on the line, and we knew he was telling the truth. Later we discovered what had actually happened. We had received some damage, especially in small ships, but nothing remotely approaching the Japanese announcements. The Kamikaze attacks against our fleet covering the landing on Okinawa had been Japan's last all-out effort. Today we marvel at the pathetic determination of those poor young Japanese aviators, who had been caused to believe that by hurling themselves into the holocaust on one-way missions they could stem the tide of defeat that was staring Japan in the face and pay back their god-emperor for having permitted them to be born.

The Kamikazes had to be escorted to their attack positions because of their lack of basic training in aerial navigation and combat, and also, in some cases, no doubt to keep their purpose and morale high. When their targets were finally pointed out to them and they were released for their final self-immolation, their more combat-wise escorts in general were to remain close enough to observe and report the results.

Japanese authorities credulously believed that distant explosions reported by the Kamikaze escorts in each case must represent the loss of a unit valuable to our side, failing to understand that the escorts were seldom near enough to report accurately, and that they had a psychological need to report successes by their idealistic young subordinates. Explosions that they believed signified loss of a ship usually represented only the explosion of a bomb when the plane carrying it hit the water. Initially, some of Admiral Nimitz's staff officers had argued against revealing the extent of the exaggerations for fear true evaluation might cause the Japanese to modify tactics that were in fact playing into our hands. On the other side of the issue, the effect of the uncontradicted claims might be bad for the morale of units at sea unable to get more accurate information. Nimitz listened gravely to both sides and finally insisted that the anxiety of the forces at sea had to have priority. This was typical of him.

I have two very personal stories about Admiral Nimitz, also out of chronology, that illustrate the kind of person he was. Similar stories are, of course, legendary throughout the Navy, but these happened to me and they have not been told elsewhere.

The war had ended, and I was a lieutenant commander. I have forgotten the occasion, and all other details, except that I was on an airplane flying from Washington, D.C., to the West Coast as one of a group of officers accompanying Admiral Nimitz, now our Chief of Naval Operations, the senior officer in the Navy, on some sort of an inspection trip. It was a long 12- to 14-hour flight in those days, in a big propeller-driven craft that could seat some 50 people. There was a railroad-type stateroom in the after section, where he and Mrs. Nimitz, who accompanied him, were quartered.

The plane droned on endlessly. Some of us had had the foresight to bring reading material, and for the rest of us it was a long nonstop voyage with desultory conversation with seat-mates our only diversion, beyond just staring at the bulkheads or out a convenient window. Somewhere in the first part of the trip the admiral's aide came forward and asked if anybody knew how to play cribbage. A number of us held up our hands, I among them. The aide, whom I knew reasonably well, fixed on me and said, "Ned, Admiral Nimitz wants to play cribbage and you're the junior man here, so you're elected. Go on back there."

I was startled, looked around me to see if anyone else had volunteered to play cribbage, but everybody's hand was already down and they were all staring stonily ahead, glad it was me and not them. I had been designated for the duty, and there was nothing for it but to get on with it. I looked inquiringly at the aide. He nodded his head. "Yes, right now." He pointed aft. I walked back to the admiral's Pullman-like compartment, occupying the entire rear of the aircraft on both sides of the aisle. He sat on one side with a little table in front of him, and Mrs. Nimitz, as I recall, was on the other side absorbed in a book. I introduced myself.

"Sit down, Beach," said the admiral, waving me to the other side of his table. "Do you know how to play cribbage?"

"Yes sir," I said, "but it's been some time since I've played. My father taught me a long time ago."

"You'll do all right," said the admiral, and held out a deck of cards. This was familiar. I cut the deck. He pulled off the top card, put it on the bottom, and began to deal, rapidly and expertly. Six cards flew out toward me. I gathered them together, gave him the poorest two, and the game began. Despite my awkwardness, it went fairly well and to my surprise I made several points. With the next hand I made more points. As the game proceeded I literally overwhelmed the CNO with my skill, pegging more points and counting higher hands and cribs than I could ever remember doing with Father. He must have taught me extremely well, I thought, when to my amazement I realized that with a little turn of luck I could skunk the Navy's CNO. ("Skunking" in cribbage is when you go around the board twice and peg out at the bottom before your opponent makes his final turn at the top of the board.) It is a prized feat needing more skill than luck, but a generous dose of both.

I was then within one or two pegs of skunking Admiral Nimitz when it became my turn to deal. Looking at my hand, it was clear I had the game won, but the dealer always counts last, and before counting there is the peg play. I thought I was sure of pegging at least a couple of holes and achieving the distinction of "skunking" the Chief of Naval Operations. But somehow I didn't quite make it. I wasn't able quite to count enough "pegging" points to peg out at the bottom. The admiral hadn't quite pegged around the top, either, but then he laid out his hand, counted it, and with a twinkle in his eyes just made it across the top.

I hadn't skunked the old man, but should not feel too badly, for when I laid out my hand I had won the first game. I felt rather pleased with myself, but there was something a bit strange that I had already begun wondering about. My hands were uniformly good, particularly my cribs. Several times I saw some rather high-ranking cards in there that I hadn't put in myself. They must have come from the admiral, and I remembered one of the dictums Father had taught me. "Cribbage is a great game," he would say, "and sometimes you can control it by making your opponent win or lose according to how you play your own cards."

I also couldn't help but notice Admiral Nimitz's ring finger on his left hand. It was missing. He wore his Naval Academy ring on his right hand, and suddenly I remembered something from my youth. I was seven years old, as I recalled, when a naval officer wearing civilian clothes came to see my father, who at that time had already been retired several years.

The two had a long conversation. I listened attentively during the moments they allowed me to be in the room with them, and also noticed that our visitor was missing his ring finger on his left hand. I couldn't help staring, and at one point asked him about it. It had been yanked off in a submarine accident, he told me. He had held it up above his head to demonstrate something, and it had been caught in some machinery and the finger was simply jerked off along with his ring.

I remembered being very concerned. "Did it hurt a lot?" I asked him. He had hardly felt it, he said, when it happened, "but I went to the doctor and after he bandaged my hand I told him it didn't hurt much, so could I go back to duty. The doctor smiled and said, 'Maybe you'd better sit here a little while.' And then it began to hurt a great deal, and I had to put my head down between my legs so as not to pass out."

The memory of this episode in my childhood is as clear to me now as it was then and I remember the lightbulb turning on in my mind.

"Admiral," I said, "excuse me for being personal but I remember as a small boy when someone came to see my father"—and I told the story.

Admiral Nimitz's eyes twinkled even more. "Yes, I was that man who came to see your father, and I was just wondering if you would remember. Your dad gave me some good advice that day, and I guess he's given you some too. You told me you wanted to go in the Navy, and I'm glad to see you did."

I remember staring at the admiral, the absent finger only too evident, and everything fell into place. No doubt he had given his aide careful instructions about whom to pick for the cribbage game, and I had provided Admiral Nimitz with a bit of distraction on a long trip.

It was my turn to shuffle the cards, we cut them again, and we played two more games, neither of which did I come close to winning, let alone even thinking about skunking the Navy's highest-ranking officer, who was also probably its best cribbage player. The score when he kindly dismissed me was 2 to 1 in his favor, but truth to tell, the first game, that he lost, had been the most fun for him.

My next yarn about the Nimitzes actually occurred on that same airplane ride. I was back in my seat up forward, and one or two of us had already settled back to try to snooze as the plane droned onward. A small bustle came from aft as the stewards made up the Pullman-car berths for Admiral and Mrs. Nimitz on either side of the passageway. It was indeed exactly like a railroad sleeping car, with curtains from top to floor. Soon, however, there came an interruption. The aide came forward again. "Admiral Nimitz has a top berth above him and he wants it occupied by somebody."

There was a moment of silence in the forward part of the airplane and then someone got up, looked around sheepishly, and said, "Well, I'm senior here, so I guess that's my berth. See you fellows in the morning!" And off he went to climb into the bunk above the admiral. The rest of us envied him his good fortune and settled ourselves for a long and restless night, but suddenly, the aide was back again. "Mrs. Nimitz has a bunk over her, too, and she wants it occupied also." Again, there was that sheepish looking around, all of us this time, and then some authoritative voice—I have no recollection who—said, "Beach, you're the junior man on this airplane. It's up to you to sleep in the bunk above Mrs. Nimitz!"

So back I went, found my pajamas in my small suitcase, brushed my teeth, and climbed the little ladder into the upper berth. As I crawled in I heard Mrs. Nimitz's cultured voice from below me. "Good night, Commander," she said, and I answered, "Good night, Mrs. Nimitz."

I slept like a baby, but somehow woke up in time to slip out of there before either of the august occupants of the lower berths, nor my senior just across from me in the other upper one, began to stir. And there's no doubt I was one of the four most refreshed passengers on that long trip when we finally landed.

Nimitz's stewardship of our Pacific war effort is legendary. There could have been no one superior to him in the way he executed his responsibility, carried out grand strategy, and maintained morale of our forces. No one else could have done it better and few, if any, could have done it as well. Some folks who saw only his kind nature and warm heart may have had difficulty visualizing him as a commander willing to risk all in battle, or willing to order others into positions of deadly peril. He combined all of these faculties, and despite his genial temperament also possessed a seldom used, well-contained, but most effective temper that not many persons experienced. Usually he let the facts speak for themselves and withheld emotion. It was reported, however, that when the *Yorktown* came back from the Coral Sea and it was estimated her repairs would take three months, his cold anger at the very suggestion she should be taken off the line at that critical moment galvanized everyone in the repair force. She was out and away in three days, as is now well known, and having that ship in the combat that ensued spelled the difference between having enough force to gain the victory or not being able to bring it off.

He had another quality that was illustrated throughout the war and contributed mightily to our success, and that was his ability to select the right person for the job that needed to be done. He relieved Adm. Robert L. Ghormley, for example, after two or three less than fully successful battles in "the Slot," not so much because Ghormley was not competent but because Nimitz wanted someone with a greater fighting instinct. Likewise, he replaced Fletcher with Spruance because he needed someone who never lost sight of the big picture, even while involved in only a portion of it himself. It was evaluation of this sort that prompted Admiral Lord St. Vincent to prefer Horatio Nelson, a junior admiral, for combat assignments over ambitious seniors less likely to see the true import of their duties for England.

Probably Nimitz would not himself have put it directly into these words, but we in the ships and submarines that were doing the fighting saw the same need: for someone in charge who had the initiative to go a little beyond stated instructions if necessary and carry the battle on his own. This is the essence of combat, whether it be a knight in armor on a powerful horse, a general commanding soldiers marching in a broad field toward the sound of guns, or the commander of fleets of ships. There has to be some sort of a zest for combat, a determined aggressiveness that sees the enemy's difficulties as well as your own and pursues them relentlessly. This is the kind of commander who can sometimes reverse the tide of battle.

The loss of our cruisers at Savo Island in August 1942 was a dreadful defeat that came within an eyelash of bringing disaster upon our Marines in Guadalcanal. Admiral Fletcher, in command of the covering carrier task force, had left the scene of action only hours before, radioing to Ghormley his intentions. Ghormley approved, ironically many hours after the disastrous battle had already taken place. Neither Fletcher nor Ghormley had a feel for combat, but Halsey did, and it was Halsey who was moved into the breach to add aggressiveness to our force posture.

This was one of Nimitz's difficult decisions. Neither Ghormley nor Fletcher had behaved badly, but neither had they carried with them the passionate combat aggressiveness that was needed. Fletcher was perhaps inordinately concerned with protecting his carriers, having lost the *Lexington* (some said unnecessarily) at the Coral Sea. Tactical instructions specified that ships should be continually topped off in fuel, whenever possible during operations, in order always to be ready for protracted combat or movement whenever such might turn up. Fletcher took this too literally, and became known, in fact, as "Fueling Jack." It was partly on account of this propensity that he managed on several occasions not to be where the action was. Halsey, Nimitz knew, would go hell-bent for battle with less concern for the fuel state. So would the coldly calculating, intellectual Spruance, tempered, however, with somewhat more of the "big picture" than even Halsey had. A combination of Halsey and Spruance was what Nimitz wanted, and he got it in two people instead of only one. Besides, keeping two fleet commanders and their staffs at full efficiency indefinitely was not a logical possibility. More than anyone, they required surcease from combat and time to plan their next moves.

Another characteristic Nimitz possessed in abundance was his willingness to delegate authority when the delegatee seemed willing and able to exercise it. Nimitz, the old submariner, at the beginning of the war had some concerns with our submarines for lack of aggressiveness. He recognized, however, that the difficulties in our torpedoes made aggressiveness somewhat moot. If the torpedoes didn't work, a hard-charging skipper would find himself in severe trouble; and many of them returned from patrol literally with their tails dragging between their legs. Nimitz had many things on his mind, but an important one was the effectiveness of our weapons. For the torpedoes, he needed the right man to lead the action. He found him in Rear Adm. Charles A. Lockwood, commanding our subs in Brisbane, Australia, who, he learned, had already made some disquieting discoveries.

Transferred to Pearl Harbor, put in charge of Pacific Fleet submarines, with Nimitz's enthusiastic backing Lockwood began to produce answers. It took him another year, during part of which torpedoes were fired at cliffs to see if they would explode on contact (some did not); fired through a series of light nets to determine exactly at what depth they ran (they ran far below their set depth, but in the process they also went up and down some 25 feet in a sort of sine wave); and made to slide down greased wires at various angles against steel plates to simulate contact hits (a "perfect" hit deformed the firing pin so that it could not fire). Finally, the "influence" exploder, the very same that I had questioned as a student in submarine school, was discovered to be too sensitive, so that it often exploded prematurely, thus giving the appearance of a hit to the man looking through a periscope when in fact the target was undamaged.

Lockwood produced conclusive evidence as to why there were problems, and he suggested the necessary fixes as well. So it is owing to Admirals Lockwood and Nimitz together, with Lockwood devising and supervising the experiments and Nimitz supporting him, that the crucial discoveries were made. Even so, not all the faults were discovered, for sometimes our torpedoes ran in circles and sank the submarine that had fired them, thus also eliminating witnesses. Not until after the war, when survivors from only seven sunken submarines came back from Japanese prison camps, was it known that two of the seven had been sunk by their own torpedoes.

We lost 52 subs during the war, 45 of them in action against the Japanese, with nearly a quarter of our operating personnel. The compendium of all submarine losses contains 28 or more whose loss cannot be correlated in any way with Japanese claims of success against our boats. Applying the two-sevenths fraction of known losses to 28 unknowns, one comes up with a statistical approximation of eight of our boats thus destroyed—with all hands. For them, there was no one to tell the tale.

Gen. Douglas MacArthur must have been an important thorn in Nimitz's side. Nimitz was winning the war in the Pacific, encroaching upon Japan, ultimately prepared to invade and seize possession of the home islands. The assault landings could have been accomplished by naval and amphibious forces alone, sending in Army troops in overwhelming numbers once the landing beaches were secure. The bypass strategy (isolating forward Japanese bases from all support, but not expending American lives and resources attempting to capture them) was working smoothly, exactly as planned and predicted in War Plan Orange. Nimitz saw no basic need to return to the Philippines; they would be cut off in any event and ultimately forced to surrender.

Readers will, however, remember the conference between Nimitz, General MacArthur, and President Roosevelt when this was discussed. The picture I remember best shows the three men in front of a large wall map, Nimitz describing planned operations with pointer in hand and a look of concentration on his face. However, this was a conference at which MacArthur won the day. The president approved of making MacArthur's return to the Philippines part and parcel of our overall strategy. Ever the good soldier, Nimitz carried out his orders, but it is worth at least another digression to consider how the war might have gone had the Nimitz plan been the one adopted.

We would have gone straight across the Pacific, completely bypassing the Philippines, possibly landing on Formosa or the coast of China—or Okinawa, as we did, in fact—to create a staging base. Nimitz would probably have planned to mount the invasion of the two home islands of Kyushu and Honshu well in advance of the 1945 schedule finally adopted, although if the atomic bomb could have been gotten ready in time this might not have been necessary. The naval Battle of Leyte Gulf would have taken place nearer to Japan, but its result would have been the same. The fighting would have been fierce, but the war might have ended sooner. Casualties undoubtedly would have been heavy on both sides, but very likely lighter than the total (including those in the Philippines) that we experienced the way the war was actually fought. Predictions cannot go much farther than this, but it will always be this writer's conviction that the war with Japan was a naval war that could have been won entirely by naval forces, including of course the Marines.

What would have become of the land battle on the mainland of Japan is the big question mark in this theory. Personally, it has always been my opinion that we could have blockaded Japan into submission: sunk her entire navy and driven her merchant ships off the seas, all of which we did. Possibly a demonstration of the atom bomb somewhere, instead of laying waste two major cities, could have been the final act. For example, one laid in the crater of Japan's sacred mountain, Fujiyama, pure speculation though this idea is, might have sufficed to prove to Japan's leaders that they had lost the war. On the other hand, Japan might have tried to wait it out, might have concluded that our supply of nuclear weapons was not great, might have staggered on a few months more.

The conclusion, in any case, was foregone. Japan lost the war when she could no longer control her own seas around Japan. She had also totally lost control of her own air space, as round-the-clock bombings were proving. What, now, if sacred Fujiyama were to belch a gargantuan mushroom cloud? Would this have confirmed the national suicide zealots, or would it have had the reverse effect?

No one can carry on this sort of conjecture for long. It is more in the realm of the novelist than the historian. What we do know for sure is that, like the punch-drunk prizefighter wandering around the ring, unable even to see his foe, let alone land an effective punch, Japan had come to the end of her rope. All that remained was to make her see this.

Not much more can be said. Through his entire life, Nimitz devoted himself to an outstanding, self-effacing, performance of duty. He reached nearly the highest pinnacle of service reward, eclipsed in his time only by Generals George Marshall and MacArthur (and believed by many to be the superior of either). Although Marshall may be said to have held much the same personal outlook as Nimitz, this cannot be said of MacArthur, whose brilliant career always carried with it elements of his own romantic self-serving personality.

No naval officer was ever so beloved by his brother officers, senior or junior, and only Arleigh Burke, some years later, came close to holding the same position in their estimate. At the time in our history when we needed them, these two stood forth as the epitome of all we have idealized. To Chester Nimitz fell the honor of being steward during our Navy's greatest challenge at arms, but Arleigh Burke's challenge was not far behind, his stewardship just as neatly directed at the problems he faced in his turn.

Chapter Seven

A Professional at Submarine Warfare

Trigger's beginning at Midway had been inauspicious. Her first war patrol had been what we learned to call a "zero": no contacts developed, no attacks, no depth charges. Our faith in our skipper was at bottom.

Like other skippers during that stage of the war, when *Trigger* was on the surface at night he had tried sleeping in the conning tower in a specially built bunk contrived with a half-round cutout where it fit against one of our two periscopes. He would lie there, basically without sleeping but not awake either, a lighted cigarette drooping from his mouth, ashes falling on his cheek. Perhaps this was part of his problem, for much of the time he seemed distant, his mind somewhere else. In Dutch Harbor, where we touched briefly en route the island of Attu, our assigned area, he organized a game of poker in a barroom in an apparent effort to relax, but at sea we hardly saw him. All night, with the ship on the surface, he dozed in the cramped bunk in the conning tower, presumably ready for any emergency, although in the circumstance it seemed hardly likely he could effectively spring into action. During the day, with the boat submerged, he stayed in his tiny cabin with the curtain drawn, sitting at his fold-down desk or lying on his bunk (the only options). Gradually we came to conceive of him as not aboard, not in the war, that he was actually trying to avoid even thinking about it.

We saw him at mealtimes in the wardroom, hardly otherwise. He never inspected the ship, never even walked through it. We junior officers did our jobs as we ourselves conceived of how they should be done. There was no guidance from him. Our exec loyally refrained from saying what he must have been thinking, but it was clear that Penrod Schneider, too, wondered about our skipper's frame of mind. His wife must have foreseen at least one of our problems: by her instruction, apparently privately given to Penrod, watch-standers in the conning tower were alerted to keep an eye on the cigarette; if the burning tip approached his mouth, or his fingers, or if he was obviously asleep, they were quietly to snatch it away.

Other than no action, even when signs of the possibility appeared, our first patrol was distinguished by only two other things: lack of sleep that we all experienced, even, no doubt, our unadmired skipper, and the patrol report he submitted. Our commanding officer, whatever his other faults, proved to be a good writer. From reading his report one would think we had covered the area well and behaved as an aggressively handled submarine should, but our superiors in the submarine force organization were not fooled. On our return to Pearl Harbor he was detached and a popular former navigation instructor at the Naval Academy by the name of Roy Benson, whom we midshipmen had dubbed "Pigboat Benny" because of the supply of submarine anecdotes with which he enlivened our daily grind in "Nav," came aboard as his relief. Things were about to change for the better.

Trigger's four war patrols under his command were all adjudged "successful," our list of ships attacked and ships sunk began to grow, and so did our count of depth charges hurled at us. "Pigboat" proved to be not only an aggressive submariner but in his less strenuous moments a light-hearted individual as well. While at Annapolis he had been a member of the "NA-Ten"— the midshipman jazz band—and many were the tales he told about it. He played the saxophone, or maybe the clarinet, or both; but not once were we treated to an example of his musical ability. So far as I knew, he never even brought his instrument on board.

Were this book aimed at describing the camaraderie existing aboard our submarines during wartime stress, it could be filled with stories about Benson. For his handling of the stressful moments during his year in command of our ship, the official records show he received two Navy Crosses in addition to lesser medals. No citations, however, can adequately depict the very personal, yet relaxed way he handled his crew, the humor with which nearly all the details of ship organization were taken care of, the truly ready wit that was always at the fore. With his arrival aboard the *Trigger*, night turned into day.

One of his first moves was to raise our morale, which he rightly evaluated as sorely needing to be raised, and this he accomplished on both the general and individual levels. One of his first moves was to cause an afternoon ship's party to take place in a nearby recreation center, with beer, steaks broiled over open fires, and a number of attractive young women who were not averse to a good steak themselves in those food-rationed years. There were not as many women as there were sailormen, however, so that each of them was continuously surrounded by a group of young sailors (average age of our entire crew was 22). We noticed also that our new skipper kept one of the prettiest more or less to himself and probably enjoyed the party better than anyone. We junior officers later found out it was through her that the others, all friends of hers, had been invited.

For our first contact with the enemy we deserved no kudos, but we learned from it. Shortly before daylight, not far from the coast of Japan, we sighted a small merchant ship. Dawn was breaking as we pursued. Benson was, of course, on the bridge, and I happened to be OOD. The ship was at battle stations. We were expecting to submerge once we had attained the right position, but it was suddenly evident that we had been sighted because the enemy ship turned away and began belching smoke, evidently hoping to outrun us.

With our four big railroad-type diesels, we knew we had more speed than he could make. "Get right astern of him," Benson said to me, "and fire one right up his arse!"

No sooner said than done. I felt it quite a compliment that Benson had not taken the conn. He could have done this at any time, but for the moment I was still handling our ship. Getting into position behind our target was easy, and we quickly settled in, our four engines at maximum power, right astern. He was maybe a mile ahead of us, and we were overtaking him fast. It would soon be time to make ready the bow torpedoes for firing; this should not be done too soon, however, for in a stern chase they would have farther to run—and at this instant, still looking fixedly through my binoculars, I suddenly saw what we should have been seeing all along. "Captain!" I yelled, "That's not his stern! It's his bow! He's coming right at us!"

The situation had dramatically reversed itself. It was now broad daylight, and whoever the skipper of this little freighter may have been, he was attacking this enemy submarine he had sighted, not trying to get away! "Collision Alarm!" I yelled down the conning tower hatch at my feet. "He's trying to ram!"

The high-pitched screech of the alarm (which I've always thought of as the voice of a ship screaming in fright) instantly came through the hatch. We could hear watertight doors banging shut under the sudden onslaught of whoever happened to be nearest (weighing as much as 500 pounds, they made a distinctive loud noise duplicated nowhere else). Then all was tensely quiet, and the voice of Walter Pye Wilson, our chief wardroom steward, assigned to steer the boat at battle stations, came up sonorously through the hatch. "Watertight doors shut below! Boat's secured for collision!"

At battle stations, black, heavyset Wilson, an old-time submariner, one of the steadiest men aboard as well as one of the most popular, was assigned to steer the ship. He had always been the proverbial tower of strength at his multitudinous duties; from wardroom to galley to handling mooring lines to battle station helmsman, he was never at loss, his cool voice under stress helping to keep the rest of us cool too. The big chrome-plated steering wheel was just beneath the hatch at our feet, so it was logical that whoever was steering should also function as a link in the communication chain. Wilson was a natural for this job.

The only hatch open was now the conning tower hatch, which would not be shut while there were men on the bridge. "Lookouts below!" I shouted. We certainly didn't need them now, and this would get them out of imme-diate danger if the ships hit. Benson and I were then alone topside, the men-acing bow of the enemy ship looming very close indeed. We were exactly end-on to each other, by this time only one or two hundred yards apart. Black smoke was pouring out of the freighter's single tall stack. Clearly he had put everything he had on the line. We, too, had our four diesel engines at maxi-mum power. At our combined closing speed of perhaps 30 knots we were due to collide within seconds.

"Right full rudder!" I yelled at Wilson. I could visualize his massive mus-cles spinning that big steering wheel faster than it had ever been spun before. "Rudder is right full!" he yelled back, a special note in his voice. *Trigger*'s bow precipitantly swerved to starboard.

This exposed the length of our port side to the enemy ship's bluff bow, and would give him the chance he must have hoped for, to hit us bows on, amidships. Sure enough, he must have put his own rudder to port, for he began to swing toward us. With our own hard-over rudder, our port broad-side was swinging toward him, exposing itself. To the Jap skipper it must have looked like a perfect opportunity. Seconds separated us from having our side smashed in.

It was like driving a car in heavy traffic, with two big differences. Ships are a lot longer than cars, and they steer from the stern, not the bow. Judging the relative motion as well as I could, I shouted down the hatch, "Shift your rudder to left full!" If Wilson's muscles had bulged at the first command, they must have gone into hard knots at this second one. We could see the rudder angle indicator on the bridge spin to the full left position, moving even faster than before. *Trigger* obediently stopped her swing to starboard, began to curve rapidly to the left. "Rudder is left full, sir!" bellowed Wilson. His voice definitely contained an unusual tone.

The ships were now perhaps 50 yards apart, water curling from both his bows as he put his full effort into turning toward us. There was nothing remarkable about him at all: just a rusty old freighter of perhaps 3,000 tons, single stack puffing out a big cloud of smoke. The only thing unusual about that old tub was the man driving her.

But we were at full speed. With our rudder now hard over toward the enemy ship and his toward us, we were spinning a circle around the same spot, passing side by side only a short distance apart. We would pass clear. I felt a quick sense of satisfaction that I had successfully dodged his assault. Already his bridge was coming abeam of ours. Suddenly Benson spoke. It was his first utterance in several minutes. "Ned," he said, "are you a hero?"

"Nossir!"

"Neither am I! Let's get out of sight!" The two of us dived for the hatch. As OOD I was the last man through it, and as I jumped below a rifle bullet zinged through the bridge side plating, making a neat hole a foot or two above my head.

"Take her down!" said Benson, and down we went with all the familiar noises attendant upon diving: diesels shutting down, exhaust valves and main air induction valve slamming shut, conning tower hatch clicking shut, its dogging handwheel being spun.

Wilson, his broad impassive face beaded with sweat, was putting the rudder amidships—another routine on diving. "All ahead two-thirds," ordered the captain. This, too, was part of the normal diving routine. Wilson turned the two knobs on the engine order telegraphs mounted in front of him, moving their pointers from the "ahead full" position, below "standard" to "ahead two-thirds." The answer from the maneuvering room back aft, where the electrician's mates on watch actually controlled the speed of our propeller shafts, was so quick it was evident they had their hands already on their own knobs.

The danger was now past. For a moment there was nothing for anyone to do, and Wilson had evidently taken more than his years of naval and submarine experience had prepared him for. "Mr. Beach," he said, great globules of sweat standing out on his expressive face, "if we're going to have a collision, can't you at least make up your mind where you want me to put the rudder?"

I stared at him for an instant, the realization dawning of what must have been his view of our recent emergency. A number of our crew heard the exchange, and for the next few days I heard comments about making up my mind, but behind the wisecracks I sensed also a hint of approving respect. Among the crew of a submarine at war, a great deal is never put into words.

And as for Wilson and me, nothing can ever take the place of that delicious moment.

Our patrol report admits that in this, our first encounter with the enemy, our target "got away." More accurately, it was a draw since we, too, got away. Still more accurately, that particular Japanese merchant skipper deserved a medal, for he came within an ace of sinking a new, inexperienced U.S. submarine.

I spent two satisfying years in the *Trigger,* and in spite of our amateurish first attack, we steadily improved in results. Our score of Japanese ships put on the bottom began to rise, and after two patrols I moved up to the post of engineering officer, in charge of our two huge storage batteries for submerged running and our four magnificent diesels for surfaced operations. I was in my element. Following our fourth patrol, we made a different sort of contribution to our submarine war effort, one in which I've always taken pride: the invention and construction of a "depth-charge-proof" bridge speaker. All subs had a built-in loud-speaking system connecting all internal compartments, and there was an extension speaker on the bridge, with built-in microphone. This was invaluable during surface operations, giving us two-way command communications at critical moments, plus an important dividend in that it kept the whole crew aware of what was going on "topside." During surface combat, as can be imagined, it was kept going full blast throughout the ship, a tremendous boost to crew morale. As we improved in our night surface attack techniques we used it more and more, and with more and more satisfaction. It had only a single drawback, but this was a very important one.

The first depth charge invariably wrecked it. Although sometimes quite distant, the first one always ruptured the speaker's sensitive diaphragm and deprived us of its use for the remainder of the patrol. Since even a surface attack usually ended with the submarine being forced to submerge, after which the drill was to evade revengeful depth charges, it had become axiomatic with us that communications with the bridge were only good for the first encounter with the enemy. After that our surface attack procedure needed to accommodate to the older system of relaying word by shouting through the open hatch.

Many were the discussions about how to fix the problem, and on the way back after our fourth "run," when conversation got around to this persistent topic, I trotted out my latest scheme. We had numerous topside stowages for guns and ammunition, and all of them had stood depth charging very well. Why not simply mount an ordinary compartment speaker inside one of these? Even if we couldn't clearly understand the words it said, I argued, a muffled speaker in a steel box would at least be better than one that was altogether dead. Besides, what if we punched holes in the face of the steel box and covered them with a strong, tight, rubber gasket? Lots of carefully smoothed small holes on the steel face of the box under the gasket ought to provide adequate voice passage and still withstand the momentary overpressure of a nearby depth charge.

The mathematics looked hopeful. At our maximum allowed submergence depth of 300 feet in salt water, the pressure would be about 135 pounds per square inch. Since a hole an eighth of an inch in diameter has a total area of not much more than a hundredth of a square inch, at that depth it would experience a little over one and a half pounds total pressure. Even a big depth charge close aboard, applying momentary overpressure of, say, 10,000 pounds per square inch, could apply only around 125 pounds of pressure on the tiny part of our gasket over each hole. Could a normal gasket, made of ordinary material, hold against that amount of pressure? It was easy to find out, right on our wardroom table. We cut the tip of a pencil to form a flat surface an eighth of an inch in diameter, put a piece of the gasket material over a piece of wood with a slightly larger hole in it, edges carefully smoothed and gently countersunk, and centered our cut-off pencil tip on the gasket above the hole. Then we began loading weight on the pencil. We stopped at fifty pounds, which seemed not to deflect the gasket very much, averring that it would obviously take a lot more pressure but there was no point in breaking the pencil.

Once arrived at Midway, we carried our results to the boss of the tender's machine shop, whom we found to be also worrying about the problem for we were by no means the only submarine complaining. Never have I seen a new idea put into hardware so fast. No one sat around "designing" our box, they simply built the thing. Within a day our idea, a round, very solid-looking iron box with an ordinary compartment speaker inside, a piece of black gasket material covering the perforated portion of one face and great bolts holding the whole thing together, was under test. To our delight, the test voice inside the contraption was clearly intelligible.

We carried our iron-bound speaker back to our ship and had it installed in place of the unsuccessful Bureau-designed one, promising to get it depth-charged at the first available opportunity and report immediately by radio. For the record, this was the only depth-charge attack I ever experienced with a certain amount of pleasure. After it was over a message went back to headquarters announcing that a better-than-average depth charging had not phased our new bridge speaker one iota. It took several more even heavier poundings during that patrol without a sign of failure, its top-flight performance was reported with every message we sent, and when we got back to port every submarine in sight had one just like it.

Trigger carried hers for the remainder of her life, and we noted an additional, unsought-for dividend. Our new bridge speaker did double duty as a reliable, if very rough, barometer, for the rubber gasket bulged out when atmospheric pressure was low, and pressed so tightly against its steel backing plate when the pressure was high that we could see the outlines of the small holes in the steel. If we were able to keep it out of the sun, which heated the box and artificially increased the air pressure inside, it enabled us to predict the weather!

In line with policy, Benson was relieved after four successful patrols that occupied a full year, and at the end he attained the dream of all U.S. submarine skippers. On the last day of our designated time on station we were off the mouth of Tokyo Bay when an aircraft carrier, escorted by two of Japan's newest destroyers, hove into view heading out of the harbor. By this time I was chief engineer, in charge of our engineering plant, and my battle station, following standard organization, was "diving officer." This put me in charge of the control room, directly under the conning tower, with the principal duty of maintaining exactly the ordered depth during a submerged torpedo attack.

This was not hard during an attack's approach phase, but because of their great weight it suddenly became a lot more difficult when torpedoes were fired, especially firing a whole bow load of six fish in a single salvo. This was unprecedented in our experience, or that of any submarine we knew of (none had had a target this important in its sights since the Battle of Midway). In the control room we all knew Benson would fire everything he had available at this most important target, yet with the conditions "topside"—smooth water, broad daylight—he would not dare increase speed to give us more

effective control with bow and stern planes. There was no need to tell anyone of this problem; we all knew it intimately. More speed meant more noise,
more disturbance in the water, a bigger "periscope feather," more chance of
being spotted. All hands feared being detected by the menacing tincans
zigzagging on the carrier's bows, just where we needed to be when firing. And
we knew in any case they would be on us the instant our revealing torpedo
wakes were in the water.

We were exactly at neutral trim, as required for submerged operations any-
time, but most critically during a slow submerged approach. Our torpedoes
were considerably heavier than the water they displaced; this was one of the
factors causing their erratic performance, we later discovered. Each of them
weighed about 800 pounds more than the water it displaced. Firing our entire
load of six bow torpedoes would lighten the forward end of our boat by
more than two tons. Without more speed, only the most prompt corrective
measures—flooding bow trimming tanks at just the right time, then blowing out just the right amount of water—could keep us from exposing some
part of our structure as our bow ballooned upward with the sudden release
of all that weight.

The torpedoes were fired by air expulsion. Momentarily we were nearly
two tons lighter forward for each fish fired, until the poppet valve for that
tube opened to swallow the air bubble, hopefully quickly enough to prevent
it from streaming to the surface and being seen by a sharp-eyed lookout aloft.
Theoretically, we became very "light" forward for a moment, then equalized
most of the discrepancy by "swallowing" the air. Nevertheless, a torpedo
tube full of water was 800 pounds lighter than it had been with a torpedo
in it. Controlling the sudden buoyancy forward from a single torpedo was
not difficult, but the carrier merited all six of our bow torpedoes. Two tons
of additional lift on our bow, with the sub creeping at minimum speed, was
more than our bow planes could manage. I knew our skipper knew this, but
I also knew that getting off a good salvo of six torpedoes at this target was
our naval duty, come what might. My job was to cause admission of just
enough water into the forward trimming tanks as we were firing to compensate for our expected sudden lightness at the bow, but not to overcom-
pensate and cause the tip of our fully extended periscope to dip beneath the
surface at that critical moment. A suddenly two-ton-lighter bow, even
though anticipated, was a lot to compensate for at creeping speed.

Tension in our tiny crew, that had reached its apparent top when we found
out what the periscope was seeing, doubled as the carrier approached, and

redoubled once again as we neared our predetermined firing point. The fire-control party in the conning tower was a deck above the control room where I held sway, and we below were not privy to all that went on up there. We had, however, developed an acute sensory ability so that, added to scraps of information passed down to us by Benson or Steve Mann, now functioning as exec, or at odd moments by the conning tower telephone talker, the entire ship's company kept itself well clued in to exactly what was going on. At one time the nearest escort, on the carrier's starboard bow, echo-ranging power-fully but steadily with his sonar equipment, headed exactly for our periscope. For a time it looked as though we must have been detected, even though he had not changed the steady rate at which his sonar searched. Simply from the efficient and modern look of this tincan, we all thought he would be sure to detect an anomaly in the water soon, would rightly evaluate it as an American sub, and would follow with a superb depth charging. But luck was with us. The enemy destroyer, evidently not "seeing" us on his sonar, continued zigzagging, swept past us unknowing.

He would be back soon, but now we had a couple of minutes. For the immediate instant it was our turn. "Make ready all tubes forward!"

For 15 minutes we had been expecting this order. I could imagine the forward torpedo room crew flooding the six torpedo tubes, working with feverish haste at the familiar task. "Ready forward!" my telephone operator announced, tension in his voice and demeanor.

A minute or two for another careful periscope look all around, and in the sky too, to spot anyone in position to come at us at this critical moment. All clear, evidently, for the periscope slithered down (but only part way, to cut down the time getting it back up). The firing point was coming near. Up went the periscope, only for an instant. In the control room we could tell that Benson had spun it around once again for a quick look at the tincan that had just passed. He would be turning around soon enough, when our tor-pedoes arrived, but would not, we hoped, see their wakes passing astern of him on their way to the carrier.

"Down 'scope!" We could hear some of the commands and imagined the others. "Open outer doors!" This order Benson had studiously avoided until now. Opening the external caps of the torpedo tubes would put sea pressure on the "fish," something they could not stand for long without flooding their engines and operating mechanisms. It was another of their deficien-cies but, considering the more serious ones of faulty depth keeping and pre-mature detonation, one we World War II submariners bore pretty much in silence. "Put me on bearing of the target!" Steve, as assistant approach officer, would do that chore for Benson, twisting the periscope to the approximately right bearing according to its azimuth ring.

"Stand by forward! Six fish!" The 'scope started up. There had been no spoken command, but none was needed. Benson had probably merely nodded his head at his periscope operator, a signalman watching him intently, with his thumb on the "pickle" control knob.

"Bearing, *mark!*" Benson's voice, precise, clipped. The 'scope started down. "Three three seven!" the equally clipped voice of our quartermaster, reading the relative bearing of the target on the periscope's azimuth circle. "Angle on the bow, starboard 45!" Benson. We were in perfect firing position.

"This is a shooting observation!" Our skipper again. "Standby—bearing, *mark!*"

"Three three seven a half!"

"Set!" Steve Mann.

"Fire!" Benson's voice, loud, commanding, pronouncing the word in a clipped way, as before.

"Flood forward trim from sea!" I ordered. We would try to replace the weight forward as nearly as possible, as quickly as the water could get there through our trim line piping. The firing procedure went on, once for each torpedo, six times in all. We had rehearsed it many times "dry," and of course had by now fired many torpedoes; but never before had we fired six all at once. I could visualize the uproar in the forward torpedo room: the whine of the starting torpedoes, one after the other; the bang of the poppet valves, opening as each fish left its tube; the sudden increase in air pressure inside the submarine as the firing impulse air popped into each tube to fire its lethal weapon, then reentered the boat via the poppet valves; the fire hydrant–size flow of water that followed the air, splashing violently into the torpedo room bilges, stopping just as dramatically as the torpedomen slammed shut each valve in turn.

Then the wait; first from the torpedo room: "All fish fired electrically!" Procedure required that each tube's electric firing switch be backed up in turn by the hand-firing key mounted on the tube itself. Next, from sonar: "All torpedoes running hot, straight, and normal!" We could all visualize our six weapons, faulty as by this time we all knew they were (though we had no idea *how* faulty), running toward our big target in a fan-shaped spread. There would be six torpedo wakes in the water, visible to an alert lookout high on the carrier's bridge, or to an escorting aircraft, or, as they passed astern of him, to the destroyer that had just now failed to detect us. He was still by far the nearest ship, only a few hundred yards away; with a quick rudder order he could be on us in minutes.

The periscope had not been idle. It had descended part way as the torpedoes were being fired: no need to increase our chances of detection by leaving it up, rubbernecking the scene. The apex of our spread of torpedo wakes would indicate our location anyway—no point in showing ourselves even more. But in the meantime, our forward trimming tanks had not been able to take in enough water quickly enough. Despite what help could be obtained from the now nearly full forward torpedo room bilges, we were light forward. Inexorably we were rising. "Full dive on bow planes!" I ordered, unnecessarily because the bow planesman, a veteran at the job, was already moving his planes into the full dive position.

But it wasn't enough. We were still flooding our forward tanks, but our depth gauges registered already a foot decrease in our submerged depth. "We need speed!" I yelled up the hatch to the conning tower. "Request two-thirds speed!" The quickness with which the annunciators clicked over was my answer. Everyone up there was just as aware of the problem as I was. Our periscope started down, bottomed in its tubular well. With the boat rising in the water there was no point in waving it up there like a flagpole.

For the record, we didn't broach, although it was a fairly near thing. Our fan-shaped torpedo wakes, laid out in the smooth water, were quickly seen, marked our position at their apex. The near destroyer came right about and gave us a dilly of a depth charging—but through it all there came also the thunderous explosion of four of our torpedoes striking their target. The carrier was done for!

So we thought, at least, and the belief sustained everyone aboard during the next few hours of desperate damage control and evasion. But of our six fish, the two at either end of our spread missed entirely, as they should have, for we had fired the spread directed by our operation order for a target of this high value: Because of fire-control errors submariners made in the tension of combat (according to our Bureau of Ordnance), or the disgraceful undependability of the torpedoes themselves (as we knew to be the case), we were always to fire one to miss ahead and one to miss astern, spreading the rest of the salvo along the target's length. We therefore expected only four hits from our six fish, and our aim having been correct, that was what we got. Of the four "hits" we heard, however, two were premature. The warheads exploded before reaching the carrier, hurting her not at all; one hit abreast the anchor chain locker doing little critical damage, and only one really injured our enemy. This was a hit in the engineroom that put her out of commission, necessitating an ignominious tow back to the harbor she had departed only hours before.

We had, in fact, achieved only one effective hit in this supremely valuable target, in spite of all the effort and the risk. Five of our torpedoes had been wasted, and we were lucky to have survived.

All this we learned later, along with the additional information that our near-success was the straw that broke the camel's back so far as our naval torpedo fiasco was concerned. BuOrd was finally forced to admit that something other than incompetent submarine skippers was at fault. Backed by Admiral Nimitz, our Pacific Submarine Force Commander (ComSubPac), Admiral Lockwood, redoubled his own experiments to determine what was wrong, and little by little the disgraceful facts came to light.

It took BuOrd, run by incompetent dunderheads (these words are used deliberately and advisedly), more than 18 months to fix the problems. In the meantime, until sometime in 1944, we submariners, led by our Submarine Force Commander in Pearl Harbor, were working on jury-rigs to solve them. Illustrative of the extremes to which this led us, we were at one point instructed to avoid the optimum firing position: instead of shooting for an impact angle of 90 degrees, we were to try to hit at about a 30-degree angle, shooting from nearly ahead or broad on the quarter.

Our aircraft carrier nonetheless spawned one anecdote that some of us love to repeat. During the last year or so of the war a story began to circulate about the submarine that was patrolling Tokyo Bay, watching construction of a new aircraft carrier, and on her last day on station began to note preparations, much to her astonishment, for launching the big warship. As the carrier slid down the ways she was greeted by a salvo of American submarine torpedoes and continued to the bottom of the harbor.

A great tale indeed! All the details corresponded with our own escapade, including that it was our last day on station, and that the carrier, newly built, rested on the bottom of Tokyo Bay, in a shallow area where it had been towed, until a drydock could be prepared to receive and repair her damaged hulk. We had not sunk her as she slid down the launching ways, but we did catch her on her maiden trials—so we were later informed. She was, in fact, about a year old and not on maiden trials, but such mundane details did not bother the Navy's public relations people. It was a great story, and to be honest about it, the specific details didn't bother us much either.

No PR effort can, however, describe how it feels to be inside a submarine while it is being heavily depth charged. We in the *Trigger* counted over 400 during my time aboard, some more distant than others. On this occasion there were about 75, and the depth chargers were particularly good. Probably the enemy destroyers, being first line, carried their newest and biggest charges, as well as their most modern sonar equipment and best operators. The combination was nearly deadly. Along with the fantastic noise (you're in a washboiler being pounded on by a giant with a giant-size sledgehammer), a series of tremendous blows is transmitted through the incompressible water. Strongly built as it is, the entire submarine structure is subjected to extreme shock, proved by marks made on the steel itself, or the machinery. It is generally known that steel is elastic, but the fact that it is much like extraordinarily stiff rubber, can be bent out of line and will then spring back to its original shape so long as it is not bent too far, is something that has to be experienced at first hand to be credible.

No experiments contemplate subjecting an observer to actual depth charging as encountered inside a submarine, but some of the unbelievable stories were proved true by high-speed movie cameras in postwar tests. I myself have seen *Trigger*'s hull whip from side to side, veritably bend in the middle and then snap back to its original configuration—and afterward, except for some paint scratches where foundations stretched past the resiliency of the dried paint, show no sign of stress at all (no one would believe me when I reported this). Steel, however, like rubber, has an elastic limit beyond which it cannot spring back to normal. Some submarines have returned from patrol with permanent deformation in their hulls, dents between frames for example, necessitating their retirement from combat; and many, like the *Trigger* at this time, received damage to machinery, such as vital air compressors or hydraulic actuating mechanisms, requiring immediate return from patrol.

This was, in fact, our experience. The foundations of both pieces of machinery were cracked, putting both of them out of commission, and it was a good thing that our time on station had expired.

On our way back to Pearl Harbor, our skipper, my former instructor in the art and science of celestial navigation, showed us the kind of man he was. Or, perhaps, this portion of my reminiscences should be titled, "Once a navigator always a navigator." In anticipation of the detachment of either Steve Mann or myself, both of us having now completed the supposed maximum of five consecutive war patrols, Benson decided I should replace Steve as navigator of the *Trigger* in order to get some probably much needed late training in the practical aspects thereof. Nothing loath, I took up the duty change with pleasure, and all went well for a few days. Then a slow-rolling drumfire began to come my way.

"A competent navigator would never miss a chance like this! Anyone who has ever navigated a ship would be interested in the subsolar point. If he had any understanding of navigation he might even shape his ship's course to pass through it, even shoot the sun right then!" Maybe Pigboat Benson, my former "navigation prof," overdid it a little. Even though new at the job, surely I didn't need a sledgehammer hint! But I'm grateful all the same.

As we approached Hawaii, the date was 21 June, and the sun was as far north as it ever got. Our course had us curving around from the southwest; we would make our landfall on Oahu at dawn of the twenty-second. Local Apparent Noon, the instant when the sun reaches its highest altitude, known by the navigating fraternity as LAN, was due, according to the time we were keeping on the ship's clocks and watches, at about 1145. To an observer in any position north of the Tropic of Cancer (the northern boundary of the Torrid Zone), the sun is exactly south at this moment, its shadow at its shortest; and to one standing on the Tropic of Cancer on the 21st of June, in the Northern Hemisphere the longest "day" of the year, just as in the Southern Hemisphere it is the shortest, at Local Apparent Noon the sun will be directly overhead.

Parenthetically, timing the precise moment of LAN on a chronometer accurately keeping the time of Greenwich, England, led, finally, to accurate determination of longitude, for the sun moves 15 degrees per hour in its daily 24-hour voyage around the world. Latitude had long been obtainable by measuring the altitude of the North Star, or the sun at noon, but not until the mid-eighteenth century, with the invention of a sufficiently accurate timekeeper, could navigators compare their own sextant-observed LAN with a chronometer maintaining the time at Greenwich (i.e., the hours, minutes, and seconds since LAN had occurred there), and thus know their own longitude: their exact position east or west of the Greenwich meridian.

The latitude of Oahu, in the Hawaiian Islands, is within a degree or so of the Tropic of Cancer. The subsolar point is, of course, that point on the surface of the earth directly under the sun, and on 21 June 1943 we were able to pass right through it. By no accident, the new navigator was on the bridge with his sextant and a quartermaster to record the times and readings, and it must be said that the hour following turned out to be one of the most fascinating in my life.

To begin with, when taking the altitude of a celestial body the sextant must be aimed at the horizon directly beneath it—not difficult to do during normal observations. When the altitude is near 90 degrees, however, the body being observed directly overhead, it becomes extremely difficult to fix on that part of the horizon where the altitude is least: it is almost the same all the way around. Second, celestial bodies are so far away that the locus of all points where the altitude would be observed to be the same is normally plotted as a straight line perpendicular to its azimuth for that moment as given in the *Nautical Almanac*. But this cannot be done when the observed altitude is very high; it must then be shown as a circle with its center at the subsolar point. I was totally oblivious of the time, took at least two dozen observations of the altitude of the sun as we passed virtually exactly under it, and when that body finally had drifted a degree or so into the west, and I quit shooting it, there was my captain, only a few feet away, hugely enjoying the whole thing.

Nor was this all, for the calculations necessary to plot my sights were totally different from any I had previously been taught by my Naval Academy navigation instructor who had become my wartime skipper, or by anyone else. Since the subsolar point was not at an infinite distance, it was in fact less than a mile away when I began shooting the sun, and we actually did pass through it at Local Apparent Noon, the conventional straight line representing the locus of our possible positions at any given sextant sighting was no longer valid.

Instead, I found myself, without need for calculation, depicting possible positions by small circles on the chart, and where they intersected, advanced for our own progress through the water between sun sights, became a perfect fix of our position. Never before (I assume) had any ship been so precisely navigated over the noon hour. My fascination with these unlooked-for discoveries must have been evident. Even my navigation instructor, now masquerading as the skipper of my submarine, evidenced interest in what I was able to show him.

When we arrived at Pearl Harbor a survey was held on our ship with the result that she was sent to the Pearl Harbor Navy Yard for emergency overhaul. I received 30 days leave in California, met, courted, and became engaged to Ingrid Schenck, a 17-year old high school junior in my own old high school in Palo Alto (recently we celebrated our golden wedding anniversary), and on return to Pearl found both Benson and Steve Mann detached. I was upgraded to exec for a newly named skipper, Robert E. ("Dusty") Dornin, who had graduated from Annapolis four years ahead of me. Part of my service in the old *Lea* had been under his older brother, who had been *Lea*'s exec when I was her most junior officer.

Dusty already had a reputation as a born fighter. He had been a noted athlete at the Naval Academy, a member of the fabled football team that had defeated West Point by three points in one of the muddiest football games ever played, had been several years in submarines, and had made his mark as TDC (torpedo data computer) operator. I quickly found that as a fighting submarine skipper he had no peer. Despite Roy Benson's great personal qualities of leadership and dedication which had rescued our boat from possibly permanent doldrums, for which everyone on board was forever grateful, it was under Dusty Dornin that she suddenly catapulted to the pinnacle of submarine capability and effectiveness.

The account, written shortly after the war ended, is to me as if it had just happened. *Trigger* began her real career as a night fighter, remaining on the surface, with her speed and mobility retaining the initiative, and in the process doing tremendous damage to the enemy. It must have been the same game German subs had been playing with our convoys carrying vital supplies to England. Dornin decided he would do best remaining in the conning tower, directing our action from the TDC, with which he was intimately familiar. This put me, as exec, on the bridge as combat OOD but subject, of course, to the skipper's overall direction. We meshed admirably. Half a century later I can still write this without equivocation, but I have surreptitiously retained copies of our patrol reports, now entirely declassified, with which to bolster my rendition of those days.

On 1 September 1943, we departed Pearl Harbor, bound for Formosa with a quick stop at Johnston Island for fuel. Dornin was anxious to get into action, so we maintained full speed on the surface all the way, diving for short periods only to "get a trim," not even submerging as we passed Wake Island of infamous memory. We passed Wake some 230 miles off with no sight of any aircraft patrol, but were due to pass Japan's Marcus Island at less than a third of that distance. As navigator and second-in-command, I consulted with our new skipper about the advisability of remaining submerged during daylight when within aircraft patrol range from Marcus, and vividly remember his reaction: "Are you afraid of the Japs?" he barked.

"Nossir," I said, "but I thought I should mention that we'll be passing pretty close."

"Okay!" he flung back. "We dive if we see any planes, but not until!"

For the record, we dived twice for Marcus-based patrol aircraft that day, the second one coming in low and fast hoping to catch us unaware and in fact unloading two bombs on us, but to me the real significance of the incident was the realization, in depth, that Dusty Dornin had no fear in his makeup. We were fighting a war, one the enemy had brought to us, and we intended to make him sorry that he had ever attacked us. The *Trigger* was back on the surface both times, running at full speed toward Formosa, as soon as the planes were out of sight.

Our first blood contact was on the night of the seventeenth, two ships proceeding in company, no escorts, but too far apart to encompass both in a single torpedo attack. We selected the biggest for our target, attained a perfect firing position in the blackest part of the night, fired four torpedoes at a range of half a mile. "Two hits seen from the bridge," our patrol report says, "both duds. Nothing heard below decks" (in other words, no explosions). "No doubt about the hits—the first was aft of the midship superstructure, and the second was on the bow. Immediately afterward, flashlights were seen on deck and over the side at the points where the torpedoes hit. The target swung towards us to ram and we went to full speed and swung away. Lights all over his decks by this time." The language on our bridge at this point was sulfurous, all directed at the U.S. Navy's Bureau of Ordnance.

The patrol report goes on:

2057, Target commenced firing deck guns. Obtained set-up to fire after tubes, but withheld fire because of poor firing data. Range now 700 yards, and with the visibility improving with approaching moonrise and the shells coming too close for comfort, at

2058, dived. Made reload. Watched target through periscope, still firing.

2100, Received three depth charges, not close.

2107, Moonrise.

2138, Reload completed. Surfaced, full speed on all main engines.

2142, Radar contact. Commenced end around on dark side of the moon. The two ships had separated, so went after the big one, hoping to be able to return for the other later.

2347, In position ahead, very bright moonlight, dived to radar depth.

September 18, 1943

0005, Target in sight through periscope. He was zigzagging radically at about one minute intervals from 030°T to 130°T. Went to 55 feet at 4,000 yards. At 2,000 yards commenced getting continuous echo ranges on him, and at

0023, fired four torpedoes, 130 port track, 1,000 yards, GA [gyro angle] 0.45 seconds later saw and heard one hit on stern. Eight seconds later sound reported another hit, but not seen through periscope (maybe another dud). However, the effect of the single hit was remarkable. Target sank in two minutes, by the stern. All hands in conning tower got a look.

0026, Target completely under.

0026½, Boilers blew up. A tremendous explosion.

0029, Made battle surface. Nothing in sight. No wreckage, no Japs. They never knew what had happened.

   Have heard of ships sinking fast, but this is the first time this ship or the commanding officer has ever experienced such a thing. It seemed very unreal.

As already mentioned, my battle station was on the bridge when we were surfaced, and on the periscope when submerged. Dusty commanded from the TDC, with which he was very familiar. I therefore had the best viewing position of anyone, and in fact aimed the torpedoes, on the bridge by the target bearing transmitter, in the conning tower through the periscope. Bearings from either instrument would be fed to the TDC, which computed the gyro angles to be set automatically on the torpedoes up to the moment of firing. My clear memory of this attack is of course reinforced by our patrol report, but the clearest memory of all was not described. One "fish" was to be aimed at the target's stern, and I clearly saw it hit right where the propeller shaft entered the enemy ship's hull. There was a big, satisfying explosion, but surprisingly no splash of water where it took place. I recall noting that the entire force of the explosion seemed to be contained inside of the target. The structure of its stern, just above the propeller, appeared beaten in—and as I watched the enemy's stern went entirely under water, his bow rose to the dark sky, and I was looking at the hull of a ship standing vertically up and down. It was sinking so precipitantly that the now entirely vertical hull still seemed to have some residual motion through the water in the original direction.

"He's sinking!" I remember yelling. "He's straight up and down in the water!"—and then I was unceremoniously shoved aside and Dusty grabbed the periscope.

He took a long look, then shouted, "Surface the boat!" As soon as Dornin released the 'scope, while the control room was blowing tanks, I propelled as many of the conning tower crew to the periscope as could be done, but within a minute was back on the dripping bridge, along with the skipper and our bridge crew, all of us armed with binoculars—and there was nothing in sight. No ship, no wreckage. During the two minutes it had taken us to get our submarine to the surface, the ship we had torpedoed had plunged completely under the water!

Engraved on my mind is the tragically dramatic picture of that big ship up-ended and sinking. I even recall seeing someone—possibly it was only imagination, but I think not—who must have jumped from the tip of her very bow as it was rising so irresistibly into the heavens; for I have the distinct memory of seeing arms and legs moving as the forlorn figure plunged 100 feet into the sea.

There was no chance for anyone to have survived. A ship sinking that fast would suck everything nearby down with it.

Dusty was nothing if not a fighter. He proved it with everything he did. We had just sunk one ship, but there was another, somewhat smaller, still in the area and still afloat. An all-out search for it was immediately begun but sadly for this narrative of submarine success we could not find it. The noise attending destruction of its larger consort may have been heard and caused a radical course change. Whatever happened, we were unable to relocate it, and the primitive radar with which we were then outfitted could not detect it.

Three days later it was a different story.

We had submerged just north of the northern tip of Formosa for a day's patrolling and in mid-afternoon, running in an easterly direction, there appeared a six-ship convoy escorted by aircraft. Because of the air cover, we could not surface to execute the classic submarine "end-around" maneuver in order to reach an attack position. We went at full speed submerged, drew our battery down heavily, but to no avail. Zigzagging though they were, they never zigged far enough to give us a chance at a shot, even a long-range one. Impotently, we had to watch the enemy ships go over the horizon and out of sight.

As night fell we prepared to surface, and right then I learned another thing about my new skipper. As I felt was my duty, I pointed out that our "can" (storage battery) had been deeply discharged during our unsuccessful submerged chase of the afternoon. Should we not put in a fast charge before beginning this new phase of our pursuit? Dornin nearly exploded. "Charge batteries? For God's sake, Ned, are you afraid of those little yellow bastards? We're chasing them right now, and don't ever let me hear you talk like that again!"

"Yes, sir!" I said, and he never did. From then onward, I felt I knew what it was to be a fighting submariner. We hit the surface at 7:30 P.M. and went immediately to maximum speed on all engines. Since the *Trigger* had been equipped with two small diesels in addition to our four big nine-cylinder railroad-type main engines, the two "dinkies" were also fired up and put to charging the batteries. They would be able to put no more than a trickle charge into the can, but Dusty found no fault with using them for what we could— and after an hour's chase we found the targets again, faintly visible in the waning daylight. Six ships there were in all, in two columns: in the right-hand column were three big tankers, in the left were three freighter types, somewhat smaller in size. It was not yet fully dark, but the darker side was to the right. That, and the location of the tankers, which all briefings had emphasized as being by far the most important of all merchant targets, made it easy to decide to attack from the starboard side.

We had rigged up a portable speaking system from the bridge to the conning tower, through which I could talk directly to the captain down below, and he to me. Neither of us gave much thought to the fact that since our speakers functioned through the ship's general announcing system our entire ship's company could also hear everything we said to each other. Among my duties was to give Dusty a running commentary of everything I saw from topside, with everyone else aboard of course listening to every word. Under the circumstances we would not have cared, but it didn't occur to us. In fact, keeping all hands so well apprised of the situation as it developed turned out to our great advantage. No crew could have more identified with what was going on than ours, for they heard every word exchanged on the command circuit. Both Dusty and I became heroes to our ship's company from that day onward. They had always been excellent; now it was as though we all possessed one single, cohesive mind. Something so powerful has to be experienced before it can be understood.

To return to our attack on the convoy, it was still fairly light; so our lookouts (and I, paralleling their efforts through my own binoculars) could see the enemy ships clearly. Our patrol report says this was from 8,000 yards away, four nautical miles. It also notes that we decided to wait a little longer before attacking. I remember marveling, at the time, at how nerveless I was. I felt none of the often-reported "butterflies" in my stomach. Fear for my own safety did not exist, nor did compassion for the innocent men we were about to kill. Now, looking back on it, I do not think this unusual. There was no "this is war" rationalization. My pulse must have been beating more firmly than ever, the adrenaline no doubt shooting through my body in great quantity. In combat, everyone undoubtedly goes through some of this change. Heroism, training, determination, capability—none of these is felt or even noticed. All, of course, are in the background, especially such intangibles as training and capability, for without them one is nothing. But these qualities are submerged in the far bigger android that, in such circumstances, man becomes. He is not a thinking being; he is neither moral nor amoral; he does what he is set to do by some order greater than his own. He thinks, of course; or more properly, he reacts as he was trained to what the enemy does, tries to stay a jump or two ahead of him, knows that this very same enemy is also doing his best against *him,* is also trained to kill. Some individuals react faster and better than others, and this can also be called "thinking," but it is not thinking of the philosophical kind. Dusty was one of those who reacted very fast indeed.

For, in this condition, man is an automaton. Otherwise he could not function. This, in its most atavistic form, is what drives the battle. This is what makes it possible to do what one must do. Few can describe it, but in its time and place it is the biggest thing in the world, responsible for everything, explaining everything, justifying everything. The civilization that we know was built on it.

Today we are trying to elevate ourselves above this, but 55 years ago, as I stood on the bridge of my submarine planning how to kill the enemy, I was an expert, practiced machine, with only one object in mind, and I discovered I was very good at it.

Yes, of course, we hated the enemy. Japan had done us the favor of making this easy by its surprise attack on Pearl Harbor. I do not speak for the POW, the front-line soldier, or the civilian residents of a captured city, all of whom had extremely special reasons to dislike Japan. We, who had never met any members of the enemy, hated them in a bureaucratic sense without much rationalization, or thought about the psychology involved. We did not, in a personal way, hate the individual members of the society or its armed forces that were opposing us. But that kind of philosophizing had nothing whatever to do with aiming our torpedoes. Here, all of us were implacable. We were dedicated to sinking ships. That this meant death and destruction we knew, of course, but I recall no consideration of that. Nor did we have anything against the people who dropped depth charges on us, to destroy us in their turn, if they could. It was a given. It was war.

From our patrol report:

2045 Commenced surface approach, planning to fire three torpedoes at the first ship, three at the second, then swing and fire four at the third ship.

2048 Nearest column of ships in plain sight—THREE TANKERS, with the big one leading. It is still fairly light. They *should* see us—but they don't.

ATTACK # 3—TANKER, 10,000 TONS—SUNK

2056 Fired three torpedoes at *TANKER #1*, 80 Starboard track (they should hit the target's starboard side at an 80 degree angle), Gyro Angle 10 Left, range 1600 yards.

ATTACK # 4—TANKER, 7500 TONS AND FREIGHTER, 6700 TONS—SUNK

2057 Fired three torpedoes at *TANKER #2*, 60 S track, GA 0, 1200 yards. Came left with full rudder and full speed. During the firing, had TBT bearings, radar bearings, radar ranges, sound bearings, and periscope bearings, all checking. [We put this in our report for the benefit of BuOrd, which still seemed to think submariners didn't know what they were doing.]

2057—10 One hit seen on after part of *TANKER #1*. Flame shot five hundred feet into the air, lighting up the whole area as bright as day. All six ships could plainly be seen. Eight seconds later the second torpedo hit her amidships; but nothing could have added to the furious holocaust already taking place.

Members of her crew in various stages of dress (most in white uniforms) could be seen running forward ahead of the rapidly spreading flames. She was still driving ahead, a brilliantly blazing funeral pyre. The men in the bow manned the bow gun and fired three or four times, but she was soon burning throughout her length. The flames were yellow-red, evidently a gasoline fire.

2058—10 One hit on *TANKER #2*. A small flash amidships, a column of smoke and water were seen, and fire immediately broke out. She was turning away from us when hit.

2058—50 One hit amidships on *FREIGHTER #2* in the far column. In the light of the burning tanker she was seen to break in half beneath the stack and sink immediately. Radar was on this target at the time, the operator having expressed a desire to see a ship sink on his screen. His wish was fulfilled, for on both the radar and PPI screens the pip was seen to diminish and finally disappear. Radar and PPI then indicated five targets.

During this time we were swinging hard left. Bridge saw *FREIGHTER #3* turn away. *FREIGHTER #1* was holding on her original course. Both remaining freighters and tankers opened fire. Range was about 1000 yards to the tanker column, 2000 yards to the freighter column. It was so bright they had no difficulty seeing us. Splashes were seen on both sides of us, but not too close. *TANKER #3* presented a 50 starboard angle on the bow, and was closing rapidly, firing his bow gun. We seemed to take a year to pick up speed. Finally steadied with our stern toward him, and at

ATTACK # 5—TANKER, 7300 TONS—MISSED

2100 Fired three torpedoes aft at this tanker, 50 S track, GA 0, 1000 yards. All missed, probably because we had not steadied enough, and he was swinging toward us, as we realized in a moment.

ATTACK # 6—SAME TARGET—HIT

2101 Fired one torpedo aft down the throat, angle on the bow zero, GA 10 R, 800 yards. Hit on the starboard bow, observed from the bridge. We were making full speed by this time, and pulling away. However, he continued firing, and was getting a little better, as was evidenced by shells whistling overhead.

2102 Dived. Slight confusion in the conning tower. The Commanding Officer fell into the periscope well and the quartermaster began to lower the periscope. Fortunately the Commanding Officer, supporting himself on his elbows, was able to make himself heard in time.

There was more to this particular episode, of course, and to the night's exploit, but this was the gist of it. By virtue of my station on the bridge during surface action, I had an enviable view of it all—and can never forget the tableau in the conning tower when we dived and I came below, dogged the hatch behind me, and turned to find Dusty half in the periscope well. When it came to writing the report of the action, I pleaded with him to tell about it. My clinching argument: "All the shore-based guys in Pearl read every patrol report. It's their biggest source of news, the closest they ever will get to the fighting. This is a great patrol, and if you let us toss in a bit of humor they'll love you forever. Besides, it's true!"

"Not all that true," growled Dornin. "I wasn't entirely in the well. The deck was wet and I only partly slipped into it!"

Our yeoman typing the report and I, drafting it, argued the point, and finally Dusty gave in, let us tell it our way. Later we heard that our report was an instant bestseller. Our skipper immediately became famous. Everyone reading it who knew him—and many who didn't—swore they could plainly see him falling into the periscope well in the middle of combat, that it was just like him. We knew differently. Dusty Dornin was a born fighter, as phenomenally successful a submarine skipper as he had been a football player. As a sub skipper he had eyes in the back of his head. This was something I could prove by instance after instance.

We made three extremely successful patrols under Dornin's command, at the conclusion of which the *Trigger* was recognized as the top-scoring submarine of the force. Then he was detached to become aide to Adm. Ernest King in Washington, D.C., and things changed. My own detachment came one patrol later, and I have sometimes wondered whether my departure, next-to-the-last man of her original commissioning crew to leave, may have had something to do with her ensuing bad luck.

I was not the last man of our original crew to depart, although I had sought that honor. It goes, instead, to our old chief steward's mate, Walter Pye Wilson. With my own orders in hand to the new-construction submarine *Tirante*, then building at the Portsmouth Navy Yard in Kittery, Maine, I had called him to the wardroom and summarily dismissed him from the ship. No one was going to be able to say he had served in her longer than I, I said, handing him a just-made-up set of orders sending him to our squadron relief crew. He had richly earned a rest, I told him, and I wanted him to get it.

Wilson, always the good sailor (except if taking orders from an OOD unable to make up his mind which way to turn to avoid being rammed), took the paper. We shook hands and bade each other goodbye. Later I discovered that as soon as I was off the ship, my Naval Academy classmate, Johnny Shepherd, who had relieved me as exec, tore it up. Wilson served two more patrols in *Trigger*, then after 12 runs in all, called it a day. By this time he could have had anything he wanted. He had become a legend in the submarine force, and maybe he had a premonition, for that was the patrol from which our old ship did not return.

Chapter Eight

Fighting the End of the War

Trigger's whole crew came to say goodbye as I threw my clothes into a newly purchased suitcase. No one could know that many of them were doomed to remain with her forever on eternal patrol, but we all understood that nothing between us would ever be the same. We had shared many risks and many triumphs together, and now that phase of our lives was ending. Combined we had been, but this was the breaking-off point, the moment when it ended. This applied to all but a few of our crew whom, in one way or another, I had managed to have sent also to the *Tirante,* then under construction at Portsmouth.

It was now late May of 1944; I had been in the *Trigger* two and a half years, having made one additional patrol after Dornin's departure to provide continuity. I was aboard during the Battle of Midway and nine following war patrols for a total of ten in all, as we counted them in those days. It had already been announced that after *Trigger*'s twelfth we would skip the thirteenth and go directly to the fourteenth. I was not superstitious, but I knew that such special things, handled right, can add up to help institutional morale. How many of our crew worried about an upcoming thirteenth "run" was anyone's guess, but this flip idea added to our cohesiveness, even though all hands knew I was probably to get orders at the conclusion of the current war patrol.

I had, however, kept one little secret to myself. On our way back to Pearl we stopped at Midway for fuel and mail, and in the pile was an All Navy Message listing promotions. My name was on the list, so I ran to the Navy-maintained Midway telegraph/cable office, and, after some difficulty con-vincing the person running it that I was indeed sending a bona-fide mar-riage proposal (there must have been some real problems to cause the query), was able to transmit, "Would you marry a Lieutenant Comman-der?" Ingrid, of course, had been receiving mail whenever I could send it, thus, although I could not tell her where I was or where I was going, had some idea of our submarine's departure and arrival times. This cable would alert her to the imminence of my return, the renewed receipt of mail, and the need to begin some fast planning.

I reached Palo Alto the last day of May with leave and travel authorized to expire at Portsmouth, New Hampshire, to discover that the *Trigger* had been sufficiently badly damaged during our just-finished patrol that she had been sent back to Hunter's Point, in San Francisco, for six weeks of repairs. My secret I could not keep any longer. Ingrid and I met the boat on its arrival, and she was greeted with cheers.

We were married on the fourth of June in the Stanford Chapel, on the uni-versity campus where Ingrid's father had been a professor of geology until called away by the war. She and I had attended the same high school, 10 years apart, and as a special concession she was graduated four days early to fit my somewhat imperious schedule. We had a week-long honeymoon in the scenic seaside resort town of Carmel, went by train to New London for me to attend the new Prospective Commanding Officer school, then pro-ceeded, via a luckily found second-hand car, to Kittery, Maine, where the Portsmouth, New Hampshire, Navy Yard was actually located.

I was to be prospective executive officer of USS *Tirante* (SS-420), nearly 200 sequential numbers in our wartime submarine construction tally after the *Trigger* (SS-237). Built to the same basic design, *Tirante*'s hull was designed for deeper depth capability and embodied many other improve-ments, among them stowage for four more reload torpedoes. She could carry a full load total of 28 fish instead of the previous 24, embodied in addition all the changes we submariners had been advocating since the war began. I remember saying she was the "Cadillac of our wartime boats," and still feel that way about her.

Our skipper was Lt. Cdr. George Street, only two years senior to me on the Navy list. I remembered him from our Naval Academy days when he and I were in the same company organization of midshipmen. He had made many war patrols as exec of the submarine *Gar*, a number before that in more junior assignments, and now, like me, had been sent late in the war to "new construction" to bring a newly built boat into combat, and incidentally have a few months restorative time in the States. I arrived at Portsmouth in July with my bride. The Navy had allowed us a break in the war, in effect a four-month honeymoon in the middle of it, demanding only an ever-increasing workload on our brand-new submarine.

I had been a war-time exec for more than a year, with a number of very successful war patrols under my belt. So had George (whom I always called "Captain," until my detachment—but then he became "George" to me and has so remained ever since). *Tirante* was his first command. Both of us had been well trained in the crucible of the biggest war the world had yet seen; the two of us meshed as though our entire careers had been planned for this combination of our respective talents.

There is much that can be written about the *Tirante*. She was the prize of the Portsmouth Naval Shipyard and became arguably its most successful submarine despite being built very late in the war and thereby able to complete only two war patrols. George Street, her only wartime skipper, was awarded the Congressional Medal of Honor for her first patrol, the ship herself a Presidential Unit Citation, and I the Navy Cross as executive officer. The "Officers' Club" at the navy yard (no longer confined to commissioned officers) was renamed "*Tirante* Tavern" after the war was over and the reports declassified.

Those of us who served aboard will never forget that first patrol.

From the report:

> Ship placed in commission at Navy Yard, Portsmouth, N.H. on Nov. 6, 1944. Lieutenant Commander G. L. Street, III, USN assumed command. Ship completed on Nov. 23, 1944, and commenced training in fog, storms, and freezing weather off Portsmouth.

> Arrived New London, Conn. on Dec. 21, 1944. Departed Jan. 8, 1945. Arrived Pearl Feb. 10, departed on first war patrol March 3.

In *Submarine!*, published in 1952, I wrote about the *Tirante* as follows,

> *Tirante*'s character developed rapidly, even before the training period was complete. Her radar was the most powerful I had ever encountered; her engines ran best when loaded to more than full rated power; she made 21 knots with ease whereas other subs of the same design struggled to reach 19. [True, we made some unauthorized modifications to her big ten-cylinder engines, rated somehow at no greater horsepower than the nine-cylinder jobs,

from the same engine-builders, that had been installed in the *Trigger*. Having been her engineer, I knew what those fine engines could deliver; *Tirante*'s, 12 percent bigger, should have been rated accordingly, and when we were done with them, they were.] She also carried four more fish than *Trigger*, and her torpedoes had been modified to eliminate the frustrations of the earlier war years. Many of *Tirante*'s crew were already veterans of the Pacific, some of them from *Trigger* herself. . . . Somehow, starting with *Tirante*'s first dive, everything seemed to work right the first time for us. Tirelessly we tinkered with our fish, and every torpedo we fired in practice hit the target except one that, on subsequent analysis, proved to have been an impossible shot.

Perhaps word of our successes reached up the line, for the day before we set out for Pearl Harbor and the war, Street was asked to take a specially donated torpedo with us and send back periscope pictures of its destruction of an enemy ship!

We worked our way through the training program at Balboa and Pearl Harbor with a vengeance and a will, finished both of them in the minimum possible time, and finally there came our area assignment: the East China and Yellow Seas, about as hot an area as ComSubPac could hand out. On 3 March we departed for Japan, via Saipan, and on the twenty-fifth we entered our area, south and west of Kyushu, Japan's southernmost island. In the next few days we sank two ships, the second one thoroughly photographed through the periscope for the Westinghouse employees at Sharon, Pennsylvania.

That night's radio traffic contained a message requiring us to rendezvous with the *Trigger*, which was patrolling the adjacent area, and carry out a coordinated patrol. This was a new thing: never in George Street's experience, nor in mine, had an ad hoc patrol coordination been ordered in this way from submarine headquarters. There had been things organized on the spot by the skippers concerned, but headquarters had always done a lot more planning than seemed to be the case here. Perhaps it knew something we didn't; possibly someone in SubPac headquarters was aware of the special relationship between *Trigger* and *Tirante*.

That had to be the answer, and I remember how pleased and excited I was. It showed that the chaps pushing the pencils in SubPac, or moving tiny submarine silhouettes around on the big magnetic wall chart they maintained, also had a special feel for the boats and the people they were dealing with.

George Street and I held a quick conference, in which I did most of the talking. Since there would be some planning necessary, there would have to be discussion between the ships; and since *Trigger* was the senior ship (her newly named skipper, Dave Connole, being a year ahead of George on the Navy list), we should send an emissary to him. As exec of the *Tirante,* I was the logical person to send, and besides, this was too good a chance to miss. I began eagerly to look forward to visiting the ship in which I had served so long, and began preparations, among other things seeing to it that everyone aboard of the old *Trigger* crew heard of the need for a crew for our rubber boat. As expected, every one of them volunteered, and from my position of near ultimate authority they were the ones selected, my only stipulation being that they must hold themselves in readiness to leave their old friends quickly when my own combined official and personal visit was over.

Three days we waited for her, searching the radio waves, patrolling ceasely back and forth in the area we had thought most convenient for both submarines and had suggested to her, but she never answered any of our messages, never appeared. When after three days we realized there was something very wrong, we sent a message stating our inability to make contact and received one saying she had been diverted to another assignment.

This fooled no one. The *Trigger* was gone, and with her many of my old friends. My feeling was deep, and so were those of the few members of the *Trigger* crew who were with me aboard this fine new *Tirante* that we had barely been able to get to sea. When I think of our old boat, and the men still serving in her, the emotion is still there.

We had indeed drawn an active area. From studying the reports of previous patrols there, we thought we could deduce where the enemy ships were going. Basically, they never crossed the open sea at night, or in the daytime either, if they could avoid it. They were becoming very scarce, and the only possible conclusion was that they were going around our designated area, in shallow water, as shallow as they could find. We laid our search scheme accordingly, and our deduction must have been right, for we found a number of single ships, and one small convoy of two ships. Our most outstanding attack, however, for which the Medal of Honor and Presidential Unit Citation were awarded, came as a result of ULTRA (secret) intelligence.

Fifty years ago the word could not be mentioned, or even hinted at. On 13 April we received two messages: the first told of the death of President Roosevelt. The second was an ULTRA informing us that an important ship, with escorts, would anchor that night off the north coast of Quelpart Island, just south of the Korean peninsula. The island was shown on the Japanese charts we carried as "Saisho To."

From our patrol report:

April 14

0000 Approaching Quelpart Island northwestern side.

0029 Radar contact. Patrol boat. Went to tracking stations and worked around him. Sighted him at 4500 yards—long and low. No evidence of radar until we were nearly around, when he turned his on (Jap 10 Cm). The patrol was evidently suspicious, probably because we came too close, but soon went back to sleep.

Continued working up the anchorage.

0223 Radar contact. Another patrol craft, bigger than the other. Avoided by going close inshore. He also became suspicious, apparently, and headed for our point of nearest approach to him. However, our tactic of heading inshore confused him (as we no doubt merged with his land pips) and he continued routine patrolling.

During the whole of the ensuing action, except while actually firing torpedoes, this patrol boat was kept on the TDC and both plots. He was always a mental hazard, and potentially a real one. . . . No soundings inside the ten fathom curve in the harbor and approaches were shown on the Japanese chart we had to use to navigate. Hoped the place wasn't mined and that none of the five shore-based radars reported on Quelpart were guarding the harbor.

0240 Battle Stations. Approached anchorage from the south along the ten fathom curve within 1200 yards of the shore line. Took "single ping" fathometer sounding every 3 to 5 minutes. The smell of cattle from the beach was strong. Bridge could not see well enough to distinguish ships from shore line in the harbor, though a couple of darker spots in the early morning mist looked promising—as did, indeed, the presence of two patrolling escort vessels where none had previously been seen several nights before during night patrol in this area.

0310 Completed investigation this side of the anchorage from 1200 yards away. There may be ships there, but cannot see well enough to shoot.

Started around the small island off the anchorage, staying as close as possible. The patrol vessel by this time was paralleling us 7000 yards off shore, still not overly suspicious, but annoying. Executive Officer on bridge could see him now and then.

0330 Having completed circuit of the small island, started in from northern side, cutting across the ten fathom curve. At about—

0340 Bridge made out the shapes of ships in the anchorage. Sound picked up a second "pinger"—this time in the harbor. Still too far (4500 yards and not sure of what we saw). Patrol heading this way. Sounding 11 fathoms. Current setting us on the beach. Decided to get in closer and have this over with. A/A ⅔. (Radar officer confirmed sharp pips of ships in anchorage).

0350 Bridge definitely could see ships. For the first time put targets on TDC, with Zero speed and TBT bearings. With assistance of TBT and PPI, SJ commenced ranging on largest ship—very difficult to distinguish from the mass of shore pips, and gave range of 2500 yards. Sounding 9 fathoms. Still getting set on. Land loomed close aboard on both sides. Patrol still not overly alerted, passing about 6000 yards away, pinging loudly, outboard of us. Land background our Saving Grace. Secured taking "single ping" fathometer readings; if those ships can get in there, so can we. Both 40 MM guns are all loaded and ready with gun crews. Since it is too shallow to dive, we will have to shoot our way out if boxed in.

0355 Exec on TBT picked out three targets, and got on largest. Backed down and lay-to. Bow toed slightly out to combat the set.

0355-30 Fired one torpedo as a sighting-in shot to dope out current using TBT bearings, range by SJ 2300 yards, gyro angle 344.30, track 90. Captain went to the bridge to get in on the fun up there. Missed to the right. Torpedo hit beach and exploded, proving there was no torpedo net.

0359 Fired one torpedo aimed at left edge of the largest target, to correct for current effect. Wake headed straight for the target.

0359-22 Fired another torpedo aimed same as the previous one—straight as a die. Exec's keen shooting eye looked right on tonight.

0401-05 A tremendous beautiful explosion. A great mushroom of white blinding flame shot 2000 feet into the air. Not a sound was heard for a moment, but then a thunderous roar flattened our ears against our heads.

The jackpot, and no mistake! In this shattering convulsion we had no idea how many hits we had made, but sincerely believe it was two. In the glare of the fire, *Tirante* stood out, in her light camouflage, like a snowman in a coal pit. But, more important, silhouetted against the flame were two escort vessels, both instantly obvious as fine new frigates of the *Mikura* class. The Captain instinctively ordered, "Right full rudder, all ahead flank," and as quickly belayed it. Steadied up to pick off the two frigates.

0402 Fired one torpedo at the left hand frigate, using TBT bearings and radar ranges.

0402-16 Fired another torpedo at the same target.

0403 Fired last torpedo at the right hand frigate.

0404 Now lets *really* get out of here!

0404-20 One beautiful hit in the left hand frigate. The ship literally exploded, her bow and stern rising out of water and the center disappearing in a sheet of fire. Must have hit her magazines. Very satisfying to watch, though not the equal of the previous explosion, of course. Possibly two hits in him.

0404-40 A hit on the other PF also—right amidships! No flame this time, other than the explosion, but a great cloud of smoke immediately enveloped her and she disappeared. We jubilantly credit ourselves with three ships sunk with at least four, probably five, hits for six fish. Not the slightest doubt about any of the three ships. Now only one torpedo left aboard. Immediately reloaded it and reset TDC cams for our MK 18.

The patrolling escort had now increased speed and turned toward the anchorage. Once more we pulled our trick of slipping undetected along the shore. As we left the gutted anchorage behind, a third PF could be seen standing out at slow speed. He did not, however, come out after us but stayed, watching the fire. So we just ran down the coast of Quelpart headed for the open sea. Transmitted results of attack to submarines in area so they could avoid the certain A/S measures to come.

The large ship which exploded was, in the Commanding Officer's mind, unquestionably an ammunition ship, or possibly a tanker loaded with aviation gas. Not much can be said about her type and size, but in the sudden glare of the explosion she appeared to be a large engines-aft vessel of from 8000 to 10000 tons. In the light of her own fire she was huge.

As we rounded Quelpart's southwestern tip, the glare from the anchorage could still be seen above the dark hills, and a heavy smoke cloud hung like a shroud over the entire western end of the island.

0513 Radar and sight contact with the other patrol, which we had avoided initially. This time he was alert, as we got definite SJ interference from him—Jap 10 CM radar. Too light to evade surfaced, so dived and evaded submerged. He came over to the spot where we had dived and dropped a pattern. Many distant depth charges or bombs were heard and planes were sighted all day. This area will be hot tonight.

2245 Surfaced, and transmitted message to Force Commander.

The message read, "THREE FOR FRANKLIN XX SANK AMMUNITION SHIP TWO ESCORTS IN ANCHORAGE NORTHERN SHORE QUELPART ISLAND MORNING FOURTEENTH X NO COUNTERMEASURES X TIRANTE SENDS X ONE TORPEDO REMAINING XX."

We headed back across the Pacific at full speed, were not happy to be directed to Midway for refit, got there nine days later. I already had in my pocket a set of orders detaching me from the *Tirante* to await arrival as prospective skipper of USS *Piper* upon return from her second patrol. *Piper* had preceded *Tirante* down the ways at Portsmouth by only a few months. I was of course delighted, my only sorrow being the necessity of leaving the wonderful *Tirante,* her great skipper, and the extraordinary crew I had had a hand in creating.

I knew that I was coming into line to have my own submarine command, and though I envied my contemporaries who got command ahead of me, this was because of my obligation to the *Tirante,* and no complaint. Nonetheless, I envied them their good fortune, but some of this jealousy evaporated when one of the first in my class to get a command failed to return from his first patrol. No one knows what happened to the *Kete.* The enemy's records do not help, and my guess is that one of his torpedoes ran in a circle. Corrections having finally been made in depth keeping, the faulty contact exploder, and the overly sensitive influence exploder that went off prematurely (thus on two separate occasions allowing me to stay alive when *Trigger's* torpedoes ran in a circle), a torpedo in a circular run was by this time a truly lethal danger. Statistics can only indicate probabilities, not show certainties, but I have already stated the statistical probability that perhaps ten of our submarines still on "eternal patrol" were sent there by our own torpedoes.

Of two of them, we have positive knowledge, for their survivors so reported when we got them back from Japanese prison camps after the war.

None of these concerns dampened my ardor, however, when my own ship finally came in. But luck wasn't with me. Although designated for one of the few productive combat areas yet remaining, in the land-locked Sea of Japan between the islands of Japan and the mainland of Asia, our departure on patrol was held up a week because Admiral Lockwood was not satisfied with tests on our new mine-detection gear. Finally, early in August 1945, he at last gave us the go-ahead. We got under way immediately, at full speed, with orders to penetrate the mine barrier the enemy had put across the Straits of Tsushima at the southern entrance to the Sea of Japan, report the locations of the mines, then have a field day against ships found in the land-locked area between Japan and the coast of Asia.

I soon realized I was racing against the end of the war, that events were taking place far beyond the ken of anyone on board. The first atom bomb was dropped on Hiroshima the same day we arrived off the enemy coast, and dispatches that night changed our orders: we were directed not to proceed into the Sea of Japan, but to lie off awaiting further instructions. For three days we wandered around, close to Tsushima, without a designated patrol area or any assigned mission except to stay out of trouble.

We did not strictly carry out that directive. We went looking for trouble, but despite our best efforts there was no action of any kind to be found. We did shoot up a couple of fishing boats one night; though doing this was in our orders since fishing boats, known to have radio transmitters, were suspected of doubling as picket boats, we were not very proud of that business. The seas around Japan were totally empty. We stayed close to the purported location of the mine barrier, diverted slightly once to penetrate into a nearby bay on the coast hoping to find a ship worth a torpedo. But we saw absolutely nothing. After three days of frustration, our radio produced orders to penetrate the mine barrier after all, enter the Sea of Japan, and begin patrol. Obviously there had been a glitch in the surrender procedure.

The second atom bomb must have detonated as we were submerged negotiating the strait (and finding not one but two rows of antisubmarine mines); no sooner had we come to periscope depth in the Sea of Japan, on the far side of the Tsushima mine barrier, than we began to hear unmistakable signs on our radio that the war was over.

Orders to terminate warlike activity filled the air. I have since many times thought over the situation and stated my own delight and that of our crew that the war had ended, and that we had survived it. But I had difficulty under-standing the feelings of despondency and frustration that descended upon me personally. It was no doubt composed of the letdown from the adrena-lin high of war service, and my own disappointment at not having had a chance to get into action on my own, added to the fact that we had almost got there but not quite. I was confident that we would have given a good account of ourselves, for the crew had trained faithfully and our record in practice was excellent. But we were denied the chance to produce the proof. Our con-tribution to the end of the war was the rescue of six bedraggled Japanese sailors from two wrecked wooden boats we found in different places in the middle of the Sea of Japan.

After the war ended, however, we had to stay in that sea until our author-ities were able to obtain a safe route out, and thus were denied any chance to participate in the surrender ceremony in Tokyo Bay, or even to be there, as were a number of our fellows. Getting clearance took about three weeks of aimless cruising around that small sea, and I had to put down a delega-tion from *Piper*'s totally bored crew seriously suggesting that since we had found a way in through the minefield we could take our chances and go out the same way. "Nothing doing," I told them, concealing the fact that I had actually thought of the same thing myself. However, Admiral Lockwood had not forgotten us, despite the temptations he and his staffers must have had to party all night. The order, with carefully prescribed routing, finally came, and we were immediately out of there, traveling on the surface.

Once past the Tsushima mine barrier, with a few stops as we went along (Guam, Pearl Harbor, Panama), we voyaged all the way to New London, Connecticut. As she entered the Thames River there, *Piper* claimed the honor of being the last submarine home from the war, and we flew a huge homeward-bound pennant, longer than the ship, from our highest periscope. Even though the end of it dragged in the water, it made for a joyous home-coming, marred in my own case only by mischance. Not anticipating war's end so soon, Ingrid and I had planned for our own homecoming to take place in California, where she had rented a cottage for ourselves and little Inga, born just before the surrender, and there I flew as quickly as I could be authorized the necessary leave and travel vouchers. A little distance, and a little delay, lessened our personal celebration not one whit.

The blow fell a couple of weeks after my leave expired. I was back in New London, beginning what I conceived as the job that now needed to be done: meshing wartime submarine practices, which at all costs should not be forgotten, with the problems of running the submarine force during peacetime. This, it seemed to me, would be obvious. I expected formal conferences, many informal discussions, in short the continuance of wartime professional exchanges about submarining (the most important thing we could possibly be doing, in my estimate). It would take place at a more leisurely pace than before, and not over liquor at the Pearl Harbor bar or in a Royal Hawaiian Hotel room, but as part of our duties now that we had the time to sort things out more carefully. The untold stories, many exchanged over drinks at the submarine base bars at Pearl Harbor, Midway, Brisbane, Perth, and Guam, would now be aired, dissected, put together into a new U.S. Navy submarine compendium of study and tradition that could only lead to better effectiveness. We could not lose what we had learned during the war. It was mandatory to assemble it, make it useful to future submariners; and the camaraderie we had found during those tremendous years would be one of the sustaining factors.

All submariners of the war would be a part of this great and obviously needed effort, I naively thought.

The reality turned out to be exactly the opposite. The war was over. The country wanted to return to peacetime, and to most individuals this meant the conditions before it began. Now, many years later, I am wondering whether elements of our prewar isolationism, the discredited America First movement, the whole gamut of national opposition to our getting into the "European war," as it was called, may not have lain dormant and now begun asserting themselves. There were instances of exuberant returning servicemen being set upon by civilian toughs, some perhaps fearing for their jobs, others driven by a complex of emotions they could not have been able to analyze.

The instantaneous and disorderly disbanding of our victorious Army in Europe was one example of this sentiment, and it affected the Navy as well. I delivered a talk to my crew in the *Piper* as we were returning from the Sea of Japan to the effect that although we had won the war we now had to "win the peace," and there was still a lot to do. We should not expect all to go straight home. There would still be a great deal of sorting out, I told them, and it was my impression that everyone on board agreed that this made sense and had to be true.

When we arrived at Pearl it turned out not to be true at all. My crew, virtually without exception, found themselves each with enough "points" to go home immediately. Their only problem was transportation. I was able to keep them aboard only because our sub had been designated for New London: a long but easy ride home. In fact, we off-loaded torpedoes and crammed in extra submarine sailors who were delighted to earn passage by bunking where the "fish" had been and standing watches for which they were qualified, thus easing that part of the load for all on board.

But the worst was my discovery that all my half-formed ideas about the postwar Navy were just that: half-formed and half-baked. So far as I could see, no one else was thinking as I was; or, to be more fair about it, all of us probably tried to conceal the disappointment. Peacetime, to the Navy, meant that prewar procedures were back in force. Wartime experience was of no importance. Despite my 12 war patrols and record of damage to the enemy, the criterion for command of a fleet submarine during peacetime had reverted to pure seniority, and I did not have enough of it. Everyone, regardless of his deserts, was to be treated according to where he stood on the Navy list.

The submarine for which I had worked so hard was given to another who, despite seniority on the Navy list, had not made many war patrols and none at all of any distinction. And I received orders to Washington, D.C., to begin a tour of shore duty.

Chapter Nine

Helping Rickover

In Washington I found myself assigned as aide to Vice Adm. Louis Denfeld, Chief of Naval Personnel—truly a top-ranking post, though how lucky
I was to draw this assignment I had no idea for some time. I had never been
"aide" to anyone, nor had my war service ever put me in contact with someone who had been—at least, to my knowledge. I had never thought about
being aide to an admiral, especially in peacetime in the Navy Department
in Washington. Had we still been at war and were I to have been assigned
to ComSubPac as *his* aide, I might have had some ideas about what I should
be doing. Not in Washington, with the war at an end, the peacetime pursuit of pulling everything in the Navy back together in full swing. In short,
I had not the slightest idea of what my duties as an aide to the Chief of Naval
Personnel might be.

The man I relieved was not much help, being himself a reserve officer several years older than I who was anxious to return to his neglected business
in Georgia and the social life that went with it. Our backgrounds were so
dissimilar that, although he did his best in the short time we had, I "took
aboard" only about 10 percent of the turnover he gave me. In short, though
I tried hard enough, I really don't think I was the ideal aide.

I soon found, however, that the basic answer to my basic question was:
"Whatever the old man wants." Every admiral was different from every other,
and it was up to me to discover and adjust to my own admiral's needs. So
much was going on in Washington, and in the Navy at that particular time,
that everyone was simply feeling his way along, just as I was.

Fortune favored me, however. Although my background in the small ships
in which I had served since graduation from the Naval Academy—one old

destroyer in the North Atlantic and three submarines on Pacific war patrols—did little to fit me for the ways of Navy bureaucracy, Washington was not inimical. It was only intimidating. Gradually (too slowly, I sometimes felt), I found my way.

Denfeld was then one of the most powerful officers in the Navy, and held one of the most important posts, the one, in fact, that Admiral Nimitz had held in 1941, from which he was sent to Pearl Harbor to relieve the unfortunate Admiral Kimmel. I had no idea of the privilege that had been given me. Being aide to the important Chief of Naval Personnel was probably the most plum assignment of shore duty that a lieutenant commander of my age could have aspired to. Not only did I have access to naval information that no one else of my grade could have had, it was a great pleasure to work for Denfeld, whom I found to be a very human person despite his high rank. It was heartwarming to me to be able to feel that I was of assistance to him.

I was in that job a year and a half, until Denfeld left Washington to become commander-in-chief of the U.S. Fleet in Pearl Harbor (Kimmel's and Nimitz's old job). With a wife, baby daughter, and the little brick house in Arlington we had had to buy to find living quarters, I wanted to stay where I was a little longer. In addition, I had become interested in the idea that it might be possible to design a nuclear-powered submarine. At this stage, such a craft was only a gleam in the eyes of (sub)visionaries, but one of my fond memories of my father was the time he held up a glass of water at the dinner table to proclaim that it contained more than enough energy, if it could be released, to drive the *Leviathan,* then the biggest oceanliner in the world, clear across the Atlantic Ocean and back.

I couldn't conceive he might be right at the time, and of course had no concept of what he was saying. He had probably read an early scientific treatise that happened to hit the nail of the future rather squarely on the head, except for the fact that uranium and water are rather significantly different.

The atom bomb had, however, changed many things in the United States as well as in Japan, and as aide to Denfeld I had seen some of the truly far-reaching thinking that was then going on. I was not the only dreamer wondering whether the tremendous power of the atom could be harnessed in more ways than only in fearsome weapons. When someone in the Atomic Defense Section of the Chief of Naval Operations' OpNav staff suggested that a nuclear-powered submarine was in the thinking stage and that I might consider moving over to them, I was convinced that this was the wave of the future, and where I wanted to be.

The move involved quite a comedown from the handsome space I had occupied in the anteroom to Denfeld's office. With my new duty assignment, I received a desk in one of the buried boroughs in "Main Navy" on Constitution Avenue. This masonry building, built as a "temporary" structure for World War I, looked substantial enough, and actually rather handsome from the street view, but over the years it had become quite a rabbit warren of meandering, unimpressive, brick wings in back. So had the Army's identical Munitions Building alongside, also facing Constitution Avenue. Although both encroached on the plaza Major L'Enfant had planned to extend from the Capitol westward that included the Washington Monument and ultimately terminated in the Lincoln Memorial, the proximity to the center of power in the nation's capital caused their retention in service long past their originally intended lives—and even these were not long enough for the exigencies of World War II, 20 years later. Still in place when I arrived were truly temporary, wooden extensions, erected in the early shadows of World War II. Some of them were on the far side of the big, shallow Reflecting Pool in front of the Lincoln Memorial, and were connected to the Army-Navy buildings on Constitution Avenue by an enclosed overhead walkway, standing on stilts in the water. Today, the functions of all these buildings have been transferred mostly to the massive Pentagon on the other side of the Potomac River, or to moderately high-rise office buildings extending along the Jefferson Davis Highway. The entire masonry complex fronting on Constitution Avenue, and all the nondescript wooden buildings nearby, plus some nearer the White House and gracing other parks, have been replaced, without dissent from anyone, by a handsome manmade lake and the now famous Vietnam and Korean War memorials.

The Atomic Defense Section of the Navy Department, known technically as "Op-36," meaning that it was the sixth portion of "Op-03," the Fleet Operations part of OpNav, as the office of the Chief of Naval Operations was known, was hidden in three or four side rooms in one of Main Navy's many back halls where policy had been hammered out for decades. I reported in with some enthusiasm for what I thought was to be the direction of my duties only to find that there was no such overall direction. I was the only submariner in all of Op-36! No one there had any background in submarines except myself. Everyone was very much at sea in his own world. Even the officer who had recruited me seemed to be somewhat in doubt as to his own duties. Possibly, I later reflected, I was intended to be the Resident Submariner, a placebo to keep the rest of the Navy believing that progress toward a nuclear engine for submarines was really being achieved.

The function of Op-36, I gradually began to realize, was really, and solely, to ensure the Navy's continued viability in the atom bomb business. Nuclear weapons were still very much of a mystery. Everyone, of course, knew the terrible destruction they could wreak. The purpose of our office was not technical development, but political. The Navy was in the fight of its life against a newly independent Air Force whose drive for its own hegemony had just been won. Full of powerful and energetic officers, the Air Force was now insisting on operational control of all aspects of the nuclear weapon. This had been true during the war, ran the argument; why change it now?

The Navy's concept was that it had fully participated in the Manhattan Project that had developed the atom bomb, naval officers were in technical "command" of both bombs that were used on Japan and flew in the B-29s that delivered them, and that use of Army Air Corps planes for the purpose was a logical necessity at the time but only incidental to the much larger question of deployment of nuclear weapons in the future. The Atomic Energy Act specified that only the president of the United States could authorize use of nuclear weapons, and if this became again imperative he manifestly should be able to employ whatever means existed to best carry out that purpose.

The argument went on that aircraft carriers could carry nuclear weapons and handle the planes to deliver them as well as the Air Force could, in some cases maybe better. Aircraft flying from carriers were already carrying bombs of equivalent weight. Their attack mission profiles would be much smaller than those of the super-long-range B-29s, and better protected. They would not have to fly as far and could be escorted by fighter aircraft from the same carrier or from other carriers in the same task force. They were consequently less vulnerable to enemy fighter planes, could be equally effective and at the same time smaller, more efficient, less obvious to enemy radar. Everyone and everything in our Atomic Defense shop was subordinate to the Navy's need to refute the Air Force contention that it alone should be the service responding to presidential directives for the employment of this tremendous new weapon.

In Op-36, our concerns were only slightly related to the new carrier from which such aircraft would fly, although we did have some particular ideas about the special magazine in the bowels of the ship where the fearsome weapons would be stowed. Mainly we spent our time refuting Air Force arguments against allowing the bombs aboard ship at all. The many penetrating congressional rules regarding access to nuclear weapons and their protection from accident or sabotage, most of them enacted since the end of the war, some of them bearing obvious marks of hurry, had either to be carefully carried out or strenuously opposed with proposals for new legislation and reasons why changes needed to be made. Much thought was given to the arrangements by which the specially mandated presidential orders for use of the weapon could be received, verified, and then carried out with speed and certitude.

One of the biggest questions from the very beginning was over the possibility that some maverick commander, in a ship at sea, isolated beyond reach of anything except radio, might take matters into his own hands and shoot off nuclear-tipped missiles in the mistaken idea of solving the world's problems by initiating the destruction of half of it. Because of its modern twist of plot, and unflagging media interest in the idea, far more thought has been expended over this scenario than it deserves. The theme, in one form or another, crops up even today, almost at regular intervals, in movies or TV shows, while people who know something about the business silently writhe in their chairs—or more likely, flip their TV remote controls to another channel.

From the beginning of the Manhattan District, early in the war, the "doomsday" nature of the atom bomb, if it could be achieved, was fully recognized. From the beginning, the Bomb has embodied the concept that only the commander-in-chief could order its use. The practical fact today is that until the right coded message comes in, no unit commander anywhere, at sea, in an aircraft, or isolated in a missile silo in the desert, knows or can figure out the entries to put into the bomb's computers. Without these it is inert. It cannot explode. In military jargon, it is "unarmed."

If dropped for any reason, an unarmed bomb might alert an enemy as to the depth of our research. It would be a coup of the highest magnitude for the wrong parties to recover it, and it would surely be dissected by experts with the proverbial fine-toothed comb. In the wrong context, it might possibly even start a nuclear war, and in any case it would doubtless give potential enemies fissionable material they might find useful. These were among the reasons why the accidental dropping of two bombs into the Mediterranean Sea during the height of the Cold War produced the tremendous—and successful—recovery effort it did.

The procedures involved in arming an atomic bomb are among the most highly classified in the world. In the two specially configured B-29s that were used against Hiroshima and Nagasaki, only the "bomb commanders," both naval officers, were able to arm the bombs.

In our Op-36 Atomic Defense shop, we had nothing to do with the details of the proposed carrier (they belonged in what was formerly the Bureau of Construction and Repair, now known as the Bureau of Ships), except in one single area. Our involvement had to do strictly with the nuclear weapons that the ship would carry—and, little by little, I slowly became aware of what an immense chore the Navy had taken on. Far better than ever before, I began to understand not only that the atom bomb was the most unimaginably fearsome weapon anyone could conceive of, but that we in the Navy were fighting for the capability to deploy it because the Navy's whole future hung on it. Even to a nonpolitical being like me, the rivalry with our Air Force hung over everything. Whichever agency controlled the nuclear weapon also controlled our entire defense establishment. So we thought at the time, and the years following have proved how right that assessment was.

As the most junior member of the Op-36 Section of the Navy Department, I could not in any way influence events in this arena. They were far beyond my knowledge and understanding, but I could see some of the things going on around me. For example, at the desk adjacent to mine, specifics for the first aircraft designed to fly with a nuclear weapon from a pitching flight deck at sea, and return on board with it if it was not expended, began to take shape. I had thought airplanes were designed by experts in ivory towers; maybe that was true, but the basic characteristics of this particular plane—determination of its operational requirements—were put together virtually at the desk next to mine. Not being a naval aviator, I understood very little of what was going on, but the occupant of that desk would occasionally show me what he was doing. Essentially, he was calculating the required performance factors for the airframe that would carry the bomb off the deck of the new carrier. The plane would have to be developed at the same time as the ship, and would need to be ready when the ship and the weapon were.

The new aircraft carrier, too, the one that would carry the arsenal of atomic weapons its planes would be able to use, was far beyond my ken. I knew next to nothing about designing or building any ship other than a submarine, and obviously all the real design work on the carrier was being done elsewhere; but in our little office there was much careful research carried out on how to handle nuclear weapons at sea, and this involved design of their stowage and handling.

We were working on basic things (it seemed to me) that would affect not only the Navy's future but also that of the entire country. The new carrier would be the biggest ship our Navy had yet built, or projected, in fact the largest and heaviest warship in the world, bigger and faster than Japan's famous battleships *Yamato* and *Musashi* of the war just ended. The careers of both of these had been ended (appropriately) by naval aircraft of the same

general types as those that had begun the war by sinking our battleships at
Pearl Harbor. This was fine, for they were already obsolete when launched,
and they deserved to be sunk because of Pearl Harbor. Our new aircraft carrier would be the new "queen of battles," and she would be the greatest warship ever built. In recognition of her value to the postwar scheme of things,
she would be given the historic and honored name of *United States*, borne
only once before by a ship of the U.S. Navy.

The name had been selected with the greatest care. It would be the finest
name that could be bestowed by the U.S. Navy, used only once before by
one of our earliest frigates, one that had distinguished herself under Commo.
Stephen Decatur in the War of 1812. The new *United States* would epitomize
everything our Navy had stood for during our entire national history, everything we hoped for the future.

Sometime around this period I also began to wonder what my mission in
the Atomic Defense Section was supposed to be, since there was clearly no
submarine interest anywhere in it.

By this time a certain Capt. Hyman G. Rickover, in the Bureau of Ships,
about eight corridors away from where I had my desk, had begun to be
talked about as researching possibilities for building a nuclear-powered submarine. The idea appealed to me, in addition to seeming within the scope of
my assignment to the Atomic Defense Section, and so I went out of my way
to seize whatever opportunities there were to listen to what he had to say. He
had been a submariner, though (probably just as well) never in command of a
submarine, had transferred in mid-career to the designation of Engineering
Duty Only, and had acquired acclaim and reputation during the war for
being the driving force behind restoration of the big electric main propulsion drive motors of the *West Virginia* and *California,* that had been submerged in muddy harbor water and fuel oil for weeks after the battleships
had been so ignominiously sunk at Pearl Harbor.

No one believed electric motors immersed for months in the Pearl Harbor
mess could be restored; yet Rickover, in charge of the Electrical Section of
the Bureau of Ships, had done it. Between patrols, when it was the *Trigger's*
turn to refit at Pearl Harbor instead of Midway, I had become accustomed
to seeing the ship my father had launched at Mare Island 20 years ago, now
lying, so terribly diminished, broadside to us at the navy yard dock across
from the submarine base.

Submariners spent little time looking across the bay, but I felt a special
relationship to that unfortunate battleship, once the pride of the fleet. So I

looked over to her more frequently than most of my fellows. Even yet, after passage of half a century, the impression of great activity within *California's* devastated hull remains with me. In the submarine base we heard only that her main drive motors were probably not repairable, that instead of trying to clean them we should spend our money and effort ripping them out and refitting her with new and more powerful turbines, as Japan had already done with some of her own older battlewagons.

To this, the man in charge of the repairs, then unknown to us, apparently paid no attention. And one day, the horribly battered battleship that had once been the pride of the Pacific Fleet belched smoke and steam from her stacks (she still had two at that time), and with the aid of tugs breasted out from her quay at the navy yard. Water churned under her stern, and slowly, under her own power, she got under way for the Puget Sound Navy Yard. It must have been a proud moment for the men who had restored her main propulsion motors, and particularly for the Engineering Duty Only Commander in charge, whose name, someone told me, was "Rick something."

I first met Captain Rickover not long after arriving in Main Navy, and after hearing at least one of his discourses, I thought it was perhaps my duty to exercise some initiative in the office to which I belonged. I had certainly contributed nothing to the airplane design initiative it was so strongly supporting. Maybe I should do a little initiating on my own. So, expecting my bosses would welcome my industry in a direction I at least knew something about, I drew up a proposal for a nuclear-powered submarine. It was a very rough idea, for I knew nothing at all about nuclear energy (nor did anyone else at that time, except Rickover). I did see that a single source of power needing no air for combustion of fuel was perfect for submarines that up to then had been confined to low-powered and extremely heavy storage batteries for propulsion while in the submerged condition. Hydroelectric plants, impracticable for ships at sea, were the only big power sources then existing that did not require tremendous quantities of air for combustion of fuel, upon which all ships depended.

The big electric storage batteries powering submarines when submerged also required no air (or oxygen), but they gave a very small amount of horsepower in return for the great size and weight involved. Additionally, this was only for a very short time, and they required daily recharge by the heavy diesel engines submarines also had to carry. In a sense, even their electric propulsion system required ordinary fuel, because the batteries needed to be recharged every night. Submarines, in point of fact, needed two complete and separate powerplants, one diesel and one electric; but the electric plant, mandatory for submerged operation, besides being extraordinarily heavy was also extremely short-ranged and good only for very slow speed.

Nuclear energy promised far more power, in less weight and space, than could possibly be crammed into a submarine in more conventional ways. An experimental atomic "Pile" at Oak Ridge, Tennessee, could theoretically make steam, or even electricity, I'd learned somewhere (probably from Rickover), and it seemed to me that this might be explored.

All this I embodied in my "tentative draft proposal," and submitted it to the head of the Atomic Defense Section, the greatly admired Adm. William S. "Deak" Parsons. He had been the arming officer in command of the Hiroshima bomb, had made emergency final adjustments to it during that epochal flight, and was now my direct superior. I believed this would show him that the lone submariner in his shop was at least trying to earn his pay.

His reaction to my paper was astonishing. I was called in to his private office and summarily raked over the coals for even thinking this way. An atomic submarine would come in due course, he said. The "Daniels Pile" at Oak Ridge was only some theorist's brainchild. It did not exist in any useful form. It was necessary first to build a bigger pile, then test it thoroughly to prove what was so far only an idea. In 10 or 15 years this might happen, not before, and if I didn't believe it I could go see Dr. Enrico Fermi, the nuclear scientist who had built the first atomic pile in the stadium in Chicago and ask him directly. Furthermore, if I persisted in this train of thought my usefulness to him would be ended.

The hackneyed phrase "I could not believe my ears" is the only one that even closely approximates that moment. I was literally on the carpet (standing on it in front of his desk), and he, his voice only a notch or so below an actual shout, was firing broadsides at me from all directions. It was as though I had done something terribly wrong. The picture sticking in my mind is that he was standing, too, or perhaps pacing back and forth behind his desk. An intellectually brilliant officer, one of the most highly regarded men in the Navy, top class in every way, he couldn't have surprised me more if he had come after me with a club!

I have since decided there must have been something else seriously bothering him at the moment, for the entire episode was uncharacteristic of the man I had come to know and admire—but I never learned what it might have been. When he finally dismissed me, I slunk away knowing the nuclear sub was not ever to be brought up, at least not to him.

As my initial hurt and puzzlement subsided, I was also struck by the incongruous idea he had expressed of my seeking out Enrico Fermi. That was one for the books. Dr. Fermi was one of the top scientists in the country, justly famous for building the first atomic pile under the football stadium stand at the University of Chicago, and having been in the forefront of the development of the atomic weapons that had ended the war with Japan. What would be his reaction to a request for an audience from a lieutenant commander in the Navy who didn't even know the lingo? I mentally played over how I would introduce myself, and recall chuckling at the thought of how ridiculous I would seem to him as, very privately indeed, I described the incident to Ingrid.

One thing did come out of the episode, however. In spite of his strange reaction to my effort, Parsons had not retracted his informal permission, given weeks previously, to pursue my contact with Captain Rickover. I soon had occasion to wonder even more about this lapse. As Parsons's tongue lashing started to wind down I was expecting such an order. It was not likely that he had forgotten. Not rescinding his previously given permission at this moment must have been deliberate, not a lapse. He may have surmised that Rickover might actually have had something to do with my idea in the first place, or even suggested it (he didn't; it was original with me, although far behind Rickover's own effort, as I was to discover). Parsons was known as an absolutely straightforward, honorable person. I was never able to guess what lay behind his strange treatment of me that day. He must have been under heavy pressure from some other source.

The next thing that happened, while I was still smarting over the reception I had received, was a summons from Rickover. In what I was beginning to learn was his usual way of dealing with people, he wasted no time with introductory niceties, said not a word about Parsons, asked nothing of my painful interview with him—and yet, all these intervening years, I have been convinced he knew all about it. Instead—and this, too, I was to learn was his normal mannerism—he greeted me with a sharp query: "Do you know what they put you in Op-36 for?" was his salutation.

"Yessir," I said. "I'm to represent submarines there."

"Right! Have you done it?"

"Yes," I said, "as well as I can."

"The hell you have! You were sent there to build a nuclear submarine. Have you done that?"

I felt like laughing. Op-36 had been heavily involved with the atom bomb business. Everyone in our office was pursuing the design for a plane that could handle such a weapon in the ways we had learned during the war, operating from a yet-to-be-built aircraft carrier. I was the only submariner in it. Certainly I could not have "built" a submarine of any kind, or even have begun to design one, during the short time I had been there. Maybe Captain Rickover felt I should have done more than merely "propose" a course of action to my boss. How could he have learned of my recent effort in this direction, I wondered.

Whatever his source of private information, Rickover did not think his question incongruous. "Well?" he barked at me.

I had already learned a few things about him, one being that junior officers had to tread carefully. Ridiculous or not, Rickover was not one to laugh at, and he gave few opportunities to laugh with him. "Well, no, sir," I said.

"So! You were sent there to build an atomic submarine, and you've not done it! Do you think that's carrying out your orders? I thought you were a submarine driver, that you had some gumption! What have you done with your time there?"

To this I had no answer, for it was clear that, so far, I had accomplished nothing at all. It would be disloyal to my boss to tell Rickover of my recent effort and its untoward outcome. Besides, clearly there were things going on of which I knew nothing. To my embarrassed admission of this, but without details about my failure so far, "Rick," as he was informally known (but not to his face), said nothing, and my recollection of the interview ended at that point.

Since then, I've wondered whether there might have been some connection between these two extraordinary encounters. Parsons and Rickover had been classmates at the Naval Academy. Totally different in temperament and method, they were not likely to have been close friends then or later, but in 1948 they could not have been unaware of each other's interest in the atom. Could Parsons and Rickover have had a set-to over me? They were in totally different lines of endeavor. I had stayed in channels. Even if Parsons disagreed with my approach to building a nuclear submarine, I could see no conflict between them that I might have caused, or, even today, any logic behind his categorical dismissal of my little idea.

Parsons, the Navy's foremost atom bomb expert, was for getting the Navy fully into the atom bomb delivery business, and this was mainly political. The bomb had been already built and proved. The big argument at that time, which the Navy finally won, was whether the newly created Air Force should gain control over all phases of the nuclear weapon itself. Not mentioned at all, anywhere in the vociferous media discussion of the issue, was that although the two aircraft carrying the nuclear weapons that ended World War II belonged to the Air Force (Army Air Corps at the time), the two bomb commanders, one in each specially configured B-29, were (then) Capt. William S. Parsons and Cdr. Frederick L. Ashworth, both of the U.S. Navy, and each in full charge of his own bomb. In the parlance created by the Manhattan District, they were the "bomb commanders." They were not pilots of the planes nor, to be technically specific, were they the "aircraft commanders." Both of these were specially trained officers of the Army Air Corps. Parsons and Ashworth were in personal charge of the bombs. No one else in the planes could even touch them.

Parsons was not even a naval aviator (Ashworth was). Command of the weapons, however, meaning all basic decisions concerning them except point of aim, was exercised by these two men, who had been with their bombs since before construction began. Now, when I knew him, Rear Admiral Parsons was the most knowledgeable man in the Navy personnel arsenal regarding the atom bomb, and in that parlous time of our history it was natural that he be in charge of the Navy's effort to retain at least some nuclear capability in the face of the determination of the Air Force to grab it all. He was, in fact, at the cutting edge of what later became known as the "Revolt of the Admirals," and had he not died prematurely of a heart attack much more would have been heard from him.

Rickover was virtually Parsons's antithesis: unpopular where Parsons was popular, doggedly and drivingly studious where Parsons was brilliant; a difficult, unpleasant goader of men instead of a leader, as Parsons was. Early in his career Rickover had been a submarine officer, served several years in the prewar S-boats, but when it came time for the submarine desk in the then–Bureau of Navigation (later Bureau of Personnel) to parcel out the submarine commands to Rickover's peer group, he was left out. No reason was given, except that there were insufficient boats to satisfy all aspirants to submarine command, so some had to be disappointed.

Within the submarine force, however, among those in the know, the story was different: Rickover was a perfectionist who drove everyone wild. His crew in the *S-48*, of which he was second in command, hated him. Not one of them—crew members or brother officers, and this included his skipper—could see that Rickover was also trying to make their boat more efficient, safer to operate, something they could be proud of. All they knew was that they would rather be anywhere else than under him.

They were, in fact, not at all proud of *S-48,* and with reason. She, the biggest of the S-boats, enlarged on the ways before she was launched, had never run well. Possibly intended to be the forerunner of the extremely successful "fleet boats" that won the Pacific submarine war for us, among the prewar submarines she was a total failure. She was different from all others in her S-boat class, not as fast, not dependable in performance, never came close to operating as her designers had hoped. This may have been why Rickover was sent to her. Detailers (those in charge of officer duty assignments) may have hoped that a driving executive officer would help ferret out some of her problems and correct them. As it turned out, Rickover was not the right man for this job, though this was not through lack of trying. He had tried hard, very hard indeed. In the process he established himself as a despot who could never be satisfied. By reputation he was a maverick who knew the mechanical details of his job well enough, but could not handle men. His treatment of everyone junior to him was demeaning. Despite Rickover's best efforts, *S-48* was a mechanical nightmare during her entire service. She was a lemon from the beginning. Under Rickover as exec, she became known as a madhouse.

The thing the whole close-knit submarine force saw most prominently, or heard, was mainly the way he drove his men. He harassed them unmercifully. Everyone under his direct orders felt his lash—and while the boat's operational problems were, traditionally, kept to the reports required, there was no such control for the personal feelings that also prevailed. Among the *S-48* officers, Rickover was not a joiner, nor was he a socializer. Except when working he kept to himself, and he seemed to work all the time. He did not bother to tell anyone his "side of the story," probably figuring it would come out in the end when the boat's improved operations were noticed. No one saw things his way or sympathized with him. No one, except possibly Rickover himself, expected the submarine high command to give him a boat when his time came.

It didn't. He was "surfaced" instead, a slap in the face to a submariner. This meant that control over his duty assignments was transferred from the submarine desk to the surface ship desk, which sent him to shore duty.

Despite the disappointment, Rickover's characteristic drive was unabated. His next duty afloat was as assistant engineer officer of a battleship, in which he set himself the goal of winning the battleship engineering competition. In this he succeeded, in the process earning the captain's admiring regard but the dislike of everyone else. Stories in the fleet told of how he shut off water for showers and removed lightbulbs from all lamps but those necessary for safe operation. One yarn that gained wide currency told of his walking into the stateroom of an officer junior to him, unscrewing the lightbulb by which that individual was at that very moment reading a book, and carrying it off in his pocket. No proof was ever offered of this story, but it nevertheless had fleet-wide circulation.

The Navy finally did find a command for Rickover, and it was almost as though it had deliberately selected the poorest ship it could find: the *Finch,* an old combination minesweeper and tug on the China station. The ship was in terrible condition, as one might expect of an ancient auxiliary in the Asiatic Fleet that had been written off long ago, and would probably have been decommissioned outright had anyone thought seriously about her. Typical of Rickover, he turned to with energy to make something useful of the old tub and began a huge program (for it and its dispirited crew) of overhauling the machinery, cleaning bilges, removing rust, scraping old paint, and repainting. While the work was going on he apparently saw the handwriting on the wall and submitted his application for the newly created Engineering Duty Only status.

Inescapably, it must be that he had finally seen the direction his talents would have to go. The officers of the regular line wanted no part of him; he understood engineering, however, and was good at it. He would have to make his mark as an engineer. As a skipper turned into an EDO he was, by Navy regulation, precluded from remaining in command, and this caused his immediate transferal to the navy yard at Cavite in the Philippines. He had been but three months in command of the *Finch* and would be two years at Cavite, ending in 1939 with transfer to the Navy Department in Washington. There, as a Navy commander (EDO), he became assistant head of the Electrical Section of the newly named Bureau of Ships.

It was while he was in this capacity that I first became aware of him, though not by name. Remarkable achievements were common during the war, but even so, submariners looking across the placid waters of Pearl Harbor at the terribly damaged hulk of the once-proud battleship *California,* inside of which her main drive motors were being cleaned of the encrustation of oil and saltwater that had been there for months, knew this job, this repair, was very special. *California* and her sisters had been built with electric drive—an engineering innovation of its time for ships of their size—and everyone in the Navy had been indoctrinated with the utter destruction that would occur if either oil or saltwater was allowed in the miles of electric windings that constituted their main motors.

Among us submariners, I remember being quite certain that repair of the ships, never to be doubted even though we had begun to doubt their usefulness, simply *had* to involve new engines. In the repairs done after the Pearl Harbor attack, we were all aware that in the *California* something very difficult had been accomplished, but none of us thought much of it at the time. I was just a bit disappointed because of my personal interest in that particular battleship. I wanted her to remain in our first line, something the repair had in a sense prevented (new, much more powerful engines, giving her more speed, might have done this), and all this came back with some force when I met the man responsible.

This was, of course, only an ancillary thought, having nothing to do with the facts of 1947. When I became aware of Captain Rickover he was the only person in the Navy actively working on designing a nuclear engine for submarine propulsion. To me there was never any question of the impressive dividend submarines would get from the tremendously powerful nuclear engine he had in mind. It would never need air to produce power, and could (at this point still theoretically) produce much more of it, in a more limited space and for an infinitely longer time, than any other machinery yet thought of. I calculated such a boat could run submerged at 20 knots for 1,000 hours instead of 2 knots for 24 before running out of battery, traveling 20,000 nautical miles at very high speed instead of a maximum of about 100 at creeping speed. I dreamed that sometime I might even have command of such a vessel. (Little did I know how overwhelmingly that ambition would be realized, all accomplished by this extraordinary but strange, disliked, difficult little Navy captain—but more of this later.)

In my early dealings with Rickover, I soon began to feel that his nuclear-powered submarine, if it could be built, would revolutionize navies and seapower. Although as a character he was an unusual one, it was clear that if anyone could build such a powerplant, it would be Rickover and his people. No one else was really trying, lip-service to the contrary; he, by contrast, was giving it everything he had.

No one else, despite occasional claims, was doing anything at all. Everyone with whom I had any contact—or heard about—was trying to fend off a determined attack by the Air Force. With the exception of Rickover and his small group of dedicated people, it was as though the Navy could do nothing but react to conditions with which it was being faced, had no capability to go out and invent or originate things on its own. Probably, for the time, this assessment was fairly correct. Most of the Navy was totally obsessed with the Air Force threat.

The Army, faced with an earlier but somewhat similar problem with its ever-more-powerful flying cadre, had solved the dilemma by divesting itself of its Air Corps, in actual fact helping the Corps become what it had always wanted to be: the U.S. Air Force. For the Navy, the threat was much more insidious: the Army could have the land, the Navy the sea, and the Air Corps would take air and space and everything that went with them. There was even fear, at one point, that England's disastrous experiment—of doing away with her naval air arm and putting the aircraft in her carriers under the Royal Air Force—would be replicated in our own Navy. To persons obsessed with organizational charts, this may have had some appeal; to naval officers who had seen action in the war, especially those charged with operating combat carriers, this would have been a sure way to lose the war against the wonderfully effective task forces deployed by the Imperial Japanese Navy.

The Navy, of course, did not agree with the Air Force proposal. Naval aviators had had a lot to do with winning the Pacific war, arguably more than the Air Corps bombing raids of its later years. Naval aviation would be equally important in the next war. It simply *had* to stay in business, and this involved access to any and all weapons that might help resolve any future war.

This was understandable. With growing dismay, however, I had to admit to myself that the whole thrust of my atomic defense division was atomic bombs, not powerplants for ships of any kind. My bosses there were apparently willing that I, as its only submariner, should maintain liaison with the Bureau of Ships and the difficult little captain with a steel-trap mind it had put in charge of nuclear power, but that was about all. My superiors were interested in naval air power to the exclusion of everything else. Undersea boats were far down the pike. So far as they were concerned, there was no incentive to divert their energies into submarine propulsion.

For myself, I realized that to get the submarine I thought we should have, I would have to throw my lot 100 percent in with Rickover, and this, little by little, I found myself doing. It was not long before I was "moonlighting" for him all over the Main Navy building. During this period I was his only working contact in OpNav. Rickover could go the high road, through his bureaucratic superior, the chief of the Bureau of Ships—and did so whenever this suited his purpose. More often his way of working was to go the "low" road: get Beach—and probably others too—to haul his chestnuts around Main Navy and then, depending on what happened, and on what level, he would deal with the results. It was a heady time for me. If there were brickbats tossed my way I don't think I even noticed them.

I spent an indoctrination week at Oak Ridge to learn some of the basics, and innumerable hours trotting around the halls of Main Navy in obedience to Rickover's bidding. It was rewarding, because I could see plans for the powerplant, a reactor to make steam and powerful turbines to use it, beginning to take shape. Day by day I could feel my enthusiasm growing. But it was difficult to keep my superiors happy with my increasing involvement with maverick Rickover. He, of course, took no notice of any of the official protocol by which lesser men were bound, with which I was having my difficulties. On the contrary, he relished every chance to show superiority to it, often impatiently summoning me to drop whatever official duties I happened to be doing at the time.

Thus it was that one day I found myself deputized by Rickover to "help get the right message" to Admiral Nimitz, then the Chief of Naval Operations. I was, after all, the submarine representative for nuclear power in Main Navy. There was no one else; Rickover's gang was entirely in the Bureau of Ships. Admiral Nimitz, well known as a dyed-in-the-wool submariner, had a couple of times gone out of his way to show friendliness to a junior lieutenant commander named Beach, whose father he had known in years past.

Clay Blair and Ted Rockwell, in their respective books, came pretty close to telling it right. As a member of the CNO's OpNav staff, I had official access to him, knew he held friendly feelings toward me (as, it might be noted, he did for all young officers trying to do their best), and they thought I might understand what might turn him on as an old submariner himself. The idea of a submarine able to go 20 knots for 1,000 hours of continuous submerged running was bound to appeal to Nimitz. So, although Rickover and his staff, in particular my close friends and Academy classmates Louis Roddis and Jim Dunford, had most to do with it, some of the words in my aborted proposal to Admiral Parsons months earlier found their way into the draft letter, prepared for his signature, that I carried to Nimitz. The result of all this is well known today, and like all of us, I am pleased to recall the small part I was able to play in causing it to come to pass.

This was the period when Rickover, always unpopular with his colleagues, was (supposedly by accident) put in an office that had formerly been a ladies' room and had been given the barest of conversions. It still had its tile walls, and you could see plaster plugging up the holes where some of the fixtures had hung. One day I received my usual sudden summons from my unofficial boss; as usual he was in a hurry, and as usual I simply ran through the many halls, made a number of right and left turns, and flung the door open into his anteroom. The route was well known to me—I had been there enough times—but the back halls in Main Navy were many and narrow, and all alike. This time my count of the right and left turns was wrong by one. The numbers on the doors were different, but I had long stopped paying much attention to these. In short, I got into the wrong hall, and ran, full speed ahead, into a real ladies' room!

It was occupied, too. Two or three women were looking into mirrors and doing things to their faces, but that was all I saw, and all I can remember. I clearly recall having the presence of mind not to continue, as I had been intending, on through the next door, the one that led to what should have been Captain Rickover's room, and a good thing, too, considering what was no doubt there. Persons familiar with movie cartoons will recall how, in circumstances like these, the characters' feet rotate furiously backward long before forward motion ceases. So was it with my own real feet, but I managed to get them back into contact with the floor, and myself very quickly indeed back out the door I had just burst through. The women at the mirrors never had a chance even to turn their heads to see what was going on, for which I was grateful, and I discovered that Rickover did have a sense of humor, for there was a small smile when I told him of my adventure.

Chapter Ten

New Submarines, Professional Success, and Family Tragedy

Duty in Main Navy right after the war might have been called "exciting," could one have looked ahead to what was in truth going on. The Navy's battle with the Air Force was in full swing. Congress was in the act with a vengeance, and although it was understood that the fight was not between military enemies but between friends who had been on the same side in the great fighting war against the Axis, it was also a battle between competing military ideologies—and the lines of combat in this different arena were drawn every bit as strong. Combat was not waged with weapons of the sort we had been trained in, however, but in the intellect, between differing concepts of what was needed for the common defense of our country. For all that, it was a bitter fight. There was a lot of shooting of words, if not of bullets and bombs, and some of them were well and carefully aimed. At their base was awareness that the real competition was for national approbation and the congressional dollar.

No one opposed the idea that the president of the United States was the only person who could order use of the terrible nuclear weapon with which we terminated the war with Japan, but the decision as to which of the military services he should turn in that extremity was also very important. That service, in everyone's estimate, would be preeminent among our defense forces. This is, of course, by no means an overall summary. A host of other considerations growing out of World War II also entered the equation, and so did personal ambitions of high-ranking officers and civilians, whom the war had produced in plenty.

Resulting animosities among the senior officers of the two services most involved in the controversy were often reflected downward to the more junior ones like me, with the consequence that the Air Force became the new enemy our Navy had to face. The rivalry inevitably produced rhetoric that, in some cases, would have been better targeted against the Axis with which we had been so recently in hot war; it was not conducive to the better management of our new Department of Defense, nor of the Cold War with the Soviet Union that was just beginning. It was, in fact, a "cold war" of its own, closer to hand and more immediate than the distant one against Russia. The caustic remarks it produced were far more direct than what we heard through the newspapers or radio newscasters about the Soviets.

This was the atmosphere in the office I inhabited. Far more invective was heard there, aimed at the U.S. Air Force, than aimed anywhere else, including the Soviet Union. By the same token, what we heard of Air Force invective against the Navy seemed at least as bad. In those days the Russians by comparison seemed to be out of the loop of controversy, at least to my eyes and ears; they certainly operated much farther away than the Air Force from the circles I moved in.

More than once, in those days, I blessed nuclear energy for the diversion of effort it afforded me. Apparently, Captain Rickover, because of my success in getting one important early letter to Admiral Nimitz's attention, looked on me as an adjunct to his office, as well as one of his low-level entry points into OpNav. His frequent calls for my services were as unpredictable as his nature or his state of mind. I reacted automatically, almost gladly, even though my own senior boss had rather explicitly told me of his displeasure (without, however, forbidding my slightly clandestine activity).

To a large degree, Rickover worked alone. He received nominal institutional support from his parent organization, the Bureau of Ships, because its head (in my view at least) had too many other things on his mind to trouble himself about the unusual activities of an unpopular Engineering Duty Only captain of Russian-Jewish descent. At Rickover's own importunation, he had been given the job of riding herd on nuclear energy for the time being, the chief of the bureau no doubt expecting that if the idea proved useful there would be adequate opportunity in due time to bring it into the mainstream of BuShips operations. No one could foresee that the energy of the atom would become so important that whoever controlled it would in time become the most important man in the Navy. Nor did the chief realize that atomic energy, under the control of a maverick naval officer, would also be useful to Congress in its enduring purpose to bend all segments of our military to its political will.

But even if these two points had been rightly evaluated, no one could possibly have anticipated that the organization this very same underestimated Rickover would build, given the opportunity, would totally overshadow the Bureau of Ships and all the successive chiefs thereof. Nor that Rickover—remaining an unprecedented 36 years in that special assignment from which no one could dislodge him—in personal fame, recognition, and reward would become the most outstanding naval man of his time.

The breaking of ground for nuclear energy came at one of the extraordinary confluences of world history: the ending of a terrible war that led to a surge of scientific and technical knowledge the like of which would have boggled the mind a few years before. It brought to civilization an electronic revolution that is still going on, that may never end, and that will change everything in the world before it is over if it hasn't already.

Not only has this electronic revolution brought tremendous change to submarines, it has done the same in all our naval ships. It is not confined to nuclear power, but it controls it, as it controls everything except, perhaps, preparation of meals. Its effect has grown so that it now encompasses everything we do, the very air we breathe; it pervades everything to the point where there is very serious thought, in high and abstruse places, about whether mankind may not today be going too far, too fast, and in too many directions in too short a time.

Such philosophical thoughts will be developed by others better equipped to do so. They deserve mention in a book devoted to my personal observations of changes in our Navy only to show that some naval officers, too, occasionally wonder about these things. It is fair, however, to note that such changes are only part of an all-encompassing, sweeping revolution going on everywhere, in what the future will probably term the most earthshaking time of mankind on this planet.

One incidental effect it has had has been the unprecedented aggrandizement of the man responsible for only an incidental portion of the tremendous changes we see today. It has lifted him to levels that were incomprehensible to any members of the Navy of 1948. Of all its important personages, he, more than any other, must be regarded as having surfaced at just the right time, in the right place, and with the right ideas.

Among my fellows, I can truly lay claim to having been one of those to imagine where he was leading our submarines, but it is silly to suggest that any-one in the postwar decades could have foreseen the position Hyman George Rickover, a despised captain in its engineer corps, would attain in our Navy.

In 1948 there came a break to my shore duty when the seniority system finally decided I had attained enough of it to command a submarine in peace-time. Just as the nuclear-power business began to heat up in earnest, I received orders to the new "guppy" submarine *Amberjack,* based in Key West, Florida.

Perhaps I should have stayed where I was, in the Atomic Defense Section of OpNav, for indeed one of my successors, whom I was able to procure for the continuation of my submarine function there, became even more involved with Rickover than I had been and grew to be one of the leaders of his effort. But I had had insufficient rank to keep my wartime submarine command; to get her back, or a first-line boat like her, was an ambition I could not deny.

Amberjack was one of the first "guppy" conversions, as we referred to our fastest and best postwar subs, to become operational. She had been modified from an uncompleted wartime submarine of the latest class and had a bigger, more powerful battery and a highly streamlined superstructure. She was capa-ble, therefore, of much more submerged speed and far greater underwater cruising range than the World War II "fleet boat" from which she had been converted. Submerged, she could run 16 knots for a couple of hours, once attained an eye-catching 19 knots for a very short time, and could cruise all day at 10 or 12 knots. With her "snorkel"—air intake and engine exhaust pipes that let us run her engines to recharge batteries while submerged—we could remain under water for weeks on end. In addition, since she still retained her excellent wartime diesels, on the surface *"Amber"* was as fast as ever. What would any World War II submariner have given to have had a boat as good as this one a few years ago, I used to think.

Driving *Amber* was an unmitigated pleasure, and I found that she could do many things we never had thought of during the war. Also, I found to my dismay that many of our old submarine traditional operating methods were still in vogue, even though long out of date.

One of them was the actual process of submerging, which still involved putting air pressure inside the entire boat to test for leaks on the way down. In a leisurely submergence, "bleeding air" into a submarine hull as a final check for its watertightness was a logical test. During the war, however, the threat of air attack mandated fast diving procedures that allowed no time for it. *Trigger,* for instance, was designed to submerge in 60 seconds. But because life depended on being able to go quickly beneath the protective sea surface, we continually looked for ways to shorten the time it took her to submerge, cutting many extra holes in her superstructure to speed escape of air at the onset of submerging, for example. Ultimately, we succeeded in cutting her diving time in half.

Better venting of the superstructure, larger water-entry holes in the bottom of our ballast tanks, bigger vent valves and a bigger negative tank all went to shorten the time it took us to get our big fleet submarines under water. *Tirante*'s shortest diving time—which we routinely recorded—was 24 seconds to a keel depth of 60 feet.

Our training, however, had always involved bleeding high-pressure air into the hull the moment the last hull opening was closed, then shutting the inlet valves and watching the pressure gauges to see that the pressure did not drop. "Pressure in the boat!" would be announced, and if it did not remain steady the boat was not airtight and, therefore, could not be watertight. In such circumstances in the prewar years it was mandatory to terminate the diving procedure and go immediately to emergency surfacing action. It was forbidden to continue the dive. Instant surfacing, followed by a search for the hull opening—the valve, pipe, or hatch—that should have been shut and was not, was required.

This procedure lost all benefit during wartime fast dives under attack from aircraft. In such circumstance the sub was usually fully under long before there was time to observe whether the artificial increase in air pressure was holding, and besides, it would have been safer to go down with some small valve open than to be hit with a bomb or gunfire. During a slow dive, with time to test for watertightness at each stage and take remedial action if necessary, the "pressure in the boat" test would give assurance that nothing had inadvertently been left open that should not have been. In a fast dive, the boat was always under before such a test could be meaningful. The air pressure test, in short, was no longer valid.

Instead, the reverse was true: once a hull opening was under water, air would no longer bubble out of it, as some ill-advised movie sequences have sometimes showed. Instead, water would pour in and compress the air inside the submarine. Thus, during a fast dive the air test might well conceal the first indication of serious flooding. This would begin to compress the air inside the sub as soon as water started to come in, which would happen as soon as external sea pressure exceeded the boat's interior air pressure—in other words, immediately. Such serious flooding would show up initially as a comforting pressure increase—except that pressure buildup would not stop when the high-pressure air inlet valves were shut.

This catastrophe had in fact happened in exactly this way just prior to the war, when the newly built submarine *Squalus* was making high-speed test dives off Portsmouth, New Hampshire. When air valves were opened for the standard air pressure test, air pressure rose normally inside her hull. That it continued to rise when the air valves were shut should instantaneously have registered as a life-threatening emergency.

Controlroom personnel took only a few seconds, less than five, to realize that something really big had been left open. The frantic report, "Engineroom flooding!" had not yet been made. The situation, back aft, was more like an implosion than simple flooding, even high-speed entry of water. The biggest, most important opening in the submarine's hull, the 36-inch-diameter, hydraulically operated main induction valve closing the tremendous air intake pipe needed to run diesels when surfaced, was open, and already under water. It had been left open or somehow (one of the suspicions) accidentally reopened during the complicated diving evolution. If this was the case, and had the controlroom crew spotted the problem during the tiny window of time they had, they might conceivably have been able to pull the hydraulic control valve back to the "shut" position and cut off the tremendous influx of water. The boat would still have sunk and hit bottom, but no one would have died, the water could have been pumped out, and the crew could have brought their submarine back to the surface.

But they lost that extremely small, vital opportunity. The big pipe, wide open, was already under 10 to 20 feet of water as the unfortunate *Squalus* leveled off at periscope depth, and the sea was roaring into the boat under fantastic pressure, forming a solid water column three feet in diameter. To the doomed men in the engineroom, the incoming flood must have seemed bigger than Niagara Falls. Within three or four seconds the after portion of the ship had already flooded beyond any hope of saving her from sinking, though not, perhaps, from being able to pump out the water later could the main induction valve have been closed, even then. She was still barely submerged, still on an even keel, had not yet begun to sag by the stern. In a minute or so, however, her stern sank like the rock it had suddenly become, hitting the bottom 190 feet down, but not before the pressure in the boat had risen far above anything anyone in *Squalus* had ever experienced. Crew members in the forward compartments were fortunate to have been able to seal off watertight doors to her after compartments before the fast-rising air pressure ruptured their eardrums. Nothing could have helped the men aft; all of them suffered excruciating pain in their ears, some surely to the point of becoming unconscious, before they died.

We had had discussions on the subject during the war, but were never able to convince senior submarine officers that the air test had become useless during a fast dive. Changing it was like changing the Submarine Operating Bible.

Amberjack was, however, too nimble a submarine to be constricted by these or other outmoded concepts. She was a tremendous improvement over the wartime submarine from which she had been converted. Now that there was also the snorkel to permit running diesel engines while submerged, we actually devised a "snorkel dive," raising the snorkel mast during the act of diving and not shutting off the diesels at all. With these new capabilities, it seemed time that the air pressure test while diving was relegated to its proper place in the routine (a slowly executed dive to test for tightness, or, for that matter, before diving at all), and at last we were able to convince our senior officers to have this point of view included in the accepted procedure.

By this time, only three years after the close of World War II, I was already well aware of the onrushing development of the nuclear submarine. With Rickover's tremendous drive, which only few of the operating submarine forces had yet been able to observe, I figured we would have this new submarine in less than 10 years, and our submarine force in the meantime would do well to consider new techniques for it. Getting rid of the air test only required official approval, which was easy once the problem was fully laid out.

The business of overcoming the fear of steep angles was more complicated, for we had to demonstrate that use of steep angles to change depth had important operational benefits.

One of the submarine concepts with which we heretofore had been indoctrinated was Simon Lake's idea that dives should be made with the boat essentially horizontal. In earlier days the Navy had two kinds of submarines, known as the "Holland" boats and the "Lake" boats. Differences in their design resulted in different operating characteristics. The Holland boats were "diving boats" because that was what their designer, John Philip Holland, expected of them. His first subs looked like footballs with a propeller on the stern, and were expected to change depth by angling downward or upward as the case might be. Comparison with photos of modern nuclear submarines will show how far ahead, and how right, Holland's ideas truly were.

Lake, on the other hand, interested in exploration of the ocean floor, designed his early boats with a wheel halfway between bow and stern, enabling them theoretically to crawl along the bottom if it was flat enough and hard enough. Manifestly, descending at any sort of angle would cause the bow to hit bottom before the wheel did, and was therefore forbidden. Lake boats changed depth slowly by use of the bow and stern planing surfaces, more rapidly (but still very deliberately) by changing ballast water: one took water into what was known as the "down express" tank (later called negative tank because it gave the submarine temporary negative buoyancy), then blew it out upon reaching the intended depth to restore the desired condition of neutral buoyancy.

In our submarine Navy, even after Lake boats were no longer built with wheels (only the first few were), they almost always submerged on an even keel or with very small angles, while the Holland diving boats accepted larger angles.

As the Navy began establishing operational requirements for the submarine contracts it negotiated, it automatically took over more and more of the design of its submarines as well. In time, Simon Lake's original company went out of business, and the U.S. Navy took over his designs and ideas. Lake plans were superseded by what was called the government design, which continued many of Lake's concepts, many of which were excellent and are still in use.

The Holland patents, by contrast, remained in private hands, newly named the Electric Boat (EB) Company, with Holland revered as the inventor but no longer in control of the company. Competition between the two types of submarines was muted but real, and for some years the privately built Holland subs outperformed the government-built Lake boats. For years we built two types of submarines, now called the "government boats" and the "EB boats," but the power of the government contract won the day, and finally, with development of the great submarines with which we fought Japan, even Electric Boat built submarines to U.S. Navy design.

EB nevertheless maintained its own design cadre, with the result that although all wartime subs were built to exactly the same basic plan, subtle, mainly cosmetic differences still existed. Fundamental was the government layout, that is to say Simon Lake's, with external ballast tanks, a superstructure designed to be free-flooding for submergence, but otherwise like that of a surface ship in order (hopefully) to permit attainment of the designated 21-knot "fleet" speed on engines. Holland had strongly opposed this feature in his rival's design, claimed it was "only for admirals to strut upon"; but admirals seldom went out in subs, and it did permit higher surface speed. Lake's wheel for bottom-crawling was gone, but internal arrangements discouraged steep angles while submerged, and our slow speed in the submerged condition on the battery would have made such angles of little use anyway.

Such were the greatly admired fleet submarines with which we fought World War II: surface ships that could submerge very rapidly when necessary. All during the war, however, we heard yarns about extraordinarily steep angles that resulted from some unexpected wartime exigency. Many tales were told at the submarine base officers' club bar of the risks encountered and the strenuous measures taken to get the boat back on an even keel. Over drinks, proof of the angles was always demanded, for between friends under such circumstances the dangers increased, and so did the submarine heroics involved. By consequence, protractor-angle measurements of where the bilge water marks reached were sometimes produced. These were usually considered irrefutable, and I recall one that exceeded 45 degrees and won a free round of drinks hands down.

These concerns carried forward into the new high-speed submarines, and many were the discussions about what would happen, and how the danger could be averted or minimized, were the stern planes, for example, to freeze in the hard dive position while the boat was traveling submerged at the high speeds we could now attain. During the war, control planes, bow or stern, had sometimes frozen in the hard dive position under depth-charge attack and had therefore led to excessively steep down angles and accompanying emergency. This had not happened often; normally, control over the planing surfaces was quickly restored because this was a casualty we drilled for. When it did happen, it was most often during a dive from high surface speed under aircraft threat. Before the stern planes could be straightened out, some boats recorded 20 to 30 degrees of down angle and all sorts of attendant dislocation of internal equipment. Some crew members were unable to remain on their now steeply slanting stations and thus could not help regain control. Great confusion always reigned at the worst possible time.

Since *Amberjack* could attain more than twice the submerged speed of the wartime fleet boat she had once been, this led to one of our first concerns. It was obvious that at such high speeds a stern plane frozen in full dive would throw us into an extremely steep down angle, might even start us into an outside loop. That aside, a frozen stern plane at high speed could well send the ship far below her authorized test depth before control could be regained.

To counter this situation became our first priority. All internal mechanisms were surveyed, many small changes made to prevent damage. We fitted extra securing straps on torpedoes, welded strategically placed padeyes on their stowage racks, and installed special turnbuckles between the racks and solid parts of the ship's structure so there could be no chance of a torpedo breaking loose. Engine crankcase oil sumps were kept at minimum instead of maximum levels to reduce chance of overflow and oil damage to main generators at the ends of their crankshafts. Since controlroom toolboxes doubled as seats for the men on watch controlling the bow and stern planes, and for the chief of the watch, who was in charge of controlling ballast and monitoring the controlroom in general, it was essential these critical watchstanders not be discombobulated by having these heavy steel chests sliding under them when an angle came on. This problem we cured by welding little corner angle bars to the decks in strategic spots. Special consideration also had to be given our cooks, so that momentarily untended pots of food would not suddenly slide off the stove, and we found that half-finished mugs of coffee, forgotten in some out-of-the-way place, inevitably would make their presence known at just the wrong time, with a crash of heavy crockery and a splattering of old, stale, brown fluid. This hazard we never fully cured.

Along with this, we worked strenuously on training our crew to regain control if the angle inadvertently exceeded what was intended. We held steep angle exercises every day at sea and very soon found that we could confidently handle an angle of 30 degrees, down or up. It was further evident that for rapidly increasing depth, especially important in emergency close quarters with other ships who hardly ever knew exactly where the submarine was, high speed and steep angles were far more effective to increase depth fast than merely flooding negative tank.

All this was reported to our superiors and received strong support because they, too, were concerned with what might happen under the visualized circumstances. Soon enough, from that source came the question of how we would handle the worst condition: if the stern planes were to freeze at hard dive with the ship at high speed and already angled downward at a big angle, say at 30 degrees. We had anticipated this challenge and had diligently drilled for it, starting with slower speeds and smaller angles and finally going to the all-out maneuvers that had been postulated.

Under the suggested circumstances: the boat in a 30-degree down angle, making 15 knots through the water, stern planes "frozen" at full dive and held there; by use of all control measures except the "frozen" stern planes, we could pull out of the dive in 100 feet of additional depth excursion, and 17 degrees of additional angle. In other words, if the stern planes were to freeze on full dive with *Amber* at 15 knots with a 30-degree down angle, and if recovery effort were begun at that moment, because of her momentum she would continue on over in her dive to a maximum down inclination of 47 degrees, and reach a depth 100 feet deeper than where she was when the emergency was recognized. But by then we would have regained control.

The stern plane operators, clearly the most courageous men in the ship, would grimly hold their planes in the full dive position no matter what else went on around them (they would reverse planes with alacrity if ordered, but this never became necessary, for we were always able to recover fully), and the maximum degree of dive angle was never more than 47 degrees. We drilled at it with enthusiasm, and *Amberjack* became known in our closely knit submarine fraternity as the "*Anglejack*." Inevitably, there came demands for some type of public show, and one day we received an official request to demonstrate our capability for the press. The resulting photograph, published in a 1950 *National Geographic* magazine, showed *Amberjack* leaping out of the water.

One of the unlooked-for effects of this highly publicized stunt was the continual question of what earthly good such a maneuver could achieve.

There was of course none, except a dramatic picture. It was purely a demonstration, but it did show what a submarine could do under water, unseen by anyone, and here, indeed, steep angle maneuvers held great tactical promise. Using them, we developed evasion techniques, screen penetration techniques, and sonar blockage procedures unprecedented up to that time. We could go from periscope depth to test depth (maximum allowed submergence) in less than a minute, and from there back up to periscope depth, ready to make normal periscope observations, in a minute and a half. If an enemy ship were to be coming directly at us at 30 knots from only 1,000 yards away, something we should by all criteria be able to hear clearly in our sonar, we could nevertheless be back at maximum submergence, from any condition including that of being fully surfaced, by the time she passed overhead. Furthermore, we could then get back up to periscope depth, take an observation, and shoot a torpedo at her before she was able to turn around for another run at us.

Many were the fleet problems in which we found we could penetrate the destroyer screen at deep depth, below the sonar layer, then come up rapidly to periscope depth ahead of the main body and in position to shoot. We proved this with periscope photographs, and whenever possible released a green flare (to represent a torpedo) aimed to arc over the target's main deck. From our point of view all this was great fun, and we wished we could have had such a ship, equipped with effective torpedoes, during the war. In one of our operations, for example, the *Amberjack* was the only "enemy" opposing a U.S. landing force of a dozen transports and half a dozen destroyers: some 17,000 people arrayed against the 80 in our little submarine. We were allowed to shoot no more than our normal load of torpedoes, 28 in all, and had to account for each shot; but we had special indulgence in that we were considered to be two submarines instead of one, and were therefore allowed 56 simulated fish in all, instead of the 28 we carried. Fortunately, we had more than sufficient green flares on board, and at the end of the operation I announced to our crew that we had sunk every ship opposed to us at least once, having deliberately sought out each one, and had not received even a theoretical scratch in return.

One high point came when the destroyer *Shannon,* in which my Naval Academy roommate and best friend, Foxy Bonner, was executive officer, steamed by our periscope. His ship was second in column, but this was too good to miss, and I let the leader go by. The green flare over the *Shannon*'s bow was a special signal to him, I told him later with great pleasure at the officers' club bar in San Juan, Puerto Rico.

Now that I reflect upon that time, however, it's clear that two other factors were also operating on my psyche. One was the end of the war, just as I was coming into my ambition to command a top flight submarine, doing the only thing I knew I could do well: combat the enemy. I had brought *Piper* home at the war's end, and then an unfeeling seniority system took her from me. Now, three years later, time-wise almost as long as the war had lasted, I had *Amberjack.* In our near daily exercises there was some of the war, some of the adrenalin-laden excitement to which I had become accustomed. It was, of course, not really the same, since we fired torpedoes only for practice and there were only light noisemakers fired back at us instead of depth charges. But the internal working of the submarine was no different, and we simulated war action daily. I drove that ship hard, myself, too.

Amberjack's home port for the entire period of my command was Key West, at the edge of the Florida Straits with plenty of deep water nearby. The location was ideal for submarine operations, and I very much enjoyed developing submarine tactics for the new high-speed "guppy" submarines our Navy was beginning to build or, more properly, into which we were beginning to convert some of our fine World War II fleet submarines. I loved the freedom of maneuver that *Amberjack*'s extra-powerful batteries and streamlined form gave us.

The big thing, nonetheless, was the knowledge that while *Amber* was a wonderful ship, she was already behind the curve. We were designing a new class of submarine that would theoretically be better, but only marginally so (and how little better I would soon bitterly discover)—but the big thing, the dream all of us who knew of Rickover's grandiose plans carried in our hearts and minds, was of a submarine powered by inexhaustible nuclear energy, able to stay under water indefinitely, run forever at speeds beyond imagination, and carry weapons that worked every time. The last part, weapons that work, will be found engraved in the soul of every World War II submariner in our Navy. That those who sent us to sea in war with unreliable torpedoes were never even identified, let alone held to account, is still a very sore point.

I was very much aware of the work going on under Rickover's direction at Arco, Idaho, where the prototype of the new nuclear submarine was built and began operating under his unremitting supervision. He was a hard taskmaster, but the fact was that everything worked right; if it didn't it was instantly torn down, rebuilt, redesigned, or whatever it took, until it worked exactly and precisely as intended. Even as far away as Key West, in the southernmost point of the United States, I devoured what little news I was able to garner, from time to time, of the progress of the new design. That it would be an epochal advance I knew, as did everyone working on it. Just how epochal no one could have guessed.

In the meantime, my command tour of wonderful *Amberjack,* projected at three years, suddenly appeared threatened after less than a year when a letter arrived from then-Capt. Arleigh Burke, one of the most highly thought-of officers in the Navy, asking me if I might consider coming to Washington to work on his staff in a special position that he termed "of high responsibility for the Navy's future."

I had entered the U.S. Naval Institute's prize essay contest the previous year; my essay did not win a prize, but it was selected for publication as an ordinary article. Possibly this was what had caught Captain Burke's notice. But I could not face giving up my ship after all the emotional payment I had made to get her, one of them not yet described. After a great deal of consideration, I wrote back declining Burke's offer, giving my reasons in some detail (though not in the same words as here), and received a return letter from the captain saying he fully agreed with me and would have done the same thing himself. It is one of my warm memories of the very human individual who was destined to grow into one of the most important figures in our naval history.

I have thought of the incident from time to time, wondering what the future might have held for me had I accepted; for suddenly, only about three months later, there was a dispatch to the *Amberjack* summarily detaching me as skipper and ordering me to proceed immediately to Washington, D.C., for duty on the staff of General of the Army Omar N. Bradley, just named to the newly created post of chairman of the Joint Chiefs of Staff. This was a direct order. It was not, like Burke's letter, a personal suggestion for my consideration.

Just-passed amendments to the National Security Act had a big effect on my own life. The post of chairman of the Joint Chiefs of Staff was created, Gen. Omar Bradley was selected to be the first officer holding this important post, and I was deprived of my submarine to become a member of his staff. In Navy jargon, there could be no "reclama." I left Key West with mixed feelings, for although professionally rewarding, Ingrid's and my time there included a personal tragedy that even now, half a century later, causes anguish in our hearts.

Our darling first-born child, a daughter named Inga-Marie, died there, one week after her third birthday. We had lived in Key West only about three months. The home movies of her birthday party, featuring her "big present," a shiny new tricycle, came back in the mail the same day we buried her. We have them safely sequestered, but neither Ingrid nor I can yet bear to look at them.

The immediate cause of her death was determined, by autopsy, to have been an intussusception of the lower bowel. An operation might have saved her, but instead, after a few tests and some outpatient treatment, including intravenous fluid injected into her dehydrated little body, she was sent home with encouraging words ("you'll see a big change by tomorrow"), and instructions that we should give her enemas. This was the day before she died, and we will never forget our desperate trip back to the Key West Naval Hospital early next morning. It may be true, as the doctors maintained, that she could not then have survived an operation, but she might have a few days before, and we can never forgive their inaction while there was still time.

Our little girl lies buried in the Key West cemetery, not far from where members of the crew of USS *Maine*, blown up in Havana harbor half a century before, also lie.

When our son Hugh arrived, 10 months later, we used the Key West civilian hospital facility and a private doctor. Hugh's birth had a great healing effect, and we also blessed the fact that our first-born son, Ned Jr., 6 months old when his older sister died, was as much in need of us as we were of him.

Upon our return to Washington, D.C., where the Naval Medical Center was considered the best naval hospital in the country, our children became regular patients of the then head of pediatrics, Dr. Thomas Cone. This caring, knowledgeable man saw our second daughter, Ingrid Alice, through difficult times as an infant. As he once wrote after receiving a Christmas greeting depicting three healthy young adults, "The picture shows I must have done something right!" Sadly, we have just received news from his daughter that he and his wife both died last year, after full and useful lives.

Chapter Eleven

The Revolt of the Admirals

According to Professor (emeritus) E. B. (Ned) Potter of the Naval Academy at Annapolis, who treats the situation in some detail in his biography of Admiral Nimitz, Secretary of Defense Louis Johnson believed the Army should take over all amphibious operations, the Air Force should manage air power and strategic weapons, and the Navy should control sea communications and antisubmarine warfare. Potter goes on to say:

> Veteran aviator Captain John G. Crommelin was the first naval officer to sound the alarm publicly. On September 10, 1949, in defiance of regulations, he publicly charged the Air Force with attempting to dominate the defense budget and take over all air power, and he accused Johnson of trying to establish a dictatorship within the Defense Department. He pointed out that two of the Joint Chiefs of Staff with a "landlocked concept of national defense" could always outvote the Navy.

The House Armed Services Committee had already been looking into the question of the Air Force B-36 bomber, successor to the B-29 that had so devastated Japan during the closing year of the war. The B-36 was designed to be able to deliver the atomic weapon anywhere in the world. Now Captain Crommelin had given that committee reason to look further into the "roles and missions" of the several military services under the recently enacted unification law. One series of hearings had been held. The Navy had made its case well, with more testimony expected, but the initial sensation had somewhat died down, partly as a result of intense pressure from Secretary Johnson.

Crommelin's defiant action had sensationalized the business to a much higher level than it had reached heretofore.

This was the situation when I arrived in Washington from Key West. None of the details had I heard at my distant post as skipper of a submarine in Key West. So far as I knew, what the press was already terming a "revolt" on the parts of senior officers in the Navy amounted to a flap between advocates of naval air and its carriers and the newly created Air Force—although I remember some slight discomfort because Adm. Louis Denfeld, my old boss, appeared somewhat unwillingly in the middle of the controversy. I could not help thinking about him from time to time. The situation must be extremely difficult for him, I realized.

The Air Force claimed general hegemony over the nuclear weapon, which it termed a "strategic" weapon (actually, the A-bomb was the *only* weapon that fit the "strategic" definition in vogue then, or at any time since). The Air Force also claimed that it, with the atomic bomb, was the service that had brought World War II to an end; that without "the Bomb" the war might have gone on much longer, with much higher loss of life on both sides. It ignored Navy arguments that Japan's merchant fleet and her navy had been totally destroyed and that she had already begun peace feelers through Switzerland, Sweden, and (amazingly) the Soviet Union. The Air Force claimed its new B-36 bomber, a development of the B-29 which had so heavily bombarded Japan during the last year of the war, was the only vehicle by which the strategic weapon could be effectively delivered, and should remain so.

The Navy's position, in brief, was that aircraft flying from carriers could deliver a nuclear weapon as well as the new and untested B-36, in many instances better, and that the B-36 itself was vulnerable to carrier-based or land-based fighter planes, or to new antiaircraft measures in general. Feelings were strong, the service partisanship extremely heavy.

I had gone into the Atomic Defense Section of OpNav, known as Op-36, when Denfeld became commander of our Pacific Fleet, and went to Key West at about the same time he came back from Pearl Harbor to relieve Admiral Nimitz as CNO. In Op-36 I had had opportunity to observe at least some of the machinations of the Air Force and the Navy in the developing controversy over control and delivery of the atomic bomb. It did not then occur to me—as it does now—to wonder whether there might have been some special significance to the use of the number "36" to designate the office in which much of the Navy's opposition to the Air Force concept of employment of the nuclear weapon, and the B-36 with which to do it, was generated.

I reported to General Bradley's office in the Pentagon not much longer than a year after I had left Op-36 in the Main Navy building on the other side of the Potomac. There I found myself nearly on the opposite side of the fence from my previous post, for General Bradley, with his Army background, had no quarrel with the decision of Secretary of Defense Louis Johnson to cancel the USS *United States* and look entirely to the Air Force for handling and control of the "strategic" weapon. On arrival, I found myself in a hotbed of activity, with little real knowledge of the forces in action around me, in the very middle of the Revolt of the Admirals.

Capt. Arleigh Burke's office, the one he had invited me to join only a few months earlier, was known in Pentagonese as Op-23. He had been ordered to Washington to create it late in 1948, and had already received considerable unfavorable press notice from a media generally reacting to Air Force initiatives. From what I read in the press or heard on the radio, Op-23 was dedicated to supporting the Navy's anti–Air Force activities during this period. It was said to be developing arguments to "shoot down" the B-36 bomber, and in general to subvert the declared intentions of President Truman and Secretary of Defense Louis Johnson to make the aircraft our primary agent of national defense. There was inference, though no direct accusation, that Burke must be breaking the law somehow, no doubt using illegal methods to support the Navy cause.

I had seen little in the news supporting the Navy's point of view. From the violence of the criticism it was fairly evident that Burke's office was carefully studying testimony and providing refuting documentation to the Navy officials who were required to testify to Congress. Evidently, from the stir being raised, he was having some undesired success in the effort.

At the same time, I began to realize with some dismay that the position of my previous boss, Admiral Denfeld, was every day becoming more precarious. He had testified in favor of the Navy's basic position, but when the president, through his secretary of defense, came down on the side of the Air Force, many high-ranking naval officers felt he had not fought hard enough. On the contrary, from what I was able to read in the newspapers or heard from radio news commentators, he was going along with the decisions of his superiors. I thought that as an appointed official of the government there was not much else he could do, but it was clear that not all naval officers felt the same.

What they expected him to do instead was not obvious, but the media had a good story in its sights and kept after it. In my view it was overly simplistic on anyone's part to describe him as "going along with it" ("it" being defined as what the Air Force or the administration wanted), but every time I saw him referred to or quoted, the thrust of the story disparagingly inferred as much. He could please neither pro–Air Force administration supporters, who wanted him to have Navy heads rolling in the hallowed halls of the Pentagon, nor the anti–Air Force zealots, who felt he should use his position to continue the battle and, if necessary, sacrifice himself in some version of Japanese hara-kiri should he be unable to convince those arrayed against the Navy. Beyond my sympathy for Denfeld, I understood next to nothing about the controversy, knowing only that in General Bradley's office I was going to be terribly out of my depth.

From the day I arrived, I found the impressions I had already received were not only correct, the ongoing discussion was a veritable hotbed of accusations. Our national policy about strategic weapons was a major issue; so was the future of the aircraft carrier, naval air, in general that of the entire Navy. Now that the war was over, the old isolationist wing Roosevelt had confronted before the war had allied itself with the effort to cut down the military budget. Added to this was the Air Force drive, recently won, for independence from the Army. With the momentum it had carried over from this fight, the Air Force was now waging all-out bureaucratic warfare for total control of all nuclear weapons. Within the Navy itself, a number of high-ranking and outspoken officers felt the CNO was insufficiently supportive of the Navy position, some of them going so far as to say he had "sold out" to the administration.

In the lower ranks there was much uninformed dissension, some of it going all the way back to the intent of the Constitution in putting the armed forces under civilian control. From what I could see, in the field there was little understanding of the problem. Naval air power had won the war against Japan; the atomic bombs had simply hastened the surrender. Why, then, did politicians want to do away with the principal means by which the victory had been won? There was far more heat than light to the arguments I had been hearing, which, after all, amounted to preaching to the choir. I had been exposed, at least, to the other side during my previous "double-banked" tour in Washington, most especially while in OpNav's Atomic Defense office, and had some idea of the complexities of the debate.

My reporting to the chairman of the Joint Chiefs produced, if anything, a strained occasion. His staff knew I had been Denfeld's aide not many years earlier, and (quite probably) also that just before coming to them I had been asked to join the Op-23 staff. I could sense bad vibes everywhere. Tension was so palpable in the office that, a few days after reporting aboard, I felt it necessary to make a speech on the subject to General Bradley himself. Asking to see him, I declared that I had been ordered to his office to work for him and for no other purpose, had yet to see Admiral Denfeld or anyone from his office, though I felt I should, and had no knowledge at all of how I had come to be chosen for the assignment.

I explained to General Bradley that I felt embarrassed because of the situation with Captain Burke. He had invited me to come work for him and had graciously accepted my declination of the opportunity. Now, only a short time later, I was not only back in Washington in the Pentagon but working, in effect, for the other side. I had now discovered that some of the media accusations were true, so far as they went. The basic purpose of Op-23, as Navy junior officers had it and as held by the media, was to defend the Navy against the Air Force political onslaught and to provide senior naval officers with ammunition for congressional testimony on the subject. Burke was doing this very carefully, remaining within all the rules regarding how such a mission could legitimately be performed.

The situation was actually propitious for me, although I didn't really understand it, when I asked General Bradley's blessing for my calling on Captain Burke. There were no rules prohibiting my going to any office in the Pentagon and asking to see anyone there (not that assent was obligatory), but under the circumstances, it was a good thing I asked.

I also stated to General Bradley that I had been personal aide to the CNO, Admiral Denfeld, in a previous duty assignment (I felt sure he knew this), but wanted to tell him that I had no knowledge of how I might have been selected out of all naval officers of my approximate rank for the post to which I had been so suddenly assigned. It had occurred to me that the CNO might have been asked his evaluation of me, perhaps even to recommend someone to fill my newly created position. My recollection is a bit vague on this exact point, but I believe it was during this short interview that Bradley sent for the admiral's letter and showed it to me.

Now, Admiral Denfeld was under fire from all sides. When I explained to General Bradley that I felt my duty to my old boss required at least that I also call upon him, General Bradley immediately agreed. "Indeed you should see both him and Burke," he said. "Give them my personal regards and tell them that I'll be only too happy to be of any assistance I can in any way."

Then he thanked me for coming to him, and said the same thing to me, that I should look to him for help and advice at any time.

When I walked out of that session with the general, there were smiles and friendly glances from his aide and his personal secretary, and very shortly I began noticing the same from all the others on his staff, as well. The bad vibes had magically disappeared. I had the distinct feeling that I had done the right thing, and that they approved.

I immediately telephoned the offices of Denfeld and Burke and made appointments. My first meeting, as I recall, was with Admiral Denfeld. I appeared in his office, he welcomed me into his inner sanctum, sat me down, and discussed various items not directly related to the issues then foremost in either of our minds: my career since leaving his office, what I thought about the future of submarines in general, my feeling about the ongoing proposal for nuclear propulsion not yet achieved. The thing that sticks in my mind most clearly, however, was the first thing he said when our conversation turned to the B-36 controversy.

Referring to the as-yet-unnamed Navy captain who, according to the press, had anonymously given out documents critical of Air Force policy "in a dimly lighted hallway of a Washington D.C. office building" (soon identified as the National Press Building itself), Denfeld said, "He ought not to have done that." I instantly felt he knew well who the unnamed captain was, and my assessment was reinforced that for him the situation was going out of control.

I think I sensed the same thing the press must also have sensed, and this was the reason why the pack continued baying at Denfeld's heels. My old boss was unsure of himself, torn two ways. Of course he wanted to keep his job as the Navy's highest-ranking officer, and of course he was well aware of his duty to support the president of the United States and all others in authority. On the other side lay all his training, all his understanding of the Navy, his personal friendships, everything he had lived for and fought for his entire life. But it wasn't that everything the Navy wanted was right, or that the Air Force was always wrong. Denfeld was in the best position of anyone in the Navy to see both sides. His problem was that he *did* see both sides, had tried too long to play fair with both. Neither side, on the other hand, was playing entirely fair with him.

Sometimes, in the great game of hard politics, a human sacrifice becomes a necessity. Kimmel was one because of Pearl Harbor. Denfeld, I began dimly to feel, was going to become another. He felt it, too, and fought against it, but there was no way out for him.

Admiral Denfeld also desired me to meet the secretary of the Navy, Francis P. Matthews, who, at the direction of Louis Johnson, was, in effect, his personal charge. Appointed after the indignant resignation of Secretary John L. Sullivan over cancellation of the new USS *United States,* given the job by the disliked Johnson, who was blamed for the heavy-handed way the business had been handled, Matthews from the start had a problem with Navy acceptance. He helped himself not a bit when, at the beginning of his tenure, unwisely thinking to add levity to an overly somber occasion, he commented that he came to the job with an open mind because he knew nothing about any ship bigger than a rowboat. From that moment, whatever he did or said, he was "Rowboat Matthews," put there by Johnson to demean the rest of the Navy.

Perhaps in the hope of somehow smoothing a little of the growing schism in the top levels of the Defense Department—my new boss being one of the big players—my old one opened the door at the side of his office and ushered me into the next one. Almost as though it had been prearranged, Secretary Matthews stepped up, shook hands with me, and repeated the formula I was beginning to hear everywhere: that I was to come to him at any time. The picture that stays in my mind all these intervening years is that he came from between floor-to-ceiling pink or rose-colored drapes. Perhaps they concealed the door to Denfeld's room so that the two could confer privately. I got the impression also that Matthews at the moment had nothing else to do. He seemed not weighed down with business and may have been glad of an interruption to his idleness, even as inconsequential an interruption as my visit.

After a few minutes of desultory talk, this interview terminated, I returned with Admiral Denfeld beyond the pink drapes, and in turn bade him good day. It was the last time I was to see him in a face-to-face manner. I carried away with me the impression that there was some small tension between him and Matthews, a sort of false heartiness in Denfeld. Having been his personal aide for two years, I had some understanding of his moods and mannerisms, and particularly noted this at the time.

In a similar way, I went to see Captain Burke. His office was located in a little-frequented area of the Pentagon's top floor, and I could see no windows. Not a prepossessing place to put a top-ranking fighting officer of the war who was deeply enmeshed, so the papers were saying, in an attempt to overcome the Air Force's inherently superior perception of the national interest.

Burke received me warmly. I said my mission was first to apologize again for having declined his good offer and then accepting a seemingly better one from a higher-ranking person. He dismissed the whole thing with a wave of his hand. "That's the way things sometimes go," he said, as I recall, "but I know you'll do your best for the Navy in whatever ways fall to you." I went on to explain my position on General Bradley's staff and to relay the general's words about being helpful in any way he could to Captain Burke in his present position. Burke said he appreciated this. So far as I could judge, the expressions from both officers, while polite and correct as might be expected, were also completely genuine. It was my opinion then, and events have borne me out, that neither Bradley nor Burke was ever motivated by anything but what he felt were the best interests of the United States. They really hardly differed in their views of what these might be. Either of them would have been outstanding as a president of the United States, had fate inclined in that direction. (Bradley would have reminded people of Abraham Lincoln, Burke of Theodore Roosevelt.)

The conversation to this stage was not important; I had made my call and expressed what I thought were the proper sentiments. Burke had just suggested that he introduce me to his staffers, and I was thinking about how to make an appropriate adieu as soon as that was over, when the phone rang on his desk. Answering it, he immediately began a long conversation with someone named Louis. Burke addressed him very familiarly, using his first name frequently but never his last name. He had been standing at this stage of our talk, intending to walk me around his suite of rooms. Now, with the phone to his ear, he turned away from me and leaned nearly all the way across his desk, his elbows resting on it as he talked, incidentally giving me a broad view of a broad part of his anatomy. The conversation proved to be a rather lengthy one, having much to do with Congress and the upcoming Navy testimony.

They talked quite some time while I stood uncertainly, rooted where I had been temporarily abandoned. I wondered, of course, whether "Louis" could possibly be Denfeld, but quickly dismissed that idea, and never did come on a logical one. Not that this mattered if it was not my former chief. At one point I made as if to depart, but Burke was nearly finished and waved me to stand fast.

He had no sooner put down the phone and turned back to me, however, when someone came and quietly said something about "the Inspector General." Burke said, "Show him in right away," and the answer, again low voiced, was that the Inspector General wanted to speak to Burke outside in the hall. The main door to the hall was left open at this point, and I saw Vice Adm. Allen R. McCann, Inspector General of the Navy, standing there solemnly and uncomfortably, accompanied by a Marine guard in ceremonial uniform and behind them a few others. McCann was a submarine officer whom I knew slightly, and I was sure that he recognized me, but he gave no such indication. His face had a severe "duty" look on it, and his eyes were concentrated on Burke.

Burke went out into the hall and shut the door, but in a moment opened it again and reentered the Op-23 reception area, followed by McCann and the Marine, and one other. McCann said, fairly loudly and clearly, "I've come to take over your office, Arleigh! Everything is to stay exactly as it is. I want all your files and papers, no matter what they are. Everything in these rooms!"

Burke said, "Some of them are personal files, and some are the personal possessions of some of my staff. They're not included too, are they?"

"Yes they are," said McCann, looking him directly in the eye. "I'm taking over your entire office as of right now." He went on to say that no one could enter or leave except for trips to the lavatories, when they would have to be accompanied. He did not know how long the process would take, but he meant to interview everyone in the place, and no one could leave until all the interviews were finished. Coffee and sandwiches would be provided. No outgoing calls of any kind could be made. No one could call home to explain the delay, and all incoming calls would be taken by one of his own staff. Behind him stood a naval officer in white service uniform whose face I could not directly see at the moment, and now I could see a number of others in the hall, most of them Marines in full uniform. There were also three or four women. All of them, McCann especially, seemed most uncomfortable. No one except the admiral was saying a word.

"I don't understand," said Burke. "Can't you come in and tell me what it's about?"

"No, I'm sorry, Arleigh. I am taking over as of right now."

"You mean you are taking over my office? You're putting me out of business?"

"That's right. Nobody can leave your office. I'm taking over all of your files. Nothing can be touched, no more work. No one may leave the office for any reason."

"This is unheard of," said Burke. "You mean you're putting me out of business just like that?"

"I'm sorry, Arleigh. As of now this door is closed, and all your other doors to the hall, too. I'll have to ask all your people simply to relax until we get this over with."

Burke looked at McCann with dawning comprehension. Then, speaking slowly, he said, "Admiral, Commander Beach, here, isn't one of my people. He has just come from General Bradley's office and our business had nothing to do with anything going on here."

In a sense this wasn't strictly true but it was a good enough approximation. Admiral McCann was a submariner, well known to the force for having invented the McCann rescue diving bell by which the *Squalus* survivors had been rescued after her disaster in 1939, and I knew he knew me by sight. He looked me in the eye and said quietly, "Beach, you get out of here!"

"Aye, aye, sir," I said to him, muttered a hasty goodbye to Captain Burke, and off I went. I later discovered that I was the last person to leave that office until two or three the next morning.

Although I had obtained General Bradley's blessing on my projected visit to Op-23, I had made the appointment privately and had not checked out with anyone before going there. I debated with myself what if anything to tell about what I had just witnessed, finally decided that it was all Navy business, certainly none of my own, that my presence had been a fortuitous happenstance, and if the Navy wished the chairman of the Joint Chiefs of Staff to know what had taken place the Navy would inform him.

It also occurred to me that although I had no idea who had ordered McCann into action, it could only be someone in a very high place, therefore either Denfeld or Matthews, no doubt with Louis Johnson pulling the strings from behind the scene. I felt no loyalty to Matthews and none to Johnson, but did have a deep sense of sympathy for my former boss. I could not have the slightest idea of all that must be driving him at this time, but if Denfeld had ordered the seizure, it was doubtless under extreme pressure. The least I could do was to keep quiet.

That was what I did, in the meantime watching the newspapers and all other sources of good or bad "dope" inside the Pentagon to see what came out. To my surprise, there was very little. There was merely a notice that Op-23, once so prominent in the B-36 fight, had suddenly begun behaving as though everyone in it were muzzled. This I clearly understood, but that was all, except for a very abbreviated account a few days later in the *Washington Post* stating that Op-23 had been disestablished by order of the Secretary of the Navy. The press either had not noticed any difference, which I could hardly believe, or as a policy matter of its own had decided to lay off.

The ramifications of the situation were extensive, as was later clear to everyone, but I recall being surprised at how little was said or printed about what had just occurred. It was nearly unprecedented, certainly so far as I knew and certainly of recent times, for an office to be summarily closed in the cavalier manner I had just witnessed. I also distinctly sensed the total lack of personal animus in the proceedings. McCann obviously was carrying out orders he deeply disliked. Burke knew this, and both officers behaved as correctly as they could under the stressful circumstances. To my surprise, I heard virtually no talk about any of this from my Navy friends or other sources. This may have been because of my association with General Bradley—no doubt that was a factor—but it is also my impression that the Navy, although shocked, had individually and by group determined to give no possible offense or other opening for attack by its critics.

There the matter rested and I heard nothing more about it until, years later, when Admiral Burke, retired after an unprecedented six years as CNO, began trying to fill in the details of that eventful day. He vaguely recalled there had been someone from some other shop with him at the moment the blow fell, but could not remember any more than that. By chance a third party related this incident to me, and I had the pleasure of writing to the admiral to refresh his memory. I should point out that by the end of that day, any usefulness the Navy secretary might have had, either to Johnson or to the Navy, had nearly vanished.

Any remaining vestiges of it disappeared entirely when General Bradley made his "Fancy Dan" speech to the House Armed Services Committee only a few days later. Because of Captain Crommelin's desperate action—as he knew it would, it cost him any chance he might have had of further promotion—the whole issue of "Roles and Missions" of the several armed services became an even hotter topic in the news media and in Congress than ever before. There were some who had hoped it would die down after the first outbreak of congressional and press interviews, just prior to my return to Washington, but Crommelin had nipped that in the bud. The dying professional dispute between the services flared up into all-out war, hotter than it had ever been.

The "Admirals' Revolt," which had been simmering down after the first set of hearings, revived to full life, more stridently than ever before. The press was full of reports about how the Navy was covertly contesting the "Will of the People," how civilian control had been specified in the Constitution for just such situations, why it was wrong for Navy admirals to want even bigger and better aircraft carriers than those that had won the war at sea, particularly now that there was no one left for our Navy to fight.

The same argument in reverse, that the B-29 had won the air war over Japan and therefore needed no successor B-36, was not even whispered (except in little-known, dimly lighted halls of the Pentagon). In the media was no recognition of the Navy's obligation to present its side objectively and fully, nor was much criticism heard of the fundamental Air Force idea that foreign policy could be managed entirely through threat or use of the atom bomb.

In honesty, I heard little talk about actually using atom bombs on countries who disagreed with us. It was assumed that our sole possession of the nuclear weapon would of itself be an implicit but benign threat, under the ominous shadow of which rational diplomacy could take place. No one addressed the future contingency that would exist when other nations, specifically the Soviet Union, developed their own nuclear weapons. This was for later, and policy-making groups like the National Security Council can be excused for wanting to deal with the immediate issues first.

Illustrative, however, of the problems involved in any lucid discussion of this period of our international concerns, the Soviet Union tested its first atomic device at this exact time, early in September of this very same year, 1949.

The big issue that grabbed everyone in the Pentagon at that time was the politics of weapons. The Soviet possession of a nuclear explosive, which meant that it would soon have a deliverable weapon, did little to change the internal fights in our own government. To the Navy, being forbidden to handle nuclear weapons meant being forbidden to store them, transport them, repair them, build facilities for them, or deliver them on target. Not only would such strictures radically affect everything the Navy did in peacetime, they would also automatically make it impossible to change under wartime pressure. Exclusive possession of the nuclear weapon by any single service thus amounted to ascendancy over the others. The Air Force believed this, too.

The Navy also pointed out the importance of flexibility, the idea that "gunboat diplomacy," a contemptuous term for the old-time use of naval forces, actually covered a lot of good uses that had served us well. Hundreds of diplomatic crises have been resolved without bloodshed simply because it became known that some U.S. naval ships had been quietly stationed over the horizon and out of sight. Hundreds more were taken care of when ships came into foreign harbors and quietly anchored, or even, in some form or other, most often at the request of the local government, sent their forces ashore to help authorities restore order. To argue that the sacred sovereignty of nations in difficulty is violated when our ships help them get things in order is to put idealistic theory ahead of the life and death of innocent people.

As an aside, perhaps we ought not to have gone into Haiti in 1915; this was a perfect example of the pejorative "gunboat diplomacy." The president of the country had enraged the people and been murdered. Everyone, including foreign diplomats, was afraid for his life, until a U.S. warship sent U.S. Marines ashore. The Marines were later withdrawn, but in the interim Haiti had the most honest government it has ever had. Look at the country today, answer if the inhabitants are better off now that our Marines are gone—and on a very personal level, what might you be reading at this moment had I not had the good fortune to be born?

What about Iceland in World War II? No Icelander liked our "invasion," but they agree it was preferable to the one by Nazi Germany which we peaceably forestalled. No one was killed or even hurt, the country was saved intact, and as soon as the danger was over our forces departed. The only lingering resentment visible in Iceland (and still sometimes mentioned, even at this late date) is over the number of lovely young Icelandic women, potential beauty contest winners every one, who married American servicemen and left the country.

Along the same line, would Cuba today be better off, or worse off, if we had prevailed at the Bay of Pigs? Would Iraq be better off if the Persian Gulf War had lasted one more day, long enough to terminate the tyranny of Saddam Hussein? How many more people will die because we did not finish the job?

Admiral Denfeld was clearly between a rock and a hard place, two little-understood forces that were beyond anything his naval training had equipped him for. He was dealing with postwar pressures that had been held back during the war years but were now free to spread out in all directions until they came up against their natural boundaries. It must have seemed to him that all the Air Force, parts of the Navy, most of the press, and most of Congress were scenting his blood and baying at his heels. He came under severe Navy and press criticism, levied approximately equally on both sides, for (it was said too often) "pusillanimously seeking to keep his job as CNO by toadying to Rowboat Matthews and via him to Louis Johnson and President Truman."

From my position at the time, having not long before been Denfeld's personal aide, it was becoming clear that he was approaching an untenable position, that the press knew it, and that he did, too. Leading segments of the Navy, principally concerned with naval air and specifically with the atomic weapon, were in open rebellion against what they saw as an unwise policy, particularly since it would depend upon a terribly vulnerable aircraft for delivery. The B-36 bomber was badly flawed. It was slow, ungainly, and easily shot down. It wasn't even a good airplane by World War II standards, much less in the nuclear age now dawning. To such criticism, the Air Force reacted by attacking those who made such observations, and did so with all the strength at its command.

Inevitably, Congress once more got in the act. It wanted to get to the bottom of the controversy, and no one disagreed with the feeling expressed by all sides that, for the good of the country, the issue should be quickly resolved.

High among the issues—and to this I was particularly attuned—was what would Admiral Denfeld do? Would he go down the line with the defense secretary and the president or would he support the Navy? I recognized his dilemma as a true one from which there was no recourse. Either way he was doomed. He had become a human sacrifice to the gods of politics. As CNO, his usefulness was fatally compromised. I knew he must be agonizing over what to do, how to handle the situation.

In the meantime, a call came for General Bradley to testify before the House Armed Services Committee. My immediate superior in the office was Lt. Col. Chester V. Clifton, whose primary job for the general was to be his front man with the press and prepare his speeches and other official utterances. I had already had some articles in national periodicals and the Naval Institute *Proceedings*. This was no doubt what had led to my assignment to Clifton as his assistant in the speechwriting department.

With the call from Congress to Bradley to be the first to testify on the now merrily boiling controversy, I expected to be involved in drafting his remarks and held the naive hope of helping the Navy somewhat in the process. This was not to be. Clifton closed the door to his office and worked on Bradley's testimony alone. He often went to see the general and then returned to his desk to work more on it. I realized I was being studiously kept out of the circle, and remonstrated with Clifton, whom I personally admired and had come to like very much. But with this effort I got nowhere.

At one point, Clifton told me plainly that this was a tremendously important matter, that what Bradley had to say would be inimical to the Navy in many ways, and therefore it had been decided that I was not to participate in drafting his statement in any way. This was Bradley's express direction, according to Clifton, in order to play fair with me and allow me to deny any connection with his testimony when queried by my Navy friends or, conceivably, in some official way by the Navy itself. Vainly I replied that I had no special fish to fry, except to support the Navy where possible, and that I hoped I might be allowed to make a contribution in terms of the testimony. I thought, as a matter of fact, that I owed it to General Bradley to supply him with any and all insights about the Navy that I might happen to have, and that indeed I had been sent to him in order to broaden his staff resources by reporting Navy views when appropriate. I hoped I would be allowed to do so, I said.

I had no such luck. The general's testimony was prepared entirely by himself with Clifton's help and that of others of his staff, and I never saw it. It was only a few days until the day when Bradley was to testify before Congress, and as he was proceeding there with his prepared testimony in his chauffeured car, Clifton handed me the manuscript with the words, "He's gone now so you can have a look at it."

I quickly read the fairly voluminous document, and almost immediately my eyes lighted on one item that seemed to jump right off the paper at me. "This is no time for Fancy Dans who won't hit the line with all they have on every play, unless they can call the signals," was what I read. I could hardly believe what I was seeing and practically ran into Ted Clifton's room. "Right here he is calling the Navy a bunch of Fancy Dans," I said. "He can't get away with that. It will raise Hell in the press and in Congress, and isn't fair to the Navy. Besides, it's totally misrepresentative of what I think the general's real attitude is."

"No, you've got it wrong, Ned," said Clifton. "Nobody's going to interpret it that way, and he doesn't mean it that way. He is not calling the Navy 'Fancy Dans,' but only referring to Fancy Dans, whoever they are, who can't take orders from the president. It's a general term not related to the Navy but only to specific rebellious officers of any of the services."

I stuck to my guns. I insisted that "Fancy Dans" would be seen as aimed directly at the Navy. I even asked if it might be possible for a phone call to intercept the general before he testified. (There might still be time for this, I thought, although not very much.)

The answer to this idea was negative. "It's too late to change it anyway. He'll know how to handle it. Don't worry."

The repercussions of General Bradley's "Fancy Dans Speech," as it became known, were instant and nationwide. The main purport of his otherwise moderate statement was lost in the flames generated by this unfortunate remark (by other versions, his testimony was not "moderate," was instead quite vitriolic). Whatever the true impression he intended, the nation can well remember the reaction of the press, the other services, the Congress, and the administration: the chairman of the Joint Chiefs of Staff had called the Navy "a bunch of Fancy Dans."

As it turned out, the unfortunate term damaged Bradley's reputation for evenhandedness, and was used by supporters of both other services as an epithet with which they delighted to belabor the Navy. I have always thought of the circumstance as one in which nobody won. Everybody lost, except me. I gained stature in Bradley's eyes and, fair gentleman that he was, he said as much. His words, in fact, were most complimentary, and I've treasured them: "Too bad we didn't let Beach see it," he said. "Maybe he'd have saved me some of this flack!"

Somewhere along here, General Bradley and Admiral Denfeld had a talk, probably by private telephone. The morning after the closing of Burke's shop, I think, Bradley knew about it. If so, he spoke of it to hardly anyone, only to Clifton, who passed on to me only the barest details. Still, I kept my little secret. It could have made no difference anyway, unless, just possibly, had Bradley had my version of what had gone on in Burke's office, he might have used slightly more sympathetic language in his testimony. As in many missed opportunities in life, one can never know what might have been.

The controversy in the media, the Congress, the Pentagon, and no doubt the White House, continued. Rather quickly the press centered on my former boss, Admiral Denfeld. He was seen as supporting the administration, contrary to the expressed disapproval of the Navy Department in general and the naval aviators specifically. The big question posed him by the press was "what side was he on?" The story was a natural—juicy in the sense that it provided plenty of grist for the (typewriter) mills of all the reporters.

In General Bradley's office, I saw the heavyhanded way in which the Navy's efforts to prepare testimony for its side of the strategic weapons controversy were being demolished. Captain Burke's office had been put out of existence, his own career jeopardized. Readers will remember the culmination of this: his name appeared on a selection list as the most junior of a number of captains selected for promotion to rear admiral. When Rowboat Matthews saw the list, which by law and custom was to be forwarded to the Senate for confirmation, he struck off the name of Burke and this nearly spelled the end of that outstanding officer's illustrious career. By good fortune, the law was on Burke's side, the Navy stood by its guns, his name was reinstated and his promotion confirmed. He later served as CNO for an unprecedented six years and is rated as one of the most outstanding such Navy chiefs.

In 1949, however, none of this had yet happened and the then-CNO, Admiral Denfeld, was under increasing pressure from two sides: the administration, to whom in effect he owed his present position—and the Navy itself, his subordinates, led by the naval air arm which saw the issue as one involving its own life, and therefore the Navy in general.

Through it all, General Bradley, who was one of the kindest, most considerate persons I have known, strove to maintain an even keel. He felt he had gone a bit too far with the Fancy Dan speech, but that could not be retracted. He stressed that as Chairman of the Joint Chiefs he had no vote in the deliberations among the three services. He testified to Congress when called, gave advice when asked to the president and the secretary of defense, always counseling moderation, gave interviews to the press in essentially the same vein, but he was powerless to stop the march of events.

Congress, in its function as determinant of the national policy, called more hearings. Bradley testified several times but carefully avoided further controversial language. The Navy would not let him forget the Fancy Dan words, but the main game was not with him. The press liked him. Everyone knew the big game would come when the CNO was called.

I remember thinking at the time that Admiral Denfeld had but two choices. One was to support the administration in its concept of the use of atomic weapons through a single agency, the Air Force. Or he could go down the line with the Navy position, which had pretty well coalesced by this time: that the use of nuclear weapons should only be a last resort and that the best way to project U.S. power across the seas in all ways, from the velvet glove to the mailed fist, was by judicious use of carrier task forces and the embedded traditional ability to act with all degrees of severity, from the mildest to the most strenuous. This contrasted with the Air Force proposals, which amounted to all or nothing.

I remember wondering what Admiral Denfeld's position would be, and recall comparing him to Hamlet, possessed of the best motives, torn between conflicting concepts of his duties, rather hesitatingly certain that whichever way he went he couldn't win. Much has been written about Hamlet, and so far nothing disturbs this analogy. When Denfeld went to testify, I wondered what he would say, but looking back on it from the vantage point of many years, I now feel that his position should have been foreseen as something he couldn't avoid.

He kept his own counsel to the very end, gave no hint of which way he was going, perhaps didn't make up his mind until the last minute. (I don't believe this; I think he simply wanted to use this last opportunity he would have for the best possible effect for the Service he had lived in all his life.) When he testified to Congress, he went down the line for the Navy, stating that the B-36 was an inadequate delivery vehicle for a weapon as important as the atomic bomb, that we in our own Navy already possessed aircraft capable of blocking B-36 missions, or of taking their place, and that foreign countries, using land- or carrier-based aircraft, would inevitably be able to do so as well.

He went on to say that nuclear missions by carrier-based aircraft had greater potential of success, in every way, than those by the B-36. Furthermore, he stated, naval air power, based on mobile airfields like carriers, gave another string to the president's bow should he decide to direct military action of any kind.

As his testimony was delivered, we in the chairman's office were reading just-delivered copies of it. When he finished, there was a mood of concern. "He has just resigned," said Ted Clifton, and that was the general feeling in our office.

It proved to be so. Admiral Denfeld's appointment as Chief of Naval Operations was summarily revoked by President Truman upon Matthews's recommendation, orchestrated by Louis Johnson. He made a triumphal exit from the Pentagon, walking down the steps in front of the building in full, but not ceremonial, uniform (to have put on official regalia, as some urged, would have struck the wrong note), before a crowd of naval officers and civilians standing there cheering him. The word had been given out in naval circles of his planned departure, and the Navy turned out en masse, for he was the sacrifice it needed. The argument that caused the "Revolt of the Admirals" was apparently ended when the CNO was cashiered from his post for having taken the position he did. The Air Force had won a resounding victory, or so it seemed.

It is now evident, however, that in fact the victory went the other way. The spectacle of the highest naval officer on active duty sacrificing himself to testify unreservedly against what he saw as a bad policy, and the undeniable sincerity of all of his adherents, had their effects on the public. The idea of resting U.S. foreign policy on the flawed B-36 and the atomic bomb soon became items of the past. The outbreak of the Korean War—and the vitally needed air power that could only be brought quickly to the pressure points by aircraft carriers and their embarked air wings—made it evident that the Navy and its carrier task forces provided a much more flexible means of projecting our national power than atomic-armed heavy bombers.

Air armadas cannot rival the influence of a naval task force anchoring peacefully—or under sufferance—in some foreign port where the citizens can have a good view of its abilities and determination; or, depending on the circumstances, patrolling at sea inside or outside the range of visibility, as concrete evidence of our national determination. Such uses of sea power, and of navies, have been traditional since the beginning of time. And now, over the years since all this occurred, it has become more and more evident that it is the U.S. Navy that can most effectively project our determination to bend events in the direction we wish them to be bent.

In other words, the Navy has, ever since 1949, been our preferred instrument for the projection of power, and this is true because it has the greatest flexibility.

The revolt of the admirals, the sacrifice of the chief admiral, the demotion or cashiering of others involved in the revolt, was one of the biggest contributions to the future of our country that could have been made. The character of our foreign policy in the years since has shown this to be true. With the examples of Admiral Denfeld, who was the sacrifice, Adm. Arthur Radford, who also nearly was forced out of service but later was recognized for his high quality by becoming chairman of the Joint Chiefs of Staff, and then Capt. Arleigh Burke, who was almost thrown on the trash heap for doing a good job, our admirals, unsung and unheralded, put all they had into the scales. Many brought official displeasure upon themselves for taking the positions they did, some were forced into premature retirement, some suffered in various other subtle ways. In the long verdict of history, as in the long fight against Japan, they won the battle. Our nation is the better for it.

Chapter Twelve

Trigger II, the White House, and Joe Blunt

I had been about two years with General Bradley when something came my way that I could not pass up. The Navy had recently laid the keel for the namesake of my old *Trigger*, and I felt a strong sentimental need to start her right. I had commissioned the first *Trigger* at the start of the war, had had four skippers and been second in command to the last two. She was lost in the area adjacent to ours just as I was coming back as exec of the brand-new *Tirante*. We had been directed to rendezvous with her, and I had planned to visit her in our rubber boat, along with a few others in *Tirante* who had also served in her, exchange plans for joint operations, and of course renew old friendships.

She didn't show up. After three days we slowly came to know she never would, that our ordered rendezvous might have been only to give her a final chance of assistance, possibly ordered by an operations officer who knew that many of *Tirante*'s crew members had once been with me in the *Trigger*.

Such a numbing realization can be appreciated only by those who have been through that special experience. It is different from any other, even from loss of a family member. The bonds between shipmates who have been in combat together, especially submarine shipmates who may be living in their own future tombs, are as intense as the storied bond between men who have huddled together in a foxhole under fire.

When I heard of the new *Trigger*, my old friends had already been gone for several years, but their memories were still very important to me. I felt I must make sure the new submarine was commissioned in their memory, in fealty and kinship to her crew still aboard on their eternal patrol. Bradley and

Clifton fully understood my sentimental need and supported my application. In due course my new orders arrived.

Looking back, on a personal level doing this was a big mistake. The new *Trigger* could have taken the place of my old boat only if she had been an operational success, which she emphatically was not. If *Trigger II* had been successful as a fighting submarine, she might have replaced her namesake. In no other way could she have symbolized the debt our country owed her. I thought, in fact, that this was the reason for giving her this name in the first place, and why the young widow of her lost skipper had been selected to be her sponsor, to send her down the launching ways splashed with champagne and the good wishes of all the ships at sea.

This ceremony did take place, and it did include all the attendant symbolism—but so far as starting the new ship on a successful career, the odds against her were too great. My sentimental approach to imbuing this first of our new postwar subs with the heart and tradition of the ship after which she had been named foundered on the sorry fact that she was unfit to serve in the U.S. Navy.

Before all these troubles developed, however, before our shakedown cruise in fact, there were a few weeks of good operations. Training the crew was easy; they were nearly all veterans of war service. With great pride I was able to wangle orders to bring our navy's newest and best submarine to the Navy Yard in Washington to show her off to the Navy Department there. *Trigger II* was the first of our postwar submarines to become operational, and getting this authorized was easy. Everyone in the submarine service wanted to get a look at this most modern addition to our fleet. To a man, wartime submariners—floating on memories of the magnificent boats in which they had fought Japan's navy and merchant marine—had their own ideas about the required characteristics of our new ones. They should dive deeper; run faster both surfaced and submerged; be more maneuverable under water; carry better sonar, radar, and fire-control equipment; be more habitable, with a better source of fresh water. They should automatically embody all the lessons we had learned during the years of combat.

The visit to Washington was a most pleasant one, well worth the difficult Potomac River passage involved. Most of the submariners in the area, retired and active, made the trip to the navy yard to look over our newest and best submarine. Except for a few questions about her unusual engines, no one foretold the many other faults in her design, or the fiasco she and her five following nearly identical sisters would become.

At that point our problems lay in the future. What sticks most in mind about that trip to Washington, nonetheless, is the aftermath—our return voyage to New London. We embarked the Assistant Secretary of the Navy James Floberg; his aide, Capt. Jimmie Thach, a well-known naval aviator; Jim Shepley, editor-in-chief of *Time* magazine; and Clay Blair, a wartime submariner, now one of *Time*'s top writers whom I had come to know during my Pentagon tours. Everyone admired Thach, an articulate veteran of much naval air combat during the war, and our few days of confinement in a submarine hull gave him an ideal opportunity to brief his captive audience, the assistant secretary. My efforts occasionally to steer the conversation into submarine matters received polite attention, but it seemed to me that Thach monopolized our wardroom talk, and it was all about airplanes and flying. I therefore welcomed Clay's suggestion that we put up a job on his own boss. It would be a welcome diversion, and give me a chance to show what my ship could do that was different from the cut-and-dried drills that were the usual fare.

Shepley had served in the Air Force during the war, and some time previously, according to Clay, Jim had inveigled him into flying with some of his old buddies in an Air Force transport plane, and during the flight had arranged a fake emergency for his benefit. The pilot announced the "emergency," directed all on board to don parachutes and prepare to jump. As Clay nervously put on the unfamiliar gear and listened to the hasty briefing given by a crew member, the plane maneuvered violently to handle whatever it was that had gone wrong. But all effort was to no avail, and the pilot finally ordered all hands to get ready to bail out. It was not until then—with Clay unhappily lined up with the other crew members, ready to make the first parachute jump in his life—that everyone relaxed and told him the whole thing had been a putup job from the beginning. Clay wanted to inflict a condign revenge. Could we fake a submarine emergency that would convince the fairly skeptical Shepley?

A whole series of war emergencies flashed through my mind, many real, others embellished by the tellers over drinks between patrols. Now I held a quick conference with key crew members, out of earshot of the wardroom. Specific jobs were assigned to each man, some of course to keep the ship under control in spite of the uproar to be generated by the others. I also did my duty by carefully briefing the assistant secretary and his aide in Jim Shepley's absence. To the trained submarine veterans I commanded, it was a great lark requiring no rehearsal. *Trigger* made a routine dive in the middle of the morning for no particular reason. It was just a morning drill, I informed our guests.

We did a few routine maneuvers, but then suddenly our bow dipped alarmingly, and without warning our normally horizontal decks were like the side of a steep hill. We were headed downward at a 30-degree angle, and everyone began to shout. The most respected sailor on board—our chief of the boat, with many war patrols under his belt and well introduced to our august passengers—yelled "Flash the blast mat!" at me, and I shouted back, "Blast the flash at once! Hurry!" A sailor ran past us in the ship's only passageway shrieking, "Married men first!" When he reached the forward torpedo room he turned and ran in the opposite direction, still screaming at the top of his lungs. One benighted heathen had a sledgehammer which he enthusiastically hammered on our steel bulkheads in my vicinity—and that of our passengers.

In the meantime, loosely stowed gear, some strategically placed with malice aforethought, had been tumbling with the huge down angle the boat had assumed. A coffee cup with a small bit of stale coffee had been left on the wardroom table, and it was now in smithereens in a little brown puddle on our immaculate floor. There was shouting from the controlroom, where the diving officer could be heard loudly ordering his planesmen to "Get the angle off, men! Come on, fellows, put your backs into it! Full rise on all planes!"—in the meantime, with quiet hand signals, ordering his crew to maintain the angle as ordered in the first place. Then a stroke of genius— "Flood down express tank! Blow negative with high pressure air! Start the turbo-blow!" "Down express" was the original name of the "negative tank," used, as the name indicates, to give the diving submarine negative buoyancy to speed up the diving process—and *Trigger*'s design used engine exhaust in place of the older "turbo-blowers" to finish emptying her ballast tanks. Of course, in the fully submerged condition the engines would not be running, nor could the turbo-blowers be used because of the pressure differential, let alone the amount of air required. But such considerations did not detract from the impressive commands, especially when given with loud urgency.

All hands had been directed that the "pandemonium drill" was to last exactly one minute, and Blair and I had stationed ourselves in the vicinity of our guests to enjoy the fun. Thach wore a solemn look, indicating to me that he hoped I knew what I was doing; Floberg had a similar sober expression as he balanced himself on the steeply sloping deck. Shepley, for whom the entire exercise had been concocted, had been caught—as intended—by surprise. Our game plan worked exactly as hoped. Clay and I can testify that Jim's lips quivered momentarily—maybe because he wanted to ask if all this was for real—but he said nothing, bore his tribulation like the true soldier he undoubtedly was. It's even possible that he half expected Clay to try to get even for the trick he had played on him with his aviator friends, but Clay and I will swear forever that the relief on his face after the expiration of the minute of uproar was as real as anything could have been.

For *Trigger*'s crew our "pandemonium drill," as we termed it, was sheer fun for everyone, with a single exception. It was a welcome break in routine; a source of stories with which to regale their friends; a chance to show a bit of originality in their truly demanding profession; and a bedrock opportunity to demonstrate their total control and command of an unusual and highly technical mechanism—the modern U.S. submarine. In this I shared with utmost delight. The exception to this general reaction was our assistant engineer, one of whose assigned duties was as "damage control officer." He had come off watch a short time before the exec and I had given the quiet briefing to our crew, was sound asleep at the time, and no one had thought to call him. He awoke when he found himself sliding out of his bunk against the forward bulkhead and found the program he had so laboriously built to cope with casualties of all kinds—in particular the unexpected—had inexplicably gone entirely to Hell! It was an hour or two before he was able to laugh with the rest of us.

But the foregoing is virtually the only pleasurable memory I can hold of *Trigger II*. My new ship, the first to become operational of a new and different submarine design for our navy, must have been designed by a neophyte committee of amateur inventors who did not test their products before installing them. From main engines to periscopes, nothing in her worked the way it should.

This is not the place, nor is there the space and time, to go through *Trigger II*'s deficiencies. They were embarrassingly numerous. One would have thought that the U.S. Navy, having built its wonderful World War II subs, would know how to build even better ones after the war, but this was not the case. The ship was a fiasco, and at the conclusion of our shakedown cruise, which consisted of a series of engineering breakdowns and was therefore also a fiasco, I felt it necessary to state plainly to my superiors, via official dispatch, that my ship, the U.S. Navy's newest and theoretically best submarine, was not fit for service. To my surprise, this brought no sympathetic approbation for forthrightness, but criticism for bringing up the unpleasant fact!

The experience gave me at least some idea of why our torpedo problems during the war took so long to fix. In both cases the persons at fault were nearer the seat of power than those complaining, and got there with explanations, though not necessarily accurate ones, much quicker.

My new submarine was the first of six sisterships of the new class to get to sea. By the time all six had gotten clear of the building yards, figuratively at least there must have been an embarrassed frown on the face of the BuShips designers. All six boats had the same problems, some worse than ours. One had to cross the Atlantic from the Royal Navy submarine base in England at the end of a towline, every one of her engines broken down beyond repair. No one, of course, thought to apologize for the bad time they had given me when I surfaced the difficulties we had faced. That came a few years later, and from an extraordinary source.

Trigger II's shakedown cruise should have been a great one, to Rio de Janeiro, but we on board advisedly called it a "shakeup" instead of a "shakedown." Afterward she was a long time in post-voyage repair, and then one day, as we were being drydocked in a marine railway and temporarily out of contact with the world, a huge crane swung unexpectedly overhead and gently lowered a ringing telephone to our deck. "For you, Captain," said the surprised sailor who picked it up. It was a call from the Navy Department in Washington, D.C. Could I be there tomorrow? No, my caller could not tell me what for.

Next day in our nation's capital I was informed that the newly elected president of the United States, Dwight Eisenhower, had asked for me to be assigned as his naval aide. The only thing I could think was that General Bradley must have recommended me to his old friend and classmate.

My four years as naval aide to the president of the United States were of course a wonderful, heady time. I quickly found, however, that President Eisenhower had different ideas about the duties of his military aides than President Truman. Truman's naval aide was a rear admiral. I was only a commander in the Navy, but I found myself relieving Rear Adm. Robert Dennison, already an officer of great consequence, in his office in the East Wing of the White House. It was evident that Eisenhower did not feel Truman's need for top-level assistants from the armed services. He was already a general, five stars at that. If he needed anything from the Pentagon, or any other part of the military, he would go directly to the top of the service involved. My job was to keep the conduits open at a lower level, to help handle the innumerable papers and phone calls that flowed across the Potomac River between the Pentagon and the White House.

I was also in charge of the *Williamsburg*, the presidential yacht, and of Shangri-La, the presidential retreat in the Catoctin Mountains. Shangri-La was operated by the *Williamsburg* crew and became famous during the war when Franklin Roosevelt announced that the Tokyo bombing raid of 1942 had come from there. (I was upset, back then, when I heard FDR's statement, on the radio, that he would "tell the Japanese where the planes had come from." I feared he would reveal it was the USS *Hornet,* and can still recall my delight when I heard the wonderful tone of voice with which he told the world that the attack had come from "Shangri-Laaah." His inflection could not have been more on the mark, and there is no way I know of to reproduce it in print. Parenthetically, this also inspired bestowing the name on a new aircraft carrier, and she actually did fly planes against Japan.)

Eisenhower very soon sampled the bucolic pleasure of the former Civilian Conservation Corps camp that Roosevelt and Truman had loved. I secretly felt that partly in order to divorce himself from his predecessors and assert his own dominance over this place he had so fully fallen in love with he ordered that Shangri-La be renamed "Camp David," for his grandson. It then fell to me to have a new wooden sign made, replacing the old name with the new (some distance off the road, however, so as not to attract tourists). A second presidential visit being in the immediate future, we had to hurry; the quickest way to get it up was to turn the old one around, with the new name carved on the reverse. The back was neatly covered with a thin slab of the same wood so that the old name could not be seen, and the rustic board rehung under its little roof. At the time I thought this an ingenious idea, since it would facilitate restoration should that later be wanted. Today the sign, no doubt replaced long since, would be a collector's item.

The *Williamsburg* was another matter. During his campaign for the presidency, Eisenhower had announced that he saw no need for a luxurious private yacht and, if elected, would have her put out of commission. He saw the matter as a campaign promise, maybe thinking of doing away with President Truman's *Williamsburg* as another means of distancing himself from his predecessor.

Truman truly had enjoyed the fine little yacht our Navy had taken over during the war. The former owner didn't want her back, and the Navy wanted to keep her in operation as a very successful "foot in the door" to the White House. She was not very large, as ships go, being considerably smaller than a Navy destroyer, with smaller engines, but she had magnificent guest quarters, and her public rooms were impeccable. The Secret Service loved her because of the additional equipment she enabled them to carry and because of the great communications service she rendered with her ship-borne radios during Truman's fairly frequent visits to Key West. Truman usually flew down, the trip being a bit lengthy by sea and also sometimes rough, but once moored in Key West the little ship was a wonderful headquarters for all the things the Secret Service had to do in serving and protecting the president and his party.

I felt it my duty at least to show the *Williamsburg* to her best advantage. With the enthusiastic help of all involved, in May of 1953 we succeeded in arranging a weekend presidential trip in her to the colonial town of Williamsburg, followed by a visit to the Naval Station at Norfolk, where the Navy promised a proper presidential reception, with full honors.

The *Williamsburg* departed Washington on a Thursday night in mid-May, proceeded down the Potomac River into Chesapeake Bay and then into the York River. We passed Yorktown in the early morning, and shortly after 0800 arrived at the naval mine and ammunition depot, a few miles upstream, where a convenient dock was located. This was close to the colonial town after which the yacht had been named. We were met there by cars that took the entire party to the city of Williamsburg. There I saw another facet of Eisenhower's character. He was toured through the preserved and restored colonial buildings, and in the House of Burgesses graciously consented to take the ancient podium. There, however, instead of saying the platitudes we all expected, he declaimed a portion of the famous Resolution of the House of Burgesses that had found its way, nearly verbatim, into the Declaration of Independence!

Following this spur-of-the-moment speech the motorcade took us for a brief visit to the famous Bruton Parish Church in Williamsburg, and then to the College of William and Mary, where Eisenhower received an honorary doctorate and addressed the student body. The motorcade then returned everyone to the waiting yacht, which promptly got under way and anchored for the night, and a good part of the morning, in Chesapeake Bay. My diary for the trip mentions two small fishing parties during these leisure hours, indulged in primarily by newsmen who had chartered a smaller yacht with which to accompany us plus, my notes say, a few members of the presidential party as well.

Everything was, of course, timed to the minute, if not the very second. At precisely 1330 on Saturday, *Williamsburg* moored to the designated pier at the Naval Station, Norfolk, and was received with full honors to the chief executive.

The Navy truly did itself proud. Our entry to the naval station was marked with gun salutes and all the other honors it could give, with white-clad sailors manning the rails of all the ships in sight. The highest naval dignitaries made official calls on the president, all carefully arranged according to protocol. Mrs. Eisenhower's mother, sister, and brother-in-law had been invited as part of the president's entourage, and it was obvious they greatly enjoyed the occasion. Navy photographers were everywhere; I still have my copy of the scrapbook they made.

The entire trip was an unmitigated success. I was proud of the Navy, and of my part in it. Not one thing had gone wrong, the *Williamsburg* had performed immaculately, our careful time schedule had been met meticulously. If anything could save the presidential yacht, this would be it! Mrs. Eisenhower was particularly warm, as were her close family members, and, indeed, everyone in the presidential party.

President Eisenhower congratulated me, too, but a day or so later I discovered he had not changed his mind. I was in the Oval Office on some errand when Mrs. Eisenhower walked in and, seeing me, immediately brought up the pending decommissioning of the yacht. I had hoped to have the chance to argue for retention, but had not yet brought up the matter when the wife of the boss did it for me. Her praise for the *Williamsburg* could not have been beaten. I could not have asked for a better advocate for the Navy's cause. But as she spoke I could see a look settle on Ike's face that, in other contexts and at other times, I have seen on other husbands' faces, and may, from time to time, have worn on mine. I was witnessing a fight between the president of the United States and his first lady, and it was over me—or at least, over the presidential yacht for which I held responsibility!

Furthermore, I could see that I had lost, even before Eisenhower said a word. Finally, as nearly as I recall, and with just a bit of a snap down low in his throat that his wife had no doubt heard many times, he growled, "I'm sorry, Mamie. I've promised, and there's nothing more to be said about it!"

Prior to decommissioning, Eisenhower authorized several special daylight cruises for injured veterans of all services, and these we did with pleasure. All that came wore their best uniforms. Many were recently back from Korea, some with awful injuries. A number had to have special nurses with them, and this I didn't even bother to ask Eisenhower about, made the instant decision that all the nurses were welcome, as well as any close adult family members in the area. The nurses, too, wore their best outfits, and the attentive care they took of their charges was great to see. We had naturally asked the president if he wanted to make one or more of the trips, but there were too many things competing for his time, and he settled instead for seeing the biggest group off and giving them a little talk.

So the final service of the *Williamsburg* was to repay in small measure some of the huge debt our country owes its young servicemen. We provided a buffet meal, music by a Navy band, and comfortable places to lie down for those who might need to do so. Many of them were so terribly wounded that it was obvious they could never return to normal lives. One in particular that I remember had lost half his skull. The skin was now well healed, but his head had a huge depression on one side, and he had lost much of his motor coordination. He was a handsome, strongly built young chap, but now he was in a wheelchair, and the attractive nurse who was with him never left his side.

Finally, sad to tell, came the day when the *Williamsburg* had to be decommissioned. It was a very solemn occasion, as are all such ceremonies, rather like a funeral. All the crew were in their best uniforms, many showing near tears in their eyes. I had, of course, had ample opportunity to recognize their high morale and devotion to duty. They had undergone the most rigid selection process before being assigned to the ship, and felt deeply their very special obligation to the White House, most particularly to the president. In everything they did, they stood proudly for the Navy. If any one of them fell by the wayside in any manner, even in common gentility, he was sent to other duty. They had built their own very special little world around this ship, done their absolute best for her, but had lost the battle in a way most of them probably hardly understood. I, too, had a lump in my throat as I ordered her flags hauled down.

A high point in my White House time was when I convinced Mamie Eisenhower that Rickover's atomic-powered *Nautilus* was going to be the most important ship launched in the entire century, and that she should accept no invitations to sponsor any ship until *Nautilus* was ready. I laid it on fairly thick, but she bought the idea, as did the president. Little by little, the event drew near. Plans were made.

Even so, it needs to be noted, through failure of being selected for promotion at the 30-year deadline, Captain Rickover was nearly forced to retire from active duty a year before the launch of his epoch-building ship. Graduating from Annapolis in 1922, he had passed the 30-year point in 1952, was extended for one additional selection board in 1953, failed of selection by that board also. The word was passed around that there were other officers in BuShips who could do the job, that, as in all military organizations, if the chief falls the next in line picks up his banner—and so on. Not in this case, and I was one of those who knew there was no one even remotely qualified to fill Rickover's shoes.

Before the selection board results are firm they must be sent to the president, who, if he agrees, must then submit the list of selectees to the Senate, usually for automatic approval by "consent" vote. The next day the list goes back to the White House for the president's signature, and this is technically the moment it becomes law. Eisenhower knew all this from his Army days, and knew also that although he could disapprove the list submitted to him in whole or in part, he could not add a name to it. The 1953 list was brought to my office by special messenger, and according to formula I prepared a forwarding memo to him, stretching things just a little by noting the absence of Rickover's name.

According to the formula, it was then sent to the Senate, where nothing happened. Several days passed. I received several telephone calls, first asking if I could expedite things, then shifting over to, "Do you know what's the matter?"

As if they didn't know. There was nothing I could find out, or do, nor would I have. Things simply had to run their course. Waiting formed its own pressures.

In a few days, Secretary of the Navy Robert B. Anderson was in the White House and came to my office. We were on good terms. Once he had asked me my thoughts about naming new aircraft carriers. He wanted now to tell me how he proposed to handle the selection board impasse. He would call a new, special board with instructions to select a single Engineering Duty captain for immediate promotion to rear admiral, and was curious as to my reaction. Advisors had assured him this was within his purview. Did I think this might get the Senate to release its hold on "the list," and how did I think "the boss" would react? I told him I thought Ike knew exactly what was going on and was obviously waiting to see what the Navy would do. It was entirely up to the Navy, I said.

I also told him that in the Navy there was a very strong anti-Rickover feeling, mainly because of his personality and rough way of doing business, and if the Senate cleared the promotion list before the Rickover matter was settled to its satisfaction, the principal incentive to do so would no longer exist. For this reason, any effort to cause the Senate to do this would be premature and counterproductive. The Senate would almost certainly not release the list, and the press could not fail to appreciate the Navy's still further loss of prestige and control over its own business.

"That's what I think, too," said Anderson. Then, sensing my chance, I brought up my main message. "The new board needs to be prevented from picking one of the others who may have been a little into atomic energy in past years but have no connection with what Rickover's doing. He's the one and only. Even if the precept can't name him by name, somehow this has to be clear."

"Don't worry about that," said Anderson. "They'll know."

For the record, that's how it came out. I don't claim having decisively affected events. That was done by the Senate of the United States, principally Sen. Henry "Scoop" Jackson of Washington State, who died in office years later. The next-built Trident submarine was given the name *Henry M. Jackson* as a memorial to him, and well did he merit it.

The day after Anderson's special board named Rickover (to the best of my recollection this "list"—consisting of only a single name—did not go through my office; it was carried directly to the president, probably by Anderson himself) the Senate's approval of the earlier list of some 20 names was also delivered. "Democracy" had worked. The press found new causes to pursue. The Navy's discomfiture did not last long, and Admiral Rickover was on the way to making history.

This was the background of my getting Mamie to expect the Navy to ask her to christen the *Nautilus* at her launching, which was scheduled for 21 January 1954. Being naval aide had its drawbacks, I immediately found. Fairly adjudicating, among all the claimants, the innumerable details that had to be handled about this launching would have driven a saint wild. It wasn't until I had gotten into the problem that I realized this was the first time, to my knowl-edge in any event, that the White House had itself launched a ship. Until *Nau-tilus,* it had all been done by the builders. In keeping with all the other "firsts" marked by that famous submarine, the shoe was on the other foot for the first time. It was the White House, for example, which told Rickover, and all other pertinent Navy and Electric Boat officials, that Mamie Eisenhower should be the sponsor. Possibly they had already decided this, for no other potential spon-sors were suggested. Secretary Anderson simply nodded when I mentioned this to him. But it was the White House that found itself, willy-nilly, deeply con-cerned with all the protocol, and nearly all of this flowed through the naval aide.

All arrangements, invitation lists, seating plans in the train, berths assigned, who went to lunch and dinner, and where they sat on the train and at the big Electric Boat lunch after the launching—everything, it seemed to me, that was in any way connected to the affair—wound up on my desk. Truth to tell, there were at least a dozen other offices also involved, each with its own VIPs, problems, and agendas, so that I had a dozen prima-donnas, not the principals but their top assistants, to keep happy. I made several preliminary trips to Groton, to the EB plant and elsewhere, learning in the process hereafter to call the place by its new name, General Dynamics, and making the acquaintance of its new chief, John Jay Hopkins. Finally, as such complicated affairs always do, but not until the last minute, it all fell together, just as for the *Williamsburg*'s trip to Norfolk, except for two items, of which more later. The designated skipper of the new boat, Cdr. Dennis Wilkinson, would, as was custom, ride his new ship down the ways, along with her crew, and I had a duty to perform for him, too. I had ridden *Trigger II* down the ways a few years earlier, but no one had thought to do anything special for Ingrid. This time, I vowed, that too would be handled right. Dennis's wife, Janice, was invited by Mrs. Eisenhower to be her matron of honor, received a large bouquet of flowers from General Dynamics, and stood with her on the platform as the first lady did her duty.

I also inquired about Admiral Rickover, received assurance that he would have a prominent spot in the stand, and that a modest place would be reserved also for Ingrid.

One of the other things I had thought to do was brief Mrs. Eisenhower on how to do this right. Several launchings I had seen had turned slightly sour at the critical moment because, with the new ship beginning to back away from the launching platform, the champagne bottle had not been swung hard enough to smash satisfactorily. Men of the sea, not overly superstitious but attentive all the same, watch over all omens, good or bad. Breaking the champagne too soon is a bad omen; not breaking it at all is worse. Best of all is for the champagne to froth violently, all over the ship's bow, just as she begins to move on the launching ways.

Mamie told me she had never launched a ship before. I carefully explained these niceties to her, somewhat to her dismay, and asked her please to have someone get her some ordinary wine bottles, fill them with water, and wrap them in a kitchen towel. Then she should smash them against something hard at about waist level.

"There's no danger from broken glass because the champagne bottle will be wrapped in a thin silver sheath, and that's what the kitchen towel is substituting for," I told her seriously, "but you'll probably not break the first one or two anyway because you'll likely not hit hard enough. You've got to hit that bottle really hard, and right in the middle against something sticking out a little, like the corner of a stone building." I pantomimed how to hold the bottle and swing it, and she promised to practice until she had the technique down well. Also, I warned her about the splash of champagne. "That's why you should put water in the bottle," I said, to give you the right feel for the weight, and to get you used to the splash. You'll get your sleeves a little wet, not badly, but that's no matter."

I also checked how she would swing the bottle, right-handed or left-handed, in case General Dynamics wanted to weld a small "hitting place" on the tip of the submarine's bow. She was a right-hander, she told me, and in a few days her secretary came to tell me that she had indeed practiced, had learned how to break a full wine bottle every time, and was grateful for the special instruction.

The timing of the launch was apparently critical because of the need to have it happen at high water in the Thames River. At a fairly laborious conference two weeks earlier in Groton, everything had been worked backward from the time of high water, scheduled for shortly before noon. I was to escort Mamie to the cordoned spot just at the bow of the ship. On the way, because of press importunations for "photo opportunity," we were to pass before a rather large set of stands reserved for photographers, and it was agreed she should stop in front of it for pictures with the beautifully sheathed bottle of champagne, which she would by this time be carrying herself. I promised to step away from her while this was going on.

Mounted on the rail of the launching platform was a small three-inch-diameter clock with a minute hand only. This was exclusively for my use. The last 15 minutes before the hour, until the minute hand stood straight up, were marked into pie slices of different colors. These were the time slots, relating exclusively to the minutes prior to the moment of launch. I had in my hand a small card bearing in large letters the exact places and times she was to pose with the champagne bottle during those critical minutes, and had carefully briefed her. The first lady was to be up there when the clock's minute hand entered the final five-minute slice of pie, give another photo-op, get herself all set, and hit the champagne bottle against *Nautilus*'s bow when the minute hand was straight up and down. My job was to get her there when the minute hand entered that last piece of pie, and make sure she was ready the moment the ship began to move.

Alongside the clock was a simple light switch, under a green cover plate. As the minute hand approached "12," I was to be sure that Mrs. Eisenhower was completely ready, then flip the switch, and fully concentrate on her, for the ship's hitherto immobile bow, towering above us, would almost immediately begin to slide away on the heavily greased launching ways. The switch would turn on a light under our platform, which would be the signal for the launching crew stationed beneath it to release the final holding clamps and send *Nautilus* down the ways. I had also been categorically promised by General Dynamics that there was no way the ship would begin to move until I turned on the light.

Simplicity itself, but here was where one of the two things that went wrong that day happened. No one, apparently, had fully evaluated the ebullience of the General Dynamics chairman who had recently acquired Electric Boat. He was a new chief executive officer, a very wealthy man, a little difficult to know. Perhaps his people had not properly briefed him. Immediately following the final speeches and benedictions, Mamie was scheduled to begin moving toward the launching platform, followed by the matron of honor with her own bouquet, ready to take Mrs. Eisenhower's at the proper moment also, and myself with the champagne to hand to her.

No sooner had the final benediction been given, however, than John Jay Hopkins, CEO of General Dynamics and therefore seated in the front row alongside her, leaped to his feet, grabbed Mrs. Eisenhower's arm, and sang out, "Let's go and do it, Mamie!" I was several seats away and one or two rows back, as I recall—too far to stop him. Thunderstruck, I ran along behind with the vital champagne bottle, followed by Janice Wilkinson carrying out her instructions to stay close to the first lady when this moment arrived.

Hopkins paid no attention to the photographers, who were clamoring for their promised opportunity, nor to his own watch, which, like mine and the pie-marked clock on the launching stand, showed a full 15 minutes before the scheduled high-water moment. Almost dragging Mrs. Eisenhower behind him by the arm, he got her to the launching platform in about one minute, far from the 10 minutes we had planned for the photographers. When Janice and I caught up with them, the whole carefully timed launching sequence had been thrown out of order.

"Give me the champagne," whispered Mrs. Ike, and she stood like the seasoned trooper she was, holding it and smiling gloriously for the now frantic cameramen. She posed like this for several minutes, turning this way and that, holding the shining silver-cased bottle so that everyone could see, then whispered, "Can I do it now?"

"Not yet. It's too soon," I whispered back. The clock's minute hand was indicating seven more minutes to go. She turned her attention back to the flashbulb-shooting media, who were still working their equipment for all it was worth. Hopkins was having his moment of glory, too, by her side, and poor Janice was hovering anxiously by. She had put down her own bouquet and was now holding only the one Mrs. Eisenhower had hurriedly given her.

The pressure became pretty intense. I had promised to flip the little switch exactly at "noon" by the minute-hand-only clock that now guided us, and there were still five minutes to go, but the First Lady of the Land was also becoming impatient. "Can't I launch her now? I'm getting tired," she muttered, slightly more strenuously in tone.

The magic moment had unquestionably arrived. The news cameramen had slowed down their flashbulbs, saving them for the climactic shot. The time was not yet, but I could feel the pressure of the Western world on my shoulders. "All right," I whispered back. Get ready!" Mamie gripped the neck of the bottle with both hands. "I'm ready!" she said.

I flipped the little light switch. Nothing happened. The ship was supposed to move immediately. Nothing. Everything was silent. Conversation had stopped, everyone was staring at the tableau before them, the cameras were poised. The ship simply did not move.

I put my hand against the bow, so that I could feel the slightest tremor of movement. Nothing. "Can't I do it now?" asked Mrs. Eisenhower. "No, ma'am," I responded. "You've got to hit it just when she starts to go!"

By this time I was pushing hard on the bow of the ship, as if I could by my own strength overcome whatever it was that was refusing to release her. Stories of ships that had stuck on the ways for days, even weeks, crossed my mind. What could we do? I pushed as hard as I could. Mamie could not have been more prepared. Unconsciously, I had put my arm behind her back so as to get her even more closely to the bow of the unmoving ship, when suddenly I felt the *Nautilus* begin to move away.

"Now! Hit it!" I yelled in her ear. Mamie was indeed ready. The pent-up emotion of the moment had gotten to her, too. She swung that bottle hard and fair. By this time the ship's bow had actually moved several inches, perhaps an entire foot from us, and to my amazement had begun truly moving fast. But Mamie was totally equal to the challenge. She hit that receding bow with a mighty blow. Champagne spurted everywhere, and her sleeves were doused with the fluid. Everyone cheered. Horns blew, lights flashed, the photographers, some of them said, had the best shot of a launching they had ever had.

Everyone commented, then and later, that the first lady looked "just super" as she did her job, that the launching was "perfect."

Some of the pictures showed the other persons up on the launching platform: Hopkins is ducking the anticipated spray of champagne, and there's a definite look of strain on my face. After all, I was trying to push the ship down the ways!

Later investigation of just what had been the holdup revealed that it was all the fault of the General Dynamics CEO. Hopkins, jumping the gun at the last minute, had gotten Mrs. Eisenhower to the launching platform too soon, and without any warning to the launching crew. Hidden under the platform, the launch mechanics knew there were 15 minutes to go and were not watching the light bulb that was to be their signal. They had simply not seen it when I turned it on. When they did see it, they hurriedly released the clamps—and they, too, were astonished at how fast the ship started to slide down the ways. It was a good thing that I had my hands on the ship's bow and was able to feel her first quickening, for there was only one chance after all the lengthy preparation: months of getting ready, reduced to a split second of mixed up timing. A very near thing indeed.

To everyone but me, however, the entire affair had been a huge success, the best launching ever, the best photographs. It was also remarked that even the heavens seemed to cooperate. It had been a dark and cloudy January day until the moment of launch, but then the skies cleared and bright sunshine flooded the area as that fortunate ship took to her element.

Electric Boat then put on a truly fabulous reception and lunch, as one might expect, following which the presidential party reembarked on its train for the overnight trip back to Washington, D.C., and here came our second unexpected problem. The first lady's sister and brother-in-law, whom, along with her mother, she had invited to the launching and who had ridden up with her from Washington, were not on board! Mrs. Doud, her mother, had gotten aboard, but the Moores had somehow missed the train. They were nowhere to be found, and our Washington-bound express was already speeding along the coast of Connecticut.

Mrs. Eisenhower was understandably upset. She had already had a very long day and had been very much "on stage." I saw a testiness in her I had not yet experienced. Something had to be done, and fast. She was near to exploding, though against whom, or what, no one could fathom. To some extent she seemed to blame me, although I had had no connection with her sister, or her plans, had not had anything to do with her seating at lunch. It was after lunch that the Moores had disappeared, as the guests went to the various buses marked for their divergent destinations.

It was soon surmised that they had simply gotten on the wrong bus, not one marked for the train to Washington—and here was where I first became aware of the extraordinary capability of the U.S. Secret Service, although, truth to tell, the first lady's sister getting on the wrong bus was their fault, too. There had been a Secret Service man accompanying them, and he must have had radio contact with one of his colleagues on the train. At all events, our train suddenly pulled off on a siding where it waited about an hour, poised on a grade crossing under which ran a fair-sized road, and at the end of that time a car appeared, stopped, and the missing pair, assisted by a couple of athletic-looking young men in business suits, climbed up the embankment and entered our train. End of problem, except that I could not get over the idea that somehow Mrs. Ike had felt it was my fault.

In my White House time there was, however, the difficulty I mentioned earlier in these pages, about which I have been reticent until now. A number of persons have from time to time asked me why I decided to retire from active duty in the Navy after a career that seemed to have been most successful, and looked pretty sure to attain high place. Why did I give all this up? A lengthy article in the *Navy Times* some years ago by Paul Stillwell, now an important member of the Naval Institute staff, went into this at some length. He came closer than he knew to the right answer in a number of conjectures, and ended with the thought that someday I might tell the story.

This is much easier suggested than actually done. How does one say, "Let me tell you how a wartime acquaintance I had once admired, a senior officer who pretended friendship, used the selection board system to achieve mean-spirited revenge because, as Naval Aide to the President of the United States, I would not employ my supposed influence to further his chances of selection for promotion to flag rank?" It was almost disloyal to the Navy and its ingrained procedures to voice such an excuse for my own personal failure.

Before coming to the White House, I had been working on a novel about submarine warfare in World War II, and I finished it while there (but not on government or White House time). The book, *Run Silent, Run Deep,* appeared in 1955. Shortly after publication, I received a phone call: "Ned, just whom did you have in mind in that character, 'Joe Blunt' in your book?"

The speaker thought he had recognized himself in the fictional character to whom I had given that name, and evidently believed I therefore owed him something. I replied that "Joe Blunt" was actually an amalgam of several submarine officers I knew, or knew of, and that the name was one my father had used for an important character in one of his own novels about the Navy half a century earlier. One of the descriptive passages about my "Joe Blunt" was that "diesel fuel ran in his veins instead of blood"—a statement that might have been applied to several persons, one of them "Uncle Charlie" Lockwood, our submarine force commander in the war. It might also at one time have been used to describe Admiral Nimitz himself. Both had once held the unofficial title of "Mr. Submarine." Possibly my interlocutor aspired to succeed to that popular accolade.

"Joe Blunt" in my novel was a fictional submarine squadron commander, a sympathetic superior to "Rich Richardson," hero of the story. The person for whom "Joe Blunt" is used here, in the pages of this book, not at all the fictional person in *Run Silent, Run Deep,* was never my skipper or squadron commander but had once been friendly to me in an unofficial way. When I first met him, shortly after I arrived in Pearl Harbor as *Trigger*'s junior officer, he was several ranks senior to me (I was a lieutenant junior grade and he a commander on the force commander staff). My first awareness of him was an unexpected invitation to accompany him on a visit to the home of friends in Honolulu. Complimented by his surprising personal attention and at the same time puzzled, since I didn't know him at all, I asked my exec in *Trigger* about it. I've never forgotten Penrod Schneider's answer, which was a clear warning: "[Joe Blunt] can be either a good friend or a bad enemy."

Years later, on the telephone in my White House office, the tone of his voice caused me to answer carefully. "As a matter of fact, sir," I said, "I combined two people I knew, and it's true that you were one of them." I had expected him to be pleased with the Joe Blunt character. Maybe he was, but from the tone of his voice I couldn't be sure.

He went on to what was evidently the real purpose of his call. He was scheduled for consideration by the Admiral's Selection Board that very year, and he wanted me to write an article for the Naval Institute *Proceedings* in support of his candidacy. The article would point out that submarine officers selected for flag rank had in the past always been fewer in number than their percentage in the grades warranted, and now that the war had ended, with the submariners having made the great contributions they had, there should be more of them selected—and didn't I think Eisenhower thought the same way?

For the Naval Aide to the President to publish such an article at such a time, especially if it inferred somehow that it reflected Eisenhower's own wishes, struck me as highly improper. For "Blunt" to ask such a thing of an officer years junior to him on the basis of past kindliness, or for any reason, made me uneasy. I remember wondering if he understood what he was asking, and even if he were fully in his right mind. Today I'm guessing he might not have been, perhaps never was.

When I told him I could not write the article he wanted, which I did as tactfully as I could, he was furious, shouted, "We'll see how that comes out!" and slammed down the telephone. I knew what he meant by that statement, but I did not believe anyone could so pervert the idealistic functions of the Navy's promotion system. When he was selected rear admiral all the same, but without help from the White House, I knew I had made a powerful enemy; that, having not cooperated with his personal campaign for promotion, I had now become a focal point for revenge. I was a highly visible target.

The next thing was quite a surprise. The captain's board was next to meet. I was a commander; barring something unusual my name would not be up for consideration. But suddenly the word began to spread that I was on the list. I heard it at least half a dozen times in one day: "They've got Beach!" The captain's board had dipped below the normal zone and selected me! I was, of course, both surprised and pleased, and also a bit concerned as to how I should take it, what I should do. After considerable thought, I decided that when it became official I would have to ask the president to release me for sea duty, since the Navy was my career. As a newly made captain, I thought, I should go to sea as soon as possible.

It was just as well I waited, for when the new captain's list came to my office for forwarding to the president, my name was not on it. Perhaps it had never been there, or perhaps it had been deleted. The rumors died even faster than they had sprung up. No doubt I should have investigated to find out what had actually happened, but I felt this was not an ethical thing to do either, so I did nothing. Another mistake.

The next year, when the captain's selection board was to meet, I was of course alert for the results; but even before the list reached my office for the perfunctory forwarding to the president, my phone rang. It was "Joe Blunt"— the first time we had talked since the business about the abortive article for the *Proceedings*. "Ned, aren't you pleased about the board?" he asked. There was a malevolent note in his voice. "Let me read you the great list of fine submariners they've got on there!" He proceeded to read the last half-dozen names on the list, the most junior ones selected, beginning with mine. After me were the best submarine officers we had, or that I could name, who were commanders junior to me. "Isn't this a great list!" enthused "Joe." "Top performers, every one!"

I could not but agree, wondering the while just what it was that I was hearing. The triumphant tone in "Joe's" voice was telling me something: he had managed to block my selection for captain the year before (no word from him about that, of course), and now he had somehow had something to do with bringing a number of top performers up to be almost exactly equal to me on the list. Some of them had been as deeply selected as I might have been the year before, and he was telling me that all of them were now positioned on the captain's list to be available as rivals for the admiral's list in future years!

In due course, this is what happened. During the next several years when it came my turn to be considered for promotion, all of these were advanced, but five successive selection boards passed me by. I am the only Naval Aide to the President of the United States to have failed of selection to the rank of rear admiral, even though, up to that point, I had an outstanding record, unblemished in any way. But I had incurred the enmity of an unprincipled individual who, though well known to be lacking in moral stature, nonetheless had clout in the submarine service, probably because of that very quality. Years later, a member of one of the boards that had had my name before it told me that "it was the submariners who did you in. If it hadn't been for them, we'd have had you on the list!"

For the record, my nemesis was probably a physical coward, too. He spent nearly the entire war at a desk job in Pearl Harbor. As an admiral he was said by some to have "done more damage to the submarine force" than any other individual. Even as idealistic an outfit as our Navy cannot avoid having some men of this caliber.

That our promotion system could have been manipulated to my disfavor was hard to take, though I guessed then, and know now, how this was managed. Several other comments, less authoritative than the one quoted above, have been in similar vein. All have pointed to machinations by the same individual, well known to the submarine force. How he managed year after year to subvert the spirit and intent of five boards, and how he could have controlled the sworn independence of judgment of the submarine members, can only be guessed, but there is no doubt he did; one of his reluctant emissaries once whispered that I "should have a Medal of Honor," and this was why.

Twice, after my retirement from active duty, "Joe Blunt" meanly confronted me to gloat over his superiority and my reduction to civilian status. Once it was in my small office at the Naval War College in Newport, Rhode Island, where I had accepted a chair in naval history; the other was several weeks later as I was hosting a small dinner party of six or eight guests in the War College dining room. Dinner was in progress when I looked up to find him staring at me, only a few feet from the far side of my table. He stood there for some time, not moving; my guests began to notice, and finally I uncomfortably got up and introduced him to them.

During the war I made 12 war patrols. My record was solid and of highest quality, then and afterward. My nomination by the Navy to be Naval Aide to the President of the United States stands in proof. I have been decorated 12 times, 10 times for war service. During the war I was in action 50 or 60 times, fortunate in having excellent skippers for the most part, and participated in sinking or damaging nearly 50 enemy ships. At the end of the war I was in command of a first-line submarine on patrol in enemy waters; during peacetime following I commanded four more important ships, and with all of them rendered useful and in some cases important service to our country. All my shore duty assignments were in very important billets, and all my reports of fitness were superlative.

But that's all long over for me, of course. "Joe Blunt" died some years ago, and had been experiencing mental difficulty long before that. *Dust on the Sea* was written several years after *Run Silent, Run Deep,* and he figures in that book too, in a less complimentary way. By author's intent, in that book he does, indeed, have mental problems. In real life, he was an example of the worst type of human being. Even an outfit as idealistic as the U.S. Navy can't avoid having some of these.

Who was the real "Joe Blunt?" Strangely, I don't seem to recall. "Joe Blunt" will have to do.

Chapter Thirteen

Salamonie and Triton

President Eisenhower's heart attack happened during the summer of 1955, while he was vacationing in Colorado. Coincidentally, I had already been wondering how long I should remain as his naval aide, prestigious assignment though it was, for I felt removed from the Navy in the rarefied, political atmosphere of the White House. I had pretty well made up my mind to ask him to release me after my third year, when news came of his illness. The immediate reaction of everyone associated with him was to remove all possible sources of stress, or even routine matters needing his attention. Expecting that he most probably would not run for a second term, I decided not to raise the question of my departure, but instead stay the full course. His recovery and reelection dictated yet another review, with the result that I asked him to let me go at the beginning of his second term in office. The warm and friendly manner in which he listened to my request is one of my great memories of him.

Leaving was a wrench, of course, but I had dedicated myself to a naval career, could not see a midrank naval officer like myself counting eight consecutive years of shore duty, and felt this was the time to go. The place for a naval officer is at sea, and now holding the rank of captain, I wanted experience with a truly big ship, back in the active line.

I explained to President Eisenhower that, although I loved being his naval aide, and the prestige and perks that went with it, I felt sincerely that my career lay on saltwater. His kindness was typical of the man. He wanted to know what kind of sea duty I aspired to, thanked me for my services, asked me how I had liked being in the White House, and told me to let him know any time he could be of assistance. I knew that it would not be quite kosher, career-wise at any rate, for a practicing naval officer to ask assistance of the president of the United States, and I knew that of course he knew this, too, but it was the measure of the man—and I flattered myself that he knew I would never ask.

Perhaps, had I been able to guess what "Joe Blunt" was about, or had I had the wit to do a little detective work, maybe ask some of my friends, I would have opted to stay a little longer in the White House. It was a position of tremendous power, and would have afforded me opportunities to block his game. No doubt he was watching carefully to see what I might be up to, and would instantly have stopped his own activities had he seen a riposte headed his way. Naively, I did nothing at all. The "system," I felt morally certain, would work the way it was supposed to. Nefarious activity would not be tolerated. Joe Blunt could not cause me any serious harm. I dismissed him from my mind.

My orders were to USS *Salamonie*, a fleet oiler displacing 30,000 tons when fully laden. She was much sought for "deep draft" command, a prerequisite for a first-class combat assignment. Based in Newport, Rhode Island, *Salamonie* had been designated for our "Sixth Fleet," operating in the Mediterranean Sea. She was an old ship, dating from 1941, and I could recall the time I had walked her decks in Hvalfjordur harbor in Iceland, while the *Lea* was fueling from her. I was unprepared, however, for the condition I found her in, 16 years later. Tender, loving care was not what she needed, but to be brought up much more strongly, "with a round turn" as the Navy saying goes, and this I determined to accomplish. She was too good a ship to be allowed just to go down the tubes, which was where she was headed.

Sadly for my perception of what the ship required, there were few in her crew who shared my view. She had been driven so hard with so little reward for so many years that they had little pride in her, and less in themselves. They gloried only in survival. In a negative sort of way, their pride lay in the deplorable shape she was in and the fact that, somehow, they could still make her do her job.

Service in our submarines had not readied me for this. In submarines there was no room for bad condition. Upkeep was always primary, for in a ship intending to operate submerged, and at times at very deep depth, the lives of all hands depended on things being as they should be. There was a tradition of being *inside* your boat, of being *with* her machinery, all her inner parts, in a very special way. Everything about her became automatically part of your own personal life. This, in fact, lay behind the specially structured qualification requirements for all submariners. Prior to being authorized to wear the dolphins of the submarine service, which signified the sought-for qualification, all crew members were required to pass rigorous tests, failing in which, after adequate time, was grounds for being "surfaced": removed from submarine duty, returned to the surface navy. Removal from the submarine fraternity, loss of special "submarine pay," went with that designation change.

I thought, at first plaintively, that if I could only have a "good submarine crew" in *Salamonie* for a few months, we could make something of her, correct her faults. Qualified submariners would not long stand for the conditions I saw, nearly everywhere I looked except in the engineering spaces. These, I thought, were up to the standards they should be. Our principal problems involved nonengineering ones: the main decks, our gun armament, the crew living quarters, work spaces in general. Masts, booms, winches, and the wire cables of fuel-handling equipment were in fair shape; the fueling hoses themselves seemed new and to be in good condition. My guides among the crew, the senior enlisted men, seemed to enjoy showing their new skipper a part of the Navy he had never seen, but they also unwittingly signaled what was wrong: material condition of our working equipment, the ship's main battery, as they several times pointed out, was good; otherwise, she was a dirty rust-bucket. She had been driven hard all her life, and it showed everywhere.

Prominent among the first things that I thought were crying for improvement were six watertight doors, closing off the crew's quarters on the main deck, that were no longer watertight. When closed as tightly as they could be, light still was visible around the edges. They were not proof against even incidental spray that, when we were heavily laden, would splash up on deck in a moderate seaway. A considerable portion of the crew lived in this large compartment, and yet, in a moderate sea, saltwater constantly came through the nominally watertight doors, splashing with real force through gaskets that could not be made tight because the doors themselves were warped out of shape. The deck of the so-called crew's living compartment was almost never dry. Little rivulets of water, often inches deep, always swished across as the ship rolled to the sea.

I looked the doors over. They were old, bent out of shape, fitted with individual dogs for closure that could no longer be properly adjusted. These were the original doors with which the ship had been built, I was told. To my surprise, however, on either side of my own cabin, two decks higher where the sea never reached, and hardly ever any spray, there were two new and very tight watertight doors, fitted with a central closing mechanism controlled from a single point that stayed in easy adjustment. Some previous skipper had become annoyed with the blasts of cold air coming through his supposedly tightly closed doors, I surmised, and had taken the obvious action.

This drove me to the telephone to use all the influence and pressure I could muster. Yes, the Navy had six doors of the type I wanted, in stock at the supply depot in Mechanicsburg, Pennsylvania, and yes, I could have them, but they couldn't be delivered for a couple of weeks and it would take two weeks to install them. We were, however, scheduled for deployment to the Mediterranean Sea. There wasn't time for this kind of delay, so more pressure was indicated. Finally it was agreed that six doors would be shipped by truck overnight, and we would have them the next day.

The repair facility at Newport, where we were based, agreed to do the job, but the foreman there warned me that it was highly unlikely his men could finish the work in the single week of availability we had left, and he was right. The doors were partly installed by Friday, but the work was not finished, and the civil servants did not work on weekends. Battle stations for me again. I went to see the skipper of a destroyer tender that happened to be in port. I knew him slightly, pled my case, offered to provide berths and food for his crew of welders and shipfitters if he could only send me some volunteers to come aboard and finish the job. He proved to be a good fellow. A crew of destroyer sailors came aboard that very day with a vigorous attitude and all their tools. Our OOD and galley crew were assigned the duty of keeping them supplied with food and hot coffee, and by midnight of Saturday the doors were fixed in place, all six of them.

This would show *Salamonie*'s crew, I thought, that a little energy and determination could take care of an obvious problem. By extension, others could be solved as easily. All that needed to be done now was to paint the new doors. This was nothing, I felt. It would take only a couple of hours. My crew, for the first time set up in the tight quarters they should have had from the beginning, would make short work of this little detail.

Not so fast, I found out. Somehow no one got around to it. Nobody cared enough. Nobody sensed that my battle for them against bureaucratic inertia obligated them to reciprocate with a little action, too. What would a submarine crew have done in this situation, I thought.

After a couple of days, with departure looming and nothing done in spite of broad hints like, "When *are* the new doors going to be painted?" I informed the ship's first lieutenant, a Naval Academy graduate who should not have needed hints, that he was restricted to the ship, was not to go ashore until painting happened. Apparently this threat created enough incentive. The doors were painted immediately, but the entire incident was an eye-opener.

I began to see that the Navy's special categories of service, such as Aviation and Submarine, had their downside, too. Use of the word "surfaced" in the case of failure to meet submarine standards inferred the inferiority of the surface navy and illustrated the problem. In a very real sense, *Salamonie*'s crew did not care whether school kept or not. Although it was through their complaints that I learned about the useless doors, it had been so long since anything had been done for them in a constructive way that it did not occur to any of our crew, or to the officers who were supposed to direct their efforts, that they, too, had an obligation to paint the new doors to prevent rusting in the salt air.

My new ship, *"Old Sal,"* as we began to call her, did have one source of pride, but it was the only one she had. She could do her job, which was to be ready at all times to service our Sixth Fleet warships, and she had two excellent turbine engines with four good boilers that had seldom, if ever, been tested at their full, sustained, overload power. It was from here that we would have to rebuild her morale. The eyes of her crew needed to be turned a little inward. They would have to live a bit more "in" her and less "on" her. Their pride in their normal performance in spite of an apparently disreputable platform (their ship) would have to become pride in doing a superior performance in a good ship.

My time in *Salamonie* would only be a year. That I already knew, because personnel policy dictated rapid rotation of deep draft commands in order to give everyone a crack at this merit badge en route to the competition for big combat commands. It was the same policy of going through the numbers regardless of capability that had cost me my wartime *Piper* and, in my opinion at least, it was obvious that this rapid turnover was one of the root causes of the ship's low morale. Allaying this, in my own case at least, was the knowledge that I had been designated for ultimate command of the big two-reactor submarine *Triton*, then under construction, and that next year I was to go into a year's nuclear training. A year would be a very short time to get *Old Sal* back on the step, figuratively back in the fleet where she belonged, and from which she had been gradually separating herself, but it had to be done, or at least started.

I began a strenuous period of at-sea upkeep during good weather, explaining to the crew that the extra work would be at sea within regular working hours, and would be paid back when possible with extra liberty time in port, or an occasional "rope-yarn Sunday" (an unofficial holiday). Salubrious "Med" weather would make working conditions not unpleasant. We would extend ourselves to the maximum to provide special services, such as carrying mail, and would be rewarded, I felt sure, by other ships in the particular ways each might find possible. *Sal's* crew was not enchanted by this announcement, but there were some old-time sailors among them, and I could feel their approval.

Foremost in our immediate needs was to scrape off the enormous encrustation of old and bulging paint that was spread on our main deck and stanchions, remove the underlying rust, and repaint with the prescribed red foundation paint and (usually) deck gray. Over the years, much old paint had been applied, usually just before inspection, by dumping a five-gallon paint tin on an unprepared deck, and spreading the puddle of paint around with mops, which would then be thrown overboard. Usually this was done right over old rust and dirt, sometimes over an occasional forgotten tool. This I proved by staging an argument with a couple of our leading men (they were not truly in on the gimmick, but they sensed I had a purpose) in which I proclaimed that what I was looking at was clearly the head of a hammer, minus its wooden handle.

They argued, as they had previously (that was why I had picked them for this little show), that it was only an unusually shaped welding bead in the deck. After sides were clearly drawn, I said, "Well, I'm captain of this here now ship, and I say it's a hammerhead, covered up with a hundred thick coats of paint. So you guys go and dig up that hammerhead, and if I'm wrong I'll pay." I hadn't figured out exactly how I was going to "pay," but knew, if my guess was wrong, a way would be shown in due time. All the same, it was worth a chance, and sure enough, when the masses of old paint were knocked off, there was the heavily rusted head of an ordinary hammer. "I'll collect a million dollars from each of you next payday," I smugly told them as the piece of junk went over the side.

When in company with other ships I was always cadging extra scraping tools from them (they wore out rapidly, especially the "cutter bundles" for our electric deck scrapers), and I spent all my small "captain's allotment" in the supply system for special cleaning and painting supplies. We were soon noted in the Sixth Fleet for the great expanses of red preservative paint that appeared all over the ship, and one day, in red block letters on our forecastle deck below the bridge where I couldn't fail to see them, were the words "RED LEAD NED," rolled out with a big paint roller. It might have been a bit of *lèse-majesté,* but to me it was indication that the light touch I was otherwise trying to employ with the crew was beginning to work. The words were entirely for my benefit, I knew, for an hour later they had disappeared under deck gray.

On another day, when fleet units came alongside to refuel, to my delight there was a message from the fleet commander: "We see what you're trying to do!" I've revered "Cat" Brown ever since, for he knew the importance of occasional encouragement, well knowing that it would quickly go all over the ship. In due course, despite some continued, but now noticeably reduced, grumbling from the crew, a few areas of good-looking deck appeared, and one day, the day before we were due to arrive in port for a week's liberty, "Rope-yarn Sunday" was announced. It was a Wednesday. Nobody did any work at all. The only thing that happened was an informal race with a civilian merchant ship through the Straits of Messina. We worked up to full throttle, full overload, and passed ahead with ease. Most of our crew was on deck in the beautiful Mediterranean weather enjoying the race, but there were others, off-duty firemen and machinist mates I later discovered, who were below decks cheering on our engineers. I also discovered that if we really tried, *Old Sal* could still churn out 21 knots.

In my search for morale-building activities our little ship's newspaper, the *Bunker Gazette,* presented some ideas. It came out once or twice a week, if the sailors editing it were not otherwise engaged, had a print run of about 50 copies, and tried to present another side of our daily lives. Early on I corralled its editors, briefed them on a reporter's duty never to reveal his sources, and volunteered to write a column for their *Gazette.* My column, authored by someone called "Old Buck" was run regularly. It spent most of its energy poking fun at the "OM" (myself, the Old Man, supposedly unidentified by anyone), and occasionally tried to deliver itself of unofficial news or some kind of worthwhile homily.

I was never sure just how this was received, nor whether anyone knew, or cared, who Old Buck was, but do remember that the editors of our epochal paper secretly bugged me regularly to get my stuff in on time. In all honesty, I felt these little things, confined (as they had to be) within the tiny community of our ship, took on an importance out of all proportion to their actual dimensions. But that's the way it always is in a ship at sea.

Then two very public things happened. Replenishment oilers always brought mail out to the fleet, but we attached more than ordinary importance to this routine service. Every time we got under way from our refueling berth in Pozzuoli, a Naples suburb, the last item on our departure checkoff list was to send an officer to the fleet mail center to pick up the last mail received for the ships we expected to meet, and we delayed our departure, if necessary, to get the very last shipment. I kept a personal tally of what we had on board, and it was segregated by ship in a converted antiaircraft ammunition locker for quick access. One day we saw a tiny stick dead ahead, over the horizon: the mast of a big ship crossing ahead of us. Careful inspection through binoculars satisfied me that it was the fleet flagship, so we fired up our 30-inch-diameter signal searchlight, high on our mast, and sent, "We have 63 sacks of mail for you."

Response was electric. Almost immediately, about as long as it took to get permission from Vice Adm. Charles R. "Cat" Brown, the distant yardarms swung perpendicular to us, and I ordered *Sal* to replenishment stations. We had barely time to get ready when the flagship *Salem,* one of the handsomest cruisers in the Navy, came boiling alongside in all her splendor. She had no other replenishment needs, so no special rigs were flown, but the word must have got out, for her decks were crowded with men looking eagerly at this unexpected mail delivery. We had our highline outfit ready, and to my surprise, all the *Salem* had was a single tall muscular sailor standing on top of her second and highest turret, just below the bridge. No "line gun" for the fleet flagship! The man on top of the turret began swinging a special heaving line—it must have had an extra-large weight—got it spinning around his head in a really huge arc, bigger than I'd ever seen a man swing a heaving line before, and with the ships about 50 yards apart, moving at 15 knots in the middle of the Mediterranean Sea, he flung the weighted end of his heaving line right onto our forecastle deck, where our enthusiastic highline crew picked it up, ran it aft, completed the connection to our highline wire, then let the *Salem* haul her "messenger" back with our wire attached and make it fast to a padeye in her superstructure.

I remember a small fear that I might have gotten incorrect information, that we might not have the mail, or maybe couldn't get it all up in the extremely short time we'd had to get ready, but I needn't have worried. Two at a time, the mail sacks were trundled across the wire cable connecting the ships, were picked up joyfully by her waiting crew members, and hustled below. In about 15 minutes everything was finished, we retrieved our highline, and the flagship tore away at 25 knots to resume her previous course.

As she broke away, there was another signal from Cat Brown: "Well done, *Salamonie!*" It was one for the whole crew to read. With satisfaction, I had noted that our decks, too, had been crowded with sightseers. It was not often that a ship of our caliber could bring the fleet flagship alongside in such an off-hand manner, I overheard someone mutter; so here was evidence of a little growing pride in *Old Sal.*

Another item was our armament. *Salamonie* still carried her wartime armament of five-inch antiaircraft guns and .40-caliber machine guns, plus numerous mounts for the smaller, but still lethal, .20-caliber guns. The bigger guns had, however, been poorly kept up. "No ship of the U.S. Navy should let her guns be in this condition," I declared, directing that our gunner's mates turn to on them forthwith. It took much labor, but their pride was stung, and there came the day when our three five-inch gunmounts and the pair of quadruple forties demonstrated they were still working. Unfortunately, the tempo of operations was such that target practice was not possible. We could shoot, but we probably could not have hit anything much smaller than the side of a barn—certainly not an aircraft—with them.

The twenties were a different story. Being smaller, they were easy to maintain. Our two were mounted on pedestals on the bridge, so it was apparent these would be the first in action should there, say, be trouble on our pier in Pozzuoli. The crew members detailed to man them, however, were also bridge telephone talkers during maneuvering watch entering or leaving port, or refueling stations at sea. Observation of both men was easy, and it was soon evident they had been picked for usefulness as telephone messenger only, not as part of a gun crew. Neither had ever shot the gun before, and I got the impression they feared it. What we needed was someone who *wanted* to shoot it.

Once decided, getting such people was easy. Already I had noticed a couple of candidates: both had little tattoos on their hands. "Was that for being in some kind of a gang when you were young and stupid?" I asked them. When they admitted as much, I asked if they would like to have one of our twenties on the bridge, and both jumped at the chance. From then on, their battle stations were the 20mm guns, and they worked on them every chance they got. At sea there were occasional chances to shoot at floating debris, or a can or box dumped from the galley. The enthusiasm of these lads assured me that orders to open fire would not need repetition. If anything, "Cease fire!" would have been a more likely problem.

Surprisingly, this element of our workup was the quickest to pay off. Soviet warships had become noticeably intrusive in the Mediterranean, and all our ships had been warned about them. Our instructions also specified how to handle some of the various possible situations, among them the notorious "shouldering" episodes that had been occurring. One night it was our turn.

We had been to port for a quick load of fuel and were on our way to rejoin our replenishment task force somewhere south of Crete. I think I was on the bridge when radar reported the approach of an unknown ship. Normally, headquarters informed us by radio of all traffic we might encounter, and this was an exception. The stranger was on a steady course, making good speed, and had a strong radar return. In addition the ship was totally darkened, not a light showing, a suspicious circumstance. By contrast we, like all ships at sea, were showing the International Rules of the Road running lights.

He would pass close by, but plot showed no likelihood of collision unless one of us changed course or speed. We were, nonetheless, plotting his movement carefully from our radar, and were at battle stations as he neared. When I sighted him it was ominously obvious he was a good-sized warship. We manned our big signal light, were ready to respond instantly should he initiate anything. Were he to crowd us, or start any of the "shouldering" maneuvers we had heard about, we were not going to give way, would shoot to hurt if he shot at us, though careful not to begin an exchange of gunfire. The young sailor with the 20mm gun alongside me had his ammunition laid out, would have loaded his gun in a second. I was morally sure the other guns were in similar condition. All had been carefully drilled not to load until ordered, and responsible officers were in charge at each station. The moment was a little tense.

Although we were as ready as we could be, my sixth sense told me that nothing was going to happen. Truculence was the order of the day; we were to give as good as we got, take no monkey business from anyone, but nobody wanted to start a real fracas. Our big searchlight was ready to flood his decks with light, and our cameramen were ready to photograph any incident, but the other ship did not waver in his course, nor did we. The moment passed.

Our closest point of approach, from memory, was in the neighborhood of two miles. Full report was of course made to our fleet commander, and some weeks later a copy of *Time* magazine mentioned the incident, but there were no other repercussions. I had the sensing that Cat Brown liked us even better, but the biggest effect of the whole episode was on *Salamonie* herself. Had things really been the way our shipboard rumor mill said, there might have been a shooting war right then. As they had it, the stranger, a huge Russian cruiser, had come within a few hundred yards, had flashed over a message, "What ship? Where bound?" We had loaded all our guns and had answered, "U.S. man of war! None of your goddammed business!" All guns were loaded and trained out on the "enemy," and we put out our running lights to show we meant business, but the other ship lost its nerve and turned away into the night. In the meantime, we had not wavered in our course. That last part, at least, was true.

It made a great yarn, but we had to dampen down the crew's relish of the incident. Calling them together, I gave them the facts as related here, cautioned them not to speak of it at all. Under the circumstances, this was a lot to ask of the American sailor, but it would at least restart the rumor mills at a less sensational level. The other effect was a big boost to my own morale: my crew was no longer ashamed of their ship. They were proud of her, for she had put down a cruiser of the Soviet navy!

I had a number of instances also to realize we had earned the regard of the fleet commander and his staff. We were hauled out of formation, once, and sent to the Straits of Gibraltar for no good reason except to follow orders received from an unknown commander of whom we had only the radio call sign. Directed to proceed "at best speed," we went all out, at the full 21 knots that *Old Sal* could deliver (she had already proved herself a mite faster than her contemporaries, and this may have been one of the reasons she had been picked for this mission, whatever it was). Just before reaching the Straits we got a message from our mysterious new boss to reverse course and head eastward at full speed along the coast of Africa. From day to day we got new instructions, and one day a U.S. destroyer came boiling from the south to refuel. As soon as it departed, another one came, then another, until we had refueled a whole division.

The division commander's flagship was the last to come alongside, and when she got there and the telephone connection was established to link our bridge with his, I asked the question that had been burning all this time. We had been aimlessly roaring at full speed twice the length of the Med. "What's going on?" I asked.

"You've got a good ship there, Ned," he answered. "Didn't they tell you? The Ruskies have sold a couple of subs to the Egyptians, we think, or maybe they're sending them on through the Suez Canal. This has been in the papers. We're shadowing them to make sure we know where they're going, and that's all I can tell you!"

We had been sent at full speed twice the length of the Mediterranean Sea without notice or preparation of any kind, and I was proud to know that we had delivered. A few days later we dropped the hook off Athens, close in with a perfect view of the Parthenon, and I wondered why we'd been favored with such a good anchorage. A visit to Fangtooth's staff ("Fangtooth" was the voice call of our replenishment task force commander) assured me it was not an accident.

Refueling at sea was a strenuous operation. Developed as a wartime necessity, it had become the standard means of keeping a fleet active in any necessary part of the world. In the days of sail, warships kept the sea for periods that were limited only by endurance of water and provisions, during which the crews suffered enormous privations. Not any more. Sailors should still be at sea as much as possible, but they should also be properly treated. During World War II we had developed the means of supporting a big fleet at sea. Instead of sending combat ships long distances for replenishment, supplies would be sent to them. It took top-level seamanship and ship handling to do it properly, but the U.S. Navy broke new ground in World War II, deploying big ships enormous distances for great periods. Today, logistic support ships like *Salamonie* and her extraordinary successors can replenish our biggest carriers in the midst of flight operations if necessary, planes landing and taking off at the same time as fuel is being pumped aboard. They can also simultaneously refuel and reprovision other ships on their other side, and send helicopters to still others hovering nearby. We have reached the pinnacle of capability.

It was not quite so yet, but *Old Sal* had her place in the panoply of our Navy's design. My last memory of her is my best. We were at last released from duty in the Med and on the way back to our home port of Newport, had barely passed the Straits of Gibraltar and entered the Atlantic, when we received word of an emergency at sea. President Eisenhower was flying to Europe for a meeting with Soviet dictator Nikita Khrushchev and other heads of state, and a division of destroyers had been deployed along his route just in case. This was usual, but what was not usual was the sudden hurricane that had overtaken the ships and the resulting emergency conditions it caused.

An unusually heavy sea had struck the flagship, a somewhat larger destroyer than the other, older ones, and had bashed in a too lightly built portion of her superstructure. Compartments were flooded, a man was dead, and the ship had left her consorts to make an emergency visit to Lisbon. The other three ships were running out of fuel in the middle of the Atlantic, the storm was still at its height, and we were the only unit of the U.S. Navy nearby. We began to drive at full speed into the midst of the storm. Huge seas were crashing on to our bows, engulfing them with solid green water (I took 8mm movies of some of them with my own movie camera, and still have them). *Salamonie* shook tremendously with each successive shock. No one who has not seen a really big storm at sea can truly appreciate the tremendous forces engaged. I could well believe the *Mahan* might have been severely damaged. We were driving with full power right into the teeth of the hurricane, not yet having made contact of any sort with the three hazarded destroyers, intent on getting to the scene as soon as possible. Although we were driving with throttles wide open, boiler safety valves almost chattering, the tremendous power of the huge seas hammering our bows took upwards of five knots off our potential highest speed. With everything on the line, we were barely logging 16 knots.

In addition to this, I could clearly see our bow shake as the seas hit it. This, too, has to be seen to be believed, for a ship is one very solid steel structure from bow to stern and is not likely to have some parts of it moving relative to other parts. Yet this was what I saw. I also saw worried looks on the faces of others as they surveyed the awesome power of the enraged sea. Finally my exec, John Oliver, spoke the thought all of us were thinking. "She can't take much more of this," he said. It was the first cautionary word anyone had said, and it was clearly his duty to say it.

"You're right," I said. "Reduce speed to standard. Let's see how well that does." Standard speed would normally be 15 knots; in the sea conditions we could log only 12, four knots less than we had been making at flank, but noticeably easier on *Salamonie*'s laboring bow. The sea began to ease slightly during the second day, but only slightly, permitting us to go back to full speed but not, in our best judgment, to "flank," our absolutely top speed. Now, however, a different problem came up. We had been maintaining a radio watch on all possible frequencies, and at this stage began hearing distress calls from an aircraft in trouble. I don't think we ever knew his specific problem, but he had two other aircraft with him, and they were all worried. We opened up to tell them our radio call sign and approximate location. They couldn't find us, and radio ranges being what they were, I never did know if they were actually in our vicinity, but for a time it looked possible.

Eventually the injured plane went down, leaving the other two circling in despair. Asking for their best estimated position, we headed in that direction and radioed Washington that we planned to divert temporarily from search for the destroyers, assuming they could last longer than a lone aviator in a rubber boat, and hoping he had been able to ditch and get into one. Within an hour we got a priority message back. Diversion was disapproved. We were to continue our search for the destroyers. The circling aircraft had dropped rubber boats but had no knowledge whether their friend had survived the crash of his plane. They finally had to leave the area because of fuel limitation, and I couldn't trust myself to tell them, without emotion, that we had been directed to cease our effort to help. With our defection went that young pilot's only chance for rescue. I never did learn his name, or what service he came from.

Around two A.M. of the next morning we made contact with the destroyers *Vogelgesang, Gearing,* and *McCard.* A very high sea was still running, and *Gearing* reported herself dangerously low on fuel. At daybreak we began to try to get the *Gearing* alongside, using the usual procedure in which the oiler maintains steady course and speed and the ship to receive fuel approaches from astern. No luck. Under ordinary circumstances no one would have tried to fuel in seas of this size. Despite everything we could do, including damage to one of our refueling rigs (a derrick and boom partly torn down), no fueling hose could be connected. We lost one of our hoses, too, when a really big sea hit *Gearing* and slammed her off course and into our stern just after she had finally got it aboard but before there was any chance to make the fueling connection.

It was actually a relatively light contact, but it punched a hole in our hull, in the crew berthing area well above our waterline; the only damage done was to habitability, temporarily taken care of with canvas and plastic sheets put in place inside the ship. The wing of the destroyer's bridge where she had hit us was well smashed, but she reported no other damage. Both ships got off lightly, and I was amazed at the extent of the local damage from a truly minor contact. It bears repeating: the forces of the sea can be dealt with, but one must make allowance for their strength. Usually they are benign, but they are implacable, more sudden, than humans can understand until they have encountered them personally.

Salamonie, having the senior skipper (me, at age 39), had been designated "on the scene commander." After several attempts to get the *Gearing* alongside had failed, I sent her on ahead and tried if we might do better with one of the others. No luck here, either. Then came a message from *Gearing* saying she had begun preparations to abandon ship! It was imperative this line of thought, which spelled incipient disaster, be stopped. I sent her the following message, made up on the spot:

> NO SHIP OF THE UNITED STATES NAVY HAS BEEN ABANDONED DURING PEACETIME WHILE SHE COULD STILL FLOAT. WE WILL NOT START A NEW TRADITION NOW. WEATHER IS MODERATING AND HELP IS AT HAND. DONT GIVE UP THE SHIP.

Back came a message forcibly declaring there was no intention of abandoning ship, and I relaxed. Whatever had caused that first message to be sent, no way would that skipper let *his* ship show the white feather any longer.

And then, while I actually had my binoculars to my eyes and was looking at the *Gearing*, dead ahead, her bridge signal light began to flash, and, blessing my Naval Academy training in signaling by flashing light, I read the electrifying message direct. "MAN OVERBOARD."

I yelled for help. "Get all our glasses [binoculars] in use," I barked out. "There's a man overboard from that tincan up ahead! All hands keep him in sight! Man the lifeboat! Alert sickbay!" I ordered a message sent to the other ships: "HAVE MAN IN SIGHT X KEEP CLEAR."

Our warrant boatswain, a dynamic chap named Curl who was responsible for all our topside rigging, came to the bridge on the run. I could now see the man in the water, about a thousand yards directly ahead of us. His head, a dot in the frothing sea, appeared and disappeared intermittently with the waves, which were still 40 feet or more in height. I knew it was a man's head, black in the gray sea, but it was in truth more like a grain of pepper in a big salad. It was imperative that we not run him down. Without thinking, I automatically took over the conn. "Right full rudder!" We began to sheer to the right. Bos'n Curl was at my elbow. "Have the man kept in sight at all times," I ordered. John Oliver, my exec and a fine officer, a lieutenant commander up from the ranks, was there, too. "Send a message to the other ships," I told him. "We're bigger and will pick him up to leeward. Tell them to keep out of our way." John's response was a single word: "Aye!"

Having got the black dot on our beam, I ordered engines stopped and the rudder full left. As our way came off I was carefully judging the direction of the wind and waves and backed both engines to kill our way through the water, exactly between the weather and the man. He was then about 500 yards away, and this would cause us to drift down on him rapidly, at the same time as it gave him a temporary oasis of comparatively smooth water. We would have to be alert to get the ship clear before the wind and sea put us right on top of him.

Bos'n Curl: "Captain, I wouldn't trust our lifeboat in this sea!" I had been worrying about that, too.

"What do you recommend?" I asked.

"I'd send a man after him and tend him from the ship. We'll bend heaving lines together, let him over the side when we're about a hundred yards from him, and pull the two of them back after he gets to the man!"

"Right on! Go to it. And you tend him yourself, but rig a phone so you can be sure I know what you need from up here!"

"Right!" said Curl.

Off he went, and I quickly became aware of hurried activity on the deck below. "The seas are so big that I think he'd better go over from the bridge deckhouse instead of the tank deck," said Curl, a few minutes later. I agreed. Seas were swamping the main or tank deck, splashing high above the cargo deck just above it. *Sal* was rolling 20 degrees to a side, a tremendous roll for a ship her size.

A few minutes later, Curl was back. "Here's our man," he said. "Gunner's Mate Second Lawrence Beckhaus, just made the rate. He says he's a good swimmer." Beckhaus was in his regular dungarees but was already barefoot, and had an inflatable lifebelt around his middle. He had a heaving line tied to the belt, held several coils in his hand. Curl held many more coils, along with a single semaphore signal flag.

"How long is the line?" I asked.

"Long enough. I've got two of them bent together here and another for a spare," said Curl, wagging the coils in his hands. His sailorman-like knots were professional. "We've got a gang of men ready to help pull the two of them back, and I've got this flag to point him right or left. We're ready to go."

"What about this belt? Are you sure it won't slip and is strong enough?"

"No problem, skipper. It's the best one we've got. Brand-new. Besides, we've got a coil of this line around his stomach just in case. Guess you didn't see that." I hadn't, but now I could see a length of the rope loosely wrapped around our sailor's middle. "Beckhaus will have to swim out to him hauling this line, but all he has to do to come back is wave to us and hang on to him," said Curl.

"Good," said I. "One thing, though. If Beckhaus loses hold of him, he's got to be able to signal you to quit pulling so he can swim back and get him."

"We've thought of that, too," said Curl.

"Give me the phone," I said. "Go to it!"

Beckhaus dived over the side from a deck some 40 feet above our normal waterline, into a big sea that reached almost to that level as we rolled to it, so that his total dive into the water was only about three feet. He swam away strongly until well clear, then took it relatively easy, occasionally looking back toward us for a signal from Curl whether to aim more right or more left. To the anxious watchers on our bridge, his little swim looked ridiculously easy as the line trailed behind him, though everyone watching knew it was far from that, particularly in the big waves which, much of the time, must be preventing him from seeing his quarry. He had to turn and look back at us a number of times, and it took several minutes, but finally he reached the tiring, half-submerged black dot representing the *Gearing*'s sailor and waved violently.

In the meantime, Curl and his deck crew had moved from the bridge deckhouse down to the main deck, where alternately they were inundated with the sea as we rolled toward, and high above it as our ship rolled away. A multitude of stanchions existed there, a great deal of ship's structure to hang on to, and beyond getting wet no one was in difficulty. Hauling in the line with two men on the end of it was not hard either, the only problem being to avoid surges associated with the ship's motion. To this, Curl and his scratch crew were well acclimated; they kept a steady strain on the line, running back and forth themselves with *Salamonie*'s deep rolls to keep their pull on the two men in the water as constant as possible. When Curl had them right alongside, he bided his time well, so that as *Sal* rolled heavily toward them, burying her lee rail deep under the sea that boiled over it, his men heaved mightily and brought Beckhaus and the *Gearing* sailor right over the rail, with the sea, and landed them safely on deck. I was fully occupied on the bridge and could not see them actually come aboard, under the cargo deck as they were, but heard it all, just as it happened, over my special telephone to Bos'n Curl. "Both men okay!" he reported. "The pharmacist's mate is here with two stretchers, and they're on their way to sickbay!"

Beyond maneuvering *Salamonie* and approving Bos'n Curl's method of rescue, I had had little part in the proceedings. The big thing was done by Beckhaus, staged and managed all the way by Curl. Our new guest was showing a little fever from his exposure to the cold Atlantic waters, according to our pharmacist's mate's report a few minutes later, and I took special pleasure in approving his proposal that the two men who had been overboard should each receive a good tot of medicinal brandy, extending the benefit, by commanding officer's prerogative, to Curl and the men with him, all of whom got soaking wet with cold December sea water down on the tank deck.

I did get a quick chance to shake hands with Beckhaus, in his bunk in the usually empty sickbay, and the same with our unexpected guest, who seemed not much the worse for wear, although indeed a little subdued and tired. In the aftermath, I proposed a medal for Beckhaus, which was delivered upon our arrival in Newport, in front of his shipmates mustered on deck. Later I had the very special pleasure of making appropriate remarks in the fitness report due on Bos'n Curl.

. . .

Once Beckhaus and the *Gearing*'s rescued sailor were on board, we had to return our attention to the job at hand, getting fuel to the three imperiled destroyers. Darkness being near, they were asked for estimates of remaining endurance, and the optimum speed and course for the night. All indicated they had enough fuel to make it through the night, so that worry was lightened. At daybreak next day we began the same drill as before, but it seemed impossible for the destroyers to make good approaches in the still heavy weather. The *Gearing*'s experience may have made them a bit cautious.

Recalling our own first efforts at fueling other ships, it occurred to me that at their present stage they might not have had much experience doing this in good weather, let alone in the conditions we were facing. By contrast, I had had much practice in handling *Salamonie* alongside ships of all types, and she was much steadier than the tincans we were trying to help. It might be worth a try at reversing the standard procedure.

Asking *Gearing*'s estimate on the best course and speed in the existing weather, I told her to steady up on it, fly the ready flag from her yardarm when fully ready to take fuel, and we would drive our ship up alongside her. This was how we did it. Because of the weather (which, however, began abating on the third day), and because of the destroyers' desire to top off their fuel tanks while they had the chance, it took us two days more to finish the whole job. The last thing we did was to return *Gearing*'s AWOL sailor, now fully recovered from his ordeal, via highline. Then we broke contact and resumed our voyage home.

The rest of our trip across the Atlantic was anticlimactic and altogether pleasant, marked, however, by serious thought on my part. I had not yet finished my self-imposed job on *Old Sal*. We had brought her a long way, I felt sure, but there was a long way yet to go. A navy yard overhaul was in the works, and an insightful skipper could undoubtedly get a lot done for her, not only preservation-wise but also in modernization. Her crew's quarters, built just as our Merchant Marine was beginning to try to improve standards in that area, were inherently superior to regular Navy design, but had deteriorated to an unacceptable low level. A good cleanup, paint, and some repair could restore them to excellent condition and be a prototype for design improvement in all Navy ships. Her armament, in which I had had so much interest, was not useful, mainly because strenuous employment of the ship prevented drill and upkeep. By this time I could truly understand the frustration of my predecessors.

My year in *Salamonie* made it clear little change in her armament could be expected, so the thing to do, obviously, was to remove useless guns and give the weight saved to increased tankage for fuel and avgas (aviation gasoline). I was tempted to ask cancellation of my expected detachment orders so as to have time to accomplish what I knew had to be done for that fine old ship. On the other side of that argument was that the bureaus in Washington worked pragmatically, not sentimentally. My reasons for wanting to do something for *Old Sal* would ring no bells there, might be counterproductive all around. After quite a bit of thought, I decided to leave things as they were.

We arrived in Newport just before Christmas, and I got home the next day, to a great welcome from Ingrid and three little children from whom I'd been absent nearly a full year.

So ends my story of the *Salamonie*. She had made an excellent record in the Mediterranean, and had received numerous accolades for being the most dependable, best-performing oiler there. Our crew, I felt, had developed a certain pride in the ship, and I was sorry to leave them. After my detachment, in the mail came a copy of one of the last issues of the *Bunker Gazette*, containing both my last Old Buck column and a "ballad" someone, probably one of the editors, had composed. Men of the sea are usually hard-boiled ornery types on the surface, but down inside there's a lot more feeling than might be expected. The ballad brought a lump in my throat, because it showed that I had actually accomplished much of what I'd set out to do:

> *Old Sal was a tanker who sailed the Med,*
> *Her crew full of guts, her Captain was Ned.*
> *Now Old Sal was dirty, and covered with rust,*
> *To chip her and scrape her and paint her we must.*
> *A more sea-going ship, we had none of us seen*
> *And the bottom of Sal will never turn green.*
> *Just mile after mile we'd sail the Med,*
> *And cover her decks with paint and red lead.*
>
> *We'd fuel ships at night, or during the day*
> *Sal's the best fueling tanker afloat, they would say.*
> *We'd give them some mail and movies and lube*
> *And when we were finished, they'd bid us adieu.*
> *All over the Med we would visit at times,*
> *And our crew walked ashore in many a clime.*

There's a lot of work with this fueling, you see.
But we'd also enjoy some good liberty.

"Shore leave will begin when the line's on the pier,
And have you some fun, and drink you some beer."
But then Ned would caution and say with a grin,
"Take care the SP's don't bring you in."

And then the Med cruise was over one day
And to fuel in a storm Old Sal sailed away.
No one could have guessed what lay ahead—
'Till in came the message: two hurt, and one dead.

Three tincans were desperately low it was learned,
And from then on all four of Sal's boilers were burned.
There were sixty foot seas and a hundred knot wind blew
When to the DD's, Old Sal carried rescue.

One man in the sea, from right straight ahead—
If we hadn't been there, he would have been dead.
Old Sal wasn't built for a lifeboat, you see,
But that's what we made her, EMERGENCY!

So listen, my hearties, and call out a cheer,
For they'll never forget that Old Sal was here.
The ship was Old Sal, and she sailed the Med
Her crew was all sailors; her Captain was Ned.

Detachment orders were in the mill, and in January of 1958 I reported for nuclear training as prospective commanding officer of USS *Triton* to Admiral Rickover with the distinction, I honestly believe, of being the only naval officer not to have been put through a grilling preliminary interview at his hands. Maybe he felt our prior association made this unnecessary, but if so he must have regretted it, for he gave me the benefit of full indoctrination from then on.

Enough has been written about Rickover, however, and said about him, that there is little to add except that the gift he gave us of nuclear power for propulsion of important ships was far more than simply propulsion. He set a perfection standard so high that the United States has had virtually no nuclear accidents of any kind, in naval plants or in the shore-based power plants that will in all probability ultimately become our main source of domestic electricity. The few small difficulties we have had are mere "incidents" in the nuclear lexicography, cannot in any way be compared to several more serious accidents in other countries, and particularly in the Soviet navy. USS *Nautilus,* impressively preserved at our Naval Submarine Museum in Groton, Connecticut, just downstream from our submarine base and a bare mile upstream from the Electric Boat Division of General Dynamics, is Rickover's monument for all time. She is the only fighting ship preserved for the man who built her instead of for the battles she fought. For the truth is that *Nautilus* fought no battles at all, except the continuous one, during her whole career, of changing the navies of the world.

Triton was the fifth nuclear submarine to be built, and we began our service in her and for her with high hearts. For a fuller appreciation of that, the reader is referred to *Around the World Submerged,* published in 1963. For an understanding of the training period under Rickover he should read my novel *Cold Is the Sea,* for that story is there accurately told though in fictional guise, in that dates and places have been shifted and names changed. It is for this reason, also, that the story of my service in the *Triton* is not here repeated. I have told it already, and it need not be done a second time.

Some points do, however, deserve notation. No one should assume that the short notice given *Triton* in these autobiographical pages indicates any the less regard on my part for that great ship and my time in her. She was in her day by far the biggest submarine in the world, the only one ever built with two reactors. Her reactors produced the most horsepower of any submarine, a then-secret 45,000 horsepower, twice as much as Dad's *Memphis, Washington,* or *New York,* and they could make the water fly by, surfaced or submerged. In either condition, there were few ships that could match her.

She had two completely separate engineering plants, driving two propellers. Submarine development has gone a different direction, to a single propeller, set in the centerline of an entirely cylindrical hull, exactly as the legendary John Philip Holland originally designed, but the *Triton* came before that. She was built for speed on the surface, and in fact was slightly faster surfaced than submerged, though capable of more than 30 knots in either condition, if we slightly exceeded the operating parameters imposed. This we did, with Rickover's approval and under his observation.

Triton was the last of our subs designed to emulate surface ship characteristics in addition to submergence capability, and in this she more nearly copied Simon Lake and the old "government" design, with her long, thin hull, and full superstructure (though no admirals ever strutted upon it), than she did the diving boat designs pioneered by Holland. We did, however, prove her out at angles up to 30 degrees at high speed, and once Rickover and Co. capitalized on this capability by asking a special reactor test with the ship at a 45-degree up angle, and another at 45 degrees down. This, done at slow speed in order to prolong the tests, was no problem at all.

Indeed, it was fairly obvious that *Triton* was built to be, among other things, a prototype for a multireactor surface-ship engineering plant. We had, for example, two "de-aerating feed tanks," standard for surface ships with normal boilers but entirely unnecessary for submarines using "steam generators," as we called our furnace-less boilers, built with no fireboxes of any kind. In the steam generators, very hot "primary loop" water from the reactor, at extremely high pressure, passes through boiler tubes on the other side of which, at much lower pressure, is the "secondary loop" boiler-feed water which becomes steam to run the turbines and all other machinery. Our powerplant showed that de-aerating feed tanks were not needed—but if they were wanted, we had developed the techniques to use them.

Our shakedown cruise, as described in my book on the subject, was to take *Triton* around the world completely submerged, accomplishing the cruise on schedule to give President Eisenhower another talking point for his forthcoming European summit conference with Chairman Khrushchev of the Soviet Union. As the world well knows, that conference was aborted when our overflying U-2 spy plane was shot down by a Russian missile.

It was comforting to feel that *Triton*'s achievement may have alleviated, to a small degree, the distressing effect on our country of that disaster which, all the same, delayed the cause of world peace for years.

Following the "subcircumnavigation," *Triton* participated in a combined "fleet problem" with the British navy, and in the process accomplished a couple of the submerged approaches that all nuclear submariners dreamed of, in those days. The entire situation is far different today, but in 1960 we still drilled at firing conventional World War II–style torpedoes at big surface warships, aircraft carriers preferred. All my wartime subs were restricted to extremely slow speed while submerged, so that a "submerged approach" consisted of starting out somewhere ahead of the target's projected line of advance, and then maneuvering so as to shoot him as he steamed by. With the early "nukes," although still shooting the same old fish, we cooked up all sorts of imaginative ways to use our heretofore unheard-of speed to improve the old-fashioned approach technique.

The exercise in which *Triton* was then engaged, from our point of view, had been most frustratingly boring. There were two British aircraft carriers in it, and we searched the war-game area for them diligently, without success, finally sending a report that I sincerely believed they were not operating in the assigned area at all. In a few hours, back came a message lifting the area restrictions, and we immediately headed out of it at high speed, in the direction we deduced them both to be. Within a day, the OOD, at the periscope watch, reported a strange object on the horizon. It looked like nothing I had ever seen, so we left it behind and continued our search. A couple of hours later, anticipating a long night, I retired to my bunk, but my mind kept churning over the details of that strange mast I had seen. Suddenly it hit me. I *had* seen it before! Leaping into our wardroom, I pulled down our copy of the latest *Fighting Ships* and turned to the photos of British flattops. Sure enough, the very tip of the highest mast of HMS *Hermes* held a contraption, presumably some sort of radar antenna, that resembled what I had seen.

In any wartime sub, even the postwar "guppy" with high submerged speed, the situation would have been hopeless. There was no way contact could have been regained. This was not so with *Triton*. Through careful study of the picture in the book, I was able to make a logical deduction of which way the carrier was headed, and even a rough approximation of her course. We rang up 30 knots and increased our running depth to the maximum allowed. For about three hours we ran thus, then slowed to give the sonar gear a good listen, and resumed speed. Repeating this procedure every ensuing half hour, I had not yet begun to worry that we might have torn off in the wrong direction when sonar reported propellers. When we got back to periscope depth it was indeed *Hermes,* looking exactly like her photograph, complete with the unusual topknot that had belatedly attracted my attention—and we were in position to execute the standard surface end-around maneuver we had used to such effect at night during the war, except that it was broad daylight.

No matter, we did the end-around submerged, keeping well out of the way of *Hermes'* escorting destroyers but otherwise without worry about being spotted. Having got into position on her port bow, *Triton* reverted to World War II approach technique, fired a theoretical salvo of torpedoes from a perfect firing position, and simultaneously lofted a green flare over the carrier's flight deck to inform her that she had been legitimately sunk by old-fashioned fish brought to bear by nuclear power. Then we put our bow back down and went again to high speed to head for where deduction, based on the location of one carrier, said the other had to be.

In due course, we found her, got off a standard attack, and saw the *Ark Royal* send off a helicopter, presumably to teach this impertinent submarine a lesson. So again we went deep, and to avoid the threatened depth charges headed directly beneath the carrier. Sonar had no difficulty hearing her powerful machinery, so that within minutes we were paralleling her course and speed, several hundred feet beneath her and of course immune to depth charging by aircraft or escorting destroyer. Here was a perfect opportunity to try another stunt nuke skippers had been talking about. *Triton*, submerged, could make more speed than *Ark Royal!*

Having tracked the carrier at 20 knots, and observing no variation in propeller beats, it was a good deduction that she had not changed speed. Once again ringing up flank, we pulled out from beneath her with a 10-knot speed advantage, ran out a mile ahead of her, slowed and fired our stern tubes. These particular fictitious torpedoes, I decided, had to be more modern versions of the World War II fish we had fired only a few minutes earlier, and also the day before at the *Hermes,* for they had to work from deep depth—and our old torpedoes could not have done that. In addition, I forbore firing another green flare. It, too, would not have functioned where we were—and hi-jinks or no, I wasn't anxious, despite our speed advantage when deep, to come to periscope depth, necessitating slow speed, dead ahead of a speeding aircraft carrier. There are times when circumspection must control. Explaining *that* collision away, assuming, if it happened, that we would have had a chance to explain anything, would have been a trifle difficult. So we pulled off the track, listened to *Ark Royal* roar by, and quietly came to periscope depth to signal her by radio that she had just been sunk a second time.

That exercise was to hold one more professional delight: in charge of the British ASW force was the same Sir Charles Madden, now an admiral, to whom *Amberjack* had been assigned as exercise target 12 years previously in Key West. It was too good a chance to miss, and I laid out a search plan, using all our speed and electronic ingenuity, to find him. Find him we did; it was perfect. *Triton* was waiting, just off his track, ready not only to shoot more fictitious torpedoes and green flares, but also to surface abeam of the flagship and use our signal light to flash over an unofficial message: "Sir Charles, we meet again," or something like that.

But it never came off. Just before we were to shoot torpedoes, he reversed course and dashed away at high speed. Raising our retractable antennae, we heard a message to headquarters announcing that the exercise was off, that a former German submarine now serving the Norwegian navy was missing, and he was off to help in the search!

Damn the Norwegians anyway, was all I could think of. But, of course, one had to admit that Sir Charles was doing the right thing, and all we could do was listen on the operational frequencies to find out what had happened. As it turned out, the Norwegian sub had merely failed to send a routine surfacing message, for which its skipper probably caught it from his regular bosses, not to mention Madden. As for me, he'd spoiled my day, and I'd have liked to tie him to the top of his own periscope and then give the classic order, "Take her down!"

Following the completion of this international fleet exercise, *Triton* was sent to Bremerhaven for 10 days of R&R. Bremerhaven had been one of the principal submarine bases during the war; German subs had been both built and based there, and many of the wartime German sub skippers lived in that now-rebuilt city. As the world's biggest submarine, the *Triton* of course made a big hit. The U.S. naval attaché met us on arrival, along with an estimated 30,000 people who came to the docks to see us arrive (an equal or greater number gathered a few days later to see us off). The local submarine captains invited our whole wardroom to a very pleasant soirée, and, at the suggestion of the naval attaché, I returned some of their hospitality by inviting them to tour my ship. This proved to be a tremendous hit, though not quite the way I expected.

The German submarine skippers were, of course, interested in what could be shown of the reactors and enginerooms, they did express satisfactory amazement at our huge turbines and the great horsepower my ship commanded, but their big interest was the periscopes, the officers' wardroom, the galley and quarters for the crew. These were not very much different from what they had been accustomed to during the war (although better, roomier, and so forth). My guests were enthusiastic about what they saw, but not at all conditioned, I felt, to appreciate the tremendous engineering advance represented by the nuclear reactors. As I recall the day, it seemed to me this may have been because they could not see enough, nor be told enough, about the reactor, while, to the contrary, all of them had had experience with steam engines, albeit not one crammed into a submarine hull.

It was a very pleasant experience, all the same, to meet and make friends with these professionals of the same branch of their navy as I was of mine. The war was hardly mentioned. The camaraderie of submarine sailors was paramount. It was clear to me that, for them, the good memories were the times at sea, in their boats, doing their duty for their country. As warriors of the sea, to these sentiments we could all subscribe, and I had continually to pinch myself to remember that in the sea stories they were continually telling, the ships being attacked and too often sunk were American or British, not Japanese.

Another occurrence during our stay in Bremerhaven was not so warming. The same naval attaché who had set us up with the local society of U-boaters came to suggest that I might pay a call on Adm. Karl Dönitz, who had been released from the prison at Spandau not many years earlier. Following his release from confinement, in 1958 he had published his memoirs of service, and in 1959 I wrote a review of his book that was published in the *New York Times Sunday Review of Books*. I had never met the man personally, although I thought I knew a good deal about him from studying his book, and welcomed the proposal. In short, it seemed to be a good idea at the time. Together, in an official car and driver, the U.S. naval attaché to Germany and I drove the two hours or so it took to reach the admiral's home in the Hamburg outskirts. He lived in the back portion of a large masonry house—built of stone, as I recall, a truly big mansion that had been subdivided into smaller living quarters. We were greeted graciously by Mrs. Dönitz, and after a few moments the admiral came in, carrying a book in his hand.

I immediately recognized the book by the paper jacket. It was a copy of his memoirs, titled *Ten Years and Twenty Days*. The reference of course was to his 10 years in Hitler's service and the 20 days following Hitler's suicide, during which Dönitz ran the country and had tried to salvage what he could from the Nazi debacle. Now Dönitz walked up to me and, without preliminaries of any kind, said, "I understand you think I should have been executed!"

So saying, he extracted from the book two obviously much-studied letters and a heavily underlined clipping from a newspaper, both of which he held out to me. I was already somewhat in shock by his salutation, and he did not give me enough time to carefully read any of the material he handed to me. One was a hand-written letter from Admiral Nimitz with an underlined passage to the effect that he respected Dönitz's loyalty to Germany, and had no reason to think he had been involved in any of the atrocities or extermination camps. Evidently Dönitz had written him to ask his support on this issue. The other letter was from Dr. Samuel Eliot Morison, our eminent historian— this one was typewritten, as I recall—in which he wrote that he accepted the German admiral's statement that he had had no knowledge of the "Final

Solution," and had not been aware of the unspeakable conditions existing in the concentration camps. Following this passage, also underlined, were these words: "Although I believe you, here is someone who does not"—and Morison had sent Dönitz a clipping from the *New York Times* of my review of his book, in which he, or someone, with a pen and blue ink had underlined phrases and passages throughout its text!

I, of course, had my own copies of the article in my desk at home, and at the moment I wished mightily that I could have foreseen this interview and studied them before coming to Hamburg. Even more, I wished the attaché had been able to warn me of the former grand admiral's feelings before exposing me to him. But, of course, he was as much taken aback as I. My review is, however, now before me as I write these words. As I recall, the passage to which the former grand admiral took most exception was near the beginning:

> The book is also Dönitz's personal refutation of the Nuremberg verdict in his case. In these less hate-filled years we may be willing to grant him the last word, but his personal bitterness at his ten years in prison gains scant sympathy when measured against the horror charged to Germany's account by millions of even less guilty people than he. Just as no law is really capable of jurisdiction over the criminal acts of a state, so does the ideal of justice for the individual sometimes prove inadequate when a state is finally forced to expiate its sins. Dönitz was fortunate he did not share the fate of some of his contemporaries.

In my eyes at least, my review was on the whole a favorable one. About in the middle, I wrote: "The American 'Neutrality Period' gets its share of attention. It is difficult today to refute the contention that here Germany was more sinned against than sinning." A little farther down, the article notes:

> Admiral Dönitz states that he was "shocked" when he learned, at war's end, of the atrocities committed by Hitler and his sadistic henchmen. This we may find a little hard to believe when the approximately 120 conferences at headquarters are mentioned. No doubt the secret was very well kept. But when Dönitz says, "I cannot say what I would have done, as a responsible member of the Armed Forces, had I known"—he but speaks the dilemma of all honest people the world over. Let the reader ponder what he himself would have done.

As I later wrote to Ingrid, "Actually, I blame Morison more even than Dönitz for the incident, for had he not written that unnecessary letter, Dönitz would have had to evaluate my review on its merits. . . . I remembered the main points of what I'd written, but was totally sandbagged, forced to rely on memory of several months back, while Dönitz was standing there with papers in his hand."

Somewhere along here Mrs. Dönitz broke up the difficult moment. "Now, Karl," she said, "Captain Beach has come to call on you, so don't go on like that."

She went out, returned with a small tray with glasses and a bottle of sherry wine. We drank a glass of the wine, and after a few minutes we left. I've since wished I had departed immediately, with a parting shot to the effect that if I thought he should have been executed, or really had guilty knowledge of the atrocities, I would never have come to see him. But the proper *riposte* usually comes to mind after the moment has gone.

A final comment on this extraordinary interview: one of Germany's top U-boat skippers, reputedly ranking number three in overall damage to our side, Erich Topp, has written a book of his wartime reminiscences. Published only a few years ago, in its pages he states unequivocally that he positively believes Dönitz was well aware of the Final Solution, even citing the time and place of the top-level conference, attended by Dönitz, in which the matter was discussed.

As for me, my original opinion of Dönitz as a worthy foe suffered severely from my meeting with him.

In my own small world, *Triton* had another effect, applicable only to me, and very possibly only the product of my own sometimes overly sensitive imagination.

Trigger II had been a disaster. Our Navy could not have built a poorer submarine if it had deliberately tried. I used to think that she must have been designed by a bunch of amateurs set up to give us an example of "design by committee," and I still bear the psychic scar of having had such high hopes for her and seeing them so terribly dashed. Now, Rickover had himself given me the *Triton*, a ship that was everything *Trigger II* should have been, nuclear-powered besides, and we had been sent on the greatest shakedown cruise any naval person could possibly have conceived of! *Trigger II's* shakedown, disaster that it was, had been to Rio de Janeiro, a fabulous destination. We had made it, barely and by the skin of our teeth, with three of our main engines totally out of commission, the fourth hardly running. Rio, a wonderful port to visit, to me has been always a memory of a terribly difficult engine repair. We got three of our four engines running, with the help of experts sent there from General Motors, their perpetrators. Nonetheless, one of these flew apart into small pieces en route home, so that only two remained in commission when we arrived back in New London.

By contrast, *Triton,* an infinitely more complicated ship, completed a much more difficult and much longer shakedown voyage without significant problems of any sort. She could have kept on going and subcircumnavigated the world a second time without stopping, except for the probability that I'd have had a mutiny on my hands. *Triton* ran beautifully all the time, and it crossed my mind that it was not at all above the Rickover I had come to know to have also thought, in a small part of his mind along with everything else, to demonstrate that he, at least, knew how to build a ship. There's no doubt in the world that if Eisenhower had directed Rickover to build the *Savannah,* instead of our maritime commission, which produced a failure similar to *Trigger II,* that nuclear-powered merchant ship, the "Peace Ship," as Eisenhower wanted to call her, would have been the outstanding success the nation deserved instead of the embarrassing klutz she turned out to be.

Such "might have beens" are useless, except perhaps for personal satisfaction. I wish now I had never seen the namesake of my old and revered *Trigger,* still whiling away eternity somewhere off the coast of Japan, just as I wish "Joe Blunt" had remained a fictional character, instead of being preempted by an unprincipled superior officer. But I did serve General Bradley, and the president of the United States, and the U.S. Senate, all of them in very special ways, and have commanded five ships, four of them of fond memory.

My father wrote 13 published books about our Navy, all of them novels for younger readers, and also commanded five U.S. naval men-of-war. I've followed his footsteps in that way, too, for this is my thirteenth published book about the Navy, if four for which I'm listed as coauthor are included in the count. On my agenda is a fourteenth book, fourth novel, soon to begin. When time comes to an end and everything is added up, I hope that his books and his ships, and mine, will be included among the things that matter.

Chapter Fourteen

Ideas for Our Navy's Future Years

As said in the beginning of this book, it began with the intent to lay out a series of thoughtful essays about our Navy, and my service in it. It was perhaps inevitable that it turn into an autobiography, and for this I offer no excuses, except that my editors encouraged it. All the same, persons like myself, who have spent a lifetime in our Navy and enjoyed it so much that they remained—in a sense—on active duty even after retirement, will also inevitably have some ideas about where our Navy seems to be going, and, in some cases, where it should go instead.

Again, this is offered with no apologies. Make of it what you will. If anything suggested in these penultimate pages strikes oil anywhere in the places where our Navy is run, or where decisions are made affecting it, I stand ready to defend what I'm about to write here, and will go to whatever legitimate lengths there may be to recommend that any or all of these ruminative ideas be folded into the pantheon of our U.S. Navy of the future.

CHANGING THE RANK STRUCTURE AND REDUCING STAFF

In numerous places and numerous ways I have argued, in writing and verbally, that our officer promotion and retention system, which was instituted with the best of motivations, has gradually grown out of hand and should now be changed. Naval philosophers might argue that this is true of any good idea. Witness the Maginot Line, built to make France impregnable against Germany, but, standing there too long, became a target which the German army studied for years and overwhelmed in days when World War II began. Witness also our democratic system of government, originated with the highest of ideals by men of heroic stature, now, two centuries later, corrupted by the need for campaign money. How long can democratic, idealistic government last if it has earned contempt from the citizens of our country?

Witness finally, and more specifically for this discussion, the U.S. battle fleet of 1941: magnificent battleships, maintained with splendor and confidence, but, like the Maginot Line, totally outclassed by the buzzing bees of carrier air power, which had ferreted out their weaknesses.

Our Navy rank structure can be compared in detail to all three of these examples. It has stood so long that its weaknesses are clear to those motivated to defeat it, it uses its assets unwisely, and it is subject to politics (Navy politics as well as national politics). Contrary to the idealistic purposes it was founded with, it has too often been perverted. Like the Maginot Line, it is ripe for a change.

The system for promotion of officers, selection by a board constituted for the purpose, has, with evolutionary changes, been in place for a century. It was created out of great need, driven by the war with Spain a century ago, when it became clear that promotion by seniority alone always resulted in "superannuation" of the most important military leaders.

By our good fortune, Theodore Roosevelt was assistant secretary of the Navy in 1898, and his enlightened insight was largely responsible for giving our Atlantic and Asiatic Fleets to top men in their prime, still in full possession of all their faculties. In the process, good officers senior to them had to be passed over. Faced with possible war, Roosevelt and his superior, Secretary of the Navy Long chose simply to appoint the best men they knew to the important posts.

Incompetence of leaders due to excessive age and other physical difficulties did trouble the Army, which apparently allowed pure seniority to control designation of which officers would be in the war saddles. Sadly, there is now good evidence that the top Navy selection of all, Admiral Sampson, the most junior of the three named to the top posts but nevertheless placed over Dewey and Schley because of the immense prestige he had accumulated, had already incurred the terrible brain malady that, in the prime of his life at the culmination of a brilliant career, made him into a bewildered old man who died four years later.

Dewey, oldest of the three and the senior by many numbers on the Navy list, turned in the best performance. Winning the Battle of Manila Bay, by Act of Congress he was named "Admiral of the Navy," and actually outlived the other two by several years (Sampson by 15, Schley by 6). The principle was, however, well established in both Army and Navy that those put in charge of important operations must be in good physical condition, in order that their performance be the best possible.

A mere commander at the time, William S. Sims, one of the then–leading lights of our Navy, picked by "T.R." to be his naval aide, recognized that one could not be sure of having a Roosevelt at the helm during war, and moreover, in spite of the best of intentions, even the great "T.R." might misjudge his man. Sims therefore led the fight to institutionalize a system of careful selection of the best fitted for promotion. By eliminating all personal variables and requiring a meticulous survey of the individual records of everyone up for advancement, this would set up the greatest surety that "superannuation" of top commanders would no longer occur.

As the years went by, however, Sims became dismayed at trends he saw developing. Competition was so keen for the higher-ranking slots, the number of eligibles so great, that the percentage chance of selection for promotion in each grade was being continually reduced. At the same time, mostly because of aviation's growing demand for enthusiastic and capable young men, the number in the junior ranks increased faster than the old rank structure could accommodate them. Yet, from the beginning, all of them had been guaranteed they would be as eligible for promotion as anyone else. He foresaw the time when selection boards would no longer be able to perform their function in the face of the influences upon them. Again, Sims got into the fray, arguing against the admission of so many young men at the bottom of the rank pyramid. Vainly, he pointed out that the growth of top billets was not keeping up with the growing size of the base, that ultimately unregulated growth in the junior ranks would so greatly reduce their proportional opportunities for the higher grades that big future problems were inevitable.

This was a battle Sims lost. He was already retired from active service, was too old to take up the controversy with his customary vigor, and died in 1936. The problem went away during World War II, naturally enough, but it returned with multiplied intensity after the war ended.

The result today is an expensive system in which, for example, about half of lieutenant commanders find their way barred to advancement because of lack of vacancies. Fully two-thirds of commanders come up against the same barrier. In such cases, having not been selected for promotion when others of their fellows are, they are officially designated as not as good: a psychically demeaning process that can only be destructive to the human spirit. In very real terms, this is one of the principal obstacles to retention of up-and-coming young officers, who see hurt inflicted on their own immediate and often much admired seniors and make their own evaluations.

For captains, however, it is worst of all. By this time they are career officers in the fullest meaning of the term; yet only 1 percent of their number can hope to advance to the rank of admiral, and this after having survived all the previous such selections in junior ranks! When instituted, the selection system failed only from a quarter to a third of eligible captains, but now the boards must disappoint all but 1 percent of the candidates, and the unsuccessful 99 percent of four-stripers will find themselves on the shelf after 30 years of service. Most of these unwilling retirees are high-quality career officers who would willingly continue in service were it possible. They must, however, be "retired," in effect pensioned off, for the rest of their lives. One measure of their loyalty to the naval service is the quiet acceptance of the unfavorable judgment of their worth. Short of another war that would recall them to active duty, this is the final service they can render to the Navy in which they have lived so long.

For the entire officer corps, only one-tenth of 1 percent of new ensigns will ultimately become admirals. As already noted, about half will not make it past lieutenant commander, the bright spot being that the younger men will have a better chance of going on into satisfying civilian careers. For 55-year-old captains with 30 years of excellent service, still coping with family responsibilities and still in the prime of their lives, the future can begin to look pretty bleak.

On the other side of the coin, proving the inequity of the formal system now in place, is the universal effort on the part of all successful officers to support the morale of those passed over by pointing out how small are the differences separating the successful ones from the others. Psychologically the difficulty is nevertheless a big one, for all instinctively recognize the basic fallacy: little though may be the difference in capability, it pales before the difference in reward. At the same time, everyone also realizes the impossibility of curing the problem without wrecking the system entirely. Despite its obvious flaws, it has succeeded in its principal purpose of putting mostly good people at the top.

It does not, of course, recognize the waste of talent, nor its cost, but the Congress will, and its legislative solution is likely not to be very palatable.

The system has grown like Topsy and apparently has been little changed from within the Navy, despite numerous well-intentioned efforts. Change must, however, be accomplished. Naval combat consists no longer of broadsides between great sailing ships, turret salvos over the horizon between fleets of gray-painted battleships, or even forays of hundreds of miles between aircraft carriers as was the case in World War II. Today, naval combat amounts to defending against electronically guided missiles, launched from thousands of miles away, and shooting back with similar missiles, programmed to seek out and destroy the ships responsible for the attack. But is this realistic? Would it not be more useful to shoot our return missiles at the seat of the enemy government that ordered them fired at our fleet? If war takes this direction, the next question will be what types of warheads to use, not only where to aim them, because they will never miss.

This prospect, too, may however come to an end because of the ability we now possess of obliterating entire countries by missiles fired from tremendous distances from submerged submarines manned by precisely trained automatons. As we view the replacement of the traditional naval gun battle, with all its imperfections and approximations, by electronically aimed devices holding destructive power ranging to the absolutely unimaginable, immaculately guided by computer chips in their electronic brains, we must also see that there can be no going back to the old ways.

Everything must change, and everything will. So far as our naval officer rank structure is concerned, wholesale overhaul is needed. This should be done with justice and fairness to those who have devoted their lives to it so far, but the changes are today moving so fast that difficult decisions will have to be made. If the U.S. Navy does not itself set this huge house in order, and relatively soon—say in the next 10 years—superior force, probably political, will do it for us.

REDUCING PERSONNEL TURNOVER—THE HOME SHIP

Recently having the privilege of hearing the Vice CNO discussing the problem of retention in the Navy, I seized the question period he offered to make a suggestion that has been coming on me gradually for several years. He seemed to think well of my spur-of-the-moment formulation of the idea and, by consequence, I addressed a letter to him in which I tried to state the proposal in a more formal and complete manner. His response, just received, was complimentary and thoughtful, but not favorable. Ship assignments must range all over the world, and he feels they cannot be made equal, one to another.

The problem addressed by the Vice Chief was that of (a) recruiting more sailors and (b) keeping them longer in service. He said that at this time the

Navy is behind all the other services in these areas. It was noted by some present that the Marine Corps (granted it has different service parameters and a totally different esprit) does not have this difficulty. It glories in its toughness, and its individual Marines individually glory in theirs. In my comment I cited the proliferation of ship reunions, pointing out that they signified not only a desire to return to the old camaraderie felt on board, but also the psychological wish to return to one's youth and surroundings. Though no one knows it at the time, I said, we all come to feel those were our best days, and the ship in which one then served turns out to have been a vital part of the same. For this reason, the ship should get a higher place on the scale of the things we do to improve enlistment and retention.

The idea is to achieve this by creating a "home ship" concept. We do it already with the home port idea. Sailors, both enlisted and officer, should have their repeated sea tours in the same ship. While this manifestly would not be 100 percent possible, one could imagine Seaman Jones serving four years aboard the USS *Neversink,* going ashore for a period of time, ideally in the same home port, and when his or her turn for sea duty comes back, priority would be to put him or her back aboard the *Neversink.* He or she would, of course, be assumed to have improved in rating (or rank) and stature during the intervening years, so the specific job would not be the same, but the venue would. Those volunteering for another ship or station aside, or found wanting in some way, sailors so identified would in time become fixtures on board, associating their personalities with it more and more as their responsibilities increase.

Institution of such things as a "service aboard" badge might be considered, even a ship's welfare council, some sort of "court of last resort" for persons with small problems, or "community on shore" organizations in which off-ship crew members could feel an affinity with a local support structure in the home port area. One could visualize a shore-based ship's office where families could turn for assistance when needed. Were things of this nature imaginatively handled, morale benefits all around would probably ensue.

If the home ship concept were to become a reality, ideally a special loyalty would be built up involving not only personnel serving on board, but their families, and it would conceivably reach far beyond the ship herself, both in time and distance. Once a *Neversink* crew member, always a crew member, for example, with career appropriately capsuled as "Seaman to Chief in the *Neversink.*" The same might similarly be done for young officers.

Were such a scheme to be put in place, a number of ramifications, and logically some problems will come to mind. The "home ship" concept could be extended to recruits in the sense that they might be allowed to choose their home ship and home port to an even greater degree than at present. This might be desirable. On the possible "con" side, it would undoubtedly "regionalize" the Navy to a greater extent than is now the case, for there would probably be a tendency to identify with location as well as with a particular ship; but this need not be seen as detrimental to the fundamental idea: to cause early identification with selected ships in order to capitalize on the loyalties that seem inevitably to grow in the later years.

NUCLEAR POWER

The great gift of Admiral Rickover to our Navy was not only the nuclear-powered submarine but also nuclear power in general. We went from sails to coal because of the manifold advantages of freedom from the wind, and infinitely greater maneuverability. With the necessity of replenishing coal bunkers came the need to return to port much more frequently than in the days of sail, and this conditioned all navies to accept short cruises as the normal state of affairs. The change from coal to oil fuel did give somewhat increased range and speed, but this was marginal. The need for fuel, despite its operational advantages, was what insidiously accustomed us to short cruises.

Now, with nuclear power, ships can stay at sea for a very long time indeed: months, perhaps years. So far as cruising is concerned the Navy has returned to the days of sail. We will not go back to the ancient privations inflicted on crew members in terms of poor food, insufficient water, and too little personal space, but it is a fact that a nuclear-powered ship can today stay at sea as long as the old sailing ships could, and travel far greater distances in the process.

This is only part of the story; the atom, combined with the burgeoning capability of replenishment at sea, has also increased the staying power of other ships: the fuel tanks of nuclear carriers, for example, carry fuel not only for aircraft but also for their escorts, so that the range of the entire task force is greatly increased. Not long ago, one of our carriers stayed at sea, deployed in one of the world's trouble spots, for a continuous six months, and so, largely, did the accompanying members of its task force. The smaller ships, though shuttling back and forth to base more than the carrier, did so to a far lesser degree than they would have normally, for the carrier was also a huge supply ship for them. Thus the usefulness of the entire task force was notably boosted, and the supporting ships reduced in number. As many have remarked, our seagoing Navy is more effective than ever before, even as it is downsizing with the end of the Cold War.

Our problem now, more than ever, is to figure out how to better handle the people, so that we can improve the potential of our downsized forces to the greatest extent possible. Here is where real ingenuity, perhaps of a radical nature (such as greatly reducing the sizes of crews but going to the two-crew concept for big surface ships deployed on distant stations), may be necessary. The old ideas of carrying extra-big crews for the sake of contingencies will have to be rethought. The "smart ship" concept may be a step in the right direction. Probably we should also look into how the U.S. Air Force handles its big bombers, which stay in the air for tremendously long hours with minimum-sized crews. Aircraft started small, with small crews. As the planes grew bigger, their crews remained small, growing the very minimum possible. Ships, on the other hand, evolved in the opposite way. Everything had to be done by hand in the sailing days, and therefore big crews were the norm (the *Constitution* in her heyday had a crew of 500 men, though she was not much bigger than one of today's smaller minesweepers). Our biggest battleships carried over 2,000 in their crews during World War II, and our *Nimitz*-class carriers have more than 6,000 aboard at this very moment.

How and whether to cut these big crews is a critically important question, and it may well be that the answer, at least for now, must be in the negative. There are here, however, huge potential dividends if they can be realized.

THE INFLUENCE OF THE SUBMARINE UPON SEA POWER

Mankind was not made to navigate beneath the surface of the sea. Notwithstanding the evolutionary link with air-breathing mammals of the deep sea, the tremendous difference between air and water creates a barrier through which man has seldom been able to pass, and then only with great difficulty.

Contemplation of the sea always brings the fascinating thought that directly beneath the huge plain of the sea great mountains exist but a few feet away, barely under that seldom quiet membrane, yet bigger than anything above it. There are also mineral and power resources in profusion, perhaps as much as three-quarters of the earth's total supply. And there are sunken ships, buried treasure, archaeological bonanzas in profusion, not to mention wondrous and fearsome creatures totally foreign to us and to our understanding.

We can record at least four centuries of attempts to probe the ocean depths, but both research and legend indicate that man has tried much longer than that. Men (and women) have dived for profit (pearl diving, shallow water salvage); for combat (a Greek father and daughter, breathing through hollow reeds, supposedly wrecked some of Xerxes' galleys before the battle of Salamis by cutting their anchor cables); for research and exploration (Halley invented the diving bell before he discovered the comet); and for many other purposes, including politics, advertising, and plain inquisitiveness. For centuries men have tried to construct special vehicles to sustain them in the hostile environment beneath the sea. Of these most were tethered, or more likely merely suspended, like the early diving bells. A few were mobile, but there was no power for submerged locomotion other than human muscle, and such craft were consequently tiny and extremely limited in speed, range, and endurance. Far more than the air above, the undersea has been fraught with difficulty and danger, and many fewer people have assayed to penetrate it.

Anything floating on the sea surface has unparalleled mobility, easily and cheaply obtained. The stratification layer between sea and air lends itself equally to peaceful commerce and to combat, the fighting being generally over who, or what political agency, is to control the commerce the sea makes so easy. In historical times—the Spanish Armada of 1588, the 1781 Battle of the Virginia Capes, Trafalgar in 1805 are prime examples—combat on the sea has also determined who is to control the land.

A century ago, Capt. Alfred Thayer Mahan, U.S. Navy, on duty as professor at the recently established U.S. Naval War College, electrified Europe by publishing his lectures at that institution in the form of a book entitled *The Influence of Sea Power upon History*. Never before had the historical importance of England's centuries-old navy been so clearly articulated. Never, either, had Germany's opportunity at the beginning of the twentieth century, as her Kaiser saw it, been stated so well. Kaiser Wilhelm II, a naval enthusiast like President Theodore Roosevelt, required Mahan's book to be read by the entire German naval officer corps, for he saw a powerful navy as exactly what he needed to consummate his long rivalry with his cousin, George V of England. Sea Power was the key, and Control of the Sea the means. A fleet of powerful battleships would be the instrument. This was Mahan's lesson, as the Kaiser understood it.

Through a whole sequence of fortuitous circumstances, beginning with his ability to state complex considerations in simple, even lyrical language, Mahan was the naval guru of his age. He greatly influenced Theodore Roosevelt, who was already very navy-minded, and most of the crowned heads of Europe as well. Germany's interpretation of his thesis was accurate enough for the time, and Mahan may therefore be held at least partly responsible, in a pedagogical way, for the naval rivalry that presaged World War I.

The central message of his life's work was that during the previous three centuries command of the sea had historically determined the outcome of international war. What sea power could accomplish, how to attain it, how it had been exercised by the sailing navies of the past, particularly that of Great Britain, constituted his theme. Control of the sea was essential, he held, attainable only by possession of a more powerful fleet than that of an opponent and using it to destroy the enemy's fleet. Ideally, this would take place in a titanic naval battle, like Trafalgar, but it could also be done in a series of smaller battles. Elimination of an enemy's ability to contest use of the sea in support of the war was the objective. As he conclusively showed, this was precisely what England had done as she built her empire.

The epitome of sea power in the early days was the wooden "ship of the battle line," the sailing battleship, the most powerful and best protected warship that could be built. The effect of the industrial revolution was to convert this "ship of the line of battle," also known as a "battleship," into a steel, steam-powered warship mounting the heaviest possible armament, protected by the most impenetrable armor that could be devised. Appropriately, this new ship, old in concept, was also called a "battleship." In the Kaiser's day, the relative size and power of navies was calculated by counting battleships, which were still expected to "stand in the line of battle."

Beginning with the ironclads of the U.S. Civil War, by 1913 battleships had developed into awesome steel monsters, possessed of a certain austere majesty that enthralled men of the sea who, despite military training and its touted pragmatism, remained largely ship-loving romanticists at heart. A goodly portion of the "battleship cult" that influenced naval thinking during the years before World War II was undoubtedly due to deep-seated sentiment for ships. Man has built few things so grand as his great sailing ships with their clouds of gray-white canvas. The modern battleship, with power limned in every symmetrical detail, in its own self is also majestically breathtaking.

During the two decades between the world wars, however, the potential of sea-based aircraft was becoming plain to forward-looking naval officers of Japan and the United States, and the debacle of Pearl Harbor solidified the ascendancy of an entirely new class of warship. Rifled cannon of huge size, able to shoot 20 miles, were supplanted by aircraft carrying bombs 10 or 15 times as far, and with greater accuracy. Aircraft carriers became the battleships' direct descendants for sea combat and, as it turned out, did much more fighting than battleships ever did. For World War II and afterward they held—and still hold—undisputed sway as the premier vehicle by which American policy can be carried anywhere in the world.

No one has yet been able to develop anything better, but the times, as always, are changing. Carriers with their air wings (for now, these cannot be left out of the equation) represent only half of the naval three-dimensional revolution. Everything below the surface is foreign to them, and a potential danger. As with the battleship before them, their prospects depend on the developments of science. The most likely scenario today, however, is that the future of navies now rests with the submarine, which can use both sides of the sea-surface membrane from what has been so far a safe sanctuary beneath it.

Mahan was familiar with the concept and design of the diesel-powered submarine that fought the two world wars. He did not live to address its success at commerce raiding, however, because his death in 1914 took place prior to development of Germany's U-boat threat to England. Had he been able to apply himself to the study of undersea warfare as it was to come, in his later years he would certainly have modified his concepts as to naval warfare. His thesis about control of the sea did indeed hold true during both world wars, but with great difficulty now that submarines were in the picture. As history has shown, victory against the German U-boat was possible only because the distant and undamaged United States was able to bring an extraordinary, totally overwhelming, force against the relatively small group of dedicated men who operated the German submarines.

In our early days, U.S. inventors built three "diving boats" that were operationally successful (they were not yet dubbed "submarines"): Bushnell's *Turtle* in 1776, Fulton's *Nautilus* in 1801, and Hunley's diving boat, named *Hunley* by the Confederacy in his honor, in 1864. All three were hand-driven by propellers, surfaced or submerged (only Fulton provided a mast and sails for surface propulsion), and all three worked (a number of others didn't, or not well enough). No portion of any of these three remains from which it may be authoritatively reconstructed (*Hunley* still exists, buried in the mud and sand of Charleston Harbor, and as these words are written has been found and may soon be raised and placed on exhibition. All three are famous historical curiosities, and have been widely reproduced in models, even in full-size replicas. The *Turtle* nearly succeeded in sinking a British warship, and 88 years later the *Hunley* sank the blockading Union

Housatonic, a first ever. For this feat the *Hunley* will live in history even though she sank also, with all hands. Her nine-man crew thus sustained greater loss than *Housatonic,* whose log showed five lost out of a crew of 160 when she went down.

Of consuming historical interest is the location of the *Hunley* wreck, found some distance from where the *Housatonic* wreckage lay. *Hunley* evidently survived the explosion of her torpedo against *Housatonic's* side, was not "sucked into the stricken hull by the roaring inflow of water," as some accounts, based more on romanticism than fact, surmised. There were other reports, really just guesses, that she might have been swamped through her open hatches by the wave of roiled water resulting from the explosion of her spar torpedo. Confederate General Beauregard, under whose orders she was operating, had supposedly directed she must stay on the surface with hatches open because there had been so many fatalities when she submerged. But this, too, is but a theory that now appears incorrect.

Hunley's attack on the steam sloop-of-war *Housatonic* took place on the night of 17–18 February 1864. We now know the boat made a totally successful attack. She rammed about 100 pounds of black powder attached to the tip of a 20-foot spar, or strong wooden pole, extending forward from her bow, against the hull of her target, detonated it, and exultantly started back to her base on Sullivan's Island, near the present Patriot's Point in Charleston Harbor. She had evidently covered much of the distance when things proved too much for her hard-working but by this time desperate crew, and she foundered. When the tiny hull is finally raised it will most likely be found that small leaks, resulting from the last-minute rifle fire of her target, let in more water than she could handle.

The boat was found by author-and-environmentalist Clive Cussler, who had invested considerable time and money in the search. Preliminary examination of the hulk indicates there may have been some damage received from the fusillade of small-arms fire directed at her upon discovery. She was detected by the *Housatonic* deck watch as she approached on her attack run, and was already too close for the Union sloop's main armament to be depressed enough to hit her. Thus, the only defense *Housatonic* could put up was from pistols and rifles, and it is probable *Hunley's* low-lying hull may have been struck a number of times. If *Housatonic's* defenders spotted the glass eye-ports she carried in her hatch coamings, or the dead-lights her finders have reported as surprisingly existing in her hull, it is logical they may have become points of aim—and if so, one or more may have been shattered or cracked.

Thus, water may have begun leaking into *Hunley*'s hull, possibly in amounts too great to overcome with the small, hand-operated pump she carried. One would expect her detachable keel (if, as reported, she had one) to have been released during her struggle to survive; so, depending on what is found when the hull is raised, this point may lead to careful inspection of the route between the two wrecks. When the remains of the *Hunley* are finally opened for inspection of her interior, there may be pathetic evidence of a desperate struggle by her doomed crew to prevent what was happening to them.

Of interest also is the account by Adm. Hobart Pasha, RN, who had been sent to Charleston by the British Royal Navy as an observer. Pasha described meeting the commander of a Confederate submarine (he so described the vessel without using that term) who was about to take her into the harbor to attack one of the Union warships. The boat's skipper invited his friend to look over his craft, and Pasha's description is very like what we know of the *Hunley,* including (now discovered in part of the wreck) something rather like a snorkel to provide fresh air to her laboring crew.

Pasha saw the boat off on her dangerous journey, and the next night again met with her commander at the same place, to learn that it had sunk with all hands except him, but through good luck he had escaped. Rather laconically, Pasha goes on to say,

> On the next occasion that same enterprising officer was employed on a similar enterprise, his efforts were crowned with complete success. . . . He started one dark night, in a submerged vessel of the same kind as that above described, and exploded the torpedo against the bows of one of the blockading squadron, doing so much damage that the vessel had to be run on shore to prevent her sinking.

What we shall discover when the little *Hunley* is finally brought back to the surface, after lying 132 or more years on the bottom of Charleston Harbor, will write some new pages in the history of underwater craft. Certainly, her intrepid crew will have to be appropriately honored, their tiny boat likewise, for they started a new chapter in naval warfare.

All nations with navies had experimented with submarines by the time of World War I, among them England, Germany, France, Japan, Russia, and the United States. All had created small submarine forces with crude boats and minimally sized crews. In that war, the giant capabilities of underwater combat ships first burst upon a startled world when the tiny 500-ton German

U-9, with a crew of 29, sank three British armored cruisers totaling 36,000 tons in a couple of hours, suffering neither damage nor loss, and very little danger, to herself. British casualties in the three big ships were about 1,500 men by most accounts, some 50 times *U-9*'s whole crew.

After World War I it was clear that an extraordinarily small group of dedicated German submariners, some 30,000, had single-handedly nearly defeated Great Britain and her navy. But what this meant to naval warfare was fully appreciated by only a few submarine zealots. Britain still held control of the sea in the sense envisaged by Mahan, and psychologically this was all that mattered to her. Almost entirely lost was the fact that traditional sea power, in the newly discovered emergency, had not been enough. The "battle line" had been in action in only one big battle, and portions of it in small ones only a couple of times. England had been saved only by timely all-out industrial assistance from her one-time colony, the United States.

Twenty years later, in World War II, there were three submarine campaigns with three very different outcomes. German U-boats, manned as before by only a relative handful of men, some 50,000 counting base personnel (an inconsequential number compared with the size of the rest of the Nazi war machine), according to accepted history nearly beat England again. For the second time in 20 years, they forced massive emergency intervention by America's industrial power. Had this not been possible, England could not have survived. (My good friend Clay Blair contests this in his latest book, but with all due respect I still see it this way.)

On the other side of the world, however, and in spite of a few brilliant early successes, Japan's submarines made little impact in their campaign against the United States. They could not have changed the outcome of the war, but they could have been better employed than they were. The assessment today is that their overall ineffectiveness was largely due to bad strategic management, not to deficiency in weapons or to poor tactical use of the boats in combat.

The third submarine campaign was that waged by the United States against Japan—and it must flatly be stated that at first U.S. submariners were the least effective of the three undersea services. This was partly because of years of the wrong kind of training, but mostly because of criminally defective weapons. Loss of the Philippines (we were able to sink only one of the Japanese invasion force) and untold suffering by her people are attributable to this disgraceful failure. The U.S. subs were excellent ships, however, and they were, at least, properly used. Torpedo problems were finally resolved (though with no credit to the U.S. Navy Bureau of Ordnance), and then Japanese maritime and naval losses began to mount.

In contrast to England, Japan had no powerful industrial ally to make up her losses, and American submarines became one of the primary decisive factors that forced her surrender.

Today we simplistically divide submarines into "pre-nuke" (before nuclear propulsion) and "post-nuke" classes, chronologically divided at the mid-century point, with, naturally enough, concentration on the present nuclear-powered era because its subs are so much grander and more powerful than everything that went before them. To the dedicated submariner this somewhat neglects the period before nuclear power, when submarines demonstrated so conclusively what they could do. The pre-nuke period, slightly longer than the first half of the twentieth century, was the growing time, and also the testing time of war. Massive improvements in diesel engines, storage batteries, electric motors, hydraulic systems, freshwater distillers, and all sorts of important internal mechanisms finally produced the outstandingly successful fleet submarines of World War II, and their contemporaries in the other navies, friendly or not. These were the boats that twice went through the crucible of war.

Twice in the first half of this century, submarines conclusively demonstrated the new element of sea power that nations are wrestling with today. Prior to outbreak of war in 1939, Hitler promised his subordinates they would have adequate time to prepare the forces they would need. To Admiral Dönitz, this meant between 300 to 400 operational submarine boats and the necessary well-trained crews. What would it have meant to England had this been the force with which Dönitz began the war, instead of the 39 or so he actually had? As already noted, in the Pacific, U.S. subs share major credit for victory over Japan. The enormous damage inflicted by submarines on both sides, roughly between a quarter to a half of all the maritime damage, was done by less than 1 percent of the forces under arms. This needs to be measured against opposition directed specifically at them that amounted to about half the total naval strength of the opposing side. And it should be noted that the submarines of all the nations involved, including those of the United States, incurred the highest percent losses of any of the forces engaged.

With the second half of the century came the nuclear-power engine, permitting submarines to remain submerged indefinitely by removing their dependence on air, eliminating the need for two dissimilar and heavy powerplants in each boat, massively increasing their power and thereby their speed. While underway they remain constantly submerged, and by consequence their upper hull form is, quite logically, no longer different from the lower. To this technological marvel have been grafted the world's most sophisticated missile systems, with guidance, range, and destructive power undreamed of during the first half of the century. These are the ships (they are not "boats" any longer but ships in all senses of the term) that today inhabit the trackless fluid covering most of our globe.

None has yet been used in war, and we have not thought much about their performance because, except when in harbor, they cannot be seen. But we *should* think about them. At this moment more than 100 very-long-range U.S. missiles are on station, concealed in the ocean, painstakingly serviced by a few hundred highly trained young men. Although this highly fluid situation (no pun here) is in deep flux because of changes in the Soviet Union, another hundred missiles (the numbers are guesswork) must be symbolically considered to be in Soviet submarines likewise hidden at sea. These are the new controlling elements of sea power, to which the first half of the twentieth century has led.

World War II was the greatest conflict yet waged by man on earth. It can be argued that the U.S. Navy was subliminally targeted toward this tremendous trial from its beginning. We are still preoccupied, however, by the mode of thought bred by that titanic conflict, and have not yet separated the lessons from the dramatic story. In a philosophical sense the nuclear submarine came too soon, for it opened new horizons before there had been adequate contemplation of how the world reached the point where we now stand.

Nor has the human mind been able to focus rigorously on the fantastic capabilities of the new "true" submarine. We go into lengthy technical descriptions, but such considerations quickly become classified so that only the professionals can know the true facts. On the PR level we say, "Try to visualize a submarine, the tiny underwater boat we knew before the war, suddenly grown to the size of the battleships at Pearl Harbor!" But few individuals, even if they grasp the technological point, will understand what may be the most important thing of all.

Eminent British historian John Keegan, for example, predicts in *The Price of Admiralty* (Viking; excerpted in the new *Military History Quarterly*) that future Battles of Jutland (or Trafalgar) will be fought underwater. With this I cannot agree. There will be no submerged battle even remotely similar to any other great sea fights. The onrush of sophisticated technology negates any prospect of repetition, even by analogy, of naval battles of ages past, any more than jet aircraft armed with heat-seeking missiles can (or should try to) reproduce the aerial dogfights between Spads and Fokkers of World War I. The new battleship-sized submarines carry weapons tens of thousands of times the destructive power of the old battlewagons, but they are not intended to fight other submerged battleships. Their targets are whole nations.

Submarine destroyers ("attack" submarines) will, of course, be sent to find them, and other submarine destroyers will protect the submerged weapons-carriers. Even before attacking them can be contemplated, however, finding the submerged battleships will be the principal problem. This is not easily done. They will not form a "battle line." The entire world ocean is their arena, and they will, each unit separately, seek out individual places from which to carry out their missions. Their threat is beyond comprehension. Their main defense is also beyond comprehension: their invisibility, until the awesome moment when their rockets fly out of a peaceful sea. One *Ohio* (the first of the Trident-class ballistic missile subs) theoretically can shoot in a single salvo more than 200 "MIRVed" atom bombs, each one far more powerful than the bomb that obliterated Hiroshima, each one independently programmed to destroy an important land target. We have to assume that the USSR *Typhoon*-class subs can dispose of approximately the equivalent. No country on earth can stand even one of these dreadful salvos. Yet the "obliteration-ship," to coin a word intended to infer much more than "battleship," has one-twentieth the crew of the greatest battleship ever built, a sixtieth of that of one of the new aircraft carriers, and the World War III we are talking about will take only a few days. There may be isolated encounters between an obliteration-ship and the attack-type submarines sent to seek her out, possibly engagements between submarine destroyers and defenders, but there will be no battles anything like Trafalgar, or, on the other side of the world and a hundred years later, Tsushima.

No one has yet dealt with the fundamental question: "Do all these marvels change sea power as we have thought of it during the past hundred years?" More specifically, in light of all this, what is sea power today?

As the twentieth century nears its end, the submarine has come of age with an éclat unrivaled by any other instrument of war, except the nuclear weapon itself. Instead of slow and steady growth, the submarine has exploded. In a very few years it has become one of the most absolutely terrifying ocean-going vehicles of all time, armed with the most fearsome, most easily concealable, most readily usable weapons ever conceived by an uneasy mankind.

Submarines, nuclear power, and the nuclear weapon were combined to form this remarkable development. Its immediate predecessors, tiny craft with only pinpricks for weapons, had lethality out of all proportion to their cost in lives and money. To neutralize them took an effort on the order of 100 to 1, and despite optimistic predictions, research since has done more *for* submarines than *against* them. The result of it all is that subs are today much harder to detect and counterattack than ever before. So far as anyone can predict, this pattern will continue. How much greater than ever before, then, is the dimension of the submarine threat!

Judging by all our experience to date, at the outset of general war between the superpowers the oceans will immediately empty themselves of all commercial-type ships. There will be no prospect of supplying overseas forces, or overseas allies, in the face of enemy determination to prevent the same, and surface naval operations of any sort will be at grave risk. Surveillance satellites will show any ship that moves on the sea, and the oceans will be totally clean—empty—save for two types of submarines: those targeted against enemy cities, and those searching for enemy ships of any kind, especially submerged ones.

We need to think of sea power in an entirely new way, for the world ocean is now a haven for surprise attack. Sea power has gone the other way from Mahan's early concept. It is less controllable than ever before. Recent history shows that formulas for the use of arms are dividing into two types. The first amounts to implementation of national policy, and the means employed may range from simple visible presence, in itself expressive of the national will, to direct use of conventional arms to enforce that will.

For this, "limited war" is the most appropriate code-word appellation, despite ambivalence of the word "war." Today, "limited" means nonnuclear. Recent years have seen numerous examples of it, whatever the linguistics involved, and there will be more. The other type of arms use amounts to totally horrible, instant destruction, visited upon huge areas of an enemy heartland in retaliation for (or perhaps in anticipation of) a similar attack by its forces. Actual use of any such destructive capability by either side is manifestly unacceptable to mankind, even though the threat of it, under the name of deterrence, has been in place for years.

It follows that the ultimate warship, the missile-firing submarine, by its very impregnability and tremendous destructive power is *right now* helping to make unlimited all-out war into a thing of the past. This is what the submarine has done to sea power and navies. One or more generations may have to come and pass from the scene before this idea will be generally accepted, but the process is going on. In the meantime we will continue to experience "limited war," for disagreements will not disappear overnight. The first thing to go will be nuclear weapons (this is happening already), and ultimately all human conflicts will be settled by other means, too. When it comes time to retire the extraordinary ships we have developed to carry the outlawed nuclear weapons, the boast will be that they were never used.

So be it. Sea Power now refers to irresistible onslaught from the deep of the sea, capable of such terrible visitation as to amount to a whole war in a single day. From this the world recoils. I believe World War II was the *last* all-out general war. World War III will never take place, though "limited" wars, carefully circumscribed as to purpose and means employed, may continue for as long as anyone alive today can imagine time. For that matter, even the meaning of the word "war" will become more carefully defined. The world is going through one of its most significant changes, for one of the purposes of man today is to avoid the final demonstration of the capabilities of the modern submarine. This would be cataclysmic, now that it is allied with the doomsday weapon.

The influence of the submarine on sea power has been, from the deep of the sea, to give new meanings to "war," and to "peace."

Index

About the Author

Edward L. "Ned" Beach, Captain, USN (Ret.), never had any other ambition than to attend the U.S. Naval Academy. He graduated in 1939 ranked second in his class, having held the post of regimental commander during his final year. In addition to his brilliant naval career described here, Captain Beach is the author of thirteen books, including *Run Silent, Run Deep,* and numerous articles. He has been awarded the Navy League Alfred Thayer Mahan Award for literary achievement, the Theodore and Franklin D. Roosevelt Prize, the Samuel Eliot Morison Award for Distinguished Service, the Magellanic Premium of the American Philosophic Society, and the Theodore Roosevelt Association Gold Medal for National Defense and Literary Achievement. The new home of the U.S. Naval Institute in Annapolis was recently named Beach Hall in honor of Captain Beach and his father, who was also a Captain in the U.S. Navy.

Captain Beach and his wife, Ingrid, live in a century-old house in the Georgetown district of Washington, D.C.